PRAISE FOR *EARTH FREQUENCY*

"For decades, I've combed books, tomes, and ancient manuscripts ⏜ travels to power places and sacred sites. Melissa's book has now replaced all other resources. I've always been a pilgrim of this earth and now I'm even more excited about my next journeys. Bravo!"

—Cyndi Dale, bestselling author of *The Complete Book of Chakra Healing*

"If you feel attracted to a place, *Earth Frequency* will help unveil the mysteries around what may be behind that attraction. Melissa Alvarez describes the phenomena and subtle energies at play that many of us feel but may be unconscious of … Dip into the history of the sacred sites listed in this book to discover more about their magic and mystery."

—Debra Moffitt, author and host of *Divinely Inspired Living*

"I love the way *Earth Frequency* takes you on a trip around the world and connects you to the energy of the earth without leaving the comfort of your home … This is a well-thought-out book that would be a great addition to your shelf!"

—Melanie Barnum, author of *Psychic Development Beyond Beginners*

"*Earth Frequency* is a perfect guide for the beginner and the advanced energy worker … This book will help you learn how to recognize energy, ley lines, vortexes, and the phenomena found in nature to establish a deeper connection with the earth … I highly recommend this essential guide for the world traveler."

—Margaret Ann Lembo, author of *Chakra Awakening*

"This is an amazing and timely book. We need this information now more than ever. I'm in awe of its brilliance! You must read this."

—Sherrie Dillard, author of *You Are Psychic*

"Melissa Alvarez has created a much-needed tome on earth frequencies. Many feel a connection to our planet, but Alvarez instructs, step-by-step, how to form a deeper connection to the earth. Her research has produced a unique approach to understanding the planet's chakras, ley lines, and other energetic points, which is invaluable to those who seek to explore and connect to our world without having to physically travel."

—Diane Wing, MA, author of *The True Nature of Energy*

EARTH
FREQUENCY

ABOUT THE AUTHOR

Melissa Alvarez is a bestselling, award-winning author who has written ten books and nearly five hundred articles on self-help, spirituality, and wellness. As a professional intuitive coach, energy worker, spiritual advisor, medium, and animal communicator with over twenty-five years of experience, Melissa has helped thousands of people bring clarity, joy, and balance into their lives. Melissa teaches others how to connect with their own intuitive nature and how to work with frequency for spiritual growth. She has appeared on numerous radio shows as both a guest and host. Melissa is the author of *365 Ways to Raise Your Frequency*, *Your Psychic Self*, *Animal Frequency*, *Believe and Receive*, *Llewellyn's Little Book of Spirit Animals*, and *The Simplicity of Cozy*. Melissa's books have been translated into Spanish, Romanian, Russian, Chinese, French, and Czech. She lives in South Florida with her family, dogs, and horses.

Sacred Sites, Vortexes, Earth Chakras,
and Other Transformational Places

EARTH
FREQUENCY

MELISSA ALVAREZ

Llewellyn Publications
Woodbury, Minnesota

First Edition
First Printing, 2019

Cover design by Shira Atakpu
Editing by Brian R. Erdrich
Interior art by the Llewellyn Art Department

Llewellyn is a registered trademark of Llewellyn Worldwide Ltd.

Library of Congress Cataloging-in-Publication Data (Pending)
ISBN: 978-0-7387-5445-1

Llewellyn Publications
A Division of Llewellyn Worldwide Ltd.
2143 Wooddale Drive
Woodbury, MN 55125-2989
www.llewellyn.com

Printed in the United States of America

This book is dedicated to Bandit. My Bandy-boy. I've never had a dog that loved me as much as you did, nor one that I loved as much as you. With every Llewellyn book I wrote, you were right by my side. Losing you so suddenly and having to finish this one without you was very difficult, but I know you are still with me in spirit. I'm so grateful for the six years we had together and for all the signs you've sent since you went back home. I miss you so much and I'll love you forever.

CONTENTS

PART 2: SACRED AND MYSTICAL SITES BY GEOGRAPHICAL AREAS

Chapter 3—Africa . . . 49

Chapter 4—Europe . . . 101

Chapter 5—Asia . . . 149

Chapter 7—United States and Canada . . . 253

Chapter 8—Mexico and Central America . . . 299

Chapter 9—South America and the Caribbean . . . 347

ILLUSTRATIONS

ACKNOWLEDGMENTS

I wish to give my heartfelt thanks to:

The readers who have taken the time to read my books for letting me know they were helpful to you through online reviews and emails.

The staff of Llewellyn Worldwide for making the process of publishing my books with Llewellyn an absolute pleasure. I so enjoy working with all of you!

Robert Coon for granting me permission to mention his Earth Chakra System and his website (earthchakras.org) in my book, and for allowing me to include the image he drew illustrating his system. Thank you!"

Lisa Erickson for allowing me to include her Planet Earth's Chakra System as she outlined on her website (https://mommymystic.wordpress.com). Thank you!

My family for their understanding when I lock myself in a room with my computer and ignore them while I'm writing. For making dinner or ordering delivery so I don't have to cook and for checking on me from time to time. Thanks guys! I love you!

Kayla Little for keeping the horses happy while I finished this book—a mermaid on land who can weather any storm, whose smile and laughter makes everyone's day brighter, and whose sense of responsibility is unsurpassed. Thank you for helping me outside when I needed it most.

INTRODUCTION

Have you ever walked into a building or across a plot of land and suddenly felt the hairs on the back of your neck stand up or gotten goose bumps on your arms? You don't know what set off your internal energy sensors, but something about the place immediately feels different. You might find yourself looking around to see if someone is watching you or suddenly feel like you need to leave the area. You may feel curious, energized, uneasy, or afraid. Or maybe you are hiking on a trail and suddenly walk into an area that feels more peaceful and balanced. Once you're aware of the effects energy has on a place, it's easier for you to recognize and connect with it.

SENSITIVITY TO ENERGY IN PLACES AND THEIR TRANSFORMATIONAL POWER

I believe that we all have intuitive abilities. We are sensitive to the people around us and the places we visit. We are able to use our intuition to come to a better understanding of those people and places. Being intuitive means you're able to sense the energy that people and places radiate, which allows you to create a deeper respect for them and an increased sense of value for the energy they bring into your life.

When you're sensitive to the energy in places, they will often feel vibrant and alive to you. There is the potential for great transformative action to occur between you and the place due to the earth frequency found there. Places have power, that's why they're called *power places, sacred sites,* or *vortexes* by a large majority of people. Some places are well known for their transformational power. When you visit them in person or by looking at pictures of the place and connecting your frequency to its frequency, your sensitivity to the place allows you to become part of its transformational energy.

Power places with concentrated, amplified, spiritual energy and transformational power exist all around the world where you can access the divine spirit of earth frequency to form a deep and clear understanding of the place and earth's power in that particular location, which can lead you to higher levels of consciousness, a deeper wisdom of all things, and the healing energy available to you from earth's frequency. If you can visit a location close to you in person to experience the power place first hand, try to do so because it can be a bit of a different experience than remote visitations.

Many power places are found in nature, so if you can't visit one that is well known, try taking a nature walk somewhere locally. Becoming one with nature can be transformational in and of itself because you're still connecting to earth frequency even if the location is not considered a popular power place. One thing to remember is that power places can exist in areas that aren't well known or even known at all. So while you're on your walk, you may wander upon a natural power place that no one else has ever come across before. How will you know? The energy will feel different and you will become aware of this difference as you walk through the area. These differences may be slight or very strong, but they will make you feel a heightened sense of sudden awareness that causes you to feel more energized and in tune with your own energy and the energy around you. You may even feel a tingling of your skin or suddenly feel hot or cold throughout your body.

Whatever happens, it will be something that immediately increases your awareness and will make you stop and think about what is happening and the changes you feel in the energy of the place. You might even find yourself doubling back again to check out the energy you just passed through. Some believe that power places must be a site of ruins or another area where the history shows a society of people who had a higher level of consciousness and deep spiritual beliefs. While it's true that places like this will indeed hold a greater field of energy and be more powerful, that doesn't mean you can't find a power place that holds transformational energy for you near where you live.

Many people are drawn to sacred sites because of the elevated levels of spiritual and healing energy. That's why thousands of people make pilgrimages to these places in order to increase their own spirituality and connection to the Divine so they will feel more in tune with their core spiritual self and more in balance because of the effect the energy of the sacred site or power place has upon them. You too can feel the same effects of a pilgrimage without actually traveling there by using your personal frequency and the earth frequency connection to the location. Sometimes it can be even more invigorating than actually walking miles upon miles to reach the destination.

The transformational power of a location helps you on many levels. After connecting with its earth frequency, you literally feel more enlightened and alive. You may feel an increase in your self-confidence, come to an understanding of how to handle situations that have been bothering you, or you may discover you're ready to make changes in your life that will enable you to move forward. Transformational places can cause a shift in your perspective, allowing you to see things in a different light. It is an awakening to something deep within your core spiritual self that you may have ignored prior to connecting with the power place. It is becoming inspired, feeling you can accomplish anything you set out to do. Transformational places can challenge you, dare you to take a different path, and give you the focus and determination to succeed. These places can heal you. Some are believed to be able to heal physical ailments while others heal the spirit or help us to evolve into the spiritual being we truly are inside but haven't acknowledged yet.

When you connect with the energy of a power place it often allows you to discover more about yourself. It can heighten your self-confidence and open your mind to possibilities you hadn't considered prior to the earth frequency connection, which can lead you out of your safe and familiar comfort zone and into areas where you felt uncertainty before but now feel you can handle with ease. In order to experience a deeper connection to yourself through the transformational power of sacred sites and power places, just take that first step. Let your barriers down by relaxing and letting go of any preconceived notions, fears, and worries that may be holding you back, if only for a few moments, so you can experience all that earth's energy has to offer. The feeling of connecting to earth frequency is enlightening, empowering, and will stay with you for the rest of your life.

Becoming one with earth's frequency often leads to soul searching and the discovery of what really matters to you and how you want to live your life. If you've been working hard and never taking the time to slow down and enjoy the little things in life, you may decide, after your earth frequency connection, that work doesn't need to consume all of your time. Instead, you may feel drawn to spend more time with family and friends or just enjoying being outside in nature. You may discover you are following your intuition and are more accepting of the things you cannot change. Earth's frequency can be transformational and bring about a greater clarity of yourself, your reason for being, and your soul purpose.

BENEFITS OF CONNECTING WITH EARTH'S FREQUENCY

Sometimes we become rigid in our beliefs and can be easily frustrated when someone else doesn't follow the same belief system. We can also become frustrated with ourselves due to the excessive amount of stress we put upon ourselves. Earth frequency can transform all of those things because when you're in the moment, when you're connecting to the energy of the place, you will often end up releasing any anxiety, fear, anger, or frustration you were previously feeling. Those feelings are replaced with acceptance, joy, and being part of something that is much greater than yourself. You'll feel yourself relax as the tension you're holding fades away. Then your mind will begin to wander through the energy, picking up information carried within it. There are messages in the energy that are just for you, that apply only to your life and your spirituality. It is divine.

This experience can bring you more happiness, joy, and lightness of being because you have allowed yourself to combine your energy with that of the place and let its energy lift you up and help you let go of emotions and worries that prevent you from reaching the levels of happiness you deserve. Too often we put blocks in our own paths and unconsciously sabotage ourselves because we feel like we don't truly deserve to be happy. Earth frequency can very effectively break down the blocks we're putting up and allows us to expand our consciousness by feeling the overflowing power of the energy in the place. When we feel, see, and experience such spectacular and spiritual energy, we can't help but broaden our horizons, making us appreciate the greatness of the world we live in and feel as though we're a vital part of the universal consciousness and energy of the planet. It truly is humbling, enlightening, and a spiritual connection to the divine when you feel the place's energy deep within your core spiritual self and in your own frequency.

ABOUT ME

I've been working with energy and teaching people about their own personal vibration, their frequency, for thirty-five years as part of my path as an intuitive coach. I've written several books specifically about frequency, including: *365 Ways to Raise Your Frequency*, which teaches readers specific ways to achieve higher levels of frequency; *Animal Fre-*

quency and *Llewellyn's Little Book of Spirit Animals*, which teach readers how to divinely connect their frequency to the frequency of all types of animals; *Believe and Receive*, which teaches readers to connect their frequency to the frequency of universal laws to achieve their greatest desires; and *The Simplicity of Cozy*, which teaches readers to spiritually connect their frequency with the frequency of simple, cozy, living. Working with frequency really is all about making spiritual energy connections. I've always loved history, and I almost minored in history in college, so it was natural for me to want to teach people how to connect to the frequency of sacred sites and vortex areas around the world.

ABOUT THIS BOOK

Being able to identify and become one with the energy of a place is the purpose of this book, and this resource will help you learn how to make energy connections to sacred sites around the world. You can even do this remotely, without physically being at the location! In fact, when I say "visiting" throughout the book, I mean either physically going to the site or remotely connecting to it through energy, images, videos, or text, so that you may have a spiritual energy experience with the frequency of the site.

In this book I've selected places from every continent on the planet and organized them by geographical areas, with the exception of Antarctica, which is pretty much uninhabitable. The only people who live there are scientists at research bases and sometimes tourists who go there on expeditions. No one lives there permanently as it is made up of ninety-eight percent ice and there aren't any cities or towns. That doesn't mean that Antarctica cannot heighten your frequency through looking at its extreme beauty in pictures—it can. It just means that there aren't any specific places that are considered sacred sites or power places in Antarctica there like there are in other parts of the world, unless you count Antarctica as a whole to be a power place.

The historical part of each entry is brief; if I wrote much more about the history and people who lived in these places, this book would be enormous. If you feel drawn to a place because of its energy or are simply intrigued by it and want to know more, I encourage you to follow up with additional research on your own to discover more about each of these places if you so desire. You are welcome to use the sources I've listed in the bibliography, website links, and footnotes or you can do your own exploration for more information if you enjoy digging into historical research.

In addition to teaching people about frequency, I also teach people how to develop their own intuition. The energy sections in *Earth Frequency* are based on my own intuition about the place. It is how I felt the frequency of the place as I connected to it during a previous physical visit or during my research while writing about the place and people who lived there. You may feel variations in the energy or something completely different when you read my words and that's awesome—go with the flow of what you're feeling and follow your own intuition, because you may be picking up on something that is important to you. For example, you may have had a past life in the area that makes the impressions you receive during the visitation session very strong and powerful. I want you to make the energy of the place your own while I guide you with my words, so veer off in a different direction if that's where you're being drawn to go.

I have also included maps that you can use to get a good feeling for where the sacred site is located in the world. Sometimes seeing the location on a map makes it easier to connect to the energy of the site because you can visualize yourself moving to the place if you physically see where it's located in the world.

HOW TO USE THIS BOOK

Before we dive into the section of the book that deals with the specific locations throughout the world, we'll first learn about how to make these connections. In chapters 1 and 2, I'll help you achieve this by teaching you how to make energy connections with a place and giving you some exercises to try before you start your sacred site visitations. It's helpful to understand the process beforehand instead of trying to figure it out once you're visiting the site.

I'd suggest that before you start reading each location, you familiarize yourself with the structure of the book and try some of the exercises in chapter 2. Then as you read about each of the locations, you can use the things you've already learned to help you visualize and connect to the frequency of each place. When you visit these places, it doesn't matter whether you're standing there in person or if you are connecting with the place from a distance, there is a vibrancy that you can't help but feel as you join with the energy of the sacred place. That vibrancy is frequency. Feel it, touch it, let it move through you and move you spiritually with its power and purpose.

In chapter 1 we'll delve into the various kinds of earth frequency and some super cool phenomenon found in nature. I'll also go over the different kinds of sacred sites you'll experience from the locations I've included in the book. I also discuss grid networks, ley lines, earth chakras, vortexes, and the 37th parallel north. I want to give you a well-rounded discussion of how earth frequency can manifest in the world and why some sites are considered sacred.

Then in chapter 2, it's time to get to work and practice. I'll go over how to recognize and connect with the energy of the places and then give you four exercises you can try before you really delve into the sites. These exercises will teach you how to connect to the frequency of a place, how to remotely connect with any place, how to use a filter shield visualization, and how to clear the chakras and disconnect from the site. These exercises are good practice to connect with earth frequency no matter where you are.

In part 2 you'll learn about the 250 places I selected for inclusion in this book. There are maps that will help you find the sacred site in the world by comparing the number in the legend to the number on the map. I've given you a brief history of each place, my intuitive impression of the frequency, and any pertinent information I thought would be helpful to you as you practice in connecting your own frequency to the frequency of the place.

Thank you for reading *Earth Frequency*. I hope you enjoy learning about the energy of this wonderful world we live in through some of the different sacred sites and power places around the planet.

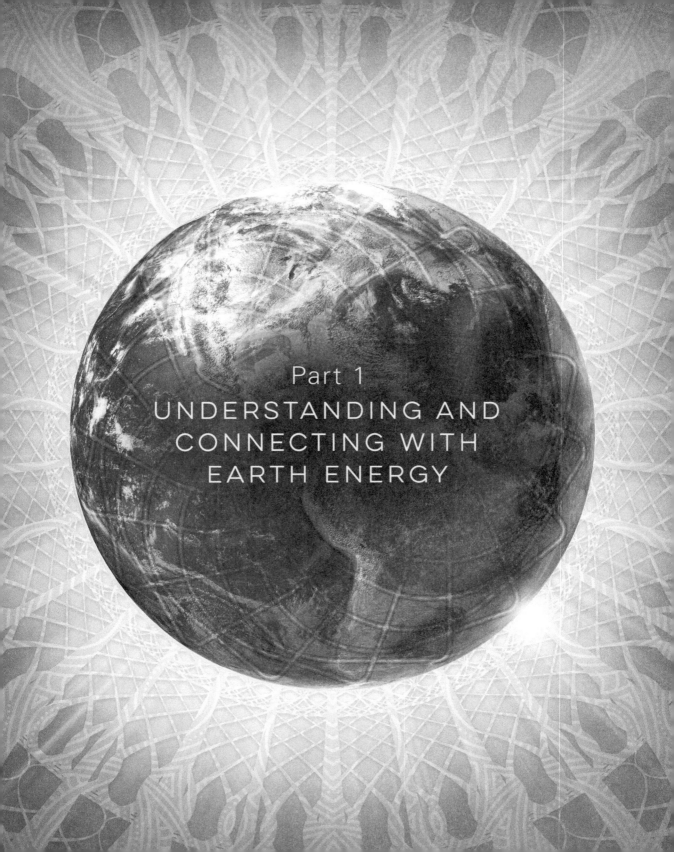

Part 1

UNDERSTANDING AND CONNECTING WITH EARTH ENERGY

Chapter 1
VARIOUS FORMS OF EARTH FREQUENCY

Have you ever stopped to consider the staggering amount of energy contained within our planet? Energy causes every change that occurs on earth. Consider the amount of energy needed to rotate the planet on its axis, the energy expelled through the eruption of a volcano, or the energy needed to move the water in the oceans. Earth's energy is complex, powerful, and constantly changing and being converted into different forms. The energy contained in earth's weather can range from a gentle breeze to a devastating hurricane. Everything vibrates, the earth included, and it is this rate of vibration that creates frequency. According to the Schumann Resonance,[1] the natural pulsation of earth's electromagnetic field ranges between 7.83 hertz to 43.2 hertz. The lowest point of 7.83 hertz is often considered the vibrational frequency of the earth. This electromagnetic field is contained within the earth's atmosphere, not within its crust or core. Earth's energy can be seen in active physical changes to the planet as well as changes to the biological systems on the earth.

There is an extreme amount of energy held within the core and crust of our planet. Even though billions of years have passed since it was formed through intensive heat, earth still contains some of that original heat. Earth is also able to create its own heat, which is generated through the process of radioactive decay. So while the earth has been slowly cooling since its beginning, it is also creating enough heat to maintain a steady temperature. Since this process is ongoing, there are times when heat, its internal

---

1. Miller, Iona, "Schumann Resonance: Excerpt from Nexus Magazine, Vol. 10, #3, April-May, 2003" https://www.sedonanomalies.com/schumann-resonance.html.

energy, is expelled. An example that everyone is familiar with is when a volcano erupts or an earthquake occurs.

At sacred sites, power places, or energy vortexes, you can feel the energy of the earth without the violent explosion of a volcano or the movement of the earth during an earthquake. These places may have mysteries surrounding them, paranormal events, or unexplained activities. People who visit these places are affected by the energy emitted in the area, usually in a positive way, and the energy there is considered more spiritual than a result of physical changes to the earth's surface.

We are also affected by the changes in the energy of the earth. It can affect our emotions, set off our sense of personal preservation, or enhance our spiritual feelings. Our own connection to earth's spiritual frequency not only elevates our own personal frequency but also connects our true spiritual selves to the ancientness of the earth and those who lived here before us.

KINDS OF EARTH ENERGY

I want to give you a basic overview of the different kinds of earth energy. Energy is never created or destroyed (the first law of thermodynamics) and it can be transferred from one object to another or converted from one form to another. Energy is usually thought of as either potential energy or kinetic energy. Potential energy is the stored energy within an object that has the ability to become kinetic energy. The amount of energy an object has when it's in motion is kinetic energy. When you add the amount of potential energy to the amount of kinetic energy, the result is the amount of mechanical energy that the object contains.

The sun provides energy to the earth in the form of solar (or photon) energy, which heats up its crust (surface) and powers the movement of the atmosphere, which distributes the energy that is important to our weather, plant, and animal life. Gravitational energy is the potential energy of an object based on how far it is from the surface of the earth. It results in the flow of rivers, the movement of air, and the movement of rocks, snow, and other matter.

The earth has four layers (crust, mantle, outer core, and inner core) and heat energy is an important part of how they interact with one another. If it were possible to dig through these layers, the hole would be eight thousand miles from one end to the other. The crust is about twenty-five miles deep and contains everything you are familiar with about the earth—lakes, oceans, rivers, mountains, jungles, forests, cities, towns, and all of the locations we'll discuss in this book. It's where the ecosystems interact with one another, where humans, animals, and insects live—it is home. The mantle is the next layer and it makes up the majority of the earth's mass. You may not realize it but there is a lot of activity going on in there. The mantle consists of mostly solid rocks that move around. The temperature of the mantle ranges from about one thousand degrees Fahrenheit near the crust to four thousand degrees Fahrenheit near the outer core. The warmer rocks move toward the crust while the cooler rocks move toward the core where they are warmed up again, then they move back toward the crust and the rocks there that have cooled down move back toward the core. This flow of energy and rock is called convection current and causes the tectonic plates to move, which can result in volcanic eruptions, the creation of mountain ranges, or earthquakes. As you move past the outer core down into the inner core, the temperature can reach thirteen thousand degrees Fahrenheit and, according to scientists, is made up of solid nickel and iron.

There are other types of energy that occur in the natural world. As the human race has progressed, we have learned how to harness some of these types of energy such as:

- **Tidal energy**—the movement of the earth's oceans that results in high and low tides.
- **Wind energy**—the power of the wind as it flows through a turbine and creates mechanical energy.
- **Chemical energy**—the energy released during a chemical reaction (like when you cook food).
- **Sound energy**—the sound that results from the vibration of an object.
- **Nuclear energy**—when a heavy nucleus splits into two light nuclei or when two light nuclei fuse to form a heavy nucleus, which is the kind of energy you find within the sun and within the inner core of earth.

All of these types of energy are part of the components of the earth and its atmosphere with help from the sun and moon. It all works together in harmony.

Humans and animals are sensitive to the energy of the earth. Think of the stories about animals running away from the ocean prior to a tsunami or leaving an area prior to an earthquake. This is because their instincts allow them to feel the earth energy connection to an upcoming event. In a 1988 study done by William K. Tong regarding abnormal behavior of animals prior to natural disasters, it was noted that positive airborne ions (carbon dioxide molecules that have lost an electron) released into the air in areas surrounding the disturbances in the earth's crust seem to have a direct correlation to animals leaving an area up to three weeks before the event actually happens.[2] These positive ions in the air cause animals to want to avoid them, so they remove themselves from the area. Positive airborne ions can cause feelings of restlessness, irritability, anxiety, make people feel sick to their stomach, or cause headaches. If you've ever felt worried or uneasy prior to a thunderstorm, it can be attributed to positive ions because an electrical storm has very high levels of them. After a thunderstorm, the air is filled with negative ions. When a molecule gains an electron, it becomes a negative ion, which has the exact opposite effect and can cause feelings of happiness, calmness, and peacefulness. Negative ions improve your mood and make you feel more energized. In nature, areas that contain more negative ions are places like waterfalls, lakes, streams, the ocean, or forests. That's why a long walk on the beach, a hike in the forest, or a day boating on a lake improves the way you feel.

It would make sense then that the air and energy in the area of power places, sacred sites, and vortexes would have more negative ions than positive ones, because they create positive feelings within you, although studies haven't proven it yet. Spiritually, it is believed that the veil between the physical world and the spiritual world is thinner at these sites. That could also explain the feelings of a heightened awareness and peace that accompany visits to these places. Think about a place you've visited that gave you a sense of awe that made you think about life and the world at a deeper level. Regardless of whether this was due to negative ions or a thin veil between worlds, I'm sure it's a feeling that has stayed with you and deeply affected you in some way, even if the location you visited was in your own backyard.

PHENOMENA IN NATURE

The energy in and around the earth can result in some pretty amazing naturally occurring phenomena. I'd like to give you a quick overview of some of nature's most awesome phenomenon to increase your awareness of them as you practice earth frequency

---

2. Tong, William K., "Abnormal Animal Behavior and the Prediction of Earthquakes," August 1988, http://www.oakton.edu/user/4/billtong/eas100/abnorm_anim_behav_earthquakes.pdf.

while visiting sacred sites, power places, vortexes, and other places covered in this book. For example, learning that volcanoes can have volcanic lightning during eruptions adds another level of energy to volcanoes or places where inactive volcanic cones currently exist. You can use this knowledge to access that additional energy as you're connecting your frequency to that location's frequency.

These are a small sampling of the many different and unique ways that earth's energy creates spectacular phenomenon in the sky, over land, and in the ocean. Some fill you with a sense of wonder, others a sense of foreboding, but regardless of the effect you feel when encountering the greatness of nature's energy, there is no doubt that there is great power created by the energy of earth and it's atmosphere. Take the time to really look at the world. By linking your frequency to that of earth's frequency, you can feel a deeper connection to the energy that is all around you.

- **Ball Lighting**—looks like a glowing ball of light in the sky during a thunderstorm. It can appear to be moving slowly like its floating to earth, quickly like a shooting star, or stationary. It can blink out as suddenly as it appears.

- **Volcanic Lightning**—mostly seen during strong, violent eruptions, this usually happens directly above the crater of the volcano amid the volcanic ash and other substances projected into the sky during the eruption.

- **Earthquake Lights**—often found near the ground but can also rise up into the air or look similar to ball lightning. Scientists believe these lights come from the electrical components of rocks released prior to an earthquake. These lights are also seen around volcanoes. They can appear in any shape or size and are often blue, multicolored, yellow, or white.

- **Aurora**—also known as the northern lights (aurora borealis) or the southern lights (aurora australis). This phenomenon only occurs within ten to twenty degrees from each of earth's magnetic poles. The light of the aurora is created when the sun's solar winds push electrically charged particles into earth's upper atmosphere. When these particles collide with the natural gas atoms in our atmosphere they give off light, which results in the beautiful light show near the north and south poles.

- **Will-o'-Wisp**—bluish lights that are often called ghost lights or corpse candles. This phenomenon is often thought to be the light of a lantern carried by a mischievous spirit whose intention is to lure unsuspecting travelers into swampy areas or to be the light created by a recently departed loved one who is lost and wandering the earth. They are also called treasure lights, because it was believed that they indicated where treasure was hidden, or fairy lights, indicating that fairies created them or that they were the light of the fairy itself. Since will-o'-wisps are primarily found over bogs, marshes, and swamps, it is now scientifically believed that they are created through the breakdown of organic matter which creates gasses that escape and burn. Will-o'-wisp are known for moving away from people and then disappearing. It is believed this happens because of the disturbance in the air as a person approaches the area, which pushes the gas away.

- **Sailing Stones**—a phenomenon where rocks move of their own accord. Scientists have now proven that they move under specific conditions that include the energy of water, ice, and wind combined to push them across the desert floor.

- **Snow Donut**—the energy of the wind and gravity along with snow that is somewhat sticky creates a snowball which rolls down a hill or incline. As the snowball gets larger, the middle falls out, creating a donut shape. The conditions have to be perfect for a snow donut to form.

- **Bioluminescence**—when living organisms in the ocean produce a glowing blue light. It's often found in algae and plankton but there are jellyfish that can also produce this type of light. In some areas of the ocean, there will appear to be blue waves coming onto the shore when algae or plankton are glowing. At greater depths, more marine life can produce bioluminescent light.

- **Lenticular Clouds**—form at high altitudes around the tops of mountains. They look like lens, fallstreak, or hole-punch clouds, which are large circular clouds with a hole in the middle; mamatus clouds, which look like they have pouches hanging from them; and morning glory clouds, which form at low levels and look like rolling tubes of clouds.

THE DIFFERENT TYPES OF SACRED SITES

Since the beginning of recorded history, people, especially elders, medicine men, shamans, wise women, people with "the sight," chieftains, and others have known about the powerful energy at specific locations because of the unique energy in the area. Over time, some of these locations became sacred because of the ceremonial or ritualistic actions of the people from the past at the location. The energy of their actions imprinted on the place, creating a unique vibration. These many different types of spiritual sacred sites around the world can be broken down into themes and categories based upon similarities between the sites. There are other reasons people believe a location is a power place or a sacred site and it has less to do with the physical location of the area than it has to do with how the energy in the site affects people. The energy between the sites may feel completely different from one another if you were to visit each one in person, so one of the links between them is what happens there in the present or the things that happened there in the past. They may also be linked by architectural design (pyramids, monoliths) or by what they can do for you (healing springs, purification sites). In modern times we often choose to visit a power place in order to increase our creativity, to pray or meditate, to amplify our intuition, rejuvenate us, help with visualization, or to bring stability and balance back to our spiritual self. Some sites can help us connect to our emotions, to feel things deeply and to clearly see our purpose. Some can help with our sense of direction in life; they can rejuvenate us or boost our energy when we connect to the energy of the power place.

Other times we might need guidance from energy animals that may only be found at specific power places through dreaming or a vision quest or by remote viewing. Maybe we need to take a pilgrimage to clear our energy and balance ourselves. There are healing and purification sites, areas that are magnetic, and medicine sites. If we can feel it and connect to the frequency of the area, then we can benefit from the sacredness of the site and its energy.

Sometimes it's important to know the history of a location before you visit it. Other times, it is important to visit it before you know the history. Most of us aren't financially able to travel the world and visit all of the sacred power places, so we have to do it from the comfort of our homes by viewing pictures and videos taken by someone who has visited the site and reading their written accounts of their visit. Doing this can be just as powerful as visiting in person and will often be a catalyst to your own unique earth frequency connection to the place.

The sites I selected for this book fall into forty-two different categories. In part 2, I have included these categories under each of the location names. This provides you with an introduction to the types of categories you'll come across. I've provided their brief descriptions here:

- **Astronomical Observatories**—These are often found at megalithic sites such as the one in Externsteine Rocks, Germany and are believed to have been used by ancient people to study the stars.

- **Bodies of Water/Waterfalls/Springs**—Large bodies of water including rivers, lakes, and natural springs are often believed to have the ability to heal people like the ones found in Wairakei Terraces, New Zealand.

- **Burial Sites**—Burial sites are considered sacred by the people who live in the area as respect to the people who have come before. These sites also give us clues to how the people lived in ancient times.

- **Canyons/Gorges**—Canyons and gorges often reveal information about times past and the ancient people who lived during those times. They often have myth and legend surrounding their existence.

- **Caves**—Caves are often sites of ceremonial and spiritual usage, where you'll find petroglyphs and rock art.

- **Ceremonial Sites**—These sites are considered sacred because they were an important part of the belief systems of the people in the area. The energy at these sites is often of very high frequencies.

- **Earth Chakras**—Several areas around the world are thought to be the chakras of the earth and show the characteristics associated with the chakra it represents.

- **Fertility Sites**—Some sites are considered to be fertility sites and it is believed that by visiting such a site will increase the chances of conceiving a child or of having a particularly fertile harvest.

- **Footprints**—These sites are where the footprints of ancient humans were preserved.

- **Forests/Trees**—In the natural world power places and sacred sites can be found within caves, on mountains, or within a forest grove. Some individual trees are considered sacred for various reasons, for example the Bodhi Tree in Bodh Gaya, India, where Buddha found enlightenment.

- **Geysers / Blowholes**—The energy at these sites is powerful, transformational, and they are often considered sacred sites.

- **Gigantic Landscape Carvings**—Done by ancient people, and some say they were completed with the help of extraterrestrial beings due to their sheer size, some of these sites like the Nazca Lines in Peru are usually best viewed from the air.

- **Glaciers**—Glaciers are reminiscent of the Ice Age when they covered large areas of the earth. Today they can still be found on many mountain tops and other locations around the world.

- **Healing Springs**—Many places with healing springs are also steeped in legend, myth, and true stories of how people were healed by entering the water or by drinking the water from the spring.

- **Impact Crater**—Impact craters hold tremendous amounts of transformational energy.

- **Islands/Reefs**—Some entire islands, like Easter Island, are considered sacred sites, while other islands have areas within them that are considered sacred. Reef systems surrounding islands fall into the same category.

- **Man-made Mounds/Mountains**—Places built by humans that look like mountains or mounds.

- **Man-made Sites**—Places built by humans are also believed to have powerful energies. These include pyramids, places of ancient ruins and astronomical observatories, standing stone sites, chambered mounds, labyrinth sites, ancient ceremonial sites, and places where man carved giant pictures into the landscape.

- **Marian Apparition / Miracle Sites**—Places where there were sightings of the Virgin Mary or where a miracle happened.

- **Medicine Wheels**—are stone circles that were used for astronomical, religious and other reasons. These circles were built by North American Indians throughout the continent.

- **Megalithic Sites**—These sites are ancient and are dated to prehistory. Megalithic sites are made of very large stones that prehistoric people constructed without using mortar. Some megalithic sites only contain one stone while others contain many stones and stone structures. Stonehenge is an example.

- **Monasteries / Temples**—Religion often plays a part in the sacredness of a location. Every religion in the world has places that are considered holy and sacred to their beliefs.

- **Mountains / Mounds / Cliff Locations**—Natural mountains, mounds, and cliffs.

- **Mythological Sites**—Areas of mythological or legendary importance, where dragons were sighted, or that had some special connection to a male or female deity, was known for granting fertility, or were important places to animals or birds. These places have moved from legend to the sacred.

- **Oracle Sites**—In ancient times, there were places where oracles would give predictive or prophetic information to the people of the time.

- **Petroglyph / Rock Art Sites**—These sites can be found at overhanging rock shelters, in caves, and along cliff walls throughout the world. Ancient people used colors found in nature to paint on the rocks, often depicting things they experienced in their daily lives.

- **Pilgrimage Sites**—Sacred places are often visited by many people during specific times called pilgrimages. These sites are often temples, mountains, shrines, lakes and healing springs to name a few.

- **Pitch Lakes**—La Brea Pitch lake in Trinidad and Tobago is the largest naturally occurring asphalt lake in the world and is included in this book. There are only two other known pitch lakes and three tar pits worldwide.

- **Power Places**—A power place can be any type of sacred site, vortex, or location in the world where the energy affects you in a powerful way. Some places are known as power places due to being so well known, for instance the locations found in Sedona, Arizona; Glastonbury Tor, England; or Lascaux Caves, France. Other places can be local to you and not known to anyone but you, but still be just as powerful in the energy.

- **Power Stones**—These locations consist of stones that are considered to exude powerful energy such as Stonehenge, Dreamer's Rock, or Easter Island.

- **Pyramids**—These manmade structures are considered power places due to their structure, the fact that they're burial sites, and because we still aren't sure exactly how ancient man built them.

- **Rainforests**—Beautiful, mysterious, and breathtaking, the rainforests contain over half of the world's animal and plant life while only covering about 2 percent of the surface of the earth.

- **Regions**—Some regions and areas of the world are considered sacred because of a variety of different types of energy locations within them—for example, the Great Ocean Road in Australia or the Sacred Valley of the Inca in Peru.

- **Relic Sites**—Places where objects that once belonged to saints or other holy people are kept are also as sacred as the objects themselves.

- **Rock Formations**—These sites are usually considered sacred due to the enormous size and the spiritual beliefs of the local people. Some examples are the Bungle Bungles in Australia, Dreamer's Rock in Canada, and Bell Rock in Arizona.

- **Ruins / Archeological Sites**—These types of sites are man-made and are often from ancient history. They are places that were sacred to the people and used for ceremony. We learn a lot from the history of the place and the ruins of these sites. The energy at these locations is often very strong and powerful due to the energy imprints made by the people who created and lived in the place before it fell into ruin.

- **Sandhills / Sand Dunes**—Sandhills and Sand Dunes are often reflective of changes, protection, and having the resiliency to absorb the impact of situations and move forward from them. Because of this they are often considered sacred.

- **Shrines / Birth or Burial Sites of Saints**—Shrines and places where an important religious figure was born or died are often sacred sites.

- **Sink Hole**—A sink hole is where an enormous amount of energy is drawn into the earth, which results in the surrounding area collapsing into the earth. The energy at sinkhole sites is very powerful.

- **UFO / Extraterrestrial / Paranormal Sites**—At some of these locations we have yet to discover how ancient man was able to create what is left behind. Some people believe there is no way some of these places could have been created without help from extraterrestrial beings. Other power places are sites where unidentified flying objects are often seen by the people in the area or where there are ancient drawings of extraterrestrial-like beings on stone. Whether you believe in ancient alien beings or unidentified flying objects or not, these areas definitely have some strange things happening and an unsettled feeling to their energy.

- **Volcanoes/Volcano Cones**—Volcanoes are considered power places and were often used as sacred or sacrificial ceremonial sites.

- **Vortexes**—A vortex is a place where the energy of the earth projects outward or is drawn inward. Vortexes are often found at many sacred sites. The energy at a vortex site is considered transformational.

As you read about each place, also consider how these categories relate to it. Is the place sacred because of the people and their beliefs or because of its characteristics such as being a volcano or a healing spring? By understanding the categories, you acquire a wider overall view of the location and the energy held within it.

GRID NETWORKS AND LEY LINES

According to Francis Hitching in *Earth Magic*, the term "ley line" was coined by Alfred Watkins to describe the invisible energy lines surrounding earth. Watkins was an English businessman who enjoyed archeology. Before he created the term, he referred to these lines as old straight tracks or archaic tracks. In other places around the world, ley lines are known as song lines, holy lines, fairy paths, dragon lines, and spirit lines. Many cultures believed these lines to be ancient, sacred tracks that form a mystical and spiritual energy alignment between land formations all around the world. Watkins believed that a ley line would start and end on a hill and the area within the straight line between the two hills would contain sacred sites and power places like ruins, megaliths, ancient monuments, churches, castles, and other man-made and natural places that contained high levels of transformational energy.

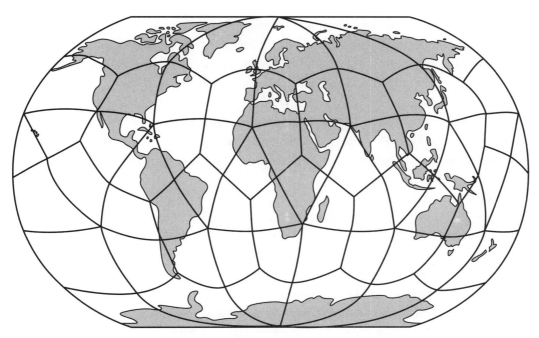

Planetary Grid System derived from Nikolai Goncharov, Vyacheslav Morozov, and Vaelry Makarov. "Is the Earth a Large Crystal?" Khimiya i Zhizn (Chemistry of Life), Science Journal of the USSR Academy of Science.

In order to understand how ley lines are a part of the universal whole, we must first look at the energetic grid networks of our planet that operates through sacred geometry, which was often used in ancient times to create monuments, sacred spaces, medicine wheels, megaliths, and churches. When the lines of the grids intersect, that's the area where you'll often find sacred sites and power places of the world. Grid networks and ley lines represent the symbolic nature of sacred geometry, that everything is part of the universal whole, all is interconnected and cannot be separated, and is a reminder of our own internal energy grids upon which our thoughts and energy travels to create our own consciousness and reality that, when connected to the energy grids surrounding the earth, allow us to make earth frequency connections through those grids and divine universal power.

Curry Model

There are several energetic grid models that are different in their belief of how the grid works. For example, the Curry model is based on earth's radiation, which makes it different from the Hartmann net, which is magnetically based.[3] The rotation of the earth and magnesium directly affects the grid. The energy runs from southwest to northeast. Curry lines are described as a mystical force field, a power life force of energy flow that surrounds earth and can be detectable by dowsing with a diving rod instead of typical scientific instruments. The lines are almost ten feet apart and are diagonal to earth's poles. The Curry net is believed to be more stable than the Hartmann net.

Hartmann Net

In the Hartmann net, the energy runs from north to south and east to west, is magnetically orientated, and rises from the ground in vertical lines that are nine inches wide. These lines are encountered every six feet six inches going north to south and every eight feet going east to west. The area between these lines is neutral. It changes every six hours and is sensitive to sunspots, moon phases, and meteorological conditions. Alternating lines are positively and negatively charged, so at grid line intersections you can find double positive or double negative charges, which are believed to be dynamic environments that are often in vibration with the rhythm of the seasons and the hours of the day and can sometimes be problematic. The Hartmann net is also described using the Chinese yin and yang with yin being the north to south lines and yang being the east to west lines. Yin represents a slow-moving colder energy and yang is a fast moving, hot, and active energy.

The Cathie Net

The Cathie net is a grid of rectangles that are forty-five square nautical miles each. These rectangles are affected by the mass of the earth, gravity, and the speed of light. The Cathie lines are believed to attract unidentified flying objects that somehow use the energy fields of these rectangles and are of special interest to UFO enthusiasts. At the end of this chapter, we'll also discuss the 37th parallel north, which is believe to be the superhighway used by UFOs.

---

3. Piontzik, Klaus, "Global Grids/Planetary Grids," http://erdmagnetfeld.pimath.de/global_grids.html

Ley Lines

Ley lines are a separate part of the energy grid surrounding the earth that send and receive energy throughout the world while connecting to sacred sites and power places along the way. While the exact way a ley line was created is considered lost information, they are thought to have been created by ancient surveying, marking off property lines in early civilization, or along pathways that primordial people often traveled, even though the roads weren't always straight, and there were well-known places along these passageways that people used as navigation points. The use of straight lines was important in many cultures where they often used mountain peaks as markers. Ley lines are believed to be man-made but follow the idea of a line of energy, similar to the grid networks, as well.

Skeptics of ley line theories say that a straight line can always be drawn between multiple places at random points and places weren't built specifically to be on an imagined line, nor could ancient man have known about the natural sites around the world that fall upon ley lines.

Using their intuition, many people can pick up on the energy at grid lines, intersections of grid lines, and along ley lines. It is believed that ancient people understood how earth's energy worked at these locations and that there is a spiritual, magical, holy, magnetic, or electrical force surrounding sacred sites and power places within ley lines or at intersecting points of a planetary energy grid.

So while you may not be able to see the energy grids surrounding the earth or the ley lines that cross from point to point, you can feel the powerful energy radiating from the intersection of grid lines and along the pathways of ley lines. Since grid lines are found within short distances, then you truly can connect to the power of intersecting lines right in your own back yard. When the human body comes into contact with the strong energy in these areas, it affects our biochemistry, our physical makeup, as well as our spirituality. Connecting with earth frequency in this way can have a powerful and transformational impact on your life. People who have experienced the energy at a sacred site express feelings of being more alive, more connected to the earth, being able to feel things more intensely and see situations clearly. They feel rejuvenated, more creative, and ready to take on challenges. They report an increase in their spirituality, a deeper knowing and understanding of the universal power that also affects earth's energy grids. They feel healed emotionally and sometimes physically.

Visiting places on ley lines or sacred sites that don't fall on ley lines and attuning to the energy of the place can help you discover different kinds of changes you'll feel when you become part of the universal whole. You may experience signs like tingling throughout your body, light-headedness, or clarity on where you are and where you need to be. Earth's frequency can be a bit overwhelming to empaths so if you feel like it's too much too fast, simply use creative visualization to put up a filter shield around you so you have more time to acclimate to the power of the energy surrounding the power place or sacred site.

You are part of earth frequency simply because you live on the planet. Isn't it time to become one with the energy that surrounds you and let it benefit your mind, body, and spirit? Earth readily gives off its energy but it's up to you to accept it.

EARTH CHAKRAS

Chakras within our bodies are small vortexes of energy that look like three dimensional wheels of light moving in a spiral along seven locations from the top of our heads to the end of our spines. In the next section we will be talking about earth's vortexes. While vortexes and chakras are both founts of energy, there are distinctions between the two. Chakras have a circular energy flow that stays within the physical body. Chakra energy movement balances the overall frequency and energy flow within the body. Vortexes are different from chakras because they are found within the earth and the energy moves either away from the land or back into it instead of only staying inside the earth. Earth's chakras are sometimes also found in areas of powerful vortex energy.

There are seven major chakras within the human body and hundreds of secondary chakras. The seven major chakras are the root chakra located at the base of the spine at the tailbone, the sacral chakra located in the lower abdomen about two inches below the navel, the solar plexus chakra located in the upper abdomen around the stomach region, the heart chakra located in the center of your chest slightly above your heart, the throat chakra located at the base of your throat, the third eye chakra located in the middle of your forehead, and the crown chakra which is located at the top of your head. Each of these chakras work in harmony with each other to help us connect to our spiritual self and become more grounded and enable us to do energy work within ourselves to transform our thoughts and our ability to be more confident, accepting, and loving and are a key part of our ability to survive on the earthly plane of existence. They can help us communicate easily, see the whole instead of just seeing the one, and once we've

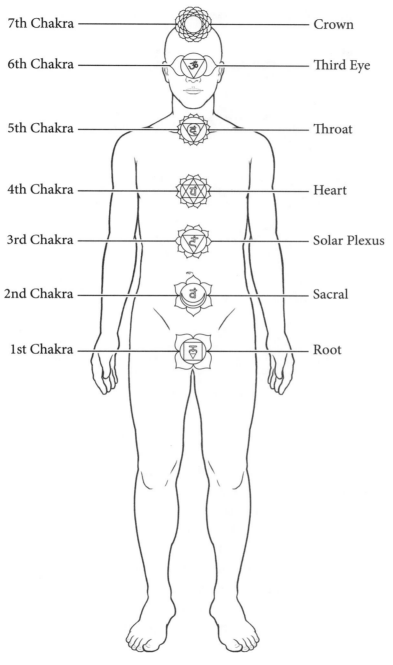

7th Chakra —————————— Crown

6th Chakra —————————— Third Eye

5th Chakra —————————— Throat

4th Chakra —————————— Heart

3rd Chakra —————————— Solar Plexus

2nd Chakra —————————— Sacral

1st Chakra —————————— Root

Chakras

connected our crown chakra to our own spirituality, then we become more enlightened through transformation.

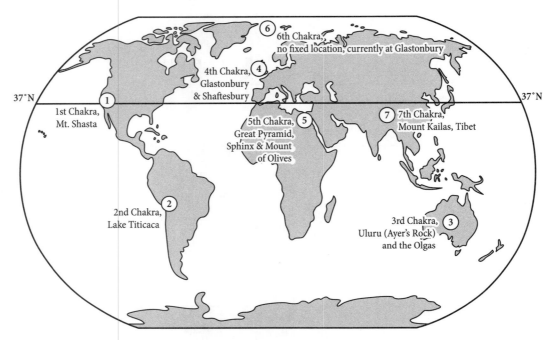

Robert Coon's Earth Chakra System

Just as every human has a chakra system, the earth also has chakras. They look similar to human chakras in that they are three-dimensional spiraling wheels of light energy. They are different in that the energy at an earth chakra can flow in two directions, either toward or away from the earth, because earth's chakras are, quite simply, powerful energy vortexes. Earth also has an enormous secondary chakra system located at sites of smaller vortexes. These smaller vortex sites of the secondary chakra system are the kinds of vortexes that you might encounter during a walk in nature. There are many different opinions and mappings on exactly where earth's chakras are located. Each one serves different people and purposes so none of them are considered right or wrong. I'm going to go over two different mappings, but my space is limited so if you find the topic of earth chakras interesting, please continue investigating on your own.

Spiritual blogger and healer, Lisa Erickson's Contemporary Earth System[4] and Robert Coon's Earth Chakra System[5] lay out details about their systems on their respective websites.

Robert Coon developed his Earth Chakra System using his knowledge of cultural spirituality, astrology, and sacred geometry. Coon believes the earth is a living being that is constantly in a state of evolution, so earth uses its chakra system to remain healthy and to transmit energy and information. This is the Coon mapping:

Chakra One (Root Chakra): Mount Shasta, North America—This mountain sends life energy outward from the earth. Numerous UFO sightings have occurred in the area. The most primal of the earth's chakras. It erupts energy like a geyser without form or structure.

Chakra Two (Sacral Chakra): Lake Titicaca, South America—This chakra is evolutionary in that it advances both new and existing species.

Chakra Three (Solar Plexus Chakra): Uluru, also called Ayers Rock and Kata Tjuta, Australia—This chakra holds the energy of Dreamtime, the era of creation from which all life came. This chakra is important in maintaining earth's vitality.

Chakra Four (Heart Chakra): Glastonbury Tor and Shaftesbury, United Kingdom, Europe— This chakra connects to immortality, willpower, and destiny and means that love can be united in a revolutionary way.

Chakra Five (Throat Chakra): The Great Pyramid, Mount Sinai, and the Mount of Olives, Egypt and the Middle East—These areas create a sphere of chakra energies by connecting with four vortexes in the area that regulate earth, fire, air, and water. Earth speaks through this chakra; it is the earth's voice.

Chakra Six (Third Eye Chakra): Aeon Activation Center, Mobile—Labeled with the Zodiac this chakra relates to the eon, which always moves westward, 1/12th of the way around the world, at the dawn of each new Aeon.

4. Erickson, Lisa, "Planet Earth's Chakras," May 26, 2009, https://mommymystic.wordpress.com/2009/05/26/planet-earths-chakras/.

5. Coon, Robert, 1967—2018, http://earthchakras.org.

Chakra Seven (Crown Chakra): Mt. Kailash, Tibet, Asia—This chakra reflects and broadcasts the true will of the earth and its purpose. Helps people find their own true will through earth energy illumination.

Lisa Erickson compared sites from many different mappings along with her intuition to come up with her own Earth Chakra System. During her studies she found that while many of the same power places and sacred sites came up in different mappings, they often corresponded to different chakra numbers and descriptions. This is the Erickson mapping:

Chakra One (Root Chakra): Grand Canyon, North America—This chakra is raw and connects to earth's core.

Chakra Two (Sacral Chakra): Machu Picchu, South America—This chakra radiates earth's rhythm, sensuality, and natural abundance.

Chakra Three (Solar Plexus Chakra): Uluru, also called Ayers Rock, Central Australia—A sacred site to the Aboriginal people, this chakra is associated with personal power and self-definition.

Chakra Four (Heart Chakra): Glastonbury Tor, United Kingdom, Europe/ Rishikesh and Varanasi, India—This chakra is where the heart of the earth is located. The England site is said to be the home of Avalon and Druid, Celtic and Arthurian legends are all linked to this chakra. The cities in India have been spiritual sites for thousands of years.

Chakra Five (Throat Chakra): Giza/Nile River/Nile Delta, Africa—This chakra is important in dreaming, expression, music, language, religion, and science.

Chakra Six (Third Eye Chakra): Mt. Fuji, Japan, Asia—This chakra offers clarity and insight to form a well-functioning third eye chakra within the human chakra system.

Chakra Seven (Crown Chakra): Mt. Kailash, Tibet, Asia—This chakra is linked to a high level of sacredness, illumination, and transformation.

Earth's chakras are transformational, and they allow us to align our own energy with that of earth frequency and connect to our higher selves. Energy moves through the universe, through the earth and through you. The energy of earth's chakras can be accessed at any time because their frequencies already live inside of you. This means you don't have to travel to distant locations to experience the powerful energy of earth's chakras. You can do it from the comfort of your own home through meditation, looking at pictures of the area, and studying the location's history and the people who lived there in ancient times.

One link between your inner chakras and earth's chakras is that you'll find yourself drawn to certain earth chakras if your own corresponding chakra feels blocked. For instance if your heart chakra is blocked due to being hurt by someone, then when you connect your energy to that of earth's heart chakra, the earth's energy can help heal your heart, so you can begin to trust and move forward again. Earth's chakras help us evolve into the true spiritual beings that we are on the inside. They help us tap in to our essential essence and align our energy with that of earth's energy to experience spiritual transformations. It doesn't matter if you visit one of the seven primary earth chakras or if you commune with and connect to a secondary chakra that is physically close to your current location. Any connection to earth's chakras will have a profound and lasting effect on your life.

VORTEXES

The term vortex refers to the patterns of powerful energy emitted from the earth that move in a rotating spiraling motion. There are two distinct kinds of vortexes—electric and magnetic—and these terms refer to the effect of the energy flow. An electric vortex means that the energy bubbles up from the earth, like water bubbles up at a geyser or hot springs. It moves upwards, away from the ground. The energy in an electric vortex is lighter, energizing, and feels as if it's lifting you into a more dynamic frame of mind. Electric vortexes are known for healing, expanding consciousness, and reaching higher levels of spiritual awareness at a universal level. Once you've experienced an increase in consciousness due to the energy of an electrical vortex, it's believed that the effect is lasting and that you'll always be more aware of the way earth frequency affects you. Because of the positivity that electric vortexes create when you encounter them, they're often referred to as positive vortexes.

Magnetic vortexes are opposite from electric vortexes. They act more like a vacuum, pulling energy back down inside the earth. This type of energy can help you feel grounded, stable, and balanced. You may feel more pensive or reflective and find yourself considering your path and changes you should make in your life. They can make you feel out of balance so that you seek a way to bring balance back into your life through change. Because they can also evoke feelings of fear or uncertainty, magnetic vortexes are referred to as negative. That being said, the energy of a magnetic vortex can affect you in different ways, both positive and negative, and it will only feel negative if you allow it to affect you in a negative instead of a positive way.

Electromagnetic vortexes have a combination of both energies which flow both upwards into the air and downward into the earth. These areas are called Vile Vortices[6] or Vile Vortexes and there are twelve of them spaced evenly around earth. They are thought to create blocks within you instead of raising your awareness and consciousness and are places where strange disappearances, electromagnetic aberrations, and other unexplained phenomena occurs—for example when airplanes or ships disappear without a trace in areas like the Bermuda Triangle after experiencing instrument and mechanical malfunctions and are never found.

The term Vile Vortices was coined by Ivan Sanderson, a Scottish biologist who was also the founder of the Society for the Investigation of the Unexplained. In 1972 he wrote an article for Saga magazine titled "The Twelve Devil's Graveyards Around the World." Sanderson believed these areas had high levels of electromagnetic disturbances caused by hot and cold air and, if over water, the sea currents. Ten of the areas are in tropical regions and fall within the Tropic of Cancer and the Tropic of Capricorn. The other two are the North Pole and South Pole and when all twelve are connected together they form a geometric, twenty-faced polyhedron called an icosahedron that surrounds the earth. Sanderson's ideas were met with skepticism and doubt.

The most well-known of the twelve Vile Vortexes is the Bermuda Triangle located off of the coast of Florida toward the Bahamas because it shows more activity than some of the other sites. According to Sanderson, the six vortexes located in the Tropic of Cancer are Mohenjo Daro (the site of the Rama Empire), the Devil's Sea (also known as the Dragon's Triangle), Hamakulia (an area near Hawaii with high volcanic activity), the Bermuda Triangle, the Algerian Megalithic Ruins, and the North Pole. The Vile Vortexes in the Tropic of Capricorn are the Zimbabwe Megaliths, the Wharton Basin (the site of the Wallaby Fracture Zone), the edge of the Hebrides Trench (near the Fiji Islands), Easter Island (Colossi), the South Atlantic Anomaly and the South Pole.

---

6. Paranormal Encyclopedia, "Vile Vortices," https://www.paranormal-encyclopedia.com/v/vile-vortices/.

Today vortexes are often sought out specifically for healing of the mind, body, and soul whether it is through a positive electric vortex or a negative magnetic vortex. Both have healing effects; they just affect you differently during the experience. In the past people didn't always understand the energy that surrounds a vortex, but because they felt the change in the atmosphere, they considered it a place to avoid. Today some people also believe they are gateways to other dimensions and spiritual realms.

Vortexes are often found on ley lines and earth grid intersections, but they can also be found in other places where there are high negative ion concentrations in the air or high levels of iron or magnesium in the ground. Since ancient times, people have believed that vortexes are sacred places and built buildings near vortexes that were used as temples, churches, or monasteries. Some areas were left in their natural state. All vortex locations were believed to be centers of spiritual empowerment.

Some of the sacred sites built on vortexes are Stonehenge, the Pyramids of Giza, Bali, and Machu Picchu. Natural places like Mount Shasta, Mount Fuji, and Ayers Rock are also considered powerful vortex sites.

One of the most well know sites with multiple vortexes is located in Sedona, Arizona—the red rock canyons, which were once a place of pilgrimages from as far away as South America and Canada. The canyons were considered a holy place that brought about spiritual growth and an intrinsic connection to universal knowledge. The veil to other dimensions is believed to be thinner in Sedona than it is at other vortex sites. Energy surrounding the Sedona vortexes is so powerful that people say they can feel it surging throughout their body, it causes the hair on their arms and back of their neck to stand up and they may experience light-headedness.

Many people engage in activities such as meditation, energy clearings, tai chi, and yoga at vortex locations. These activities enable you to make higher consciousness connections to earth frequency at the vortex, which results in a deeper transformation on a personal and spiritual level.

When visiting a vortex, even if you're with a group, find time to sit alone and absorb the energy and beauty of the vortex. Close your eyes and pay particular attention to your breathing. Slow it down by taking deeper breathes; imagine your heartbeat slowing as well. Feel yourself become one with the power of the place. As the energy moves through you, pay particular attention to how you feel physically. Do you feel a tingling sensation in any part of your body? Or maybe an area where you experienced a previous injury feels uncomfortable. If you feel uptight, then make an effort to relax into the energy surrounding you. Open your heart and quiet your mind. Only when you feel at one with the area, and fully embraced by its energy, should you let your mind drift to questions you would like to have answered or consider situations in which you're unsure of the best way to move forward. As you think about each question or situation, trust in your intuition and the energy that is moving through you. Whatever you see in your mind's eye, hear clairaudiently, or simply just know—that's your answer. The way will be clear to you. To finish your session with earth frequency at the vortex, slowly feel yourself returning to the present. Feel the rock, grass, or whatever you've been sitting on. Allow your senses to tune into the smells around you. When you feel that you're ready, open your eyes. When you leave this place, the energy of the vortex will stay with you and continue to positively affect you.

THE 37TH PARALLEL NORTH

There is another area that is an invisible energy line that encircles the earth. It's been called the Haunted Highway, the Paranormal Highway, and most recently, the 37th parallel north, because it is found on the circle of latitude that runs along the 37th latitude line, which is thirty-seven degrees north of the earth's equator (see the previous image under chakras). It crosses North America, Europe, Africa, Asia, the Atlantic and Pacific Oceans, and the Mediterranean Sea. This "paranormal highway" extends down to the 36th parallel and up to the 38th parallel with the central area being the 37th parallel. It is an area with a great deal of unexplained phenomena surrounding it. While many types of paranormal activity can occur anywhere on the planet, the energy surrounding the 37th parallel, especially in North America, seems to draw more than the average amount of activity to it.

In the United States, the 37th parallel runs along the northern borders of Arizona, New Mexico, and Oklahoma and the southern borders of Utah, Colorado, and Kansas. It also crosses Santa Cruz, Gilroy; Madera, California; Colorado City, Arizona; the Ubehebe Crater in Death Valley; and an area known as the Four Corners. The Four Corners is the only place in the United States where the corners of four states meet. These states are Colorado, Arizona, Utah, and New Mexico.

The 37th parallel is well known in UFO circles because it is believed that alien spacecraft use the energy along this paranormal highway almost as an airstrip. There are many strange animal mutilation occurrences, a higher level of earthquakes, unusual lights near the ground and in the sky, cave systems, and unusual anomalies, UFO sightings, ghosts, hauntings, and encounters with sasquatch just to name a few. But the 37th parallel doesn't just contain the weird, strange, or the unexplained. There are also sites of higher learning, governmental areas, monoliths, and sacred sites included as well. Off of the coast of Sicily, there is a monolith similar to Stonehenge located at a depth of 131 feet in the Sicilian Channel. It is believed to be man-made about ten thousand years ago. In Athens, Greece, there is Aristotle's Lyceum, a philosophical school that he started and where he would walk around teaching others. Also in Athens is Plato's Academy, another philosophical institution, which originally began in a public garden just outside of the city. In Turkey there is the Göbekli Tepe temple, a megalithic site that is believed to have been built six thousand years before Stonehenge and is possibly the world's first temple. Granada, Spain, is the location of a well-known 1976 UFO sighting, and in Asia, the 2011 earthquake that measured 6.6 magnitude occurred in Fukushima, Japan, on the 37th parallel.

In North America there are other strange things that have occurred or are still happening today along the 37th parallel as well—for example, the Great San Francisco earthquake of 1906. In Joplin, Missouri, there is a long history of the Spook Lights, also called the Joplin Hornet Spook Lights, which are unexplained lights that move around, flicker in changing colors, and grow in brightness and intensity. There are cave systems throughout the 37th parallel in Oklahoma, Arizona, California, and Kentucky that are thought to be used by UFO pilots. Death Valley, California, has thirty-two caves that are believed to contain the remains of giants that were between eight and nine feet tall. And then there are the government conspiracy theories that surround Area 51, a top-secret military base in Nevada, and the tunnels believed to be underneath the Pentagon in Arlington, Virginia, and at Fort Knox, Kentucky.

In the United States, specifically in the Western regions, there are hundreds of UFO sightings along the 37th parallel. Some UFO enthusiasts also believe that alien travelers may even have bases within the caverns located along the 37th parallel at Dulce and Taos in New Mexico. There have been UFO sightings in Owensboro and Irvington, Kentucky; Aztec, New Mexico; and Cape Girardeau, Missouri.

Area 51 is one of the more well known places along the 37th parallel, especially to UFO, aviation, and conspiracy theory enthusiasts, because of its remote location, the highly classified security, and secrecy surrounding this U.S. Air Force base. Area 51 is located about one hundred miles from Las Vegas, Nevada on the 37th parallel. Its air space is restricted and pilots who knowingly enter the airspace can be court marshaled, dishonorably discharged, and even go to prison. According to the U.S. Air Force, the facility is for testing technologies and systems training in order to keep the United States secure. It is known that nuclear tests were performed in the area. In the past any satellite images of the area were deleted from the government databases, which added another layer to its secrecy. Many wondered what was being hidden in Area 51. One of the most popular theories about the activities at Area 51 is that an alien spacecraft crashed in Roswell, New Mexico, and that the ship and aliens were shipped to Area 51 to be studied. UFO enthusiasts believe that Area 51 is connected to other secret sites by a plethora of underground tunnels. It is said that there are large storage facilities that contain many spaceships, and some believe they have aliens who were on the space craft living, alive and well, at Area 51. The U.S. Air Force has denied any association with aliens or spacecraft even though there have been people who worked there previously and said that the aliens are there.

The 37th parallel in North America is also home to many sites that are sacred to Native Americans. Some of these locations are at the Comanche National Grassland in Colorado, the Cimarron National Grassland in Kansas, the Monument Valley Navajo Tribal Park in both Utah and Arizona, the Canyonlands National Park and Zion National Park in Utah, Cahokia Mounds in Illinois, the Chaco Culture National Historical Park in New Mexico, and the Mesa Verde National Park and the Navajo State park located in Colorado. Native Americas also mention star travelers and sacred sites like Chaco Canyon and Cahokia Mounds seem to support their beliefs. The Chacoans architecture and their observational sites indicate that they watched the sky and had a great understanding of the sun, moon, and stars. They had ceremonial sites around Chaco Canyon with the primary one being a petroglyph called the Sun Dagger that was developed to determine sun cycles.

The 37th parallel is an energetic line around the world where people have experienced everything from the weird to the wonderful, the strange to the spiritual, and everything in between. If you're inclined to go look for spaceships in the night sky, or if you'd like to visit a sacred site to help you grow spiritually on your path, then planning a visit to any of the locations along the 37th parallel may be an interesting way to gain insight into phenomenon that you may not be able to find in other areas of the world.

Chapter 2
BEGINNING YOUR PRACTICE
WITH EARTH ENERGY

People who can sense energy from others and the environment are empaths, meaning they actually absorb the energy, whether knowingly or unknowingly. I've always believed that being an empath is the most difficult intuitive ability to have because it can be very draining on your own frequency. Sometimes you're bombarded with energy and you're not sure if it's fluctuations of your own frequency or if you're sensing energy belonging to another person or to your surroundings. For many empaths, it's difficult for them to be in crowded places because they simply get overwhelmed by the energy of the people. If there is energy associated with the place as well, then you can see how challenging it can be to sort through it all. With places, you might pick up energy unexpectedly from any structure you visit whether it's a mall, church, tour stop, or somewhere outside. The important part is to recognize the energy of the place. So how do you do that?

RECOGNIZING AND CONNECTING WITH
THE ENERGY OF A PLACE

As you begin your quest into earth frequency, you must first begin with your own frequency. If you know what your own frequency feels like at your soul essence, in the core part of your spiritual being, then it's easier to tell when other energy is affecting you. Since we're all connected and part of the whole, being able to recognize energy and purposefully connect to the higher frequencies around you so that it affects you positively instead of you taking on the negative energies of others enables you to connect on the highest possible levels of frequency. Higher frequencies make you feel stronger and more balanced. There are some steps you can take to connect to your frequency to earth energy around you. It begins with awareness of noticing the powerful frequencies around you and then sorting through them. If you're empathic, you might have to set up barriers or boundaries to keep other energy away or muted until you have a chance to evaluate it, and then, if you choose to feel its full intensity—like you'd probably choose to do at a sacred site or power place—then you can lower any shields you've built and open yourself up to fully connect to the energy of the place.

Being able to tell the difference comes from an attentiveness of the energy around you at all times. The energy from people usually has emotions associated with it. You may pick up on anger, happiness, sadness, fear, disappointment, or any other human emotion. These energies often feel as if they're coming from outside of you instead of being an internal emotion that is truly your own. Connecting to the energy of a place can also cause you to experience emotions, but the difference is that they are emotions you feel and own *because* of the place's energy, not the emotions of the other people who may also be visiting or residual energy left over from past inhabitants.

As you walk through a place, earth frequency may feel like it's in the air or radiating up from the ground. To gain a deeper connection to earth's frequencies, which results in a very spiritual experience that elevates your own personal frequency, just stop for a while, find somewhere to sit down and mediate for a few moments. Think of the history of the place and the people who lived there long ago because the remnants of their energy can also affect the frequency of an area. Allow your own energy to reach out to the energy you feel in and around the place. As you make the connection, be aware of how it affects you. Do you see visions of things that might have happened in the past? Or maybe you feel a deep spiritual connection to the earth through a portal of its inner frequency moving upward from the ground and into the air.

When you connect to earth frequency, you may feel more alive or as if you've been here before. Quite often you may be drawn to an area where you lived in a past life. Visiting that area in person can be a very spiritual and moving experience that you'll never forget. Being able to experience places that call to us is the reason people travel all over the globe. I know I feel a deep connection to Ireland and the Scottish Highlands even though I haven't been there (yet). There's a specific mountain that I always see in my mind's eye and when I think of it, I can smell the fresh clarity of the air and feel the wind blowing across my face. I know this is a past life memory and that it draws me to the Highlands.

Think of some of the places you feel drawn to—not a place you'd like to visit just to see or take a vacation—but a place where you feel its energy connects with your own. You feel a pull toward it, a knowing of what it would be like to walk across the land, or swim in the ocean or lake. Make a list and then look at pictures of the area. While being there in person is the best way to experience the location's true power, you can still connect to its frequency even if you're thousands of miles away.

As you experience earth frequency, remember to remain clear and focused in your intention; be aware of and understand that recognizing the energy of place is the first step. Knowing how it is different from the energy of the people around you and being able to separate the two with your own intuitive abilities will help you sort through the energies. Once you can tune in to just the earth frequency and leave the people energy behind, then you're well on your way to experiencing an exhilarating connection to the place.

When connecting, take note of how the area looks. Are there unique plants and trees? Are there animals you've never seen before? Think about how the air feels—is it crisp and fresh, hot and arid, or damp and cool? How does the place smell? Is it earthy, does it smell of rain, or does it smell like flowers? Imagine yourself touching some of the things in the area and notice how they feel, the texture, color, and moisture levels. You can accomplish all of this either by visiting the place and connecting to its energy in person or by using visualization techniques or meditation. Remember that energy has no limits, no borders, and it can stretch across time and space. Unleash your frequency to connect to the frequencies of locations all around the world.

STARTING YOUR OWN PRACTICE

Now it's time to practice connecting to the energy of a place. In this chapter I've included four exercises that you can do that will help you get the most out of your earth frequency connections. I'd suggest reading all of the exercises first, then selecting one to try. If you want to keep up with your progress, I'd also suggest getting a notebook or journal where you can write down your experience, emotions, and how the frequency connection felt to you. This is a great resource to refer back to in the future, especially after you've visited many sites, to see how much you've grown spiritually or the transformations you've made since you started on this journey.

These exercises do not have to be completed in any particular order. Feel free to pick the one that calls to you and try it first. I've started with a short exercise to get you going, then included a longer creative visualization exercise to take you more in depth. Then I teach you how to filter a site's energy by using a filter shield visualization, how to clear and balance your chakras using earth frequency, and how to disconnect from the site when you're finished doing the exercise.

EXERCISE: CONNECT TO THE FREQUENCY OF A PLACE

So here's a short exercise that will help you connect to the frequency of a place, whether you are there physically or not. In the next section is a longer creative visualization exercise you can also use for each individual place in the book. For this first short exercise, run your fingers along the edge of this book until you intuitively feel that you're at the right place. Now open the book to that page and start reading about the place on those pages. As you're reading, pay attention to how you feel and how the energy of the place is affecting you. You may also choose to stop reading for a moment and meditate about the place while imaging that you are there.

Notice any physical reaction you have to the place. Does your skin tingle or are you breaking out in a sweat? Also notice any intuitive impressions you receive. You can even make notes about all of your emotions, physical reactions, and intuitive impressions if you want too. Once you feel you have a good connection to the place, decide if your impressions were right or if any other information comes to you. You may discover that while you're reading you begin to get impressions that have nothing to do with the text you're reading. This is great because it means you've obtained a deep frequency connection and are receiving additional information that is specific to you and your energy relationship with the place. This often happens in the case of past lives lived in a location. You may remember specific information that no one else might know simply because you've lived there before. Trust in these impressions and the frequency connection that you've developed during this exercise.

You can do this same short exercise using the internet if you want to experience a connection with a place that isn't included in this book. Search for the location you want to connect with and look at pictures of it before reading about it. What do you feel while looking at the pictures? There are other times that you may want to know about a place first. For instance if you want to seek out a place that has healing waters then it may be helpful to know why the waters are thought to be healing prior to doing the exercise.

Whether a location is naturally made from the earth or made by man, it is often the lore, legend, and beliefs of the people who lived in the area that makes it a special place of power today. All one has to do is walk into or mentally connect with a sacred site to feel the change in the energy. There is a feeling in the air that lets you know this place is like no other, its energy is unique and special to this location. And when you leave the area, you can feel the change in the energy just as easily as you can feel drops of rain on your arm. This is a short exercise to get you started but I highly recommend that you also try the next exercise which is much more in depth.

EXERCISE: CONNECT REMOTELY WITH ANY PLACE

This exercise can be used for each of the locations in this book. For some of the places, you may experience very powerful feelings and emotions as you do this exercise, and for that reason, I recommend that you do only one location a day if that happens. Take your time to process the experience before moving on. For other locations, the emotions and frequency may not be as strong. In those cases it's fine to try more than one visualization exercise in a day. Many times when the connection to a place is very strong it can be indicative of a past lifetime in that location. That's why it's important to pay close attention to your intuitive impressions of the place. After you read the information about the location, think about what you've just read. You may even want to record yourself talking about the place during this exercise and then replay it back later. To do the exercise begin by closing your eyes and imagining yourself standing in the location.

Feel the sacred frequency surrounding you. Imagine the energy moving from the core of the earth, through the layers of dirt and rock, until it reaches your current location. As the energy moves into the area where you're standing, feel it move upwards from your feet, through your body, to the tips of your fingers, and exiting at the top of your head. Let the energy flow through you, surrounding you, encasing you in its ancient sacredness. Feel not only the energy of the earth but the spiritual essence of it combined to create the frequency of this unique place. Once you are in tune with the way the energy moves, the way the frequency is vibrating, and how your own frequency has merged with it, slowly open your eyes in your mind's eye.

See yourself standing in the location, feeling its energy pulse through you. As you look around, you notice the terrain of the land as it was described. It may be rocky or mountainous or you may be standing in the middle of a large field with lush grass. Pay attention to any plants, trees or bushes that you see. Reach out and touch them with your hand. Now take a deep breath. What do you smell? Does the area smell fragrant with flowers? Or does it smell earthy, like the forest? Do you smell water, rain, or the morning dew? Is the wind moving or is it still? Take note of the time of day by looking at the sky. Is it early morning or twilight? Is it cold or hot? Is it in a busy location filled with other people or are you alone in a remote location? Take a deep breath. Notice if the air feels dry or moist. Feel the frequency of the place in the air as you breathe it in. Feel yourself connecting to this energy, becoming one with it as you connect even more deeply with this place.

Once you have a good feel for your surroundings, pay attention to the lay of the land, natural structures, or buildings in the area. Walk around the site. Look at the specific details. If it is a mound, walk around it and over it and find yourself in its center. Does the center feel different than it does at the edges or is the frequency the same strength throughout? If you're in the mountains, does the elevation affect the frequency? Do you feel lighter? Maybe your connection is deeper because of the sheer age of the mountains. If it is a building, run your fingers over the structure; can you feel the vibration within it? If not, imagine your own energy reaching from your core out to your fingertips, radiating into the structure to connect with its energy. Notice any intricate details drawn on the structure by ancient man. Are there carvings or other notable distinctions? Look at them, consider their importance, feel the energy that vibrates within them.

If the location contains historical landmarks, what is your first impression of them? Open yourself and let your intuition guide you. Trust in what you're sensing, feeling, or seeing in your mind's eye. The ancientness of these sites can take you back in time, connecting you to the frequency of the past as well as the current frequency of the place. Allow it to happen. Allow yourself to feel the shift of time and place within your spirit. Try to see the place as it was in its glory. Imagine what it was used for, the people who lived in that time and how they felt about this place. Through your frequency connection, allow the site to share its knowledge with you.

Whatever it wants you to know, to see, or feel, trust in your impression, know that they are right and that the sacred site is sharing this information with you because it's important for you to know.

As you continue your journey around this site, look for anything unique and unusual. Do you notice certain patterns, or are there bodies of water nearby? Stroll around, enjoy the view. How do you feel? Are you calm and peaceful or is there something about this place that makes you more alert and aware? Do you feel curious, like an explorer on a quest? Take note of how the frequency of this place affects your emotions, your sense of balance, and your spiritual self. Remember this feeling and know that you can return to it at any time that you desire simply by thinking of this location and its effect on you.

Now close your mind's eye to this location. Connect to your own frequency as you disconnect it from the location and bring it back into yourself, elevated from the experience. Let the world behind your closed eyelids go dark as the images of the location disappears in your mind's eye. Feel the chair you're sitting in, become aware of the sounds around you. Do you hear the whirring of the air conditioner or the heater in your home? Maybe there's a wall clock ticking somewhere nearby. How do your clothes feel? Are they soft or scratchy? Take a deep breath as you allow your complete awareness to return to the present while remembering your experience. When you feel totally aware and back in your own reality, open your eyes. Notice the room you're in. Does anything in this room remind you of your connection to the location? If it does, make note of it in your mind. Then, when you look at this item in the future, it can remind you of your visualization exercise to this location. When you feel ready, you can continue reading or you may decide to stop for the day and write down your experience and allow yourself to go over details of the visualization exercise throughout the remainder of the day.

EXERCISE: FILTER SHIELD VISUALIZATION

Sometimes the power of a place can be overwhelming, especially to highly sensitive people like empaths or intuitives. If you're visiting a power place or sacred site and feel completely overwhelmed by it, then this exercise can help you gradually acclimate to the energy in the area. First, if you're physically at the location, walk away from the area until you feel that the energy is at a level you can handle without any type of filter shield in place.

If you're remotely viewing the location, do the same thing by retreating some distance in your mind's eye so that you feel there is a comfortable space between you and the location or by walking away from the pictures you're viewing and looking at them from across the room. Now, using creative visualization, build a circular brick wall about six feet away from you, then close it up into a cone shape over your head. You can also use wood, metal, or any other material that you feel will work best to protect you from the onslaught of energy. Whatever the material is, it moves with you as you walk around and stays exactly six feet from your body.

Now, either physically or in your mind's eye, move back to the area of high energy that you just left. You can no longer feel the energy because of the wall's protection. When you feel ready, imagine little holes being created in the brick or whatever material you used to create your protective wall. You'll feel the energy of the location moving inside your barrier a little at a time. The holes act like a filter, only allowing in as much energy as you can handle. As you adjust to the energy flow, create more and more holes in the material. If at any point you feel like it's too much, just imagine some of the holes closing up to reduce the amount of energy coming through and stop at that point. During your visit, try to increase the number of holes in the barrier until you can completely remove it. In this way, you've filtered the energy through a shield until you're able to handle its strength. If you feel that you need to leave some of the filter shield in place during your visit, then do so.

EXERCISE: CLEARING CHAKRAS
AND DISCONNECTING FROM SITE

Try this exercise to clear blocks from your chakras while visiting a sacred site or power place. First walk around the site, either physically or in your mind's eye, and find a place where the energy feels the strongest to you and sit down or imagine yourself sitting down. Close your eyes and feel the energy as it slowly moves upwards from the earth, into your body and to your root chakra. The earth energy opens the chakra and moves in the same direction as that chakra's energy, wiping out any negativity that may be hiding or residing within the chakra. Once it feels as if all of the blocks have been eliminated, imagine the energy flow moving in the opposite direction, against the directional flow of that chakra's energy. Give the energy the intention of looking for any other blocks or negativity that may have been missed. Once you feel the energy is moving smoothly and there isn't anything else to remove, then allow the energy to flow back in the same direction as your chakra energy for a few more moments, then move up to the next chakra. Repeat this process at every chakra. When you finish with the crown chakra, imagine the energy flowing upwards and out of your body, high up into the sky or even out into space, taking any negativity with it and releasing it into the universe to dissolve. Feel the energy move back down toward you, its vibration clean and clear. As it moves into your crown chakra, imagine the energy closing the chakra, retaining part of the earth frequency inside of it. Allow it to move from chakra to chakra, down your body, closing each one as it goes. Once it closes the root chakra imagine the energy disconnecting from your body as it flows back into the earth. You can still feel the energy below you, but it's no longer flowing through you. Feel how earth's energy has attuned your chakras; balanced and cleansed them. Thank the earth for sharing it's frequency with you. When you feel ready, open your eyes and stand up, and then enjoy the rest of your time at the site.

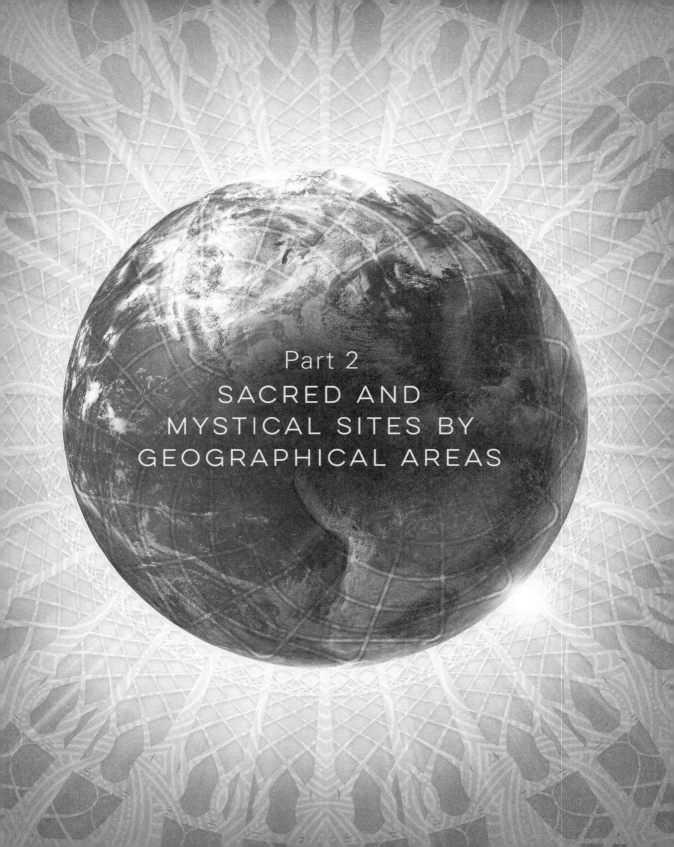

Part 2

SACRED AND MYSTICAL SITES BY GEOGRAPHICAL AREAS

Chapter 3
AFRICA

When you think of Africa, images of lions, giraffes, large herds of zebras or wildebeests, and other wild animals living in wide open spaces might be the first things that come to mind. Yes, Africa is alive with the energy of the Serengeti, but there is so much beauty and intense earth energy in this wonderful continent.

As we visit Africa, we will experience the energy of some very well-known sacred sites like the ancient Great Pyramids of Giza, the Sphinx, Luxor Temple, and the Valley of the Kings in Egypt. We'll also check out the energy of Mount Kilimanjaro, the Sahara Desert, and Fogo Island. From Madagascar to Mauritius to Olduvai Gorge in Tanzania. There are many interesting sites that were sacred to the ancient people who inhabited this land and are still sacred to the people who live there today. Sites like Vredefort Dome, the largest impact crater on earth, and the Chapel of the Tablet, where it is believed the Ark of the Covenant is secretly protected, are intriguing due to their history and the mystery or legends surrounding the site.

This can help you grow personally and spiritually when you connect your frequency to the energy of Africa's power places and sacred sites. Exploring Africa, a land filled with splendor and exceptional energies, is a journey that will enlighten and inspire you.

Map Key

1. Ambohimanga—Madagascar
2. Bandiagara Escarpment—Mali
3. Carthage Archeological Site—
   Tunis, Tunisia
4. Chapel of the Tablet—Ethiopia
5. Chirundu Fossil Forest—Zambia
6. Coffee Bay—South Africa
7. Dashur: Red Pyramid & Bent
   Pyramid—Dashur, Egypt
8. Fogo Island—Cape Verde
9. Great Zimbabwe Ruins—
   Zimbabwe
10. Karnak Temple—Luxor, Egypt
11. Laas Geel—Somalia
12. Lake Fundudzi—South Africa
13. Lake Malawi—Malawi
14. Lalibela—Ethopia
15. Luxor Temple—Egypt
16. Mauritius—Indian Ocean
17. Meroe's Ancient Pyramids—
    Sudan
18. Mount Kilimanjaro—Tanzania
19. Mount Nyiragongo—Congo
20. Mount Ol Doinyo Lengai—Tanzania
21. Mysterious Granite Obelisks—
    Axum, Ethiopia
22. Observation Hill—Kenya
23. Olduvai Gorge—Tanzania
24. Pungo Andongo—Malanje, Angola
25. Rhumsiki—Rhumsiki, Cameroon
26. Sahara Desert—Northern third
    of the African Continent
27. Senegambia River Stone Circles—
    The Gambia/Senegal
28. Sevilla Rock Art Trail—South Africa
29. Sossusvlei Dunes—Namibia
30. The Amphitheater—
    Drakensberg, South Africa
31. The Great Pyramids of Giza—
    Giza, Egypt
32. The Sphinx—Giza, Egypt
33. Tipasa—Tipaza, Algeria
34. Tsodilo Hills—Botswana
35. Valley of the Kings—Egypt
36. Vredefort Dome—Free State
    Province, South Africa

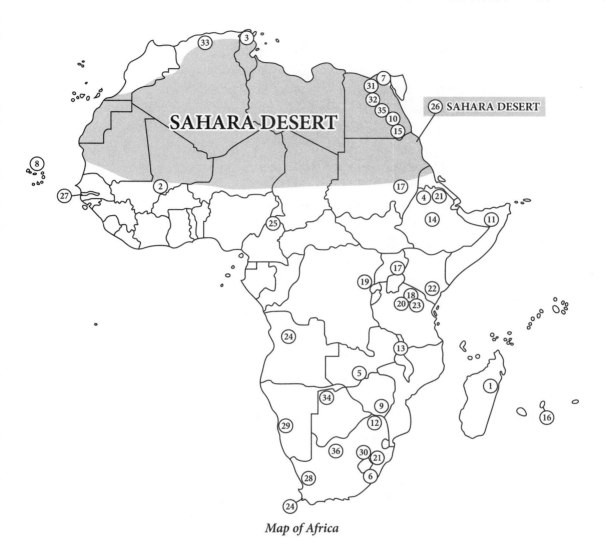

Map of Africa

1. AMBOHIMANGA–MADAGASCAR

Categories: Islands/Reefs, Mountains/Mounds/Cliff Locations

Ambohimanga, also known as the Royal Hill of Ambohimanga and meaning blue hill, is located in the municipality of Ambohimanga Rova in the Province of Antananarivo Avaradrano in the Highlands of Madagascar, the fourth largest island in the world, located off southern Africa's eastern coast in the Indian Ocean. It is the most sacred site in Madagascar, an important historical walled village that includes the royal palace. The Malagasy people still worship at Ambohimanga and consider it a sacred place of cultural identity for them.

There are twelve sacred hills of the Imerina people that look over Tana, the capital city of Madagascar. Ambohimanga is the tallest of the twelve and it is surrounded by thick forest, which is also considered sacred. The first evidence of the hill being used was in the fifteenth century when it was called Tsimadilo. It is known as the Royal Hill because it was where the royalty lived, reigned, and where they are buried. The palace at Ambohimanga is a prime example of how the royalty lived in the eighteenth century and how their close affiliations with the French people affected their construction, even though it is beginning to decay now. The buildings still contain the original items used during the eighteenth century, including beds, wardrobes, sofas, pots, spears, knives, and other items. There's even an ancient swimming pool. In a small courtyard near the end of the road that goes to the Rova, where two royal dwellings are located, the rulers would give out their decrees and sentences to the people. At the foot of the Rova, they held ceremonies and celebrations.

When kings ruled Ambohimanga, they closed the gates to the palace each evening. They rolled these enormous stones into a dug-out section of ground in front of the gate. Legends say it took seventy soldiers to push it closed. There are seven separate entrances into Ambohimanga, with gates in place of the slabs, but the slabs are also still there.

The ancestors of the Merina people who built Ambohimanga came to Madagascar approximately six hundred years ago from Indonesia. Rice was their primary food and they grew it in terraced sections they built within the city. The people believed in ritual sacrifice of animals, often a zebu, and there is a sacrificial altar at the site. There is a large stone called the Ambatomiantendro rock that was a landmark so Ambohimanga could be easily located. The king also played a Malagasy game called Fanorona at the rock, and grids from the game that they carved into the stone are still visible today.

The energy at Ambohimanga is quiet and still. It moves like a calm breeze in a linear and upward motion. There is an undercurrent of turbulence that causes spikes in the frequency, which then smooths out into an even tone. This energy will affect you in the same way. It touches any turbulent emotions within you, bringing them to the forefront so they can be addressed and dealt with until they are resolved. Once you resolve them, your personal frequency elevates and rises to a higher level, energizing and rejuvenating you spiritually.

2. BANDIAGARA ESCARPMENT—MALI
Categories: Caves, Mountains/Mounds/Cliff Locations

Located in the Mopti Region of Mali, West Africa, in the Bandiagara Circle, the Bandiagara Escarpment, also known as the 8.57 Cliff of Bandiagara, consists of both sandstone cliffs and plateaus. The cliffs are over 1,500 feet tall and the escarpment is over one hundred miles long. Due to its size, it is geographically diverse and there are areas where you'll find waterfalls and rich vegetation and other areas that are in the plains region and are a desert. The area has flash floods, so the people who lived in the area took to living in the cliffs to protect themselves during a flash flood, store their grains, and bury their dead at a higher elevation, so they wouldn't be washed away by violent waters.

Humans have lived in the region since Paleolithic times. The Tellem people lived in caves along the cliffs for over two thousand years but were overrun by the Dogon people in the fourteenth century. Their homes are known as the cliff villages. They live simply, their homes are rectangular shapes they've carved into the sides of the escarpment at the base of the cliff, and some live in villages that are on the plateau. According to their oral history, the Dogon people took advantage of the natural tunnels in the Bandiagara Escarpment to protect themselves from their enemies and to conduct surprise attacks on them. The Dogon people believed the Tellem people could fly and that's how they were able to build their homes, funeraries, and grain storage areas so high in the side of the cliff.

Today there are more than 289 Dogon villages across the escarpment.[7] The villages are set up with earthen family homes with thatched roofs. Those without thatched roofs blend into the cliff, making them virtually unnoticeable. All of the family dwellings are

---

7. Smithsonian Institution, "The Cliff of Bandiagara Land of the Dogon," http://worldheritage.si.edu/en/
sites/bandiagara.html.

windowless, typically have two stories, and are built very close to one another. Beautiful carvings are often made on the structure. There are separate granaries for both women and men, with the women's containing personal items and the men's containing food for the family such as millet and sorghum. There are other buildings in addition to the houses, including mosques, totemic sanctuaries, shrines, and the Togu Na, which is a meeting place with a very low roof that is specifically for the elders of the tribe. The purpose of having such a low space for their meetings is so everyone remains seated if they get into a debate. Masks also play an important role in the Dogon culture and they use them in their ceremonies, especially funerals.

There are several museums in the area that document the history, architecture, and the cultural heritage of the Dogon people in order to preserve their cultural heritage. They include sculptures that date to the fifteenth century and are similar to the carvings on the doors, locks, and walls of their houses today.

The energy at the Bandiagara Escarpment, specifically in the Dogon Country, moves at a medium pace and flows in a wave. It is peaceful, mysterious, and light. It is deeply connected to the earth and there is a deep rhythmic thump within the frequency that reflects the heartbeat of the planet. Peacefulness, love, and the oneness of the universe fill the energy of this area. It is a reminder that releasing the number of things you have to do in a day and simplifying all areas of your life can truly lead to more joy and happiness and less stress.

3. CARTHAGE ARCHEOLOGICAL SITE—TUNIS, TUNISIA
Categories: Mythological Sites, Ruins/Archeological Sites

The Carthage Archeological Site, also known as the Archaeological Site of Carthage, is located in the District of Tunis in the country of Tunisia, in the northern part of the African continent.

Carthage was founded by the ancient Phoenicians. There are two theories regarding its beginning. Ancient texts cite it between 1215 and 1234 BC while modern researchers place it between 846 and 813 BC. According to legend, the first people who settled in Carthage were from the city of Tyre in Phoenicia. The leader of the settlers was Princess Elissa, who was also known as Dido in Roman mythology and the Queen of Carthage, who escaped from Tyre when her husband was killed by King Pygmalion, who was also Princess Elissa's brother. She founded the city of Carthage, and then in order to protect the people who lived in the city, she committed suicide, so her brother would not go to war with Carthage because of her. In another legend, it is said that she killed herself by jumping into a burning pyre so that she wouldn't have to marry the King of Libya. According to Virgil in the Aeneid, she was in love with Aeneas, whose ship had wrecked at Carthage. When he left Carthage to go to Italy, she was devastated and threw herself to her death on the pyre.

In the ancient world, Carthage was an important trade center especially in the fifth to sixth centuries BC. It was a popular port town and explorers and merchants alike brought great wealth to the city. Carthage was run by these wealthy nobles and merchants even though there was a senate—magistrates and judges who held a lot of power. One of the main problems in Carthage were the disagreements between the people who owned land and the maritime families, which predominantly controlled the western part of the Mediterranean. Rome challenged Carthage's rule during both the First and Second Punic Wars. It was during the Second Punic War because of the division between the landowners and maritime families, which prevented the shipment of the supplies needed to win the war, when Carthage was finally defeated by the Romans. During the Third Punic War the city of Carthage was completely destroyed, but then Romans, led by Julius Caesar, built a new city over the ruins of the old city. Over the centuries the city of Carthage has been inhabited by the Phonecians (Punic), Romans, Vandals, Paleochristians, and Arabs, all of which left their own imprint on the city.

The ruins that are located in Carthage today are primarily Roman structures although archaeologists have discovered a few of the original Carthage cemeteries, fortifications, and shrines. The ruins you can visit today include the Antonin baths, the aqueducts, the amphitheater, the chapel, the necropolises, the theatre, the circus, the residential area, the basilicas, the Malaga cisterns, the Punic ports, and the acropolis of Byrsa.

The energy at Carthage is laid-back, yet it has a sense of power and danger woven within it. This energy has a slow, easy pace as it meanders through the area yet it can increase in speed as it twists and turns with accuracy through the ancient ruins of the city. This energy is helpful to you when you need to address a situation with a sense of calmness and patience, yet you also need to strike quickly and with stealth to ensure your success. This energy is especially beneficial when it comes to business dealings, and it is a clear sign to keep the paths of communications open to avoid arguments, which can cause the collapse of what you're trying to achieve.

4. CHAPEL OF THE TABLET—ETHIOPIA

Categories: Man-Made Sites, Relic Sites

Located in Aksum (also known as Axum) in the Tigre region of Ethiopia in eastern Africa, the Chapel of the Tablet, which is another name for the Church of our Lady Mary of Zion, has legends about it that say it contains the holy artifact called the Ark of the Covenant.

The name Aksum comes from the Aksumite Empire that was prevalent in the area between the first and sixth centuries AD. During this time, the empire was well known for its trading power and naval strength. The Church of Our Lady Mary of Zion has existed in the same location within Aksum since the fourth century, although the church itself has been destroyed many times since its original construction, it was always rebuilt in the same spot. According to legend, the son of the Queen of Sheba brought the Ark of the Covenant to Aksum and placed it in the Church of Our Lady Mary of Zion, where it remains to this very day.

According to the Bible, the Ark of the Covenant holds the stone tablets containing the Ten Commandments given to Moses by God on Mount Sinai. In the book of Exodus and 1 Kings in the Bible, the Ark of the Covenant is described as being fifty-two inches long, thirty-one inches wide, and thirty-one inches tall, was made of wood from the Shittahz tree, and covered in gold with another layer of gold molding over the first layer. It had four rings of gold attached to each corner through which two wooden staffs covered in gold would be placed, one on each side. On the top were two cherubim, whose wings were spread toward the middle of the Ark, and it was between these two guardians that God would appear. The Bible says the Israelites carried the Ark with them everywhere after Moses built it. When they were traveling, the Ark was always covered so it could not be seen because it held divine power, which was also believed to have caused the deaths of many people. When they weren't traveling, it was placed in a sacred tent called the Tabernacle.

There is a great mystery surrounding the Ark of the Covenant. It is unclear as to exactly when it left Jerusalem and was taken to Ethiopia and no one seems to have actually ever seen the artifact. At the Temple of Jerusalem, only the high priest saw it. At the Chapel of the Tablet in Aksum, it is said to be stored in the catacombs and is only seen by the Guardian of the Covenant, whose job is to protect the Ark of the Covenant. The Guardian of the Covenant is a virgin selected by the previous guard before they died.

Once a person is chosen to be the Guardian of the Covenant, it is a lifetime commitment and they can never leave the Ark unguarded, which means they can never leave the Chapel of the Tablet.

The energy surrounding the Chapel of the Tablet is pure and divine, with a deep spiritual connection to universal energy. It is inspirational and inspires a deep dedication within you at a spiritual level. This dedication is to exploring the realms of the divine, feeling true meaning of your own spiritual essence, and embarking upon a path that will expand your horizons to that which cannot be seen, only felt, and known unequivocally as truth on an individual level and in the grand scheme of universal consciousness.

5. CHIRUNDU FOSSIL FOREST—ZAMBIA

Category: Forests/Trees

The Chirundu Fossil Forest is located in the area of the customary land of Chief Sikoongo off of the Lusaka-Chirundu Road, in the Gwembe District and the Southern Province of the Republic of Zambia in southern Africa, approximately thirteen miles from the border of Chirundu.

The Chirundu Fossil Forest contains fossilized and petrified tree trunks from the Karoo ice age, which occurred between 360 to 260 million years ago. According to scientists, the fossilized tree trunks are coniferous trees that grew in the area approximately 150 million years ago. Some of the trunks are over thirty-two feet long. These species of trees are now extinct in the region. Over time, permineralization preserved the wood. This process is when all of the organic materials, such as cellulose, are replaced with minerals, usually silica, a colorless compound that occurs in quartz, sandstone, and other types of rocks, which turns them into fossils. Based on examination of the fossils, scientists determined that when the trees were alive, there was a moderate climate in the area with seasonal changes, according to the varying degrees of coarseness of the bands in the trunk. The current vegetation is more suitable to the hot climate that typically occurs in the area in modern times. These fossilized tree trunks are a physical representation of the climate changes that occurred in Africa over time.

Scientists believe some of the petrified tree trunks have barely moved from the place where they fell 150 million years ago. These are extremely well preserved. Others were moved by water from streams and were damaged when they hit one another while in the water.

All portions of the fossils located within Chirundu Fossil Forest are protected by law, which means that it is illegal to collect, break, or take any portion of the petrified tree trunks out of the area. It is also illegal to cut or remove any of the trees or shrubbery that is currently growing in the forest. You are required to stay on the designated pathways when visiting the Fossil Forest. It is important to have respect for the area and not participate in any acts of vandalism. Not following the rules will land you in prison or with a heavy fine.

The energy surrounding the Chirundu Fossil Forest feels smooth, strong, and primeval. It flows very slowly, the movement almost imperceptible. You'll feel it is a change in the atmosphere when you walk closer to the area of the Fossil Forest. The air feels a bit heavier, and you may feel a chill, even though the weather is hot. There is a sense of inner knowing and interconnectedness between your spiritual self, your physical self, and the universe as a whole. It feels as if you stepped back in time, when time didn't exist, and life was lived in the moment. This energy will help you to live in the moments of your life and to appreciate everything around you.

6. COFFEE BAY—SOUTH AFRICA

Categories: Bodies of Water/Waterfalls/Springs, Caves, Mountains/Mounds/Cliff Locations, Regions

Located on the Eastern Cape Province of South Africa approximately 155 miles south of Durban and near the mouth of the Mthatha River in an area known as the Wild Coast is a small town with a population of 258 people named Coffee Bay. It is said to be one of the most beautiful places to visit on the Wild Coast. Some people say the town gets its name because of the hundreds of coffee trees that once grew in the area although there are no longer any coffee trees in Coffee Bay. Others say the town received its name when a ship that was carrying coffee beans as its cargo wrecked near the coast of, or ran aground in, Coffee Bay. Regardless of how the name came about, there are some interesting and fun things to see and do in the area.

People come to Coffee Bay for the gorgeous beaches, hiking trails, camping, and coastal forest, but most of all to enjoy the relaxed, casual atmosphere of the town where eating outside in the hot, open-aired lounges is preferred along with casual beachwear attire. Other things to do in Coffee Bay include spear-fishing, sunbathing, surfing, collecting shells, horseback riding, golfing, hiking, fishing, snorkeling, or scuba diving. The town is known for its delicious and fresh seafood, so after a day experiencing the relaxing energy of the beach or a hiking adventure, enjoy a fresh seafood dinner (mussels are a specialty) to tantalize your taste buds. This laid back ambiance is beneficial to connecting with the energy of Coffee Bay because it puts you in a peaceful state of mind, which enables you to feel the frequency at deeper levels within yourself.

One of the most well-known rock formations is called the Hole in the Wall, a cliff of shale and sandstone that has volcanic dolerite on top of it that juts out into the ocean. An archway has been cut out of this cliff by the ocean, which also amplifies the sound of the waves. It's a three-hour hike from town and you'll spend some time resting or swimming in the ocean, connecting with the energy of the water and surrounding area, or perhaps trying to climb the cliff before heading back. Local legend says that the lagoon was landlocked from the ocean by the cliff. The hole was created when a beautiful girl from the village near the lagoon fell in love with one of the sea people, who looked human but had flipper-like hands and feet. The girl's father found out that she was in love with one of the sea people and forbade her to see him again. One night when the tide was high, the sea people got a large fish to knock a hole out of the cliff, then they swam into the lagoon and scared the villagers, creating a distraction so that the girl and her lover could escape into the sea. Local lore says that at certain times you can still hear the sea people playing music and singing.

If you're up for some excitement and aren't afraid of heights, you may like to take the hike to Mapuzi Caves. The area where the caves are located is naturally secluded. This hike will take you through fields along a narrow path on the side of a cliff above the caves where the energy is serene and refreshing. At this point, if the tide is in, you can jump off the cliff into the water. Even if you decide not to jump into the water, you can explore the caves.

The energy of Coffee Bay feels liberating and free. It moves at a high frequency and at a quick speed that spirals around the bay and upwards. There is a sense of peace and serenity that will have you setting your troubles aside as you absorb the positivity of the energy. If feels like a weight has lifted from you, leaving you feeling relieved and relaxed while experiencing a quiet mindfulness of simply being. The energy of Coffee Bay will intensify your ability to connect to your higher self. Your intuition is heightened and you'll see past the physical into the spirituality of the place.

7. DASHUR: RED PYRAMID &
BENT PYRAMID–DASHUR, EGYPT

Category: Power Places, Pyramids

Dashur is located in Monshaat Dahshour, Al Badrashin, in the Giza Governorate of Egypt approximately twenty-five miles south of Cairo. The Red Pyramid and Bent Pyramid are about one and a quarter miles south of South Saqqara where the Mastaba Faraoun, also known as the "Bench of the Pharoah," marks the grave of King Shepseskaf, who was the last-known Egyptian King of the Fourth Dynasty. South Saqqara is a complex of ten pyramids and tombs.

In Dashur there are five large pyramids to see. There isn't as much visitor traffic in Dashur as at some of the other larger complexes, so you will be able to explore and experience the pyramids without fighting a crowd. These are the Black Pyramid, the White Pyramid, the Red Pyramid, the Bent Pyramid, and a satellite pyramid.

Snofru (also known as Snefru), the first ruler of the fourth dynasty, who reigned between 2575 and 2551 BC, is believed to be the builder of several of the pyramids in Dashur, including the Red Pyramid and the Bent Pyramid. According to scientists, the base of the Red Pyramid is only a little smaller than the Great Pyramid of Khufu at Giza, but it is shorter because of a higher degree of slope to the sides. Even with this increased slope, it is still the fourth tallest pyramid ever built in Egypt. It is also called the Shining Pyramid, and gets its name from the red quarried limestone used within its casing stones, which were made of Turah limestone that was polished, making it shine. Scientists categorize the Red Pyramid as the most successful, and probably the first, cased pyramid built in Egypt.

The Red Pyramid is the only pyramid in the area that you can enter, and you can do so at your leisure as the entryways are unmanned. After descending through the northern entrance, there are two underground chambers with corbelled roofs, which means that they arch to a point at the top. These two chambers are connected by one tunnel. Another separate tunnel leads you to the third chamber, which rises into the body of the pyramid to a height of approximately fifty feet and also has a corbelled roof. The Red Pyramid is unique in that it is anonymous, which means that there are no inscriptions inside, however some inscriptions made by the workers who built it, including dates, were found on the back of some of the casings.

The Bent Pyramid is one of the best preserved in the area because a lot of its original casing is still in place. Archaeologists have studied the Bent Pyramid in depth and they believe there could still be some undiscovered rooms. It is called the Bent Pyramid because of an angle change halfway up the structure from 52 degrees to 43.5 degrees to the top. The reason for this degree change is unknown although archaeologists suspect that they realized the slope was too steep so they made the required adjustments at the halfway point, or they might have just wanted to finish the pyramid faster. Another unique feature of the Bent Pyramid is that it has two entrances. One leads to the upper chamber and the other to the lower chamber. Most pyramids only have one entrance.

The energy at Dashur is peaceful, easy going, and light. It moves in a drifting type of flow, slow and steady. The energy here is uplifting, motivating, and inspiring. It feels warm, silky, and smooth. This energy is especially helpful if you need to find your focus to deal with situations in your life. It can help you with balance, with experiencing a positive flow instead of a negative one, and will help you keep negative energy, feelings, and people at bay.

8. FOGO ISLAND–CAPE VERDE

Categories: Islands/Reefs, Volcanoes/Volcano Cones

Fogo Island is located in the Cape Verde Islands approximately 375 miles off the coast of West Africa. Fogo Island consists of nine inhabited islands, one uninhabited island, and eight islets, all of which were originally volcanoes that rose out of an oceanic crust that scientists believe to be 140 million years old.

Fogo Island's volcano is still active and is named Mount Fogo. The caldera area is named Pico do Fogo and is the highest point of all the islands. The last time it erupted was in 1995, which was a vent eruption within the caldera that created a massive sinkhole within the caldera. The main cone last erupted in 1675. Inside the caldera is a small village called Chã das Caldeiras, which had to be evacuated during the 1995 eruption. The people who live in the village grow exotic fruits and grapes. They make wine with the grapes and due to the scarcity of wood, they store it in old petroleum drums, which gives it an odd taste. Since Fogo Island is primarily for agriculture, the slopes of Mount Fogo are used by the islanders to grow coffee, oranges, tobacco, beans, and peanuts on both the west and north sides of the island because the land is humid and fertile on that side. The south side of the island is arid, barren, and dry, which makes it unsuitable for crops. The people also use lava stones in the construction of their buildings. Much of the coastline of Fogo Island is black lava from previous volcanic eruptions.

The cone of Mount Fogo is still intact and people are allowed to climb it. It is a very steep climb and takes about four hours to reach the top. The view allows you to see panoramic vistas of the island and if the climb up didn't take your breath away the view will. It's the perfect place to raise your frequency. The descent will take less time due to the incline of the volcanic cone and you'll find yourself moving faster. It's important to be careful so that you do not fall down the slope

The main city on Fogo Island is São Filipe, which is where you will also find the airport. The other city on the island is Mosteiros. In São Filipe there is a museum housed within a restored colonial home. It has a collection of objects from everyday life, old furniture, and a library which contains many books, travel logs, and other material written about Fogo Island, some of which are centuries old.

Ferry services are available from Fogo Island to the other Cape Verde Islands. There are bus routes to take visitors to various places on Fogo Island, however, they leave regularly during a small window of time. Because of this, it's easy to get stranded on one section of the island so it's important to know the bus schedules.

The energy of Fogo Island feels positively charged and moves in a long flowing arc. There is an undercurrent of anticipation, of being prepared for the unexpected, and of taking action when needed, even at the spur of the moment. This energy can make you feel a little bit hyper, as if you need to do something and do it right now. When applied to your daily life, the energy of Fogo Island can help you get things done quickly and efficiently and enables you to accomplish more during your day. It can inspire you, especially your creativity, and raise your personal frequency so that you see the situations in your life with more clarity.

9. GREAT ZIMBABWE RUINS—ZIMBABWE

Category: Ruins/Archeological Sites

Located near the town of Masvingo and Lake Mutirikwe, in the Masvingo Province in the south eastern hills of Zimbabwe, Africa, where the Bantu civilization of the Shona people lived during the Middle Ages, is the Great Zimbabwe National Monument, also known as the Great Zimbabwe Ruins. They are also located between the Limpopo and Zambezi Rivers.

According to legend, these ruins are what are left of the capital city of the Queen of Sheba, a very beautiful woman who was powerful and extremely wealthy. She is known in many different religions worldwide because of her visit to King Solomon. While there are different versions regarding her visit based upon the religion, she went to ask questions about King Solomon's religious beliefs and his connection to the Lord God Almighty, who had given King Solomon the gift of wisdom. All of the Queen of Sheba's questions were answered by King Solomon and they had dinner together. She was very impressed by his knowledge and gave him gifts of gold and riches and then returned to her own country. However, archaeologists have not been able to prove that the Queen of Sheba ever lived in this location.

The first mention of the great Zimbabwe ruins in history was in 1531 when a Portuguese army captain named Vincente Pegado wrote down a description of them. It is believed by archaeologists that the complex was used by the kings of the time as their courtyard, home, and protection from enemies. Ancient theorists believed that the Great Zimbabwe Ruins were built by Phoenicians or the Egyptians, who had lived in the area during the eleventh and fifteenth centuries; however, archeologists determined this complex was built by the Shona people who lived there at the time, not the Egyptians or Phoenicians. The African architectural structure includes towers, platforms, turrets, and sculptured stairways. The walls are built without mortar and the largest wall, which is called the Great Enclosure, has almost a million blocks in the thick outer walls. Only the king and his first wife lived inside the great enclosure. His other 199 wives lived in the queen's chamber.

Today there is a small museum at the site that displays some of the archaeological finds discovered during excavations, most of which show that the Great Zimbabwe Ruins were where great traders from other world nations lived in ancient times. Some of these items are Arab gold coins from Kilwa, porcelain from Persia, glass beads from China, pottery shards, and ironware.

The Great Zimbabwe Ruins are a sacred site and still in use today by different tribes and communities in the area for religious or spiritual ceremonies. The energy in this area, specifically within the ruins, is very upbeat and positive. It moves in a fluid motion, spinning upwards in a tight circle. There is a feeling of happiness here, of joy and laughter, the essence of which has lasted through the ages. Any time you're feeling down or you need a pick me up, connecting to this energy will lift your spirits and put a smile on your face.

10. KARNAK TEMPLE—LUXOR, EGYPT

Categories: Bodies of Water/Waterfalls/Springs, Ceremonial Sites, Man-Made Sites, Monasteries/Temples, Pilgrimage Sites, Ruins/Archeological Sites

The Karnak Temple is located in Al-Karnak, Luxor, in the Luxor Governorate of Egypt. The Karnak Temple Complex is one of the most famous sites in Egypt. Most commonly referred to as simply Karnak, the complex is home to several different types of buildings including pylons, temples, courts, and chapels, all of which are connected to create the largest building ever made for religious purposes in the ancient world.

The structure is built on two hundred acres, with dimensions of one mile by two miles, and dates back to 2000 BC. It is a sacred place and was the site of pilgrimages for approximately 2,000 years. It took 1,300 years to build beginning in the sixteenth century BC and approximately thirty different pharaohs added their own personal touch to the complex in one form or another, which enabled it to reach its tremendous size. Each pharaoh may have built a new pylon, temple, a new shrine, or they added new hieroglyphic inscriptions into buildings that were already constructed to proclaim the great deeds of that pharaoh.

The Karnak Temple was dedicated to the god Amun, his wife Mut, and their son Khonsu. Each member of the family had their own area, which was called a precinct. There is also a precinct for the falcon headed local god named Montu. Amun's precinct was the largest and the grandest of all the precincts. Karnak Temple is also connected to the Nile and every year three sacred barges, called the Theban Triad, would take the statues of the gods (Amun, Mut, and Khonsu) on a trip to the Nile during the annual Opet festival. This festival took place yearly during the second month of the first season, at the end of the agricultural period. They believed that during the course of a year, the gods and the earth became tired and needed to have their energy replenished. The Opet Festival lasted for twenty-seven days in order to accomplish this replenishment. The festival was also a way to celebrate the connection between the god Amun and the current pharaoh. The festival was held when the fields were flooded by the Nile, which meant the common people who typically worked those fields could enjoy the festival since they were unable to work. However, they were limited to participating in the festival at the Sun Court and weren't allowed into the rest of the temple areas.

Some of the other important structures within Karnak Temple are the First Pylon, which was built in 656 BC but never finished. The mud brick ramps used to build it are still there. Today, this is the entryway into the Karnak Temple Complex. Hypostyle Hall is 54,000 square feet and includes the main sanctuary, a sacred lake, and several smaller temples. To date it is the largest room in any religious temple or building anywhere in the world. The Sacred Lake is lined with stone and has stairs that descend into the water. The sacred geese of Amun swam on this lake and it was a symbol of the life giving water from the Egyptian creation story. The Temple of Khonsu has a colonnade lined by a row of sphinxes, twenty-eight columns, several chapels and a staircase to the roof. Khonsu was a moon god who could drive out evil spirits.

The energy at the Karnak Temple Complex is broad, open, and inviting. It is clear and bright. It switches between a left to right movement to a right to left one. This change in direction keeps the energy of abundance, regeneration, respect, and spiritual awareness flowing throughout the area. Connecting to the energy will help you clear out any negative thoughts, patterns, or behaviors within your character and your spiritual self. It is freeing and will lighten you so that you feel as if a weight has been lifted from your shoulders. If you need to rejuvenate yourself physically, emotionally, or spiritually, then the energy found at Karnak will speed the process.

11. LAAS GEEL, SOMALIA

Category: Petroglyph/Rock Art Sites

Laas Geel (also spelled Laas Gaal) is located in the Horn of Africa, in Somaliland, which is in the northwestern part of Somalia, approximately thirty-four miles northeast of Hargeisa, the capital of Somaliland, in an area known as the badlands. Somaliland declared independence from Somalia in 1991 but it is not an officially recognized state internationally. Laas Geel means "where the camels once watered" and it is located between two dry river beds. The region is no longer green so people don't take their livestock there to graze anymore even though some of the natural areas will fill with water when it rains.

There are many rock shelters in Laas Geel that contain rock art from the Neolithic age, five thousand years ago. Scientists believe these paintings are some of the oldest rock art in Africa and are among the best preserved. The rock art is within twenty different natural rock shelters in Laas Geel, most of which were protected from the elements because of the natural rock overhangs. Archeologists and scientists believe that the rock art at Laas Geel could be up to eleven thousand years old. Some of the rock shelters and alcoves contain up to 350 different paintings of humans and animals, with a large majority of cows, some of which have wide long necks and others wearing ornaments, and a dog-like animal often with a human drawn beside it. There are drawings of monkeys, giraffes, antelope, hyenas, and jackals, some of which are no longer found in the area. There are also drawings depicting humans drinking milk from the cattle, which gives insight into how these ancient people survived.

Based on the scientific analysis of these drawings, it is believed that they were created when the Horn of Africa was flourishing with green plant life and an abundance of animal life, which would have been during the interglacial period. The paintings show the things that these ancient nomadic people encountered in their daily lives and also include different tribal art markings. There are differing opinions on the reason the ancient people drew these figures. Some say they were just being artistic while others disagree and say that they were drawn during rituals and ceremonies.

The people who live in the area today avoid Laas Geel because they believe the rock art was drawn by the devil and the whole area was haunted by evil spirits, including demons. Since they didn't understand what the rock art was, they stayed away, which also inadvertently helped keep the art preserved because no one bothered it. Some of the paintings have become distorted, erased, and smeared due to water getting to it or by animals who touched them.

The energy at Laas Geel is vibrant and moves at a somewhat elevated rate. It's not fast but not slow either, more of a medium tone and speed but filled with a pulse that is energetic and lively. This energy will get you moving physically and will also put your mind in motion so that you're thinking about the situations in your life. Once action is taken in this way, then it acts as a catalyst to creating positive changes in your life. If you're feeling stuck, and need a way to break out of a rut, then accessing the energy of Laas Geel can help you break free.

12. LAKE FUNDUDZI—SOUTH AFRICA

Categories: Bodies of Water/Waterfalls/Springs, Rainforests, UFO/Extraterrestrial/Paranormal Sites

Located in South Africa's foothills of the Soutspansberg Mountains, in the Venda region of the Limpopo province, lies a true inland lake, of which there are few in the region, called Lake Fundudzi. This is a sacred lake to Venda people, known as the Vhatatsindi or the People of the Pool, who live in the area. The lake is steeped in legend as is Thathe Vondo, a nearby sacred tropical rainforest.

Scientists believe Lake Fundudzi was originally created by a landslide that changed the course of the Mutale River. Legend has it that the landslide was a curse upon a Kraal who wouldn't offer shelter, food, or aid of any kind to a leper. There are three rivers that flow into the lake and no outlet for water to leave the lake, but the lake never overflows and it's water levels will rise and fall without reason regardless of the amount of rainfall in the area. One of the stories of the Venda people, to prove the sacredness of the lake, has to do with the mysterious water levels. It is said that a resort developer tried to build on the shores of Lake Fundudzi but after they started construction, the water levels of the lake rose and flooded the site. The developer moved to a different location on the lake and again, the water levels rose and flooded the site. The developer gave up and once the crews were gone, the water levels went back to normal.

Lake Fundudzi is believed to be protected by the Venda python god who lives in the mountains surrounding the lake. After bathing in its waters, he'll hit the large stones on the shore as if they were drums, which creates a sound that the people in the area often hear. Because of its sacred status, the waters of Lake Fundudzi cannot be looked at directly when you approach, instead, it must be greeted by all visitors in the traditional way of the Vhatatsindi people, which is called the ukodola. To perform the ukodola greeting, you must stand with your back to the lake, bend over, and greet it through your legs saying a specific Venda phrase, then you spit on the ground and throw a small stone through your legs toward the lake as a gift.

The Vhatatsindi also believe that the spirits of their ancestors live in the water of the lake and are guarded by a white crocodile. They believe that when their kings died and their bodies were placed in the lake, the crocodile would spit up a stone, which had to be swallowed by the new king. There are many other legends about Lake Fundudzi that have been passed down through the generations. Today ceremonies and rituals are still performed at Lake Fundudzi. Most often these are to ask for rain and a good harvest and they will pour beer into the lake as a gift to the python god.

The energy at Lake Fundudzi is mystical, magical, and filled with a high frequency of knowing. Accessing this energy will enable you to expand your intuition, especially clairvoyance and mediumistic abilities. The energy here moves in a strong circular flow from the bottom of the lake upwards to the sky and back down. It spins like a fast moving wheel. You'll often experience an increased amount of paranormal and intuitive experiences when you're connecting to the energy at Lake Fundudzi.

13. LAKE MALAWI–MALAWI

Category: Bodies of Water/Waterfalls/Springs

Lake Malawi, also referred to as Lake Nyasa, is located in southeast Africa and in the central and southern regions of Malawi and also borders Tanzania and Mozambique. Lake Malawi is one of the Southern Rift Valley freshwater lakes located in Malawi and Tanzania. It is the second deepest lake in Africa, the ninth biggest lake in the world, and the third largest lake in Africa. Lake Malawi National Park, a World Heritage Site, is located at Cape Maclear in South Malawi. The scenery at Lake Malawi is simply majestic. With deep, clear, blue water and mountains in the background, it will delight you, especially if you enjoy photography.

Discovered just 150 years ago by David Livingston, who nicknamed Lake Malawi "the Lake of Stars" because you can see the reflection of all of the stars in the lake at night. It's also known as the "jewel in the crown" when describing tourist attractions in Malawi. Another interesting name for Lake Malawi is "the calendar lake." It received this nickname because the lake itself is 365 miles long and 52 miles wide. The lake is extremely deep. In the northern section, it is about 2,300 feet, which came about because of the natural fault lines (some have a slight slope while others are very steep) in the Great Rift Valley region where the lake is located. Scientists date the lake between forty thousand and two million years old. Fourteen rivers feed into Lake Malawi with only one river, the Shire, flowing out of it. Lake Malawi has three separate water layers that do not mix, which makes it a meromictic lake. There are also two islands within Lake Malawi named Chizumulu Island and Likoma Island, both of which are inhabited.

People have fished the waters of Lake Malawi for thousands of years. There are perch, lake salmon, catfish, yellow fish, and others that are large enough for a meal. Most of the fish in Lake Malawi are tropical cichlids and there are over one thousand species of them living in the lake. Many people like to keep these brightly colored tropical fish in their aquariums and the ones found in Lake Malawi are shipped around the world. The various species of cichlids are usually divided into three main category types commonly known as peacocks, haps, and mbuna.

There are many different things to do at Lake Malawi. Taking a boat out on the lake to go fishing is always a popular activity as is sailing, water skiing, snorkeling and scuba diving. Lake Malawi is well known for its beaches where you can relax or take a dip in the energizing waters of the lake. You'll also encounter a lot of different species of wildlife who also enjoy visiting Lake Malawi. These include the hippopotamus, baboons, hyrax, crocodiles, antelopes, monkeys, and numerous birds such as herons, cormorants, fish eagles, and kingfishers.

The energy at Lake Malawi is lively, cheerful, and bright and yet it has a powerful, ancient strength that moves through it. The energy here helps you to see the bright side of situations, to look at the positive instead of the negative. It helps you to find balance in all things. Spiritually, it will lift you and open your senses to the greatness of the world we live in and the higher consciousness that guides you through your daily life. It will give you strength to endure any issues you encounter and the powerful insight to make deliberate choices, both of which will bring you more happiness and joy.

14. LALIBELA—ETHIOPIA

Categories: Ceremonial Sites, Man-Made Sites, Monasteries/Temples, Pilgrimage Sites, Regions

Located in northern Ethiopia in the Amhara region is the town of Lalibela, which is known internationally for its eleven monolithic churches.

The exact date of construction isn't known because the records were lost, but it is told through legend that the churches were built during the twelfth century AD during the reign of Gebre Mesqul Lalibela. He was the King of Ethiopia who ruled for forty years and was part of the Zagwe dynasty. Legend also says that he had a vision about the city of Jerusalem and tried to recreate it by building the churches with his own hands and with angels helping him. This was during a time when pilgrimages to Jerusalem were prohibited so King Lalibela decided to make his own version of the city. Another version of the legend says an angel came to Lalibela and asked the king to build the churches and it took twenty-four years to complete them all. He had men working during the daylight hours and the angels took over the work at nighttime with Saint George supervising the creation of the Bet Giorgis church. However, archeologists dispute the legends because they believe that three of the churches, named Danagel, Merkorios, and

Gabriel-Rufael, were carved five hundred years earlier but became associated with King Lalibela over the years.

These are the largest monolithic churches ever built. They were carved both externally and internally out of one block of granite with all of the roofs stopping at ground level. Each church was carved to look unique and different from the others. They all have different entryways and doors, various styles of roofs, columns, and decorative motifs carved into them, and are all several stories tall. Inside, they also painted the church walls. Between the churches are ceremonial passageways, which also go to catacombs and caves, trenches, and drainage ditches. Archeologists have not been able to determine what happened to the rock that was carved out of the temples or where they took the dirt that was dug out from around them during the construction because it was never found.

Today the churches are classified as being in grave condition. The drainage ditches weren't kept clear for several hundred years, which resulted in water damage. Seismic activity in the area caused further damage especially to the bas-reliefs and sculptures.

In ancient times, people would make pilgrimages to Lalibela to celebrate Christianity. Even today monks and priests continue to live there. People still make pilgrimages to the churches especially during the religious festivals and celebrations. They always wear white clothes, which is representative of their status as a pilgrim.

The energy at Lalibela is of a high frequency that feels hot, active, and yet calm and soothing. It feels as if it is moving in opposite directions at the same time. The flow is smooth and even. This energy is connected to the center of the earth, from which the volcanic rock of the churches was formed. There is an ancient awareness in this area that encourages your spirit to seek more knowledge and to form a connection to that which you cannot see but feel deep in your soul. It will enable you to create a deeper relationship with your higher self and your true spiritual essence.

15. LUXOR TEMPLE—EGYPT

Categories: Man-Made Sites, Monasteries/Temples, Power Places, Ruins/Archeological Sites

Luxor Temple is located in the city of Luxor on the east bank of the Nile River, in south east Upper Egypt approximately five hundred miles south of the Mediterranean Sea. Luxor is the capital of the Luxor Governorate. Within the city of Luxor, you'll find the ruins of the city of Thebes, including the Luxor Temple. Thebes was also known as the City of a Hundred Gates and was the capital of Egypt in ancient times. Thebes also used land on the west bank of the Nile River to bury their dead in a necropolis (cemetery) of elaborate funerary complexes for both private citizens and the royal family known as the Tombs of the Nobles.

Luxor Temple has been called the world's largest outdoor museum. The Luxor Temple was built between 1390 and 1352 BC by Amenhotep III. As they came into power, other pharaohs added to the temple including Tutankhamen, Horemheb, and Ramses II. Alexander the Great is also represented here with a granite shrine at the rear of the temple. Other rulers also made repairs to the temple during their reigns.

Because of the methods of building in ancient Egypt you will find similarities between Luxor Temple and Karnak Temple. Both were dedicated to the god Amon, his wife Mut, and their son Khonsu. Most Egyptian temples are built facing east to west but Luxor Temple was built so that it would face the Karnak Temple, so it has a north-south orientation and is 1.2 miles away. During ancient times, there were sphinx statues with ram heads on them lining the road, which was used for processionals, between the two temples.

The Luxor Temple is extremely well preserved in many of the relief carvings, statues, and the structure that remains after thousands of years of exposure to the elements. It is most known for its amazing features starting with the entrance pylon that was built by Rameses II, which consisted of six gigantic statues of Ramses (four of him standing and two of him seated, of which the two seated and only one of the standing statues remains) and two obelisks. This entryway is decorated with scenes of his battle of Kadesh and other military accomplishments. Other important areas within the Luxor Temple are the Amenhotep III Colonnade (where seven pairs of open flower papyrus columns stand at a height of fifty-two feet tall), the Court of Amonhotep III, the Court of Ramses II, and the Avenue of Sphinxes.

In addition to the Egyptians, other people in history, including Alexander the Great, the Romans, and Muslims, also used Luxor Temple. Historians and scholars report that since it's construction over three thousand years ago, Luxor Temple has been continuously used as a religious center by a variety of people.

The energy at Luxor Temple feels flat, sturdy, and unending. It moves in low, short waves close to the ground. There is a trembling sensation associated with the energy as if a great power is about to erupt all around you. When connected with this energy you will detect its strength within that you have never been conscious of before, and which will enable you to reach whatever goals you set for yourself and allow you to rise above any negativity or disturbing situations you find yourself involved in. The energy here will strengthen and embolden you to embrace all life offers.

16. MAURITIUS—INDIAN OCEAN
Categories: Islands/Reefs, Mountains/Mounds/Cliff Locations, Regions

Mauritius, also known as the Republic of Mauritius, is an island nation approximately 1,200 miles from the southeast coast of Africa in the Indian Ocean and 500 miles east of Madagascar. The nation includes two main islands, Mauritius and Rodrigues, and several outer islands, some of which are still disputed territories.

Mauritius formed due to volcanic activity millions of years ago. It is well known internationally for its tropical vegetation, awe-inspiring mountains, brilliant white sandy beaches, sugarcane plantations, lush flora, and crystal-clear lagoons. The island itself is forty miles long and twenty-eight miles wide and is home to 1,300,000 people who come from a variety of backgrounds including Indian, French, English, South African, Chinese, and Creole. English is the official language of the country but French, Hindi, Mauritian Creole, Tamil, Marathi, Hakka, and Bhojpuri are also spoken here. Mauritius can truly be considered a melting pot of people from all around the world.

In Mauritius, you'll hear Sega music at night, which is festive calypso-style music that is often played all night which adds to the casual and unique energy of the island. There are plenty of activities to keep you busy on this beautiful island. There are seven fantastic golf courses, many opportunities to go deep sea fishing, and too many water sports available to mention, so whatever you fancy is right at your fingertips. If you enjoy mountain hiking, biking, cycling, kayaking, or other types of land sports, including horseback riding tours, many companies offer a variety of these types of activities to suit the needs of the visitors to the island so that they can immerse themselves in the positivity and exciting energy found here. An interesting fact about Mauritius is that it was home to the Dodo bird, which became extinct when the last one was killed in 1681. The dodo was a type of pigeon that lived on the island for more than four million years. Because they didn't have any predators on the island, their bodies became quite large and they could weigh up to fifty pounds, their wings became quite small, and they lost their ability to fly. When other animals were introduced to the island while it was under

Dutch rule, such as monkeys, pigs, and rats, these animals would eat the eggs the dodo laid, which contributed to its extinction. Due to their large size, humans often killed the dodos for food.

The energy at Mauritius is high frequency, vibrant, and will lift your spirits. It is nearly impossible to feel down, upset, or stuck in a rut when connecting to the energy of this place. It moves in a side-to-side rhythmic motion that is both empowering and inspirational. Any time you feel the weight of the world pressing down upon you connecting to the energy of this island nation will free you from the pressures and stress that you are facing. It will put a smile on your face, laughter in your heart, and gratitude in your soul.

17. MEROE'S ANCIENT PYRAMIDS—SUDAN
Categories: Islands/Reefs, Power Places, Pyramids, Ruins/Archeological Sites

Located along the banks of the Nile River in eastern Sudan, Africa, is the Archaeological Sites of the Island of Meroe. The city of Meroe was the capital, and a wealthy metropolis, of the Nubia (aka Kush) Kingdom in ancient times. Archaeologists believe that the city was founded in 590 BC when the Nubian's moved their capital to Meroe. It was considered an early state within the middle Nile. It received the name Island of Meroe because of the water flowing around it.

At the Archaeological Sites of the Island of Meroe, you will find the ruins of more than two hundred ancient pyramids from the Kush Kingdom. These tombs were built on a smaller scale than those in Egypt and they are the final resting place of the Meroitic kings and queens. This style of construction called a Nubian pyramid, which means they have steeper angles on the side and a smaller, narrower base between twenty to ninety feet on each side. Imagine the Giza pyramids in miniature with a more teepee styled appearance. The pyramids include decorative designs that were popular in Greece, Rome, and Pharaonic Egypt during ancient times. The Meroitic royals of the Kush Kingdom ruled this area of the Sudan for more than nine hundred years until the Aksumites conquered them around 330 AD.

Nubia's trade included imported gold, even though they had their own gold mines, copper, ebony, ivory, incense, and exotic animals. During the time of the Middle Kingdom, Egyptians expanded into Nubia in an effort to control trade routes and built fortresses down the Nile that were permanent trade bases.

While there is some written history of Meroe, to date no one has been able to decipher the written language. What is known is that they believed the king's health was connected to the land's fertility. The priest had the power to determine if the king was still fit to rule and if not he would send a message to the king telling him that his time on earth was finished and he must die. The kings of Nubia would listen to the priests and take their own lives thinking it was best for the people they ruled. However, according to Diodorus, Ergamenes disagreed with this ruling by the priest so he came to them with an army, slaughtered them all, and put his own rules regarding the length of time a king should rule in the place. Some say that this is a myth while others decree that it is historical fact.

Unfortunately, the Nubian pyramids were damaged by tomb raiders looking for treasure. Some of these tomb raider's actually blew up whole pyramids just to see if there was treasure inside. In an effort to preserve these ancient pyramids, many of them have undergone reconstruction, making them look new again. It is an ongoing task to remove the sand that accumulates against the pyramids when the sandstorm winds blow across the desert.

The energy at Meroe is gritty, hot, and dry, and moves in long flowing arcs. This is the energy to connect to when you really just need to do hard physical labor. It helps you connect the physical to the spiritual. Sometimes the act of manual labor can free and open your mind to things that are new, unpredictable, and sometimes not of this world. The energy at Meroe is a reminder that sometimes big things come in small packages. Take the time to look at the small things in life, to smell the roses along the way, and to feel the warmth and love in everything you do.

18. MOUNT KILIMANJARO—TANZANIA

Categories: Mountains/Mounds/Cliff Locations, Mythological Sites, Pilgrimage Sites, Power Places, Volcanoes/Volcano Cones

Mount Kilimanjaro is located in the Kilimanjaro Region of Tanzania, which is in the southeastern part of Africa. It is the highest point on the African continent. Mount Kilimanjaro stands alone and is not part of any mountain range, which earns it the title of being the tallest freestanding mountain in the world. It is approximately 750,000 years old.

Mount Kilimanjaro is comprised of three extremely large stratovolcanoes named Shira, Kibo, and Mawenzi, that sit in a northwest to southeast direction. It is 19,340 feet tall at the summit. Shira is the oldest cone that forms the broad section to the west northwest while Kibo is the central stratovolcano, and Mawenzi is on the southeast side and has a sharp peak called Uhuru. The caldera is not circular but is more horizontal in shape. It is approximately one and a half miles wide and two and a quarter miles long. The summit of Mount Kilimanjaro is almost always topped with ice due to its elevation.

Scientists have determined that the majority of Mount Kilimanjaro rose from the earth during the Pleistocene age with the exception of a few summit craters that they believe formed during the Holocene age. There are no known eruptions of Mount Kilimanjaro in recent history; however, scientists believe that it may have erupted at some point in the past ten thousand years. There have been no earthquakes in recent history that would give any indication that there was some sort of activity going on underneath Mount Kilimanjaro.

It is one of the Seven Summits, which are the seven tallest mountains in the world, one from each continent, so it is no surprise that adventure-seeking people would want to climb it. Every year more than thirty-five thousand people climb to the summit. There are two ways to get to the top of Mount Kilimanjaro; one takes between eight and ten days just to reach the base camps, which are below the summit. A faster route takes four to five days to reach the base camps; however, this route is more dangerous because there's more of a chance that you will get altitude sickness. It is important to understand the weather conditions from the base to the summit for the time of year that you plan to climb Mount Kilimanjaro.

The volcanic mountain is surrounded with folklore, myths, and legend. One of these tales is that mountain pygmies the size of small children live in the ravines and caves. Another is that gorillas live in the forests of Mount Kilimanjaro. To date, scientists haven't been able to prove either of these stories. The local people believe the mountain was the way to heaven and God. It is also believed that portals to the underworld are on Mount Kilimanjaro so you shouldn't venture into the forests or you could find yourself instantly transported there because you unknowingly stepped through a portal. There are many groups of people worldwide who make pilgrimages to Mount Kilimanjaro for a variety of spiritual reasons.

The energy at Mount Kilimanjaro is cleansing, restorative, and a powerful catalyst to moving you along your own spiritual path. It is radiant and clear in purpose and acts as a guide to get you back on track if you've lost your way. Its energy feels like a warm embrace that captivates and holds your interest while opening your mind. It is quiet, yet speaks volumes to your soul.

19. MOUNT NYIRAGONGO—CONGO

Categories: Mountains/Mounds/Cliff Locations, Volcanoes/Volcano Cones

Mount Nyiragongo is located in Democratic Republic of the Congo in the Virunga Mountains in the volcanic region of Virunga National Park. It is near Lake Kivu and the western branch of the Rift Valley.

Mount Nyiragongo is one of the world's most active stratovolcanoes, which are the most dangerous and deadliest of all volcanic types, and it tends to erupt approximately every thirty years. Since 1882 it has erupted thirty-four times. It's most recent eruptions occurred in 1977 and again in 2002. When its lava lake empties, it flows like water, which makes it difficult for the people living nearby to escape in time to avoid harm. During the 1977 eruption, it was flowing at sixty miles per hour and can move even faster. It is the fastest flowing lava in the world. In 1977, it took less than an hour for the lava lake to drain completely. The lava moves so quickly because it has low silica content. It happened so fast that people were taken by surprise and unable to escape the lava flow. The 2002 eruption resulted in over 200,000 people fleeing the lava flow, which destroyed many homes and businesses. Very few volcanoes in the world today have lava lakes as active as the one found in Mount Nyiragongo.

The lava lake in Mount Nyiragongo is now active again and it's only a matter of time before it has another eruption. Approximately six months after the 2002 eruption, it erupted again and has been continually erupting ever since, however, the eruptions are contained within the crater inside the new lava lake that formed below the previous lake. Scientists and volcano experts believe that Mount Nyiragongo has the deepest lava lake in the world so they keep a close eye on this volcano's lava lake activity, which is currently classified as an erupting volcano with continual effusive eruptions within the summit's crater lava lake. In order to see the lava lake, you have to hike 11,400 feet to the summit where the crater is located. This trek takes approximately five hours to complete because of the steepness of the side of the volcano. The return trip is also a challenge for the very same reason.

For the people who live in the area, carbon dioxide poisoning is a real concern because it can leak from cracks in the earth, killing the people who encounter it. If the wind is blowing, it disperses the carbon dioxide but residents must always be aware of the signs of this silent killer.

The energy of Mount Nyiragongo is ancient, commanding, and potent. It is forceful and strong, demanding, and purifying. Connecting to the energy of this volcano will cleanse you on many levels, which will bring a clear and precise vision of where you should be and where you're going. This energy will radiate all through your physical body and spiritual self. Whenever you feel that you just can't shake off the negativity around you, and need to break free, the immense energy contained within Mount Nyiragongo will erupt through you and put you back on your spiritual path.

20. MOUNT OL DOINYO LENGAI—TANZANIA

Categories: Mountains/Mounds/Cliff Locations, Volcanoes/Volcano Cones

Mount Ol Doinyo Lengai, which means "Mountain of God" in the local Maasai language, is located in the northern part of Tanzania in the eastern Rift Valley of eastern Africa. It is a 6,562 feet tall stratovolcano but it is unique in that it is the only volcano in the world whose lava is a natrocarbonatite. This means the lava contains sodium, potassium, gregoryite, nyerereite, and carbonate minerals instead of the silicate materials that you would find in other volcanic lava flows. The temperature of the lava is much cooler and will range between 932°F and 1,112°F instead of the normal temperatures of silicate based lava, which range between 1,300°F to 2,200°F.

Because of this vast difference in temperature and composition from other types of lava, there are visual variances that can be seen immediately during an eruption. Instead of having a red appearance, the lava looks dark brown to black. It flows like water instead of lava, and when it cools the minerals become unstable when exposed to the moisture and oxygen in the atmosphere. It does not have the strength of the silica-based lavas, which turn to rock, instead, it will turn into a white powder within a few hours of the eruption and will weather rapidly instead of being extremely hard and long-lasting like other volcanic rock. At other times, the change in color may take longer depending upon the weather on the earth's surface. The wetter it is, the faster it happens.

Scientists believe that the current cone of Mount Ol Doinyo Lengai is approximately fifteen thousand years old. The known eruptions have not been large events. They usually occur within the summit crater, and because of this, it has changed the interior of the crater from having tall, steep sides to appearing almost flat because the lava has filled it up. Since 1998 the lava has been flowing over the rim of the crater.

According to legend Mount Ol Doinyo Lengai is said to be the home of the Masai god. Locals believe that the volcano is the source of life and that its eruptions kill ticks and parasites that harm their livestock. It is also thought to be the source of life for humans, and the people would often pray and offer sacrifices to the Masai god for the women in their tribe who are having difficulty getting pregnant to become fertile and with child. They also pray for the sick to be healed, for rain, and for anything else they need, want, or desire.

The energy of Mount Ol Doinyo Lengai quivers and moves in a quick jagged motion. It feels cool and somewhat fragile, ancient, and unpredictable, healing and engaging. The energy from this volcano encourages you to keep a cool head, to look at things from a different perspective, and to always be the unique individual that you are on a soul level. It inspires you to let your own creativity spring forth, to allow your uniqueness to shine, and to always go with the flow of the situations you find yourself in. It encourages you to be strong but to realize when a situation is fragile and needs extra care to turn it into the positive success you desire.

21. MYSTERIOUS GRANITE OBELISKS—AXUM, ETHIOPIA
Categories: Burial Sites, Ruins/Archeological Sites

The city of Axum, also known as Aksum, is located in the Tigrai Region of northern Ethiopia, in the Horn of Africa. It was an important city of the Aksumite kingdom between the first and eighth centuries AD. The city was well known for ivory trade during ancient times. Today, it is known for the ruins, which include the palace, royal tombs, and the mysterious granite obelisks, also known as stelae. Legend says that Axum was the home of the Queen of Sheba and the Ark of the Covenant.

In ancient history, obelisks were often used to mark the burial sites of important people including kings and queens. Archaeologists have yet to determine if the Axum obelisks were used for this purpose, although it is quite possible. Another thought is that they held religious significance for the people of the time and were an important part of religious ceremonies. Unfortunately, their purpose isn't known for certain. The obelisks at Axum are some of the tallest monoliths ever erected during ancient times. They were made from a single piece of stone. The tallest one fell at some point and archaeologists suggest it may have fallen as they were trying to erect it and was broken into six pieces, where it still lies today. Its height when it was still a single stone was 109.25 feet and it weighed approximately 500 tons.

Of the obelisks still standing at Axum, the tallest is 80 feet, and has a rounded top. It is named the Obelisk of Axum, is 1,700 years old, and has a unique history. In 1937, it was cut into six pieces and shipped to Rome, where it was displayed in the Porta Capena Square near the Circus Maximus.[8] It was taken by troops who were occupying Abyssinia. The Obelisk of Axum weighs more than 150 tons. In 1947, Italy signed an agreement with the United Nations to return it and after a lot of negotiations it was finally given back to Ethiopia in 2005 but it had to be cut into three separate pieces before it could be returned. Once it was back in Ethiopia, restoration began but it was complicated due to the trauma suffered by the stone over the years including a lightning strike.

The Obelisk of Axum contains many carvings on the sides. At the base there are carvings of doors that have locks and knockers while higher up are carvings of windows, and horizontal lines that appear to represent nine individual floors, or stories, of a building. Each horizontal line also has circles carved across it. There are other obelisks at the site but all are much smaller than the Obelisk of Axum.

The energy at the site of the obelisks is of a high frequency. It moves quickly in a tight upward spiral from the ground into the sky. It then spreads out into a larger spiral and gently flows back to the ground and repeats this movement over and over. It feels hot, energetic, and empowering. This energy gets you moving at a spiritual level by making you think about your own spiritual purpose, your reason for being, and what kind of a difference you can make in the world. You will find yourself analyzing your path and probably making changes if you feel that you have deviated from your true purpose. Looking up into the sky and feeling the energy wrap around you as you take in the monolithic single stones that create obelisks, you will feel a sense of humble appreciation for the vastness of universal consciousness and the wonders that the world has to offer.

---

8. Alluring World, "Obelisk of Axum," http://www.alluringworld.com/obelisk-of-axum/.

22. OBSERVATION HILL—KENYA

Category: Mountains/Mounds/Cliff Locations

Observation Hill is located in the western part of the Amboseli National Park in the Loitoktok District of the Rift Valley of Kenya, in Kajiado County, South Africa. There are five different habitats within the park including the open plains of the savannah, woodlands, Lake Amboseli, (which is now just a dried bed where the lake once was, although there are other lakes with water in the area), swamps and marshes in the wetlands (that also have sulfur springs in them), and rocky thorn bush areas. From the park you can also view Mount Kilimanjaro in the distance on clear days.

The only place in the park where you are allowed to get out of your car and walk around is at Observation Hill. It is the highest point in the otherwise flat land of the park. Observation Hill formed during the Pleistocene period and is shaped somewhat like a pyramid.

To get up to the top of Observation Hill, you'll climb a staircase that was carved out of the volcanic rock. The park officials have placed information panels where you can read about the formation of Observation Hill, the habitats, animals, and plants within the park. When you reach the lookout areas there are 360° views where you can see many of the things you read about on the way up. A large portion of the park is dry and dusty and to the east are the Enkongu Narok marshes that are green and vibrant. You will also see the headquarters of the park rangers and the abandoned Ol Tukai Lodge, which are within a fenced off area of the park.

Observation Hill is one of the best places to view African wildlife. Remember to bring your binoculars so you can see some of the smaller animals and birds that are harder to view than the large African wildlife, which at times is also far away and difficult to view without binoculars. Some of the wildlife that you can see are large herds of African elephants walking throughout the area or enjoying the wetness of the marshes. There are over nine hundred elephants who live in the park and they are one of the most popular attractions. Hippopotamuses are frequently found around and in Enkongu Marok marsh. Buffalo roam throughout the park along with giraffes. While more difficult to spot, you can also see prides of African lions either lounging during the heat of the day or on the hunt. Wildebeest abound in very large herds and is quite possible to see them on the move. Herds of zebras and antelope are also in abundance and can be seen from Observation Hill. There are also cheetahs, impalas, and gazelles living in the park. You may also hear the laughter of hyenas, the roar of the lions, the call of the monkeys, or the sounds of any of the other animals.

Visiting Observation Hill is a unique experience. It is recommended to visit during sunrise or sunset due to the amazing views that happen in conjunction with the position of the sun and Mount Kilimanjaro as a backdrop. Remember to bring your camera to capture memories for a lifetime.

The energy at Observation Hill is relaxing, invigorating, and raw with an underlying presence of wildness and danger. It will move you spiritually, make you feel a sense of awe, and will inspire you simply through the vast interconnectedness of the habitats and the animals who live there. This is an excellent location to practice animal frequency to connect to the energy of the animals. An additional underlying energy moves in a gentle flow with small undulations as if it's being carried on the wind. It can settle you, help you find balance, and allows you to experience happiness and joy.

23. OLDUVAI GORGE—TANZANIA

Categories: Canyons/Gorges, Power Places, Ruins/Archeological Sites

Olduvai Gorge is one of the most important paleoanthropological sites in regards to human evolution. It is located in the northern part of Tanzania, which is on the eastern coast of Africa, in the eastern Serengeti Plain within the Ngorongoro Conservation Area. Olduvai Gorge is a two-branched, deep ravine located in the Great Rift Valley between the Serengeti National Park and Ngorongoro Crater and twenty-eight miles from Laetoli, another significant paleoanthropological site. If you combine the lengths of both branches of Olduvai Gorge it is approximately 30 miles long and 295 feet deep. The gorge is approximately thirty thousand years old and was formed by streams in the area and changes in the earth.

In 1929 Mary and Louis Leakey set up an excavation site at Olduvai Gorge along with research programs. Between the two of them they made many discoveries that changed the way people looked at human development in history. In the ravine, the Leakeys found remains of early hominin species. These include Australopiths including Zinjanthropus boisei, Homo habilis, homo erectus, and homo sapiens. During their archaeological work they found four different layers of fossilized remains within the gorge and surrounding areas of what is now known as the Ngorongoro Conservation Area, one of which was a twenty-five million year old skull of a Proconsul primate, which was discovered by Mary

Leakey. In 1959, Mary Leakey discovered parts of another skull and some upper teeth. When all the four hundred pieces were recovered, they formed almost a complete skull which dated at 1.75 million years old. They named it Zinjanthropus boisei. In 1968 a member of the Leakey team, Peter Nzube, discovered a female skull that dated at 1.8 million years old. It was named Twiggy, because it was flat and had to be reconstructed, and it was believed she died as a young adult because her third set of molars did not have much wear. One of the most significant finds at Olduvai Gorge was a female discovered by a team of American and Tanzanian archaeologist in 1986. They uncovered 302 bones and teeth from the female's skeleton, which dated at 1.8 million years old.

The work done by the Leakey's and other archaeologists and paleoanthropologists over the years has resulted in significant finds regarding hominin evolution over millions of years. Louis Leakey referred to Olduvai Gorge as the "Cradle of Mankind" because he firmly believed it was the location where early man as humans evolved.

The energy at Olduvai Gorge feels busy. It moves in a haphazard, kind of shaking motion, and feels sort of like a bee buzzing by your ear. This energy is of very high frequency, is sizzling and in constant movement. It opens your awareness, creates new insight, and will place possibilities in front of you just to see what you will do with them. This is an energy of new opportunities, of growth, and of following your passion. When it is time for you to discover more about your own spiritual self, or to embark on new adventures, start a new project or business, then connecting to the energy at Olduvai Gorge will bring you success.

24. PUNGO ANDONGO–MALANJE, ANGOLA

Categories: Mythological Sites, Power Places, Rock Formations

The small town of Pungo Andongo is located in the northern part of Angola, which is in the southwestern part of Africa and borders the Atlantic Ocean. Pungo Andongo is about seventy-two miles from the town of Malanje, which is known for its open-air market. Pungo Andongo is famous for its black stone geographical formations known as the Black Stones of Pungo Andongo, the Malanje Black Stones or simply the Black Stones. They are millions of years old and their composition is consolidated sedimentary rock including sandstones and conglomerates. Geologists aren't really sure of their formation and they seem out of place in the flat savannah.

The Black Stones of Pungo Andongo are associated with many legends and myths according to the native tribe in the area, the Mbundu people. These ancient rock formations are very unique in that they are shaped like animals and other items. The most popular is Pedra Homen, the male stone. Legend has it that if a man touches the Pedra Homen stone, his male parts will start to grow. Age does not matter, therefore you'll find men of every age visiting the stone. But it's not limited to just the men. Close by Pedra Homen is another stone called Pedra Mulher, which is the female stone, but the locals don't say what happens to a woman when she touches the stone. Another legend is that during the sixteenth century King Ngola Kiluanji and Queen Ginga Mbandi ruled their Kingdom of Ndongo at Pungo Andongo. One day the queen was bathing in the stream that ran along the base of the stones when Portuguese soldiers happened to show up. She ran away and the stone carvings are believed to represent her footsteps.

If you choose to visit the Black Stones of Pungo Andongo, there are a few traditions of the Angolian people that you should be aware of prior to visiting. It is customary to greet the elders first when meeting a group of people. You should make a low bow as a show of respect. People in the area avoid direct eye contact, especially when a woman looks at a man, they should never look him directly in the eye. Even when speaking with other women, it's advisable to only look at them indirectly. The people in Angola are not concerned with giving someone else their personal space. They'll get right up in yours during a conversation and think nothing of it. Backing away from them to regain your personal space could be considered offensive to them, and since they are a very hospitable people who wouldn't want to offend you, they'll just step right back into your personal space. So if you're visiting Angola, leave your personal space at home.

The energy of the Black Stones of Pungo Andongo are solid, fixed, and vibrate with a low-pitched frequency. They represent strength, endurance, respect, and staying strong under erosive elements. This energy will give you the strength and persistence needed when striving to attain your goals or make it through a difficult time.

25. RHUMSIKI—RHUMSIKI, CAMEROON
Categories: Mountains/Mounds/Cliff Locations, Volcanoes/Volcano Cones
The country of the Republic of Cameroon, is located in the west-central portion of Africa with its coastline on the Atlantic Ocean. The village of Rhumsiki is in the Far North Province of Cameroon in the Mandara Mountains, a three million year old volcanic mountain

range that is about 120 miles long that runs along the border of Cameroon and Nigeria. The highest elevation is at Mount Oupay, which is 4,900 feet above sea level.

Rhumsiki is one of the most popular locations in Cameroon and the Mandara Mountain range due to the abundance of volcanic plugs, also called volcanic necks or lava necks, that are scattered across the landscape, which is also made up of basalt rock formations in addition to the volcanic plugs. The landscape is reminiscent of the moon's landscape or that of an alien planet and is extremely beautiful in its uniqueness.

A volcanic plug is formed when an active volcano erupts and the magma hardens inside a volcanic vent, the plumbing system of an active volcano, instead of flowing out of it. Depending upon the activity level of the volcano, there can still be molten magma underneath the volcanic plug. If this is the case, and the volcano erupts beneath the plug, the eruption can be very violent and explosive. Once a volcano is inactive, the magma beneath the plug will also harden. As the surrounding volcano erodes over time, the volcanic plugs remain visible because they don't erode at the same rate as the rest of the volcano. They often contain dense rocks that contain a lot of magnesium and iron and less silicon because they come from the deep crust or the upper mantle of the earth, which takes a long time to erode. Volcanic plugs, like the ones found in Rhumsiki, after millions of years of erosion look cylindrical and often jagged in appearance. The largest volcanic plug in Rhumsiki is known as Kapsiki Peak, which is 4,016 feet tall.

The Village of Rhumsiki is welcoming and it is not unusual for the children in the village to show you around so that you have lots of photo opportunities with their acclaimed volcanic plugs. The Kapsiki ethnic group lives in Rhumsiki and the valley surrounding the village in stone homes with thatched roofs. The local crafters will meet with visitors to show them their expertise as blacksmiths, potters, weavers, and spinners. You can enjoy a performance by the local dancers or have your future told by an intuitive who uses a crab that moves around pieces of wood, which determines what your future holds.

The energy in Rhumsiki is happy and joyful and yet quiet and calm. It moves in an upward motion from the earth to the sky in almost a straight line. It feels as if it pulsates, which could be a shadow energy of the great volcano that was once active at this place. There is a sense of sacredness here, of being one with the planet. It encourages you to embrace your own uniqueness and to step out of your comfort zone, to be different but true to your spiritual essence, and to see the uniqueness in everything and everyone around you, instead of walking through life with blinders on.

26. SAHARA DESERT—NORTHERN THIRD
OF THE AFRICAN CONTINENT

Categories: Regions, Sandhills/Sand Dunes, Volcanoes/Volcano Cones

Located in the northern part of Africa, the Sahara Desert covers 3.6 million square miles, approximately one third of the entire continent. The borders of the Sahara Desert are the Atlantic Ocean on the west, the Red Sea in the east, the Mediterranean Sea in the north, and the Niger River valley in the south. It covers most of many countries in northern Africa including Algeria, Chad, Egypt, Libya, Mali, Mauritania, Morocco, Niger, Western Sahara, Sudan, and Tunisia. It is the largest hot desert in the world. The normal temperature during the hotter months is usually 122 degrees Fahrenheit, or even hotter, while the average temperature is about eighty-six degrees Fahrenheit. At night, the temperature is often below freezing due to the lack of humidity. Rainfall ranges between 0.79 to 3.9 inches per year depending upon the location within the Sahara.

When you think of the Sahara Desert, the first things that may come to mind are enormous shifting sand dunes, which it does have, and they are called ergs. Some of the dunes in the Sahara can shift to 590 feet tall. The sand is orange in color due to its iron. The wind in the Sahara is called the Sirroco wind and can blow at sixty-two miles per hour consistently. This creates massive sand storms that constantly change the topography and the height and shape of the dunes and can even be viewed from space. However, ergs don't cover the whole of the Sahara. The majority of the Sahara has very little sand and is mostly barren land with rocky plateaus called hamada, gravel mixed with sand over the plains, dry mountains, oasis depressions, and shallow basins. The tallest point in the Sahara Desert is an inactive volcano crater called Emi Koussi, which is 11,204 feet above sea level and the lowest point is an oasis depression called Egypt's Qattara Depression, which is 436 feet below sea level at the deepest section.

There isn't much plant life in the Sahara, only five hundred known species, which have adapted so they can grow in the desert's harsh climate. Most of the plant life is found in the Tibesti Mountains and the Jebel Unweinat Mountains where the temperatures are lower and there is more rainfall. There are animals that have also been able to adapt to the harsh conditions in the Sahara and that can live for extended amounts of time without drinking water including the African wild dog, the golden jackal, the ostrich, the Saharan cheetah, the fennec fox, the pale fox, and the dorcas gazelle. There is also a species of white antelope called the addax that can go an entire year without drinking water but only five hundred are left in the wild and are critically endangered. The desert monitor, scorpions, the scarab beetle, the horned viper, the black-throated firefinch, the African silverbill, and desert crocodiles can be found in some parts of Chad and Mauritania. The only domesticated animals that live in the Sahara are goats and camels.

The energy in the Sahara Desert is in constant motion at a high frequency. It is hot, dry, and moves in an undulating wave that is slow at times and fast at other times. This encourages you to find your own balance within and to move quickly when necessary but to always take the time to slow down. This is a good energy to connect with when you have to do without something that you think you absolutely need in your life. The energy here awakens you to knowing that you may not need what you think you must have and can help you adapt to expected and unexpected changes that occur in your life.

27. SENEGAMBIA RIVER STONE CIRCLES— THE GAMBIA/SENEGAL

Categories: Burial Sites, Power Stones

Located in the countries of the Republic of the Gambia and Senegal in West Africa are the Senegambia River Stone Circles also known as the Megaliths of Senegambia. Except for the Gambia's coastline, the country of Senegal wraps around the Gambia, which looks like a sliver of land inserted into Senegal from the Atlantic coast on the west and that stretches about three quarters of the way through the Senegal following the Gambia River. The Senegambia River Stones are so named because they are situated in both countries and are located north of the Gambia River and south of the River Senegal. Archaeologists have also divided the whole area of the stone circles into four main locations, which are Wassu and Kerbatch in the Gambia and Wanar and Sine Ngayene in Senegal. The Senegambia River Stone Circles are "the largest concentration of stone circles seen anywhere in the world" according to the UNESCO.[9]

Archaeologists have yet to determine the identity of the ancient people who built the stone circles because they predate the arrival of the Manding people who currently live in the area. They also do not know when they built the monuments, which includes

---

9. UNESCO, Stone Circles of Senegambia, https://whc.unesco.org/en/list/1226.

the stone circles, multiple burial mounds and other markers which total approximately 2,000 individual sites spread over thousands of square miles. There are 1,053 stone circle sites which, when combined, contain 28,931 individual monolithic stones. There are also 17,000 individual monuments. Archaeologists think the sites were probably built sometime between the third century BC and the sixteenth century AD. They also think that the custom of burying their dead in the stone circles was long-standing and that the stone circles continued to be built over a period of two thousand years.

The stone circles have a unique construction and sometimes you'll find a smaller circle of stones inside of another larger circle of stones. The stones themselves are typically the same size in height, about six and half feet tall with each individual stone weighing up to seven tons. The openings to enter the circle all face east and the stones themselves are grave markers. Archaeologists have discovered that the burials of these people involved several steps. They would first bury the person in a shallow grave until only the skeleton was left, then they would select specific bones, usually skulls but sometimes other bones, and then bury them altogether within the stone circle. In the cases of sites with two stone circles, pottery was found on top of jawbones, which may have been a type of food offering for the afterlife. There was also metal found around some of the stone circles. Archaeologists believe this would've been a festive religious ceremony when the bones were removed from the shallow burial sites and taken to the stone circle and that a lot of ritual was involved with the construction of the stone circles, monuments, and at the individual burial mounds.[10]

The energy that surrounds this large location is steady, cool, and thought-provoking. It sounds like a deep toned humming vibration that moves slowly but steadily in one direction before switching to the opposite direction in a continual pattern as it moves over the two thousand acres. The energy here feels like a solid foundation and lasting stability. When you're trying to establish something new in your life, connecting to the energy of the Senegambia River Stone Circles will give you a strong basis from which to build.

---

10. National Geographic Video, African Stonehenge?, June 17, 2009, https://www.youtube.com/watch?time_continue=174&v=9o7S0l7Q76w.

28. SEVILLA ROCK ART TRAIL–SOUTH AFRICA

Category: Petroglyph/Rock Art Sites

The Sevilla Rock Art Trail is located on Traveller's Rest Farm, which is about twenty-two miles from Clanwilliam in the Cederberg Mountains, in the Western Cape of South Africa approximately 186 miles north of Cape Town.

Traveller's Rest Farm offers accommodation for visitors with twenty-nine cottages of various sizes that offer all of the comforts of home. The farm is privately owned so the owners charge a small fee for a permit to walk the Sevilla Rock Art Trail and view the famous artwork of the ancient Sans people. A permit is also required because it is a UNESCO World Heritage Site. The trail is about three miles long and it will take you approximately two and a half to three hours to complete. As you walk the trail alongside the Brannewyn River, you'll be able to see a wide variety of the indigenous plants and different species of animals including but not limited to birds, lizards, small game, baboons, and rock hyrax, which the locals call dassies.

There are nine separate sites of rock art paintings on the trail. The early inhabitants of the area were the San, also spelled Saan, who were also indigenous hunter-gatherers, primarily nomadic Bushmen. The rock art in these nine sites is estimated to be between eight hundred and eight thousand years old and were created using ochre, egg whites, gall, and blood. There are images of people, elephants, and other animals, and handprints of both adults and children.

While the Sevilla Rock Art Trail paintings are the easiest to access, there are more than 2,500 rock art paintings created by the San people in the Cedarburg region. When visiting the Sevilla Rock Art Trail remember to be respectful of the rules set forth for these precious artifacts. Touching or wetting the paintings is strictly forbidden because it will cause irreparable damage to their integrity. They have been here for thousands of years so it is important to preserve them so they will be here for a long time in the future.

The energy at the Sevilla Rock Art Trail moves in a fluid rocking motion and vibrates like a medium pitched humming sound. The energy here feels wise, protected, and worry free. It is laid-back, relaxing, and balanced. Connecting to the energy of this place will enable you to gain more wisdom, which creates a levelheaded, calm approach to life. If there are times when you're feeling hotheaded, worried, frustrated, or like you're about to crawl out of your skin, then allowing this energy to move through you will calm and settle you. It will help you release pent up energy so you can see things from a clearer perspective. Sometimes you might have to walk away from situations you find yourself in and calling on this energy will give you the ability to remain silent, turn, and put one foot in front of the other.

29. SOSSUSVLEI DUNES—NAMIBIA

Category: Sandhills/Sand Dunes

The Sossusvlei Dunes are located in Namibia, in south western Africa on the Atlantic coast, in the Namib-Naukluft National Park, the largest conservation park in Africa, in the southern region of the Namib Desert. The Namib Desert covers the entire Atlantic coast of Namibia and is said to be the oldest desert in the world. The contrast of the red orange dunes against a cloudless, deep blue sky is very dramatic and draws visitors from around the world.

Sossusvlei when translated means "dead end marsh" and applies to the salt and clay pan area, which in geology means it is a depression in the ground where water collects and where salt will remain after the water evaporates. When it is dry, Sossusvlei looks whitish gray which is in direct contrast with the orange red color of the dunes surrounding it. Sossusvlei is located at an area where the dunes connect and block the Tsauchab River. Typically the Tsauchab River doesn't flow into the harsh conditions of the desert, but if the rainy season gets more rain than normal, the pan can fill and will hold the water for a year. This creates a photographer's dream because of the way Sossusvlei is situated between the dunes, causing them to reflect in the water, which results in amazing photographs.

Big Daddy, at a height of 1,066 feet, is the largest sand dune in the Sossusvlei area and the second tallest in the Namib Desert (Dune 7 is the tallest at 1,257 feet). Geologists believe that the sand in the pan area is between three and five million years old. While the area is dry and harsh, there are a number of plant and animal species that have adapted to survive in this desert's conditions including Hartman's mountain zebra, oryx, springbok, Burchell's zebra, bat-eared foxes, and many species of lizards and insects.

Today people refer to the whole area as Sossusvlei. While visiting, there are several ways to experience the orange-red dunes. You can take the easy route and book a flight or balloon ride to view them from above, or you can travel around on horseback or climb directly to the top of the dunes. The climb is not for the faint of heart and is very strenuous, but once you get to the top, the views are absolutely mind blowing. The open spaces you can see from the top of the dune will make you feel like a wondrous part of this amazing world. Stargazing at night at the Sossusvlei Dunes is an incredible experience you know you'll never forget as you view the millions of stars in the blackest night.

The energy at the Sossusvlei Dunes is intriguing, mysterious, and ancient. Just think, you're standing on sand that is at least three million years old. The energy here moves as the wind blows, fast and strong with dips and curves. This is beneficial to you when you need to take quick action without hesitation. It will also keep you humble if you start feeling too proud or sure of yourself. Connecting to the energy here will help you adjust to whatever life throws at you. Just move as the wind does and curve or dip as needed.

30. THE AMPHITHEATER–DRAKENSBERG, SOUTH AFRICA
Categories: Bodies of Water/Waterfalls/Springs, Canyons/Gorges, Mountains/Mounds/Cliff Locations, Power Places, Rock Formations

The Amphitheatre is located in the Drakensberg Mountain Range in northern Drakensberg, South Africa, in the Royal Natal National Park of the KwaZulu-Natal Province.

The Drakensberg Mountain Range (*Drakensberg* translates to "Dragon's Mountain") is the tallest mountain range in all of South Africa, and at its highest point it is 11,424 feet above sea level. The mountain range is 621 miles long and made of a top layer of basalt that is nearly 5,000 feet deep and beneath that is sandstone. The range goes into Lesotho where the mountains gradually become smaller and less rocky.

The Amphitheater is a cliff face that is very dramatic in its appearance due to its sheer length and height. It is located in the northern part of the Drakensberg Mountain Range. The Amphitheater also has the second highest waterfall in the world, Tugela Falls, which flows from the Tugela River down the craggy face of the cliff into Tugela Gorge below. The water of Tugela Falls drops 3,100 feet from the top of the Amphitheater to the bottom of the gorge and has five separate leaping points where the water surges away from the rock face of the cliff on the way down. The amount of water flow you'll see at Tugela Falls depends on the weather. If the area has seen little rain, the river sometimes completely dries out and the falls are nonexistent, but during times of heavy rainfall, the falls are so large they can be seen from far away. To ensure you're visiting during a time when the Tugela Falls are in their splendor, check with local officials in regards to the weather and the flow of the falls.

If you're adventurous you can take the five hour hike to the top of the Amphitheatre. You'll start at the car park above the Witsieshoek Resort and climb until you reach Mount Aux Sources peak. At this point you'll encounter chain ladders. If you decide to brave these ladders and continue to the top you'll experience phenomenal, breathtaking, and amazing views of the African landscape, of the mountain range, and the gorge 3,100 feet below. From here there is also a trail that goes to the bottom of Tugela Falls, and also includes another chain ladder you'll have to climb down. If you are afraid of heights, this climb is not for you. I highly recommend that you take a look at videos of people climbing these chain ladders prior to visiting so you'll know what you're in for before reaching them.[11]

The energy of the Amphitheater is ancient, powerful, and remote. It vibrates in a slow-moving, yet high-frequency pattern that sounds like a repetitive tapping. The energy of this place will help you when you need to stand strong, to be firm, and not sway from your beliefs. It will help you remember the truth inside you, whether you let the world see that truth or keep it private and to yourself. If you find yourself feeling weak or alone, connecting to the energy of the Amphitheater will enable you to find the strength within through your connection to the age-old wonders of the universe.

31. THE GREAT PYRAMIDS OF GIZA—GIZA, EGYPT
Categories: Burial Sites, Earth Chakras (Throat), Man-Made Sites, Power Places, Pyramids

The Great Pyramids of Giza are located near the city of Cairo and are on the Giza Plateau. The Great Pyramid was built over a twenty-year period under the reign of Pharaoh Khufu during the Fourth Dynasty, between 2589 and 2566 BC. When you think of Egypt, some of the first things that may come to mind are the Great Pyramids of Giza. There are three pyramids on the Giza Plateau. The largest, oldest, and tallest of the three is named the Great Pyramid and was built by Pharaoh Khufu. The middle pyramid is more toward the background and was built by Pharaoh Khafre, Khufu's son. The third pyramid is situated toward the front and was built by Pharaoh Menkaure.

---

11. Govertical Mountaineering, "Climbing the Chain Ladders, Northern Drakensberg Amphitheatre," April 20, 2010, https://www.youtube.com/watch?v=FN1wT0DxZnM.

The only surviving wonder of the Seven Wonders of the Ancient World is the Great Pyramid. At its base, the pyramid measures 754 feet on each side and its point is at 479 feet. There are over two million blocks of stone precisely laid within the pyramid, some of which are enormous. Its construction is not completely understood today because the ancient people who built it did not have access to machinery to move such colossal sized slabs of stone. Many different theories exist as to how the ancient Egyptians were able to construct such a massive undertaking. Regardless of how it was actually constructed, the majority of archaeologists believe it was built to be the tomb of Pharaoh Khufu as a monument that would last forever. Others think it was a temple or holy memorial.

Ancient Egyptians believed the soul remained with the body after death and the pharaohs became gods in the afterlife, thus the reason for such detailed mummification. They also included everything that the king would need in the afterlife inside the tomb with him such as riches, furniture, food, pottery, tools, and weapons. They believed these items would take care of him and his family members, who were often buried nearby or in the tomb with him.

The Great Pyramid's entrance faces north and is fifty-nine feet above ground level. According to archeologists, it leads to an underground chamber that wasn't finished. It splits and goes to the Queens chambers. At the top of the queen's chambers is a narrow and long passageway going to the king's chamber, which is the actual burial room. The walls and roof are made of granite stone and from this room there are two shafts that go to the exterior of the pyramid.

The energy of the Great Pyramids of Giza is positive and enlightening, which draws people from around the world to visit it even in modern times. The energy here sparks a deeper sense of desire for enlightenment, personal change, and spiritual transformation. The energy moves with ease and flow around the exterior of the Giza Plateau and then in between the pyramids themselves. The energy is uplifting and inspiring, which can be beneficial to you in any situation. Experiencing the energy in this place can evoke strong emotions at a spiritual level.

32. THE SPHINX—GIZA, EGYPT

Categories: Man-Made Sites, Monasteries/Temples,
Mythological Sites, Power Places

The Great Sphinx of Giza is located on the west bank of the Nile river in the Giza Plateau in Egypt. It sits alongside the Great Pyramids of Giza and is closest to Pharoah Khafre's valley temple. The Great Sphinx is a national symbol of Egypt and one of the most well known ancient monuments in the world.

Pharaoh Khafre built the second pyramid of Giza and the complex surrounding his pyramid included the Great Sphinx, around 2530 BC. The Sphinx has the body of a lion lying down, paws facing forward and the face of a man wearing the headdress of the pharaoh. Archeologists believe that the face of the man is that of Pharoah Khafre himself and that the Sphinx is his self-portrait, although there is some dispute regarding the date of its actual construction. Some archeologists believe it could have been buried in the sand long before Pharaoh Khafre came into power and the sand was dug away from it. Some evidence suggests that it once had a beard but the pieces found dated during the New Kingdom times so this isn't conclusive. They also believe that the Sphinx was built to watch over Pharoah Khafre's pyramid complex. Legend says the Sphinx was a merciless protector of the temple complex and would keep evil spirits from entering the area. In Arabic it is called *Abu al-Hawl*, which means "Father of Terror." In Greek mythology, a sphinx would ask riddles and if the correct answer wasn't given, it would eat the person.

The Sphinx is about 240 feet long and 66 feet high and carved out of a massive ridge of limestone. It was built by excavating the outcrop and by then removing some of the large blocks of stone. The lower body was constructed using some of these huge stone blocks, which were also used in other parts of the temple complex. Once this was cleared away, the remainder of the Sphinx was carved out of the remaining rock. It is located in a shallow depression south of Pharaoh Khafre's pyramid. The limestone of the body is softer than that of the head so the body erodes faster. The face has suffered a lot of damage, not only from erosion. Soldiers used it for target practice during the French occupation in the early 1800s, which archeologists believe may be the reason why the nose and lips are missing, although this can't be confirmed. With these important features missing it makes the face look flat and there has been some debate as to whether the Sphinx was really a self portrait of Pharaoh Khafre or if it was a woman's face. Three tunnels were also built within the Sphinx but they are short and if they went to rooms similar to the pyramids, these passageways have filled over time and aren't accessible. It may also be that the builders started cutting out the tunnels and then stopped for some reason.

The energy of the Sphinx is hot, protective, and enlightening. It moves in a quick tempo like a wave around the monument. It is purifying, cleansing, and connected to the Divine. The energy encourages you to seek your own divine connection to universal consciousness through purification and cleansing, by letting go of that which no longer serves you, and embracing enlightened thoughts and ideals. It can make you feel a lightness of being, a oneness with universal energy, and brings about a profound knowing within your spiritual self.

33. TIPASA—TIPAZA, ALGERIA

Categories: Man-Made Sites, Monasteries/Temples, Power Places, Ruins/Archeological Sites

Tipasa is located in Tipasa Archaeological Park in Tipaza, Algeria, which is in the northern part of the country, approximately fifty miles west of Algiers in the Commune and Wilaya provinces. Tipaza was founded and named during the pre-Roman era and spelled with a *z*. Today, many people spell it with an *s* and both spellings are often used interchangeably. It borders the Mediterranean Sea and has forty miles of coastline. Algeria is in the northwestern section of the continent of Africa. In ancient times it was also within the area known as Mauretania, and the original inhabitants of the area were from Berber lineage and were know as the Massaesyli and the Mauri (Moors). Today the city of Tipasa is known for not only the Roman ruins at the site but also for the influences that the Phoenicians, Byzatines, and Christians had on it.

Tipasa was originally settled by Phoenician sailors who were looking for a port during long trips at sea. Archeologists found Phoenician tombs that date to the sixth century BC, which is believed to be around the time it was settled. Other items were also found at the archeological sites that suggest the Phoenician's traded with Greece, the Iberian Peninsula, and Italy. The Romans overtook the town and, under the rule of Septimus Severus between 193 and 211 AD, it became a prosperous Roman port town. The Romans annexed the town into the Roman Empire in forty AD and built a wall around the town to protect it and keep out invading armies. In later years, after the

Roman rule, Tipasa was often attacked by the Berbers and the Vandals and was finally abandoned in the sixth century AD.

When visiting the site, the first thing you will encounter is the amphitheater of which only the oval walls of the arena are still standing today. In this amphitheater, the ancient people would have gladiator fights and enactments of naval battles. There are two main roads through the town that will take you to the temples, forum, theater, baths, tombs, and two basilica, one of which was the largest North African Christian building of the time, the Grand Basilica. Another building, the Villa of Frescoes, was one of the largest houses of the area, at one thousand square feet, built during the second century AD.

The city of Tipasa was discovered again in 1856 by archeologists and there have been continuous excavations since that time. During their excavations, archaeologists have found human remains on both the inside and outside the large wall that the Romans built around Tipasa, including a paleo-Christian cemetery that is one of the most important finds in North Africa. Archaeologists also found mosaics built into the floor of the bath complex.

The energy of Tipasa is vibrant and alive. It is a complex intermingling of separate frequencies that are all at various high levels of vibration, and when they come together, it sounds like a sweet song, and will motivate, inspire, encourage, and enlighten you on many different levels. The energy here encourages you to be true to yourself, your spirituality, and your moral values, while being understanding of those same qualities within others. It speaks of open mindedness, and not putting limits on others. Connecting to the energy of Tipasa means to walk through the world with your eyes wide open and your heart full of love.

34. TSODILO HILLS—BOTSWANA

Category: Petroglyph/Rock Art Sites

The Tsodilo Hills are located in the southern corner of Botswana, Africa, in the Kalahari Desert near the Namibian border within the Okavango Sub-District. It is a difficult location to access and you will need a four-wheel-drive vehicle during the last leg of the journey.

Tsodilo Hills are world renowned for the amount of rock art contained within a small region. More than 500 individual sites contain over 4,500 ancient rock paintings.

This is significant because the depictions within these paintings show human activities, wildlife, and changes to the environment that these people experienced over a period of more than one hundred thousand years.

The hills themselves are four massive quartzite rocks that rise up from the desert sands. To the bushmen of the area the largest rock is the male, second largest is the female, and the smallest is a child. Legend says that the fourth rock was the first wife of the male hill. He left her for a younger wife, who is now the second largest rock, and now the first wife remains in the background behind the rock family.

Because these hills are where the spirits of the ancestors rest and where the bushmen's gods live, legend says that after the world was created, the creator said his first prayer from these hills. Because this is a sacred place, legend also says that if anyone hunts or kills anyone or anything near the hills, the gods will curse you with bad luck and hard times.

The rock art scene contains some interesting pictures such as whales, rhinos, giraffes penguins, a zebra (that is now used as a logo for the Botswana National Museum and Monuments), and one of the pictures containing humans shows males who are sexually excited dancing around. In addition to the rock art, there are other things you can see at Tsodilo Hills. One of these is a weird looking little tree at the beginning of rhino trail that is located near the female hill. This tree is called the tree of true knowledge. There is also a natural cistern off of Cliff Trail, which always contains water, called the Horned Serpent.

The San and Hambukushu people who live nearby believe that ancestral spirits often visit Tsodilo, which is also a place of worship. The waterholes, landscape, and hills are all considered sacred. The quartzite rocks that form Tsodilo Hills are known to have healing and stabilizing properties.

The energy at Tsodilo moves in a rapid upward motion. The energy here is uplifting, stable, and a solid foundation on which to build a spiritual base. As you make changes on your spiritual path and become open to inner growth and universal enlightenment through a connection to the cosmic energies of the universe, you will find that the energy at Tsodilo will help you regulate and find a new balance as your own frequency elevates.

The energy here encourages rapid growth in both the understanding and involvement of new abilities such as intuition, empathy, and mediumistic tendencies. Call on the energy of this place when you feel a rapid increase of your own personal spirituality in order to maintain balance during times of spiritual growth.

35. VALLEY OF THE KINGS—EGYPT

Categories: Burial Sites, Man-Made Sites, Power Places, Regions

The Valley of the Kings, which is also sometimes referred to as the Valley of the Tombs of the Kings, is located on the west bank of the Nile River in Upper Egypt, west of Luxor, Egypt. In ancient times it was part of the city of Thebes. During the eighteenth to the twentieth dynasties, which occurred between the eleventh to sixteenth centuries BC, almost all of the pharaohs were buried in the Valley of the Kings. Currently, sixty-three tombs and chambers have been discovered. A necropolis means *city of the dead* and the Valley of the Kings is considered one of the first examples of a necropolis. The Valley of the Kings is a burial place of all of the great pharaohs from the New Kingdom and high-ranking officials such as the queens, elite members of the royal court, and high priests.

Some of the tombs found in the Valley of the Kings are simple pits while others, like KV5, are massive and complex with over 120 chambers. The tombs were dug deep into the mountain in order to conceal them from grave robbers because they buried many treasures with them when they died. Things needed in the afterlife and pets, such as dogs, gazelles, and baboons, were often found buried near the person. The builders often used the geological features of the earth to their advantage to make building the tombs easier. Archaeologists believe, based on ancient Egyptian writings, that there may be some nobles who would've been deserving of a tomb in the Valley of the Kings but whose tombs haven't been located yet.

The tomb of Pharaoh Ramses VII was the first one discovered in the Valley of the Kings and has the distinction of being named KV1, the KV stands for Kings Valley. However, the first Pharaoh to be buried in the Valley of the Kings was Thutmose I in 1493 BC. The most recent discovery was in 2008, which consisted of a tomb that had a sarcophagus, flowers, linens, and pottery but there was no mummy inside. It was named KV63 and is thought to be an embalming tomb.

Today you can visit some of the tombs in the Valley of the Kings but the majority of them are not open to the public. Many of the tombs contain Greek and Latin graffiti written by people in ancient times. Approximately 2,100 graffiti markings were found with half of them located in KV9. The oldest dated graffiti is from 278 BC.

The tomb of Ramses III is the most visited tomb in the Valley of the Kings. The tomb of Tutankhamen is probably the most famous and was the most intact Royal tomb discovered although it also showed signs of grave robbers previously entering the tomb.

The energy in the Valley of the Kings is somber, respectful, and quiet. The frequency is high and moves like an arc then dips through the valley. The energy here encourages you to realize your greatest potential while on the earthly plane because in reality you can't take the physical items you accumulate with you into the afterlife. The energy here will help you realize the importance of growing on your own spiritual path by determining your own inner truth within yourself and allowing that truth to grow into something beautiful and long-lasting. It is being known for who you are, what you believe, and how you treat others and not by a monetary value or the physical things you accumulate.

36. VREDEFORT DOME—
FREE STATE PROVINCE, SOUTH AFRICA

Categories: Impact Crater, UFO/Extraterrestrial/Paranormal Sites

Vredefort Dome is located in the Free State Province of South Africa approximately seventy-five miles from Johannesburg. The Vredefort Dome is an astrobleme, which means that it is an enormous crater that was created when a meteorite or comet impacted the surface of the earth. Vredefort Dome is a World Heritage Site and is one of only a few impact craters on earth that has multiple rings due to the force of the impact, which melted rocks in rings around the center of the impact similar to ripples when you drop a rock into water. These rings are still visible from space.

Geologists estimate that this event happened approximately 2,023 million years ago, which makes the Vredefort Dome astrobleme the oldest one found on earth to date. The crater is 186 miles wide with the Vredefort Dome making up the center of the impact crater. The crater is named after the town of Vredefort, which is located inside the center of the crater, and the dome shape created during impact at the center point, thus the name Vredefort Dome. Today only the crater floor is still visible, everything else, including the rim of the crater and the actual dome itself, has eroded away in the millions of years since the event. Scientists have determined that in order to make an impact crater of this extreme size the meteorite or comet would have been traveling at a speed of 22,369 miles per second and it would have been about six and a half miles wide.

A unique and lasting effect that still lingers at the impact site is the magnetism. If you walk around the dome with a compass it will move all over the place, never giving the correct direction. Scientists think this happens because of varying magnetic fields in the area.

There are tours available where you can walk through the area and learn more about it. While the general tour is the one that most people take and gives an overall view of the geology, culture, and history of the place, there are also individual geological tours, bird tours, history and cultural tours, and educational tours available for students and the public. These tours run between five and eight hours each.

The energy of Vredefort Dome is of an extremely high frequency, it is somewhat volatile, and moves in waves away from the center. When connecting with the energy of Vredefort Dome, it acts as a catalyst in your life. It encourages you to take action, can help you make quick decisions, and enables you to deal with the ripple effects of the decisions you make. This energy gives you the confidence you need to own your actions, choices, and beliefs. Spiritually this energy will impact you on many levels. You may feel an intensity regarding your spiritual self that you've never felt before, or experience an increase in all of your senses, including your extra-sensory perception, in regards to people and their motives, behaviors, and how they're affecting your own energy. You may notice an increase in intuition and other abilities, or find yourself feeling more déjà vu or having paranormal experiences. The energy here is a catalyst that will get you moving in the right direction to grow spiritually and on a personal level.

Chapter 4
EUROPE

Megaliths such as those found at Stonehenge in England, Carnac in France, and the Neolithic Astronomical Observatory Externsteine Rocks in Germany have been an enigma to those of us living in the modern world. Who built Stonehenge, lined up all of those monoliths at Carnac, and carved out the observatory at the Externsteine Rocks? What purpose did they serve? And the question most asked—how did they move giant rocks that weighed several tons and sit them upright?

Europe is also home to sites like the Carne Abbas Giant and White Horse Hill, both of which are located in England. These enormous drawings in the earth are an amazing example of human artistry. Lascaux Caves is filled with rock art from ancient times, there are pilgrimage sites such as the Pilgrimage Church of Maria Straßengel in Austria, Saint Winefride's Well in England, and the Basilica of Our Lady of Fatima in Portugal. There are also ruins from the ancient world including the Parthenon and the Oracle at Delphi in Greece as well as naturally occurring places like Mount Olympus in Greece, Mount Shoria in Russia, Pulpit Rock in Norway, and Saana Fell in Finland.

The countries that make up Europe are all filled with both power places and sacred sites that will lift you up and raise your frequency. They will enable you to connect with the history of the place while experiencing the tremendous earth frequency and sacred power held within the energy of the location.

Map Key

1. Ale's Stones, Sweden—Ystad, Sweden
2. Aquae Sulis and the Abbey of Bath—England
3. Avebury—Wiltshire, England
4. Basilica of Our Lady of Fatima—Portugal
5. Carnac—France
6. Carne Abbas Giant—England
7. Cathédrale Notre-Dame de Chartres—Chartres, France
8. Cumae—Italy
9. Drenthe Province—Netherlands
10. Ggantija Megalithic Temples—Maltese Islands, Olympia, Greece
11. Giant's Causeway—Northern Ireland
12. Glastonbury Tor—England
13. Gog Magog Hills—England
14. Irish Round Towers—Ireland
15. Las Médulas—Spain
16. Lascaux Caves—France
17. Lindholm Hills—Denmark
18. Men an Tol—Cornwall, England
19. Mount Olympus—Greece
20. Mount Shoria—Russia
21. Mynydd Carn Ingli—Wales
22. Neolithic Astronomical Observatory Externsteine Rocks—Germany
23. Newgrange—Ireland
24. Parthenon—Greece
25. Pilgrimage Church of Maria Straßengel—Austria
26. Pulpit Rock (Preikestolen)—Norway
27. Saana Fell—Finland
28. St. Winefride's Well—Holywell, England
29. Stone Forest—Lake Varna, Bulgaria
30. Stonehenge—England
31. Temple of Hera—Italy
32. The Alps—Switzerland
33. The Oracle at Delphi—Greece
34. The Paps of Anu—Ireland
35. Wawel Chakra Vortex—Poland
36. White Horse Hill—Uffington, England

Map of Europe

1. ALE'S STONES, SWEDEN—YSTAD, SWEDEN

**Categories: Burial Sites, Megalithic Sites, Mountains/
Mounds/Cliff Locations, Power Places, Power Stones**

In Österlen, Sweden, on a high hill and cliff overlooking the Baltic Sea, 104 feet above the fishing village of Kåseberga and east of Ystad, is Ale's Stones (Ale's Stenar in Swedish). The megalithic monument is called a tumulus, an ancient burial ground in the shape of a ship that is 220 feet long and sixty-two feet wide and is believed to be from the Iron Age (500 to 1000 AD). Each of the fifty-nine stones used to create the megalith weighs about two tons.

The majority consensus is that Ale's Stones is the 5,500-year-old tomb of King Ale, a Stone Age chieftain. In Scandinavian legend, Ale the Strong ruled Uppsala for twenty-five years until Starkad the Old, through a treacherous plan, killed him. When archeologists examined the site, they determined that the tomb was actually forty feet away from the ship-shaped megalith and the stones used in the ship outline were probably taken from the burial site, where they found imprints of enormous boulders that were previously removed. There are marks cut into the stones that are similar to the ones found at other comparable ancient sites and are thought to be where food or other symbolic offerings were placed.

Another theory that surrounds Ale's Stones is that it is astrologically aligned with the summer and winter solstices and the sun rises and sets over specific stones. While there are other sites that are aligned with the summer and winter solstices around the world (for example: Stonehenge, Hagar Qim, Newgrange, and the Great Amun Temple), scientists do not put credence in this theory in regards to Ale's Stones. They believe the alignment with the solstices may have been accidental or the ship outline may have faced the sea simply because the deceased person buried there asked that his tomb overlook the sea because he loved it so much and wanted the sun to rise over his face and set at his back. We will never know; but it is an interesting situation to think about, isn't it?

At Ale's Stones, the energy is clear and pure. It moves in a jagged way from the sea then across the land and then back again. It seems to move on the wind yet still be grounded to the earth. Looking over the spectacular cliffs at the ocean is a moving, spiritual experience because there is a sense of belonging to, yet being distant from, the world as it was thousands of years ago. The energy feels like it is a deep hum that moves through you, catching your attention so that you notice it. It's a working energy, the kind that gets you thinking and keeps you thinking until you reach a resolution, whether it takes days, weeks, or months. It is progressive and grows over time, making you dig deep within to find answers.

2. AQUAE SULIS AND THE ABBEY OF BATH—ENGLAND
Categories: Healing Springs, Monasteries/Temples, Power Places

Located in Bath, Somerset, United Kingdom, are the Roman Baths, also called the Aquae Sulis, which is the Roman name for Bath. At the Roman Temple of Aquae Sulis, natural springs produce water that is 120°F at the rate of 250,000 gallons per day. These springs have been used for over ten thousand years. They were originally considered sacred by the Celtic people, who were the first to build shrines at the site, then by the Romans who built additional extravagant bathing complexes, and finally by the Christians, who built many churches next to the springs, which is the site of Bath Abby today.

The main feature of the Roman Baths is what is called the Great Bath. This structure is unique because it is built like a massive pool. It has a lead lining made up of forty-five sheets, and is filled with hot spring water that flows over a large flat stone, known as the diving stone, into the bath. In ancient Roman times, the Great Bath was enclosed by a large building with vaulted ceilings. The Great Bath is 5.25 feet deep and has steps on every side.

The Roman baths have long been considered sacred because of their healing abilities. We now know, after examining the water from the springs, that there are forty-three different types of minerals including potassium, copper, iron, and magnesium, all of which would have had positive effects on those soaking in the water.

The energy at the Roman baths is indeed very healing. Imagine soaking in the hot water of the springs with your eyes closed as your body absorbs the minerals within the water. Meditating while surrounded with this positive, healing energy would be helpful in finding balance within and connecting to universal consciousness and your higher self while releasing stress and relaxing.

Bath Abbey is next door to the hot springs of the Roman baths. There have been churches at this location since 757 AD. There was an Anglo-Saxon monastery in the beginning, which was then replaced by a Norman Cathedral that was there between 1019 and the late fifteenth century. In 1616 the ruins of the Norman cathedral were repaired and built into the abbey that is in the location today.

Since the beginning of its history, kings and queens (in addition to the common people) often visited the churches in the location of Bath Abbey. In 973 the first king of England, King Edgar, was crowned at the site.[12] The ceremony was the first in a long series of coronations for all future kings and queens of England.

The energy at Bath Abbey is one of solemn reverence. It is peaceful, loving, and feels as if it could support you through any problems or ordeals you may encounter in life. It is transformative, meditative, and connects with the Divine. Allowing the energy of Bath Abby to flow through you will bring about contentment and happiness within your own core spiritual essence.

3. AVEBURY–WILTSHIRE, ENGLAND

Categories: Megalithic Sites, Power Places, Power Stones, Vortexes

Avebury Henge is located twenty miles north of Stonehenge, in Wiltshire, England. Like Stonehenge, it is both a henge and a standing stone circle, also called a stone ring. Avebury Henge is quite possibly older than Stonehenge and is the largest stone circle discovered in the world to date. Computer software can visually reconstruct the site due to the large amount of the structure that has survived over the years. Archeologists think Avebury was a gathering place for people of the community and surrounding areas. It is likely they held festivals and other types of rituals inside the stone circles.

The construction of Avebury includes an outer circle that is twenty feet high and 1,396 feet wide. Most of the outer circle stones are missing. Inside the outer circle is another circle of irregular shaped stones, which encloses twenty-seven acres and two additional stone circles, called the North and the South Circles. It is believed that the South Circle was used for many different types of rituals. The North Circle has a double ring of stones that may have been used for funeral rites.

Recently, archeologists made a new discovery within the south circle. Using ground penetrating radar technology to look into the earth, they found a square of stones with another line of stones extending from it located in the center of the South Circle. Archeologists weren't previously aware of its existence but believe it to be a Neolithic house. It is thought that the two smaller circles were built first around 2600 BC and that the large outer circles were built one hundred years later around 2500 BC. Some of these standing stones weigh as much as forty tons. In 1724 William Stukeley, who had access

---

12. Bath Abbey, "History," http://www.bathabbey.org/history.

to ancient texts through the Masons, surveyed Avebury and the surrounding areas and theorized that it was part of the shape of a snake. Avebury Henge and the two circles inside were the serpent's body, with the head a mile and a half away on Overton Hill.

The energy at Avebury is mystical, potent, and spiritual. For thousands of years people have thought of Avebury as a sacred place. They have visited to connect with the earth energy and the energy of ancient awareness and to infuse Avebury's energy into their own frequency. Some archaeologists believe the land of Avebury was used for spiritual ceremonies for centuries, since the Mesolithic period, before the actual stone circles were built. Today visitors to Avebury Henge can walk around the area by themselves or take a guided tour. The energy described by visitors is said to be magical, mysterious, enchanting, and strange. Placing your hands on the ancient stones is an excellent way to truly connect to the energy of the place. You can feel the vibration move from the earth through the stone and connect with your own frequency.

4. BASILICA OF OUR LADY OF FATIMA—PORTUGAL
Categories: Marian Apparition/Miracle Sites, Pilgrimage Sites, Shrines/Birth of Burial Sites of Saints

Located in the small town of Fatima, Portugal, is the Basilica of Our Lady of Fatima, where, in the early twentieth century, the Virgin Mary appeared.

In 1917, three local shepherd children (ten-year-old Lúcia dos Santos, her nine-year-old cousin Francisco Marto, and her seven-year-old cousin Jacinta), said they saw the Virgin Mary appear on the thirteenth day of every month between May and October. These children also said that the previous year they also saw an angel of peace. Lucia said Mary told them to do penance in order to save sinners and to say the rosary every day because that was the way to find peace in the world and within oneself. In order to accomplish the penance, the children would not drink water during hot days and they would tie cords so tightly around their waist that they were painful. During the June 13 apparition, the Virgin Mary told Lucia that her cousins were going to die but she was going to stay a little longer so that she could make the Virgin Mary well known and loved on earth. During the July apparition, the three secrets of Fatima were given to the children, which were prophecies about the future. The first secret was a vision of hell, the second told the end of World War I and the beginning of World War II, and the third couldn't be told until after 1960 according to Lucia. The Vatican decided to keep it secret until the year 2000. The secret was vague and some believed that it predicted the 1981 assassination attempt on the pope. On October 13, 1917, over seventy thousand people gathered to see the arrival of the Virgin Mary. During this event, only the children saw her but others saw what is now known as the Sun Miracle of Fatima, when the rain clouds parted, the sun changed colors and looked like it was spinning and then went completely dark before looking as if it was crashing to earth. Many believed the events of that day to be a miracle. Lucia lived to be ninety-seven years old but her cousins died during the 1919 flu epidemic. They exhumed their bodies in 1935 and in 1951. Francisco's had decomposed but Jacinta's was incorrupt.

The energy at the Basilica of Our Lady of Fatima is very spiritual and holy. It is positive and uplifting and can be transformative. It shows the power in faith and the manifestation of miracles. After the appearances of the Virgin Mary, a Marian shrine was constructed at the site in 1919. Each year over four million people participate in a pilgrimage to Fatima in the hopes of seeing an apparition of the Virgin Mary. People make this pilgrimage on the twelfth and thirteenth day of each month between May and October in recognition of the original appearances of the Virgin Mary.

5. CARNAC—FRANCE

Categories: Megalithic Sites, Power Places

Carnac is a town located in the Morbihan Department in Brittany, France. Geographically it is on the northwest coast. The town of Carnac is internationally famous for having the largest number of megaliths in the world, which are believed to have been placed in their current positions by Neolithic farmers.

The town of Carnac is divided into two sections—Carnac-Ville and Carnac-Plage. The Museum of Prehistory is located in Carnac-Ville and the area in a seven-mile radius of this part of the town is where you find the majority of the megaliths. Carnac-Plage is a resort area by the sea that has a modern, state-of-the-art thalassotherapy center, which is using the sea and marine environment to promote health, healing, and wellbeing through physiotherapy, algotherapy, and hydrotherapy. Carnac-Plage also has another booming business: oyster farming.

Over the years, many of the stones were removed to either be used in the creation of other buildings or to simply get them out of the way so roads could be built. In Carnac-Ville, they took great measures to make sure that the monoliths were preserved.

They decided to offer public visits in order to maintain control of the area containing the stones. It is now fenced off so people can't gain unauthorized access or damage the stones. Today, if you would like to see the standing stones, you'll have to book a guided tour. In the standing stone area, there are over three thousand of them that are in straight lines. These stones carbon dated to 4000 BC and were dug up in the area where they now stand, which is why they are all different sizes. It's unclear as to why they were stood up and placed in lines. Archeologists theorize that it was for cultural or religious reasons and that possibly the stones marked pathways for people to walk through during ceremonies.

In addition to the three thousand lined-up standing stones, there are also over one hundred different types of monuments based on the arrangements of the stones. Some of the types of stone monuments are dolmens (vertical stones topped by a flat stone), mounds (individual tombs), enclosures (circles or other shaped spaces created with stones), alignments (parallel rows of upright stones), cairns (stacked piles of smaller stones usually found over a burial site), and menhirs (individual freestanding stones that were placed in a hole with a wedge stone on the bottom to keep it stable). Archeologists found many artifacts at Carnac including pottery, necklaces, copper tools, beads, and flint arrowheads to name a few.

The energy at Carnac feels like it pulsates and moves in both a circular and linear pattern. There are theories that the stones act as energy conductors and are moving earth's energy through the series of megaliths. It affects you in an enlightening way and can lead to heightened intuition, deeper meditation, and altered states of consciousness where you can connect to the Divine. Experiencing the type of energy found at Carnac can open your awareness and has transformative power.

6. CARNE ABBAS GIANT—ENGLAND

Categories: Fertility Sites, Gigantic Landscape Carvings, Monasteries/Temples

In the chalk downlands of southern England, you can find huge figures carved into the chalk of the land. Near Dorchester in Dorset, above the village of Cerne Abbas, is the world famous Cerne Abbas Giant (also known as the Cerne Giant and the Rude Man), an ancient chalk figure sculpted into the hillside of a naked man with an erection and holding a club. The Cerne Abbas Giant is Britain's largest chalk hill figure, at 180 feet tall and 167 feet wide. There is a mound beneath the Giant's left hand, which archeologists believe could have possibly been a severed head or a lion's skin, which the grass has since covered up. Above the giant is the Trendle, an earthwork believed to be the site of an ancient temple, that has been dated to the Iron Age. Local dancers use the Trendle today during May Day celebrations.

All of the chalk figures in the area were created by cutting away the grass and making a trench so that the chalk underneath was revealed. Then they added more chalk into the trench so the grass would not grow into the figure. The trench that forms the giant is one foot wide and one foot deep. In 1924, the Cerne Abbas Giant received official status as an ancient monument and is now under the control of the National Trust, who replaces the chalk every few years to keep the monument intact. After episodes of vandalism to the monument, it was fenced off so the public can no longer access the area.

The Cerne Abbas Giant is quite the mystery. No one knows the reason for his existence. The first written mention was in 1694 by the churchwarden of St. Mary's church in the village who paid three shillings to have the giant repaired. There are predominantly three theories regarding the origins of the giant. The first and most popular theory is that the giant is a prehistoric symbol of fertility or a Celtic fertility god. The second theory is that it is an illustration of the hero Hercules. In history Hercules is often depicted holding a club, naked, and with a lion skin over his left shoulder. Experts who examined the giant through scientific tests believe that something was draped over the left side at one point in time. If this theory is correct, archeologists believe the Emperor Commodus had the giant drawn between 180 and 193 AD. The third theory is that the Benedictine monks of the Cerne Abbey drew the giant.

Regardless of how the Cerne Giant came into existence, the energy at the site is fruitful, uplifting, fertile, and inspiring. Connecting to the energy of the Cerne Abbas Giant can help motivate you to move forward on your path, enhance your spirituality, and bring about good changes in every aspect of your life. It can bring success in all ventures.

7. CATHÉDRALE NOTRE-DAME DE CHARTRES— CHARTRES, FRANCE

Categories: Pilgrimage Sites, Relic Sites, Shrines/Birth or Burial Sites of Saints

Chartres is a medieval city located in the northern part of France in the Eure-et-Loir Department sixty miles southwest of Paris. One of the most famous buildings in Chartres is the Cathédrale Notre-Dame de Chartres, also known as the Cathedral of our Lady of Chartres. In its early days, the cathedral was the center of activity for daily life, special events, and for the economy of Chartres. Today the cathedral is the seat of the Diocese of Chartres.

It is one of the world's best examples of Gothic architecture. Construction began on the cathedral in 1145 and again after the fire of 1194. It took twenty-six years to reconstruct due to two fires, riots, revolts at the site, and the wars in the area. The building itself included new techniques for high elevation construction with the cathedral's floor plan created in the shape of a cross. Construction of the spires on the front of the cathedral happened in two different centuries: the plain pyramid spire in the 1140s and the taller, more intricately detailed spire in the early sixteenth century. One of the most awe-inspiring features of the cathedral is the stained-glass windows. The cathedral houses the largest collection of medieval stained glass in the world. Royalty, lords, trades people, and even local everyday people donated the windows to the cathedral. These stained-glass windows add to the positive, thought-provoking, and transformational energy you will find inside of the cathedral. Walking through this massive building with its high arched walls and roof will make you feel humble. The play of color inside of the building from the stained-glass windows gives you feelings of hope, lightness, and inspiration.

Since 876 AD, the site where the Chartres Cathedral sits today has been in possession of a tunic said to belong to and worn by the Virgin Mary. According to legend, Charlemagne received it as a gift while in Jerusalem during a crusade and he gave the relic to the cathedral. Others believe Charles II, King of France and Holy Roman Emperor, donated the relic. People have made pilgrimages to the Cathedral of our Lady of Chartres for hundreds of years to view the tunic. Prior to the building of the current cathedral, several other wooden cathedrals said to possess the relic were located at the same site, all of which burned down. The cathedral is still a popular Marion pilgrimage site today.

There is another legend associated with the cathedral, which is the belief that they secretly kept the Ark of the Covenant hidden in the crypt of Chartres for many centuries. There is a carving on a pillar on the exterior of the cathedral at the north door, which is supposed to show a wheeled vehicle transporting the Ark of the Covenant into Chartres Cathedral.

Visiting Chartres Cathedral is like stepping back in time. The detail put into the construction of the cathedral is awe-inspiring and quite incredible. The energy here is confident, engaging, and flows from a deep connection to universal consciousness. It is a place where you can connect to your inner essence and experience transformational spiritual growth.

8. CUMAE—ITALY

Categories: Caves, Oracle Sites, Monasteries/Temples, Ruins/Archeological Sites

Cumae is an ancient Greek colony in the western part of Italy about twelve miles west of Naples. In 750 BC Greeks from Chalcis founded the city. Sometime between 428 and 421 BC the Samnites overtook the city and eliminated their currency, language, and almost everything about the Greek culture, replacing it with their own. In 338 BC Rome conquered Cumae and by 1207 AD the city was destroyed by Naples because it had become a refuge for pirates and bandits. Cumae gained notoriety as the home of the Cumaean Sibyl, a priestess and prophetess who presided over the Apollonian oracle there. In ancient times there were a number of prophets at different locations who would give answers to questions asked. Today a Sybil would be the same as a seer, oracle, or intuitive. The Cumaean Sibyl became famous with the Romans after they conquered Cumae.

There is a legend that surrounds the Cumaean Sibyl that says she lived in a cave with a hundred openings, gave her prophecies through song, and would write prophecies on oak leaves and then arrange those at the entrance of her cave for people to find. She would also help people cross over to Hades through Lake Avernus, a nearby volcanic crater lake that was believed to be the entrance to the underworld. This sibyl made a pact with Apollo where she exchanged her virginity for an extended life, which was one thousand years. But she forgot to ask for eternal youth, so she grew old and feeble and then became smaller and smaller until they kept what was left of her in a jar. Eventually the only thing left was her voice.

In Cumae, there is a 430-foot underground corridor at the site of the cave where the Sibyl once lived. The cave has multiple entrances but not the legendary one hundred. There is limited access for safety reasons so the public and visitors can only look in from the outside. There are also plaques around the base of the temple of Apollo (only the base survives today) that contain parts of the Aeneid, an ancient poem written by Virgil, where he asked the Sibyl to take him to the entrance of the underworld so that he could visit his father's spirit. Other plaques placed around the base explain the construction of the Temple of Apollo at Cumae.

Today the cave of the Sibyl is part of the Cumae Archaeological Site. There are many ruins left of the city where you can visit and experience an increase in your frequency as you connect to the intuitive energy that remains in the area from times gone by.

The energy of Cumae is powerful, insightful, and intuitive. It can heighten your own psychic and intuitive abilities, can help you see situations as clearly as they are, and can heighten your connection with the Divine. The energy can help you see the world, and the people in it, from a sense of knowing, through the energy and its link to the universe's collective consciousness.

9. DRENTHE PROVINCE—NETHERLANDS
Categories: Bodies of Water/Waterfalls/Springs, Burial Sites, Regions

In the northeastern portion of the Netherlands is Drenthe province, a scarcely populated, heavily forested region. Many of the forests were made national parks to protect them. Today, much of this area is primarily used for agriculture and farming.

People have lived in the Drenthe province since prehistoric times, according to the artifacts found in the area. Some of the oldest artifacts found are from the Wolstonian Stage, which occurred 150,000 years ago when there were three different periods of glaciation.

The Netherlands has fifty-four dolmens in the country and fifty-three of them are located in Drenthe province. Dolmens are one-chamber burial tombs built by placing two megaliths in an upright position and then placing a large flat stone across the tops. The structures look like stone tables, which is also the meaning of the word dolmen. The dolmens in Drenthe are believed to have been built around 3500 BC and, due to the amount of them found in Drenthe, it is also theorized that Drenthe was the most populated place in the country during that time.

There are two towns in Drenthe province that offer other ways to connect to the energy of the area. In Emmen, the Wildlands Zoo is one of the most popular places to visit. Here you can connect to the energy of the animals from the area and from other parts of the world. In Assen, the capital of Drenthe, you can immerse yourself in the province's history by viewing some of the ancient artifacts at the Drents Museum. This art and history museum houses permanent collections such as bog bodies of the Emmer-Erscheidenveen Man, the Weerdinge Men, the Exloërmond Man, and the Yde Girl. Bog bodies are preserved corpses found in peat bogs that tell us a lot about ancient history. The museum also has artifacts from the Funnelbeaker culture including the Pesse canoe, which dates between 8200 and 7600 BC and is the world's oldest recovered canoe. The museum also hosts temporary exhibitions as well.

Drenthe has an energy that is in harmony with the nature of the place. It moves and flows like the wind through the trees, the water flowing in the rivers, and yet can be quiet and still. It is profound, divine, and seeps into the recesses of your soul, awakening you to a heightened sense of enlightenment. The energy here can be transformational on a spiritual level because of the strong mystical qualities, the vibe you get when walking through the forest, or visiting one of the dolmens. The area draws people who enjoy spending time in nature due to the incredible forests, lakes, and rivers in the area. Biking, horseback riding, and hiking are popular activities in Drenthe province. Biking is recommended because many bike trails have been built so that people can experience the small villages in the province as well as its natural beauty.

10. GGANTIJA MEGALITHIC TEMPLES— MALTESE ISLANDS, OLYMPIA, GREECE

Categories: Fertility Sites, Islands/Reefs, Megalithic Sites, Monasteries/ Temples, Oracle Sites, Pilgrimage Sites, Power Places

Located in Xagħra on the island of Gozo, the second largest island in Malta, are the Ggantija Temples, two prehistoric megalithic temples. The Ggantija Temples are older than the Great Pyramids and Stonehenge and are considered to be the second oldest man-made religious site in the world. Göbekli-Tepe in Turkey currently holds the top spot as the oldest. The Ggantija Temples are believed to be about 5,800 years old and were built sometime between 3600 and 3000 BC. The temples were made out of the coralline and globigerina limestone found on the island. Some of the stones used in the construction of the temples weigh over fifty tons.

As with most things ancient, the Ggantija Temples are surrounded with legend and mystery. *Ggantija* is Maltese for "giant's grotto," and according to legend, a giant named Sunsuna built the temples in twenty-four hours (one day and one night) while nursing a baby. It was believed that only giants could lift or move such heavy stones. Legend also has it that the bones found on the island were those of the giants, when in fact they belong to elephants and hippopotamuses. Another theory is that the giant was actually a goddess and the baby was a girl so the larger temple represents the goddess and the smaller one the daughter.

While little is known about the exact religious practices at the temples, it is believed they were shrines to the great Earth Mother who was a goddess of fertility. Some theories regarding the religious ceremonies are that liquid offerings were poured through libation holes as an offering to the gods, the spirit of the place, or in memory of those who had died. It is thought to have been a place of healing. Based on the evidence obtained at the site, archeologists believe people made pilgrimages from the other islands, Sicily, and even North Africa to visit the temples, possibly to visit with the oracle who lived there and who would give prophecies to the people while in a trance.

If you look at a view of the temples from above you'll notice that they are built using curved architecture with two large round rooms one above the other. These are the ritual rooms and it is believed they are a physical representation of the Earth Mother with the top room representing her breasts and the bottom room representing her hips. Based on evidence from the site, the temples in their original state were covered with domes that were painted red on the inside. The larger of the two temples has altars, a stone hearth that was believed to be used for a sacred fire, libation holes, relief carvings, and niches with altars. The smaller temple does not have any of these items.

The energy at the Ggantija Temples is peaceful, loving, and abundant. Experiencing the energy here is purifying. It can help you release any negativity you've been holding on to and embrace the positive, pure energy of the earth. It is an energy of birth and rebirth, of connecting to your soul essence as it is in the spiritual realm. Feelings of completion, of blessings, and of being loved are abundant at the Ggantija Temples.

11. GIANT'S CAUSEWAY—NORTHERN IRELAND
Categories: Mountains/Mounds/Cliff Locations, Mythological Sites

Giant's Causeway is located on the northern coast of Ireland between Benbane Head and Causeway Head on the edge of the Antrim plateau in the Ulster province. The unique, polygonal rock columns of five to seven sides were formed here fifty to sixty million years ago when multiple lava flows met the sea. The columns are made of basalt, which is a dark volcanic rock high in iron and magnesium content but low in silica. This type of lava is hotter than other types of lava and it cools from the bottom upwards and from the center outwards, which forms the columns. Each column is between 15 to 20 inches wide and of varying heights, with the tallest being 82 feet. They are located beneath cliffs, some of which are 330 feet high. There are approximately forty thousand columns that look like steps at Giant's Causeway.

Opposite of the Giant's Causeway in Staffa, Scotland, you'll find the same type of basalt columns on the northern shores. These columns were made by the same lava flow that created the Giant's Causeway, which leads us to a short version of the legend of the area. There was once a great Irish giant named Finn MacCool who wanted revenge against the Scottish giants. Finn built a causeway from Ulster to Staffa made out of honeycombed, six-sided cobblestones. One day he challenged the Scottish giant Benanodonner to cross the causeway and fight him. As Benanodonner crossed the causeway, Finn realized that he was bigger than he'd thought so Finn ran home. Oonagh, Finn's wife, made him lie in the bath and covered him with sheets. When Benanodonner arrived, she told him Finn was hunting and tricked him into thinking that Finn was enormous. She then showed him their baby, which was Finn, and Benanodonner quickly retreated. If the baby was that big, then how big was Finn? Finn followed and scooped up a chunk of earth to throw at Benanodonner. The hole filled with water and became Lough Neagh. The dirt missed Benanodonner and fell into the sea creating the Isle of Man. Finn and Benanodonner tore up the causeway only leaving the ends on their respective shores, which are still there. And that's how the stones became known as the Giant's Causeway.[13]

As you stand on these unique lava formations, it's easy to imagine that they were created by giants. The energy surrounding the area is very strong and powerful, just

---

13. E2BN, "Finn MacCool and the Giant's Causeway," 2006, http://myths.e2bn.org/mythsandlegends/textonly5639-finn-maccool-and-the-giants-causeway.html.

as giants would be. It also feels structured and organized, like the column formations. As you stand on these structures, you can connect to the ancient energy of earth's formation. Feel the heat of that time course through your frequency, revving it up with power. Feel it flow into you from your feet, energizing and revitalizing you with its purity from the origins of the earth. There is a feeling of mystery and intrigue at Giant's Causeway, which connects to the mystery of your own spiritual origins. Breathe it in, absorb it through your body and let it lift you to higher levels of awareness just as it lifted the columns from the earth toward the sky.

12. GLASTONBURY TOR—ENGLAND

Categories: Earth Chakras (Heart), Mythological Sites, Power Places, Ruins/Archeological Sites, UFO/Extraterrestrial/Paranormal Sites

Located in Somerset, Galstonbury is a small town that is abundant in historical sites, ruins, mythology, and legend that goes back hundreds of years. In the fifth and sixth centuries, Glastonbury was known as the Isle of Avalon. It was surrounded by water and what is now known as Glastonbury Tor overlooked the area known today as the Somerset Levels. The water was drained long ago so the land could be used for agriculture.

It is believed that Excalibur, King Arthur's sword he pulled from the stone, was forged in this area. King Arthur is believed to be buried in Galstonbury or the surrounding area and the abbey monks have claimed they discovered the bones of both Arthur, and his queen, Guinevere. It is believed that Joseph of Arimathea, the man who buried Jesus after his crucifixion, walked these lands. Glastonbury is a location where ley lines are believed to converge. It is home to those with New Age, Neopagan, and Neodruid beliefs and is a well-known New Age community.

Glastonbury Tor is a large cone shaped mound that rises 521 feet above the town and can be seen for miles. Sitting atop the tor is the tower of the Church of St. Michael, which is the only surviving part of the fourteenth century structure. There are seven levels around the tor that have been dated to Neolithic times. Glastonbury Tor is also believed to be the final resting place of the Holy Grail. It is thought to be at the bottom of the tor underneath the Chalice Well. There have also been reports of strange and mysterious lights that flow in an arching and writhing motion from St. Michael's Tower to the ground close to Chalice Well. Could this be a connection between the Holy Grail and the remnants of the ancient church?

There are many places to see in Glastonbury including the abbey, temples, museums, and other historical sites. Glastonbury is also known for its yearly five-day music festival, which draws huge crowds. It is held on nine hundred acres in the Vale of Avalon and upwards of 200,000 people will be in attendance. While the site itself is six miles outside of the town of Glastonbury at Worthy Farm, the town also sees an increase in visitors during the festival.

The energy in Glastonbury is powerful, magical, and timeless. Being in the area feels as if you stepped into another dimension of mists, mystery, and infinite possibilities. It's positive, uplifting, and inspirational. It swirls around you, pulses from the earth into your feet and throughout your body. It feels like the wind brushing against your skin, as if the ghosts from times gone by are standing with you as you look out across the land. The energy leads to moments of enlightenment, epiphanies, spiritual awakenings, and sometimes paranormal experiences. Was that Merlin you just saw in your peripheral vision? The energy of Glastonbury will affect and change you on a spiritual level.

13. GOG MAGOG HILLS—ENGLAND

Categories: Power Places, Regions

Gog Magog Hills are located southeast of Cambridge, England. They are also known as Gog Magog Downs and, simply, the Gogs. These low, rolling chalk hills are several miles long.

Gog Magog Hills received its name from the legend of the giant named Gogmagog. The legend says that the Roman Emperor Diocletian had thirty-three daughters who were married. They all plotted to kill their husbands in their sleep all on the same night. Because of this crime, they were given six months of rations and set adrift in a boat. They drifted to an island that they named Albion after the oldest daughter. They stayed on the island and, with demons by their sides, they created a race of giants. Later, Brutus along with his champion and best warrior, Corineus, fled the fall of Troy and arrived at the same islands. He claimed the islands for himself and today they are collectively known as Britain. Gogmagog was the leader of the giants and he fought with Corineus for the island. Corineus threw Gogmagog from a high rock to his death. Corineus was given the western half of the island, which is known as Cornwall. The area where Gogmagog landed is what is now known as Gog Magog Hills.

There are several places of interest within Gog Magog Hills. At Saint Wendreda's church in the civil parish of March, which was built during the fourteenth and fifteenth centuries, there are a total of 120 roof figures including angels, martyrs, and canopied saints. The energy in St. Wendreda's is one of a slow-moving flow yet a powerful and reverent spirituality. The energy here feels pure, warm, and iridescent. If you would like to visit a chapel with a different kind of energy, you might like to see the leper chapel in Cambridge, also known as the chapel of St. Mary Magdalene. In the past, it was used as both a hospital and a place of worship for those who had leprosy. This is thought to be the oldest building in Cambridge and was built in the twelfth century. The energy at the leper's chapel is calm, soothing, and healing. It is an ideal place to visit if you are sorting through problems or want to connect with a healing energy on a deeper level.

Another popular power place to visit is Wandlebury Hill Fort, which is a few miles south of Cambridge. It has a circular shape so it is also known as Wandlebury ring. It was built during the Iron Age and you can still see the earthworks that served as defensive barriers against invaders. The Earl of Godolphin constructed the buildings currently inside the ring in the early eighteenth century. The burial site of the stallion that was the foundation sire for the Godolphin Arabian horses is under the arch on the premises. Wandlebury Hill Fort is said to be haunted by knights in silver armor who would do battle with you if you called out to them, and there are many unexplained happenings in the area. The energy here is stoic, calm, and deep. It feels as if you stepped into a deep pool of positivity, of certainty, and planning. The energy here can help you determine the next step you need to take in any endeavor in life. Its strength makes you pause, reflect, and decide the direction you wish to take.

14. IRISH ROUND TOWERS—IRELAND

Categories: Man-Made Sites, Relic Sites

The Irish Round Towers are scattered all across Ireland and are shrouded in mystery. While there are many theories on their origins, no one is quite sure of all their uses. Research puts the construction of the towers between the seventh and tenth centuries AD because it can be confirmed that churches built between the fifth and twelfth centuries AD also have a round tower in that location. Based on artifacts and research, the round towers were thought to be primarily used for bell ringing, but they were also thought to be grave markers because bones were found at the base of many of the towers. In Irish Gaelic they are called *cloigthithe*, which means "bell houses."

There are currently 65 sites remaining, in various states of ruin, but it is believed that there could have been as many as 120 to 130 towers in total. The towers vary in size, some being up to 130 feet tall and 40–60 feet in circumference at the base. The towers also have a double wall with Roman block and mortar construction. The space between each wall was filled with smaller stones for reinforcement. The doors are often between six to ten feet off of the ground. Dirt filled the base of the tower to the level of the door, which helped to create a solid, strong foundation. Inside there were wood floors built all of the way up through the tower with stairways leading from floor to floor. At the top were four windows and a cone shaped roof made of stone and mortar, which was presumably where the bell was housed. The windows would allow the sound to travel throughout the countryside.

Some of the theories surrounding the Irish round towers are that they were used as hiding places for people when the Vikings were pillaging the area. They were also thought to be storage places for religious relics, watchtowers, belfries, lookouts, safe houses, granaries, astronomical marks that mirror the stars in the northern sky during the winter solstice, or used for energy conducting, storage, and transmission. No one really knows for sure and they could have been used in all of these types of situations over the years.

The Round Tower of Kilmacdaugh is the tallest of all of the round towers at 111.54 feet. It is part of a complex that includes the cathedral, Temple Mary Church, the Grebe House, O'Heynes Church, the Church of St. John the Baptist, and the Round Tower. The tower has a slight tilt to it. The energy at this tower is calming and peaceful, reflective and inspiring. As you walk through the area you'll feel as if time has stopped, that you're one with the energy of the place and inspired by the positivity that the completeness of the tower radiates. While each of the towers may give off a slightly different energy frequency, they are always positive in nature and will enable you to focus within, to connect with your true essence, your spirituality, and will balance, motivate, and guide you forward on your path, always lifting you upwards.

15. LAS MÉDULAS—SPAIN

Categories: Bodies of Water/Waterfalls/Springs, Regions

Located in the El Bierzo, Leon, region of northern Spain is a very unique land formation called Las Médulas. At the base of this area is the small town of Las Médulas where you can visit the archaeological learning center to find out about the history of the site before beginning the hike, which is somewhat difficult, to the top to view it. The site is considered a cultural landscape and is a World Heritage site.

Las Médulas is a two-thousand-year-old historic site where, for over two hundred years, the Romans mined for gold. In an area of 3.86 square miles, they used a mining method called *Ruina Montium*, which used controlled water flow to mine the gold from the hills. They built canals and aqueducts to force river water from the Eria and Cabrera rivers, which were more than sixty-two miles away from the site, into the mine to soften the lower levels of earth until it collapsed. The Lake of Carrucedo was formed due to the water flow through the earth. There are large caves where the water once flowed underground that you can walk inside. One has even been turned into a museum. The old canals are now roads that people use for both transportation and sometimes to move livestock. Chestnut groves that the Romans introduced into the area are still abundant today.

Today the site consists of many red hills in a variety of unique shapes that formed when the land collapsed. Often pointy and with a swirling appearance, these red rocks are all that is left of the mountains that the Romans condensed into an uneven landscape. One interesting feature are the horizontal lines made during the mining process that are still visible. As you look at the remnants of the mountain with these horizontal lines, you can almost feel the powerful rush of the water as it flowed against the earth. While the process was destructive to the mountain, the energy was a potent force that reshaped the land in a positive way, leaving beauty in its wake. You can connect with the positivity of this energy especially if you're in a place in your life where you're ready to make big changes. If you've been going through a difficult time with changes being forced upon you that you may not have wanted, try to look at them as a process you're going through, just as the mountain went through the process of mining, and then examine yourself to find the beauty that the situation has left in you. What have you learned, how can you move forward? There may be twists, spirals, points, and caves, just like you'll find at Las Médulas, but they are part of you. Embrace them all because we never go through life unchanged.

16. LASCAUX CAVES—FRANCE

Categories: Caves, Petroglyph/Rock Art Sites, Power Places

Lascaux Caves are in the southwestern part of France near the small town of Montignac and the medieval city of Sarlat, in the department of Perigueux and the region of Nouvelle-Aquitaine between the Lorne Valley in the Pyrenees and the Dordogne region of France and the area known as Lascaux. Lascaux cave is a twenty-thousand-year-old cave like no other.

In 1940 four boys were out for a walk through the forest when their dog fell into a hole. During the dog's rescue the boys discovered a prehistoric Palaeolithic cave with almost 600 paintings and 1,400 engravings of animals on the walls and roof.[14] The majority of these paintings and engravings depict animals but there are also abstract symbols and even one picture of a human. There are drawings of horses, deer, bison, ibex, aurochs (large extinct cows), and some cats. This artwork has been dated to 17,000–15,000 BC which makes it part of the upper Paleolithic era. It is believed that the front of the cave may have been inhabited but the area of the cave with the artwork was only occupied while the artists were working.

Based on the findings within the cave it is known that the area was lit by sandstone lamps and fireplaces and they used animal fat as fuel. There were also tools and shells worn by the artists found within the cave. Some of the tools were made out of flint while others were made of bone. Reindeer antlers were found and it is thought they were used to mix the color pigments with water. An interesting tidbit about the cave is that while reindeer and the woolly mammoth were the main food source for the people, there are no pictures of these animals on the walls of the cave. Archeologists and researchers think the animals and other pictures depicted on the walls of Lascaux have a spiritual meaning.

In 1948 the cave was opened to the public. In 1963 visitors were no longer allowed because the carbon dioxide from people breathing caused visitors to pass out inside the cave and the humidity in the air was damaging the paintings, causing algae to grow. In

---

14. Ministère de la Culture, "Lascaux, the Discovery," http://archeologie.culture.fr/lascaux/en/discovery.

order to preserve the paintings, the French government built an almost perfect replica of the cave next to the original at a cost of $64 million.

Today, even though you can no longer visit the original cave, you can still experience all the emotional and energy effects of the original by visiting the replica since they are so close in proximity. The energy at the Lascaux Caves is intense and focused. It's as if you can feel the spiritual essence of the animals depicted on the walls along with positive creativity of the people who made the art. The energy here can give you the initiative to embrace your own creativity and inner vitality. The energy is enduring and can help you attain your own long-term goals in regards to your own spiritual nature and what you would like to accomplish in the physical realm.

17. LINDHOLM HILLS—DENMARK
Categories: Burial Sites, Ruins/Archeological Sites

In Denmark, Lindholm Høje is located on the north side of Limfjord across from the city of Aalborg. It is a narrow chalk hill that was formed by ice during the Cretaceous period. Between 400 and 1000 AD, the site was used as a Viking and Iron Age burial ground.

The area was excavated between 1952 and 1958 and seven hundred graves were discovered. Graves located at the top of the hill date to 400 AD and the graves of the bottom of the hill date to 1000 AD. It was customary during this time to bury the dead where they would have a beautiful view in the afterlife. A unique feature of the graves is in their construction. The Iron Age graves were often topped by a mound of earth while the Viking graves had stones placed around the edge of each person's gravesite and the person's corpse was placed on a wooden funeral pyre and cremated within the gravesite. It was thought the cremation set the person's soul free so it could move quickly to the next life. After the cremation, dirt was thrown over the remains to create the grave. The Viking graves were made in two different shapes. The men received a stone outline in the shape of the ship or triangle while the women's graves had an oval or round stone border.

The ruins of two villages are also on the site with the northern one dating between 700 and 900 AD and the southern one between 1,000 and 1,150 AD. The buildings in the villages were small and evidence suggests that the people of both villages moved around to live in different places on the hill. There were quite a few artifacts found in the area that gives us glimpses into the life of the people who lived there. Some of the artifacts found are weapons, buckles, arm rings, rivets, whetstones, pearls, glass beads from the Iron Age, combs, toiletry items, and earthenware. People were buried with things they might need in the next life. The hill is currently used for sheep grazing which adds to the feeling of peacefulness and contentment. There are markers with information about the history on small sign posts throughout the site.

The energy at Lindholm Høje is tranquil and serene. There is a surreal and mysterious energy that pulls your thoughts back in time as you look out over the hill of rocks and across the fjord. This feeling is even stronger when mist is flowing in from the sea and over the hill.

While it is free to visit Lindholm Høje, there is a charge to visit the museum. However it is quite worthwhile to be able to view the Viking artifacts that are on display. There are replica jewelry pieces and other souvenirs for sale in the shop if you want to take home a memento of the energy you felt in this area. If you choose jewelry you can white light cleanse it and program it while standing on the hill so the energy at Lindholm Høje fills the piece.

18. MEN AN TOL—CORNWALL, ENGLAND
Categories: Burial Sites, Megalithic Sites, Power Places, Power Stones

Men an Tol is located in Madron, Cornwall. The name *Men an Tol* translates to "holed stone." It is also sometimes called the Devil's Eye or the Crick Stone. It is a formation of four granite stones. There are two upright stones, and between them is a circular stone with a hole in the middle (like a donut). There is another stone that has fallen near the base of the Western upright stones. It is thought that the stones of the site may have been rearranged due to previous documentation by William Borlase in the eighteenth century where he said they formed a triangular shape.[15]

Several recumbent stones found under the ground gave rise to the theory that Men an Tol was part of larger stone circle. Another theory regarding the stones is that they are part of the remains of a tomb created three thousand to four thousand years ago during the Bronze Age. During this time holed stones were often used as entrances to burial chambers but it was rare to find circular stones with the center hole during the

---

15. Cronwall's Archaeological Heritage, "Men-an-Tol," http://www.historic-cornwall.org.uk/a2m/bronze_age/stone_circle/men_an_tol/men_an_tol.htm.

Bronze Age. There's only one other site known to have one, which is at Tolvan Stone. The only artifact to have been found at this location was a flaked flint found in 1885.

It is also believed that there is spiritual significance to the stones at Men an Tol and that the stones have healing properties. Centuries ago, some of the rituals performed at the site were to cure illness. For example, a child with tuberculosis or rickets would be passed naked through the hole of the stone three times and then they would pull them across the grass toward the east three times to cure the disease. The site was given the name Crick Stone because of its ability to cure backaches, rheumatism, unexplained fevers with shivering, and spine trouble in adults if they crawled through the center of the stone nine times against the sun. Others believed the stones would protect them against those who wished them ill or witchcraft and that the stones could help foretell the future.

The energy at Men an Tol is of a high vibration and appears, on a spiritual level, as white light. It is bright, pure, and can connect you with the Divine. It is an energy you can access for physical, spiritual, and emotional healing, and to help you grow on your spiritual path. Looking through the hole of the circular stone and seeing the vertical stone through the center, as if it's in a lens, is a connection to what has come before. While it is quite possible that the stones were moved, it is also possible that the center of the round stone was used as a lens in the past to look at other objects. The positivity of the energy at Men an Tol is uplifting and can heal what ails you.

19. MOUNT OLYMPUS—GREECE

Categories: Mountains/Mounds/Cliffs, Mythological Sites, Power Places

Mount Olympus is located in Greece in the Olympus mountain range in the Olympus National Park. It is the highest mountain in Greece at 9,570 feet. It is near the Aegean Sea and the Gulf of Thermaïkós. Due to its height, Mount Olympus is often snowcapped between November to May, and it has a lot of cloud cover year-round. There is a high diversity of plant life on Mount Olympus and over 1,700 different species are on the mountain. The different elevations and the closeness to the sea encourage the growth of different types of trees and plants at various elevations. Summers on the mountain are warm and dry while winters tend to be very wet. Regardless of the season, if you hike up the mountainside, the temperature decreases the higher you go.

According to Greek mythology Mount Olympus was home to the gods and was where the throne room of Zeus existed. The highest peak of Olympus is called Mytikas today but in the ancient world it was called Pantheon and the people of that time believed that the twelve Greek gods would hold meetings there. It was also believed that all of the gods lived on Mount Olympus within the Alpine ravines unless they were traveling. The exceptions were Poseidon, who lived in the sea, and Hades, who lived in the underworld. These twelve gods, known as the Twelve Olympians, were Zeus, Hera, Poseidon, Demeter, Athena, Aries, Apollo, Artemis, Hermes, Aphrodite, Hestia (who gave her place to Dionysus), and finally Hades or Hephaestus, depending on the myth.

Today Mount Olympus is a national park with an abundance of activities. Hiking is one of the park's most popular activities and they have created many different types of trails for all levels of physical activity. You can also stay overnight at one of the refuges. Other activities include cultural and athletic events and religious gatherings. If you do decide to hike Mount Olympus, be on the lookout for wildlife. There are many animals that live on Mount Olympus including deer, fox, wild cats, wolves, jackals, woodpeckers, eagles, and a wide variety of butterflies.

The spiritual significance of Mount Olympus, and the myths associated with the mountain, brought travelers from around the world for centuries. Many monks and hermits chose to live on the sacred mountain either in caves or within the forests prior to the arrival of Christianity in the area, which suppressed the belief in the old myths and legends of the Greeks. The monks did this in order to submerse themselves into the sacredness of the energy at Mount Olympus. The energy here is transformational, ancient, and a connection to the Divine. It is deep, solid, and seeps into you as you draw upon its unlimited strength and wisdom. The energy at Mount Olympus can increase your intuition, and can help you connect to your soul's true path. It encourages you to look deep within to see the truth of your inner self and to live that truth every day in positivity, joy, and happiness.

20. MOUNT SHORIA—RUSSIA

Categories: Mountains/Mounds/Cliff Locations, Power Places, UFO/Extraterrestrial/Paranormal Sites

Located in Kemerov, in the southern Siberian Mountains of Russia, is Gornaya Shoria, which translates to "Mountain Shoria." At this site, there are what appear to be huge megalithic granite stones in the shape of rectangles with flat surfaces that look as if they've been cut and stacked upon one another. The site was discovered in 1991, but due to a lack of funds, the first exploration of the area didn't happen until 2013. The stones are quite impressive to look at due to their gigantic size. They are extremely large individual stones, which measure around sixty-five feet long and twenty feet high. Some are thought to weigh between three thousand and four thousand pounds. The sides are flat and smooth although you can find some that have more pointed edges. Researchers and geologists have compared them to the Egyptian pyramids and Stonehenge, causing it to become known as the Russian Stonehenge.

Since its discovery, many different theories have surrounded the megaliths. Are they signs of a lost ancient civilization of giants, evidence of extraterrestrial visitations, or a prehistoric man-made wall? Or, quite possibly, could it just be Mother Nature's work that created this amazing phenomenon through an upthrust, which is when the earth's crust thrusts upward during mountain forming. With a granite upthrust, the cracks can form straight lines, both vertically and horizontally, and over the years, erosion wears down the stone at the cracks. This makes it look like the stones were cut and placed there when they were thrust up from within the earth millions of years ago.

At this time, scientists have not done any kind of dating on the stones or any excavation in the area. More geological research will have to be performed before any definitive answers can be obtained about the origins of these blocks of granite on Mount Shoria.

Just because we don't know how this stone structure was formed or when it came into existence doesn't mean that we can't benefit from the energy of the area. The energy here feels soft, smooth, and flowing. It vibrates at a high frequency but can dip to a low thrum of vibration at times, as if time itself is slowing down, or as if the area is going into hibernation. This energy can help you find your inner balance so that you're thinking and feeling on an even keel. It can bring emotions back to center so you can deal with situations without becoming distraught and high strung or feeling down and as if you just don't care. Just as the blocks of granite at Mount Shoria are balanced one on top of another, the energy of this place can help you find that same sense of structure within yourself. It can help you solve problems you're dealing with or propel you down new paths by bringing structure, organization, and beauty into your life.

21. MYNYDD CARN INGLI—WALES

Categories: Mountains/Mounds/Cliff Locations, Ruins/Archeological Sites

Mynydd Carn Ingli, which translates to "Angel Mountain," is located in Newport, Pembrokeshire, Wales. It is 1,135 feet above sea level and easily accessed by hiking up from the town of Newport. There is also a parking lot about a mile from the summit if you prefer a shorter hike. Once at the summit you can see the hills of Snowdonia National Park, almost all of Cardigan Bay, and a long view across St. George's Channel of the Irish Sea.

At the summit are the remains of a Bronze or Iron Age stronghold, a hill fort of which only the stone walls and ramparts remain intact on the north side; the remainder has turned into rubble over the years. The size of the ruins makes it one of the largest in the country. In the area around Mynydd Carn Ingli are quite a few ruins of ancient villages and settlements, hut circles, round barrows and cairns, and standing stones.

The hill fort is believed to have been build prior to the twelfth century, when it was first recorded as Mons Angleorum, where Saint Brynach had conversations with angels. It is also thought to have been destroyed by Roman invaders because they ruined the places they conquered by pushing down the walls, which looks like what happened to these ruins.

Saint Brynach was known to spend several days at a time at the summit of Mynydd Carn Ingli communing with God and the angels. It is said that he would live in one of the still standing huts while he was there. People of the area noticed that when he returned from Mynydd Carn Ingli, he had a unique appearance, as if he had been in the presence of God. They thought he picked this location due to the height toward the heavens, the beautiful view, and because the energy is peaceful and filled with the positivity of spiritual guidance. It was through his connection with the energy of this place that Saint Brynach gained the respect of the local people, which enabled him to follow and fulfill his own life path of being in service to others in the ministry of God's love.

The energy at Mynydd Carn Ingli is indeed peaceful, settling, and enables you to find calmness within during stressful times. Just the act of hiking to the summit, being surrounded by nature, and exercising your muscles as you move helps to relieve the stress of any situation that you may be going through. The energy at Mynydd Carn Ingli feels like a warm blanket wrapping around you. Just as Saint Brynach spoke with the angels from high atop the summit of Mynydd Carn Ingli, you too can connect with the angels, your spirit guides, and your higher self as you embrace the energy found at Mynydd Carn Ingli. Imagine yourself by the sea, with the wind blowing around you, and the occasional cry of a bird as the only sounds you hear. Reach upwards within your own spiritual essence to find the place where your higher self lives in the spiritual plane of existence. Embrace the part of you that always stays behind to watch out for yourself as you make your way on the earthly plane.

22. NEOLITHIC ASTRONOMICAL OBSERVATORY EXTERNSTEINE ROCKS–GERMANY

Categories: Astronomical Observatories, Megalithic Sites

Located in the northwestern part of Germany, between Dortmund and Hanover and to the west of Horn-Bad Meinberg in the Teutoburg district, lies a Neolithic astronomical observatory called the Externsteine Rocks. This area is often referred to as the sacred heartland of Germany.

The Externsteine Rocks are approximately seventy million years old, date back to the Cretaceous period, and are at the center of the Thuringian megalithic area. They consist of five columns of rock that look like pillars rising out of the forest. Up until the eighth century AD, there was a large and sacred Irmensul tree located at the top of the Externsteine Rocks but Charles the Great cut it down. The Externsteine consists of seven main sandstone blocks that are approximately one hundred feet tall. At the top of the main rock you can still see where the Irminsul tree stood. This area is a natural sanctuary, which was believed to have had a roof at one time. At the bottom there is a relief carving of the shape of the tree. The monks also carved out steps on the pillars.

Archeologists believe the Externsteine was used for religious ceremonies for more than four thousand years by people of various religious beliefs. However, it was also used for different things at other times, possibly including a fortress or prison.

The temple of rocks at Externsteine were built according to astronomical calculations. From the ground opening in the rock you can view the sunrise during the summer solstice and the moon at the extreme north. In ancient times, caves were dug into the base of the spires and in later years were enlarged so hermits, monks, and other Christians could live within them.

Today a festival is held at Externsteine each year during the summer solstice. The site attracts a large crowd during the festival, but it also has quite a few visitors during the rest of the year. If you decide to visit this area, you might try arriving early in the morning or staying late in the afternoon to avoid some of the crowds and to experience the energy flow in the early morning and late evening.

While a lot of the history is unknown, the site has drawn people over the millennia who felt the pull of the energy in this area. Because it has always attracted religiously minded people, it is an indication of the strength and power of its spiritual energy. Walking up the hand-carved steps or stepping into one of the chiseled out caves creates a connection to a deep energy that feels as if it is bound to earth's frequency. It is strong, powerful, and can boost your frequency to higher levels while keeping you grounded to the earth. The energy is steady and means that this is a strong foundation during times of change. When change comes you will be ready for it. Just as the rocks have experienced many changes over the years, you too will experience change in the near future. By connecting to this potent and stabilizing energy at Externsteine you will be able to quickly adjust and move through those changes with positivity, light, and purpose.

23. NEWGRANGE—IRELAND

Categories: Man-Made Mounds/Mountains, Monasteries/Temples

Newgrange is located at Donore, County Meath, in the Boyne Valley. Newgrange is a Neolithic monument built 5,200 years ago in 3200 BC. It is a circular mound that is 279 feet in diameter, 45 feet high, and has a 63-foot passageway that leads into a central chamber. There are also three alcoves inside. There are 97 kerbstones that surround its base, with the entrance stone being the largest and most impressive due to the carvings etched on it. This is quite impressive because during the time that these carvings were done, the people didn't use any type of metal yet. The final phase of the building was the stone circle that surrounds Newgrange. Researchers believe it was made up of many more stones than are there today. Excavation found that the stones are on top of an Early Bronze Age Pit Circle. This circle is also thought to have either a geometrical or astronomical purpose or it served as part of the death rituals performed by ancient people.

Over the years Newgrange was damaged by people carving their names into the stone and removing stones to use them on the nearby roads that were built. It was during the removal of some of the stones for road construction that the entrance to the interior tomb was discovered. In 1962, the site was excavated and the white quartz frontage was rebuilt on the structure to restore it to its original form.

One of the most unique aspects of Newgrange happens during the winter solstice, the shortest day of the year. There is a roof box over the entrance of Newgrange and when the sun rises on the morning of the winter solstice the sun's rays go through the roof box and into the passageway, lighting up both the passageway and the chamber at the end with the light of the sun. The entire event lasts for seventeen minutes. Sometimes a day or two before or after the winter solstice you can also experience this illumination event.

Classified by archaeologists as a passage tomb due to the layout of the area inside, Newgrange is also considered an ancient temple because of the astrological and spiritual aspects of the cairn, tomb, and surrounding area. It was a site built by the people in a farming community, a place of religious ceremonies and spiritual worship. A place where people of importance were respectfully buried. Newgrange was built with great care and even today, it is waterproof.

The energy at Newgrange is ancient and healing. Quartz crystals used in the creation of the mound signifies being open and willing to receive communications from the spiritual realm. It amplifies the energy of people who wear the crystal and it also amplifies the energy surrounding the place. It is believed the people who lived at Newgrange worshipped the sun and quartz crystals and were particularly effective in amplifying the sun's energy. In the ancient world quartz crystals were used in funeral rites, to get rid of evil, and were used to promote healing and the development of spirituality. Connecting with the energy of Newgrange can help you in the advancement of your own intuition and spiritual growth.

24. PARTHENON—GREECE

Categories: Monasteries/Temples, Ruins/Archeological Sites

The Parthenon is located on the Acropolis in Athens, Greece. *Acropolis* means "high city" and refers to any complex built on a high hill. It is also referred to as a "city in the air." The name came from *Athena Parthenos*, which means "Athena the virgin" and also means "house of Parthenos," which was used to describe the smaller room where the Athena sculpture was kept.

The acropolis was built over seven acres on a hill that is 490 feet above the city of Athens during the fifth century BC at the height of the Athenian Empire's power. Pericles, a statesman and general of Athens, oversaw the planning and construction and put Phidias, one of the best sculptors of the time, in charge of the project. Every four years the Panathenaic games, which were a religious festival with cultural events and athletic competitions, were held in Athens. During the games of 447 BC on July 28th, the first stone of the Parthenon was laid.

The Parthenon was the biggest building within the complex of Acropolis. It was built as a monument to honor the goddess Athena and to house the new statue of her. It replaced two smaller Athena temples built on the Acropolis. The Parthenon became the largest Doric Greek temple and mixed the new Ionic architectural style with the older Doric style. It used more than 22,000 tons of pentelic marble, which was pure white and had a very fine grain, from Mount Pentelicus. It also contained more sculptures than any other temple previously built.

For over one thousand years the Parthenon was used as the religious center of Athens but was converted into a church by the Christians in the fifth century AD. They made changes to the original structure; for example they built a bell tower and put windows in the walls. In its remodeled form it stood for another thousand years. In 1687 the Venetian army seized the acropolis from the Turks who had stored explosive powder inside. On September 26, a Venetian shell hit the Parthenon and the resulting explosion blew out the walls, collapsed columns, and then the Venetian army destroyed it even more. Over the years, people took parts of the building as souvenirs. Some of the sculptures were saved by the seventh Earl of Elgin, Thomas Bruce, who purchased it from the Turks, which he then sold to the British in 1816. Today it is in the British Museum of London.

The energy at the Parthenon is still very powerful. The goddess Athena was known as the goddess of wisdom and war who exemplified courage, justice, strategy, rational thought, and strength. Other qualities she was said to have were wisdom, inspiration, compassion, and generosity. The energy of the Parthenon can connect you with all of these qualities within yourself. It is pure and purposeful and rises from the earth into the air in a flowing, yet rigid, manner. It can help you become stronger than you think you are, while inspiring you to become all that you can be.

25. PILGRIMAGE CHURCH OF MARIA STRAßENGEL–AUSTRIA

Categories: Pilgrimage Sites, Relic Sites

In the district of Graz-Umgebung, northwest of Graz, Austria, high on a hill called Frauenkogel, overlooking the town of Judendorf-Straßengel is the Pilgrimage Church of Maria Straßengel.

The first documentation of the church was in 1208, but legend states that in 1157 Markgraf Otaker III brought a picture of the Virgin Mary (which he said had to be made public) with him to the monastery as he made his holy pilgrimage from Palestine. The founding year of the pilgrimage is said to be 1158. The original picture of the Virgin Mary was destroyed at some time and the current image was painted between 1420 and 1425. This image of the Virgin Mary is considered one of the church's relics. The other relic is a piece of a fir tree root that is shaped like Jesus on the cross that was found in 1255. The beard and hair are made up of root fibers while the body, face, and cross are made up of solid root. Analysis has shown that this root has not been carved in any way and is a natural formation.

The current high Gothic church building began construction in the fourteenth century. The first stone was laid on December 8, 1346 but it wasn't completed until 1355. The church still has seventy-seven of the original fourteenth century stained glass windows. It went through various restorations in the mid to late 1970's, in 1984/1985, 2007, and 2010 on different parts of the building.

The Pilgrimage Church of Maria Straßengel is considered one of the most important churches in all of Austria. The church is filled with symbolism from the images in the stained glass windows to the altars, the reliefs, and even in the towers themselves. The church's position high on a hill also gave it levels of defense because you can see all across the valley below. This served as an early warning system in times when the church needed to protect or defend itself.

The energy at the pilgrimage church of Maria Straßengel is peaceful, serene, and feels as if you're cocooned in safety. The interior of the church feels as if you've stepped back in time as you gaze upon the beauty within. You can also take a walk around the grounds and experience spectacular views of the town below and the mountains in the distance. The energy here can help you become more grounded and connected to the earth's energy that quietly flows through this area. It can help you become more in tune with your own spiritual nature, enhance your own connection with the Divine, and lead you to an inner sanctum where you can learn more about your true spiritual self. The energy is meditative, and experiencing the strength of this quiet energy can lead to deep transformative thoughts and visions as you feel the positivity and love that flows throughout the church and grounds.

26. PULPIT ROCK (PREIKESTOLEN)–NORWAY
Categories: Mountains/Mounds/Cliff Locations,
Power Places, Rock Formations

Located in the Forsand municipality of Rogaland county along the Lysefjord coast of Norway is Preikestolen, which is also known as Pulpit Rock. It is a mountain plateau of a relatively flat topped rectangular stone that juts out of the rocky coastline. It is one of the area's most popular attractions because it is used as a viewing platform. Pulpit Rock received recognition as one of the places in the world that has the most phenomenal views. The flat top part of Pulpit Rock is 1,982 feet above the fjord.

According to Innovation Norway,[16] around 1900, gymnast Thomas Peter Randulff was traveling on the steamship Oscar II along the Lysefjord when the captain pointed out the rock and said it looked like a pulpit. Once he saw the rock, Thomas decided that he was going to climb up there. After his initial ascent, Pulpit Rock became a popular destination for hikers.

If you are afraid of heights, this location is best viewed virtually—seriously. You can even see it from Google Street View,[17] which is really cool, even though it might make your knees weak (as it did mine). To get to the top of Pulpit Rock, it's a strenuous two-hour hike each way over rocky terrain and it is recommended that you're in good physical condition in order to make the climb because there are times when you'll walk right along the edge of the cliffs. Once you reach the top there is a crack across the entire width of Pulpit Rock that you'll have to step over to get to the square part of the viewing area. The top isn't completely flat. It is flatter at the outer edge but before you get to that part there is somewhat of a slope to the rock. If there is snow on top of the mountain it is recommended that you book a guided tour so that you access the site in

---

16. Innovation Norway, http://VisitNorway.com.

17. Google Street View, 2014, https://www.google.com/maps/@58.9864172,6.1888647,2a,75y,102.04h,72.2 9t/data=!3m6!1e1!3m4!1s8a_ZNUuyxTQUH8ajgGh_2A!2e0!7i13312!8i6656.

the safest possible way. Pulpit rock can also be viewed by taking a boat tour along the Lysefjord if you don't feel up to a four hour hike or if heights bother you. There are also combination tours where you can take the boat tour and hike to the top of Pulpit Rock.

The view from the top of Pulpit Rock is absolutely spectacular even in videos. I'm sure physically standing on the top of Pulpit Rock would take your breath away with its sheer beauty. The wind and the scent of the water in the fjord below is a catalyst to feeling part of the whole of creation. The energy here is strong, peaceful, and very empowering. It can help boost any type of spiritual work that you are doing within yourself and is a prime example of how small we are compared to the whole. The energy at Pulpit Rock can help you grow within your spiritual self and to see life from an expanded perspective instead of having tunnel vision.

27. SAANA FELL–FINLAND

Categories: Bodies of Water/Waterfalls/Springs, Mountains/Mounds/Cliff Locations, Power Places, Vortexes

The fells of Finland are located in the upper northwestern portion of the country between the Norwegian and Swedish borders. A fell is a mountain or other barren landscape in a high altitude. Saana Fell is located in Finland at Kilpisjarvi Lake and has a barren summit that is home to many rare species of butterflies. In 1988 the west side of the fell was protected by the government to preserve these butterfly species. At the base of Saana Fell is the village of Kilpisjarvi.

There are several fells in the area, however Saana Fell stands out as unique due to its shape. Saana Fell gets its name from a Saami word that means fungus or mushroom. While it does look like a mushroom it is more often described as looking like an overturned boat. The Saami are the indigenous people who live in the northern areas of Sweden, Finland, Norway, and Russia. They are the oldest living culture of people in the world and have lived in this area for approximately four thousand years. It is believed that they were here even before the Vikings. They live in Saami Land, which is practically barren, with the majority of the population living in the part of Sami Land that is in Norway. The Saami are a peaceful culture that survives by hunting and fishing. Reindeer is their primary food source. They are nomads and during the summer often move around with their animals and teepee homes.

Saana Fell is sacred to the Saami people, who burned fires to the god of thunder on its summit. According to legend, giants lived in the area long ago. Saana fell in love with Malla and they were going to be married by Paras, who was also a magician. But Pältsä, who was also in love with Malla, tried to stop the wedding by having evil witches come to Kilpisjarvi. They made a strong northern wind that froze the land and the wedding party. Saana pushed Malla into her mother's arms (Big Malla). The freezing cold killed all life in the area and the giants fell down, creating all of the fells in the area. Malla cried as she died and her tears formed Lake Kilpisjarvi between Saana and Malla fells.[18]

If you'd like to hike to the summit of Saana Fell, it will take a minimum of two hours. At the steepest part they have built Finland's longest staircase which has 740 stairs to aid in the climb. These steps do not have handrails and each step is made of three two-by-four boards. There are also flat landings built into the staircase so you can rest at several points along the way.

The northern lights over Saana Fell are a beautiful sight that embraces the energy of the fell with its undulating and flowing movement. While the area itself is cold and barren and often covered in snow, the energy here is in a constant state of forward motion. It feels as though it cycles through the fells, the lake, and the air, creating a vortex of energy that flows from one fell to another and back around again. The energy at Saana Fell can help you when you're trying to reach specific goals by spiraling you forward, with a deep surge of energy that will propel you toward your goal.

28. ST. WINEFRIDE'S WELL–HOLYWELL, ENGLAND

Categories: Healing Springs, Pilgrimage Sites

Saint Winefride's Well, also known as the Lourdis of Wales, is located in Holywell, Flintshire, North Wales. St. Winefride's is a pilgrimage well and is open to visitors throughout the pilgrimage season, which is from Pentecost to the last Sunday in September. Throughout history many of the kings of England have made pilgrimages to St. Winifrede's Well beginning with Richard I in 1189.

The legend of the well is that St. Winefride was about to be raped by a man named Caradoc and he cut off her head with a sword. The spring erupted from the ground at the place where she died. St. Winefride was brought back to life due to the prayers of

---

18. Grandma in Lapland, "The Legend of Saana and Malla Fells in Kilpisjarvi," September 28, 2013, http:// grandma-in-lapland.com/the-history-of-saana-and-malla-fells-in-kilpisjarvi/.

her uncle, Saint Beuno. After her rebirth she lived as a nun for twenty-two years until she died a second time. St. Winefride was a real Welsh woman who lived in the seventh century. Since her death, she received sainthood because she was martyred and her well at Holywell became esteemed as a place of healing and pilgrimage for the past thirteen centuries. Written records of cures that happened due to the healing waters from St. Winefride's Well date back to the twelfth century. The shrine even has a collection of crutches dating from the late nineteenth and early twentieth centuries on exhibition at the well. These crutches were left behind because the people were cured by the healing waters and no longer needed them. Within the museum there is a library where they keep all of the letters they received over the past hundred and fifty years from previous visitors to the well, which detail how people who visited the well were healed through the intercession of St. Winefride while they were visiting the well.

All visitors are welcome to bathe in the healing waters should they so desire during the specified bathing times. People have been bathing in these healing waters for over one thousand years and there are many incidences that indicate that these waters do indeed have the power to heal what ails you. You are also allowed to bring empty water bottles so you can fill these from the well and take the healing well water home with you. This is especially helpful if there are people you know who are ill and unable to make the trip to the well themselves.

The energy at St. Winefride's Well is tranquil, peaceful, and serene. When you walk into the area of the well you can sense the sacredness of the energy. There is a loving, warm, and healing sensation that you will feel as you connect to the energy of this place. You may experience an increase in your intuition and a deep connection to those who previously visited to be healed because the depth of their belief in the miracles they experienced is part of the energy that remains here and will affect your own energy. This is a therapeutic place of healing and can help you spiritually awaken.

29. STONE FOREST–LAKE VARNA, BULGARIA
Category: Forests/Trees

The Stone Forest is located about eleven miles from Varna, Bulgaria, going west toward the capital of Sofia. It is also known as *Pobiti Kamani*, which translates to "Stone Forest."

These all-natural stone columns vary in height and width, with some being up to thirty feet tall and some almost ten feet wide. These columns are not part of the bedrock.

Some are hollow and were filled with sand while others are solid. All are loosely stuck into the sand. The pillars themselves are very porous. Some are still standing upright but a lot of them have fallen and are on their sides. Many have crumbled due to the effects of erosion.

The stones were first documented in writing in 1828 but archeologists think they have been in this location since ancient times. In the late 1930s the site was designated a national landmark.

There have been many theories about these limestone columns and how they formed. Bulgarian geologists Peter and Stefan Bonchev Gochev (who are brothers) believe that these columns are from fifty million years ago during the Cenozoic Era. During that time oceans covered this part of Eastern Europe. The brothers believe that the sediment that settled on the seabed created these limestone pillars. Methane gas seeped up from the bottom of the oceans and created hollowed sections within the limestone, leaving behind long tubes. Today we see what remains from the erosion of the limestone and the seabed. This is just one of many theories, but is quite possibly the most accurate one at this time, even though there are still some factors regarding the columns that are unexplained within this theory. An interesting local legend says that the pillars are petrified bodies of giants.

The Stone Forest was named a protected site in 1938 because it is the largest inland sand habitat, with unique plant and animal life, and it is the only place where archaeological evidence of humans during the Mesolithic era has been found within Bulgaria.

The energy at the Stone Forest feels timeless and ancient, as if you stepped back to the beginning of the world. As you look at the limestone columns, imagine that you're standing at the bottom of the ocean over fifty million years ago. Think for a moment how the world above must look. Imagine the plant life and animal life on the surface. Look up at the perfectly formed columns all around you as you imagine the Stone Forest in its original state. Notice any fish swimming around in the water, the temperature of the water, and imagine that you are part of the beginning of time, which as a spiritual being, you are. Connecting to the energy at the Stone Forest can enable you to expand your consciousness to encompass universal concepts as you connect to the spiritual energy of these columns standing in sand that have been there for millions and millions of years. Take off your shoes, walk barefoot through the sand, and obtain a deeper connection to the remnants of an ancient world all around you.

30. STONEHENGE—ENGLAND

Categories: Burial Sites, Megalithic Sites, Power Places, Power Stones, Vortexes

Stonehenge is located near Amesbury, Wiltshire. It is among the most well-known Neolithic standing-stone monuments in the world. Shrouded in mystery, the five-thousand-year-old structure is made of approximately one hundred stones placed in a multi-layered circle. Archaeologists believe it took nearly 1,500 years to build. They have traced the inner stones to bluestone quarries approximately two hundred miles away in the Preseli Hills. The question remains as to how these ancient builders moved these massive stones such a great distance. They also traced the outer stones to local quarries. Archeologists think that the inner circle of bluestones was built first and the outer ring was added later and that the inner circle of bluestones were rearranged multiple times. The largest stone in the outer circle, also called a sarsen, is twenty-four feet tall and weighs over forty tons.

They also think Stonehenge was once used as a burial site. There are legends that Merlin of the King Arthur tales used his sorcery to create Stonehenge and Uther, King Arthur's father, and King Aureoles Ambrosias are buried there. The construction of Stonehenge predates these legends by thousands of years. Other theories include that Stonehenge was built by the Danes, Greeks, Egyptians, Saxons, or maybe the Romans. Currently archaeologists believe that Stonehenge was built by several different tribes of people over thousands of years based on the artifacts found at the site.

Because there are no written records, archaeologists really don't know why Stonehenge was built or exactly who built it. Some of the theories include that it was a memorial to people who were slain by the Saxons, that it was used for ancient astronomy, that it represents the Giant's Ring (a magical stone circle with healing powers in Ireland), a Druid temple, a landing pad for space aliens, and a healing center. We'll probably never know for sure why Stonehenge was created or the purposes it served over the thousands of years it has been in existence.

Stonehenge is also believed to have been created over an area of the earth were ley lines converge. The inner circle is the outer part of the spiral, which goes to the middle but not the exact center of Stonehenge where an altar stone is located. The altar is located at the point in Stonehenge where the earth energy is the strongest.

The vortex energy of Stonehenge is healing and often attracts animals that will sleep inside of the circles. During an experiment in the late 1940s, World War II veterans slept in the same place that a cow or sheep had previously slept and found that they were cured of any ailments. The energy of Stonehenge will not only help you heal your aches and pains, but the energy of the earth that is radiated up into and throughout the site gives you strength and brings about enlightenment into the divine spirituality of the universe. The energy at Stonehenge is very strong and can affect you in positive ways in all areas of your personal and spiritual life. All you have to do is be open to these positive forces and willing to see the path you should take.

31. TEMPLE OF HERA—ITALY

Categories: Ceremonial Sites, Fertility Sites, Monasteries/Temples, Mythological Sites, Ruins/Archeological Sites

In the ancient city of Paestum, Campania, south of Naples in the Parco Archeologico di Paestum, there are two temples built to honor the goddess Hera. These two temples are the Temple of Hera I and the Temple of Hera II. Hera, queen of the gods, was the wife of Zeus, king of the gods, in ancient Greek mythology. Hera was the goddess of fertility and creativity. Legend says that Jason and the Argonauts started the city. Before it was called Paestum, the city was known as Poseidonia, and was believed to be a ceremonial site honoring the god of the sea, Poseidon. There is also a third temple at Paestum honoring Athena. Let's look at the two temples of Hera individually.

The Temple of Hera I is also known as the Basilica. Archaeologists have dated it at approximately 550 BC and it is built in the Doric architectural style with nine columns across the front and eighteen along the sides. When it was rediscovered during the eighteenth century it was named "the Basilica," which also means "town hall" because it was not thought of as a temple at that time. The pediment and entablature did not survive over the years so the building looks short and wide, and more of a meeting place than a temple. The columns of the temple use a design that was prominent in the early classical Greek temples called entasis. This is when the columns are wider in the middle and smaller at the top to give an energetic feeling of lifting upwards. The builders at that time also believed that this form of architecture created an optical illusion, which made the columns appear straight. Artifacts consisting of many small figurines of the goddess Hera were found within the structure.

The Temple of Hera II, also known as the Temple of Neptune, is located beside the first temple. It was built between 460 and 450 BC and is the most well preserved of the temples. It is also built in the Doric style. Across the front there are six fluted columns and fourteen columns down each side. Inside are two rows of smaller columns used to create aisles called the cella. The entablature and pediment have survived on this temple. This temple is almost an exact copy of the layout of the Temple of Zeus at Olympia.

The energy of both of these temples can help you become more creative and artistic. It is positive, warm, and moves in an undulating fashion and twists horizontally as it circles around the area. Because Hera was the goddess of fertility, many people still visit the temples in the hopes of ensuring pregnancy. The energy of Paestum can help you obtain success when you start something new. It is the energy of birth and rebirth, of inspiring hope, of awakening to your own true essence, and of amplifying your creative nature. Whatever it is that you're trying to accomplish at this point in your life, connecting to the earth frequency of this ancient place will give you a boost in your forward motion and pull success toward you as you strive toward your goals. The energy here can also help you during times of rebirth, times when you want to change things in your life. It can help give you the motivation to stay the course and the ability to succeed on your path.

32. THE ALPS—SWITZERLAND

Categories: Glaciers, Mountains/Mounds/Cliff Locations, Power Places

The Alps are the largest mountain range in Europe and are located in northern Italy, southeastern France, some of Austria, some of Yugoslavia, and in almost all of Switzerland. If you were to look at the Alps from an aerial view the mountain range creates a broad arc across Europe. The Alps are 750 miles long, cover 80,000 square miles and are between eighty and 140 miles wide. While most peaks range between 6,000 and 10,000 feet, the highest is Mont Blanc at 15,782 feet.

There are many things to do in the Alps regardless of the country. Mountain climbing, also known as mountaineering, is a popular activity during the summer. There are also places in the Alps where you can go swimming or boating in emerald-colored lakes. Winter activities include skiing, tobogganing, and ice-skating. However, in order to experience the energy of the Alps, finding some of the sacred places is a must and there are many of them across the mountain range.

Mont Blanc, the highest peak in the Alps, is on the French and Italian border. The name means White Mountain. Because it is the highest peak in the Alps it draws the attention of those who like mountain climbing. The ascent is difficult and due to the height of the peak, there are some incidences of altitude sickness. You don't have to climb to the top of the mountain to benefit from the energy surrounding it. The energy at Mont Blanc is vibrant and can fill you with a sense of excitement. Underneath lies a strong, powerful, and serene energy that can help boost you in any endeavor you are trying to achieve. The energy here pulses, almost like a heartbeat, and if you stand really still you can feel the pulse on a spiritual level.

Visiting a part of the Alps where you can view glaciers is an unforgettable experience. The Aletsch Glacier is the largest and also the longest in Europe. It is a little over fourteen miles long. It is located in the high Alps, where it begins in the Jungfrau region, and flows down to the Massa Gorge. The energy at the Aletsch glacier is solid and secure. It vibrates at a slow yet powerful rate. Connecting with the energy of this glacier can help ground you and inspire you to stay strong and steady in your movement toward your goals instead of rushing ahead.

Regardless of where you visit in the Alps, you will undoubtedly leave with a sense of inspired positivity. The height of this mountain range, the beauty of its snowcapped peaks, and its ability to make you look inside and consider your own inner truth, your spiritual essence, and how you fit in to the wonders of the world, makes the Alps, from one end to the other, a spiritual place of power.

33. THE ORACLE AT DELPHI—GREECE

Categories: Mythological Sites, Oracle Sites

Delphi is located on Mount Parnassus near the Gulf of Corinth. It is one of the most popular archaeological sites in Greece. It is an easy daytrip, approximately 112 miles, from Athens.

According to Greek mythology, Zeus released two Eagles and sent them in opposite directions. The place where the two Eagles met was said to be the center of the earth. Delphi was that place. Delphi also had a sacred meaning because they believed it was where you were closest to God. Even in ancient times, Delphi was believed to be the center of the earth by the people living at that time. Apollo was worshiped at Delphi. He was one of the most complex gods and was revered with high importance. He was the son of Zeus and the Titan Leto. His twin sister is the goddess Artemis. People worshipped Apollo because he was god of many things. These included being the god of medicine, music, art, poetry, knowledge, and prophecy. He was also the god of light, oracles, plague, and archery. This means that while Apollo could help heal you or give you success, he could just as easily bring a deadly plague against you.

Apollo is considered an oracular god and he communicated to the people of Delphi through the Oracle of Delphi—Pythia, which means priestess. There are stories that the Oracle existed within the chasm before Apollo was worshipped there. According to the legend a shepherd noticed that his goats were acting strangely so he went close to the chasm where the sheep were. Suddenly he was filled with divine energy that put him into a frenzy and he began to prophesize. Eventually word spread about the chasm and many people decided to visit to have their own futures told. Unfortunately, people kept falling into the chasm so the people decided to elect one woman to act as the prophet and deliver the messages that came forth from the chasm. They had her sit on a tripod type of chair so that she wouldn't fall in. It was said that vapors would rise from the floor when the prophecies were delivered. Today it is believed that cracks in the ground were releasing ethylene from within the earth, which is a sweet smelling gas that could have acted as a hallucinogen for the oracle.[19]

Connecting with the energy of the Oracle of Delphi will enable you to increase your intuition, your clairvoyance, and all other psychic abilities. The energy here moves at a swift, fast flowing rate as it whirls around between the mountaintops and over Delphi. The energy can lift you up to great heights and offer you clarity of purpose and extended visions. It can make it easier to understand your intuitive abilities, and can assist you in using them in a way that is perfect for you on your own spiritual path. Each individual's path is different and our levels of intuition are different from one another and are dependent upon our unique purpose and path in this lifetime.

34. THE PAPS OF ANU–IRELAND

Categories: Mountains/Mounds/Cliff Locations, Pilgrimage Sites

Located in County Kerry, near Killarney, are two barren mountains that, when viewed from the north or south, are in the smooth shape of a woman's breasts, thus the name

---

19. Nevins, Jesse, "Coastal Carolina University: The Oracle at Delphi," https://www.coastal.edu/intranet/ashes2art/delphi2/misc-essays/oracle_of_delphi.html.

"paps," which means "breasts." They are named after the ancient mother of the gods of pre-Christian Ireland, Anu, who is also known as the goddess of Munster, and as Danu, by the Tuatha Dé Danann people. Anu is connected to the Mor Riogach, a name that means war fury or great queen. Together with two other goddesses, Badbh and Macha, the three together were known as the Morrigna who could change into ravens. This area is well known for the large number of ravens that live in the area even today.

The Paps of Anu is considered one of the most sacred places in Ireland by people of different religions. Over the past seven thousand years, it has been a place of religious ceremonies. May Day is often celebrated in the City of Shrone, also known as Cathair Crobh Dearg, below the Paps of Anu and it is considered a pilgrimage site.

On top of each of the mountains are pre-historic cairns, manmade stacks of stones. The cairn on the eastern pap is bigger than the one on the western pap. It is approximately thirteen feet high and sixty-five and a half feet wide. The cairns represent nipples but they are also thought to be ancient graves.

To experience the energy of the Paps of Anu, hiking to the summits of both mountains takes between seven and eight hours. There is a trail between the two mounds but the dip in between is often wet. The climb is steep and you should be in relatively good physical condition to hike this trail.

To see the Paps of Anu in all of their glory, there is an interactive map where you can view the area online.[20] Here you'll find a virtual reality screen where you can explore the whole area by clicking on icons and scrolling around within the picture. Put your monitor at full screen to get the best experience. You'll feel like you're right there at the top of the cairn looking out across the valley below or in the City of Shone, looking up at the Paps. You can also travel around the ancient City of Shone and see a primeval holy well, a mound, the city walls with ancient carvings, and lots of other interesting features. This video really helps you to connect to the energy of the place.

The energy at the Paps of Anu is ancient, calming, and will help you feel settled within yourself. If you're encountering problems in your life, connecting to the energy here will help you come to a clear resolution by making you look within as you view the area and feel the soothing vibrations at the Paps of Anu.

---

20. Voices from the Dawn, "The City and the Paps of Anu," https://voicesfromthedawn.com/city-and-the-paps/.

35. WAWEL CHAKRA VORTEX–POLAND

Category: Pilgrimage Sites, Power Places, Vortexes

Wawel Chakra Vortex is located in the Krakow Royal Castle in Krakow, Poland. The Wawel Chakra is thought to be an actual stone built into the foundation of the Renaissance castle, or that it is one of seven stones placed in different locations around the world, or that it is some other type of physical object. However, no object has ever been found that people could say, "This is the Wawel Chakra." Because there is no evidence of a physical object, many people believe that the term Wawel Chakra describes a vortex of energy in this location.

During the eleventh century, the Polish rulers lived on Wawel Hill in an early Romanesque stone building. Over time the building was expanded repeatedly especially during the fourteenth century when major additions and renovations occurred. The remains of the original eleventh century building are still located in the northern wing of the castle. Today the castle is known as the Wawel Royal Castle–State Art Collection and is a museum that hosts exhibitions and conferences. It is a national cultural institution that underwent a complete restoration during the end of the twentieth century.

In the past, people believed the Wawel Chakra was stored in the basement of the castle, specifically underneath the west wing. In order to connect to the energy of the chakra, people will lean against the walls of the west wing for hours at a time in the hopes of absorbing some of the chakra's energy. The castle staff tried to prevent this from happening by putting up signs, roping it off, and even posting guards to keep people off of the walls. Tour guides are asked not to discuss the chakra stone, and the Catholic Church dismisses the chakra stone legend.

People are drawn to the vortex energy in this area regardless of how much others want to prevent it. The energy calls to you because it is pure, powerful, and of the Divine. It can help you make transcendental changes within your spirit that will last a lifetime. It forges a deeper connection to your core spiritual essence and a clear line of communication to your higher self. This can be extremely helpful if you're having difficulties understanding your life purpose, contacting your spirit guides, or finding positivity while living in the earthly realm. The energy here feels like releasing a sigh. It's a feeling of coming home or becoming one within yourself. Because this vortex energy is connected to the earth chakras, you can also connect your own chakra frequency to this energy to clear your chakras, to raise your frequency, and to remove any blocks that may be keeping you from achieving all you desire.

36. WHITE HORSE HILL—UFFINGTON, ENGLAND

Categories: Burial Sites, Gigantic Landscape Carvings

Located in Oxfordshire, Uffington, alongside the Ridgeway between Dorset and the ridges of Brookshire Downs, White Horse Hill is an ancient complex of four prehistoric sites.

Uffington Castle is at the summit of White Horse Hill. It is believed to have been built in the Iron Age and was a hill fort. It sits at 860 feet above sea level with long views. Currently over six counties can be viewed from the top of this hill. The design of the Uffington Castle was basic. It had one ditch and one rampart. Archaeologists have found post holes in pits that indicated that structures were built within the castle. These were probably round huts large enough to contain an extended family group. This was a common practice in the Middle Ages. Pottery and coins from the time period were also found in the burial chambers.

The Uffington White Horse is thought to be over three thousand years old. It is the oldest chalk cut hill in Britain. What we see today is a stylized version of the horse with the lines looking thin and artistic. However, researchers believe that there is a more standard and larger version of the horse underneath the ground. The changes in the topsoil at Whitehorse Hill have reduced the image of the horse to what we see today. Others believe that it has always looked exactly as it does today and that there is not a larger version of the horse underneath it. The purpose of the White Horse is unknown but it is thought that it could've been a landmark for those traveling, representative of the tribes who lived there, or simply people from the past being artistic.

Also on Whitehorse Hill you will see the Manger, which is a dry valley with ripples that were created during the last ice age when the permafrost retreated. These ripples are calls the Giant's Steps.

Dragon Hill is also part of the Whitehorse Hill complex. It is to the east of the Manger and it is said to be the site where St. George slew the dragon. Legend says that the dragon's blood poisoned the ground and left a scar on the earth for everyone to see in the form of white chalk. Dragon Hill is a small, round hill with a flat top. Perfect for fighting dragons.

You can also see Neolithic burial mounds from White Horse Hill. The largest of these burial mounds contained forty-seven skeletons. Make sure to look carefully for these mounds as you walk from the car park to the area of the Uffington White Horse.

Recently a chalk figure in the shape of a duck was discovered a short distance away from the White Horse of Uffington on a nearby hill. It was named the Uffington White Duck and it is approximately 360 feet tall. There are plans to restore the duck to its original appearance by removing the grass that has overtaken it over time and through the use of special mapping technology and with the knowledge of experts in this type of conservation work.

The energy at White Horse Hill is soothing, calm, and gives a sense of inner peace. Connecting to the energy here is opening yourself to the freedom to being who you are at your true spiritual level. Whether it's spreading your wings like a dragon flying through the air or flying across the ground with the beat of thundering hooves, you too can soar and feel the exhilaration of these types of flight. Embracing this energy will allow you to soar, to reach your dreams, and to fulfill your life purpose by becoming all that you are supposed to be in this lifetime.

Chapter 5
ASIA

Asia brings to mind mountains, caves, and bodies of water in the countryside as well as bustling cities. As we travel through Asia on our quest to experience earth frequency, we will encounter many mountains, including Mount Fuji in Japan, Mount Everest in Nepal, and Mount Ararat in Eastern Turkey. We'll also go underground in India to visit the Ajanta Caves, in Sri Lanka to visit the Dambulla Cave Temple, in China for the Yungang Cave Shrines, and on Gharapuri Island to experience the Elephanta Caves. There are breathtaking bodies of water in Asia such as Ha Long Bay in Vietnam and Klayar Beach in Indonesia, and there are also healing waters such as the Dead Sea in Southwestern Asia. There are many shrines and monasteries in Asia including the Taktsang Monastery in the Himalayas, the Ise Jingu Shrine in Japan, and in Angkor Archeological Park in Cambodia. There are many locations throughout Asia that have deep, ancient connections to spirituality and earth frequency. These places of power will help you experience a deeper connection to your own spirituality so that you can grow within yourself and immerse your physical being with your higher self and spiritual essence. The sacred sites found in Asia are will expand your horizons and knowledge as they touch you at a soul level.

Map Key

1. Angkor Archeological Park—Cambodia
2. Ayutthaya—Thailand
3. Baalbeck—Lebanon
4. Bagan—Myanmar
5. Bodh Gaya—India
6. Borobudur—Java Indonesia
7. Bukit Timah Forest Reserve—Singapore
8. Dambulla Cave Temple—Sri Lanka
9. Elephanta Caves—Gharapuri Island, India
10. Ha Long Bay—Quang Ninh, Vietnam
11. Ise Jingu Shrine—Japan
12. Jeju (Cheju) Island—South Korea
13. Kanyakumari—India
14. Khongoryn Els (Singing Dunes)—Bayankhongor, Mongolia
15. Klayar Beach—East Java, Indonesia
16. Kyaik Pun Paya—Near Pegu, Burma
17. Kumano Kodo Pilgrim Trails—Japan
18. Lumbini —Western Tarai, Nepal
19. Lycian Rock Tombs—Turkey
20. Mount Api Pinnacles—Sarawak, Malaysia
21. Mount Ararat—Eastern Turkey
22. Mount Everest—Nepal
23. Mount Fuji—Japan
24. Mount Kailash—Tibet, China
25. Mount T'ai Shan—China
26. Pagoda Forest—China
27. Plain of Jars—Laos
28. Socotra Island—Republic of Yemen
29. Taktsang Monastery—Paro, Bhutan, Himalayas
30. The Ajanta Caves—India
31. The Dead Sea—Jordan/Israel/West Bank, Southwestern Asia
32. The Lake of Heaven—Tibet, China
33. The Somapura Mahavihara—Bangladesh
34. Yazilikaya—Turkey
35. Yungang Cave Shrines—China

Map of Asia

1. ANGKOR ARCHEOLOGICAL PARK–CAMBODIA

Categories: Man-Made Sites, Monasteries/Temples, Mythological Sites, Power Places, Ruins/Archeological Sites

The Angkor Archaeological Park is located in northwestern Cambodia near Siem Reap City. It contains the ruins of Angkor, which include the internationally known Angkor Wat Temple, the Bayon State Temple located in the walled city of Angkor Thom, the Preah Khan, the Neak Pean, and many other ruins of ancient temples. The park is situated on 249 square miles of land between the Kulen Mountains and the Tonle Sap Lake. Siem Reap City is located south of the Angkor Archaeological Park and is where you'll stay if you visit the park. There are no hotels or restaurants inside the park; instead, they are all located within Siem Reap City.

The temples located within the Angkor Archaeological Park were built between the ninth and fifteenth centuries AD during the Angkorian-era Khmer Empire and served as the capital city. In addition to the ruins within the park, there are also ruins outside of the park. More than a million people lived in Angkor during the height of this ancient civilization. The buildings and temples constructed during this time represented the wealth, prestige, and eye for artistic detail of the Khmer people. The Khmer people made up the majority of the population of Cambodia in ancient times, just as they do today.

It is highly suggested that Angkor Wat and Bayon are must-see sites during any visit because they represent the most magnificent examples of the architecture and art of the ancient city. Let's take a quick look at both of these temples.

Angkor Wat is the most famous of all of the temples in the Angkor Archaeological Park. Angkor Wat was built between 113 and 115 BC. Structurally it is massive, is built out of stone and is the best preserved and the largest of all of the temples in the Angkor complex. It is the world's largest religious monument. It is contained within an area of five hundred acres in the shape of a rectangle enclosed within a large wall. It has three levels with a central tower and four surrounding towers that are 213 feet from ground level and are intricately carved. It is surrounded by a moat that is 656 feet wide with a bridge that crosses it to the temple. Both the interior and exterior of Angkor Wat have bas-relief carvings that tell stories from the Hindu mythology, apsara carvings, and a giant reclining Buddha on the third level. Angkor Wat is known for having the best examples of art carvings from the Angkorian era.

The Bayon Temple was built about one hundred years after Angkor Wat in Angkor Thom, the capital of King Jayavarman VII, and served as the state temple. His successors added their own additions to the temple so it also contains Theravada Buddhist and Hindu elements in the design. What makes Bayon Temple so unique are the over two hundred gigantic stone faces that were placed in sets of four identical faces each that point in the same direction. There is some dispute over whose face is portrayed all over the building. Some say they are all images of King Jayavarman and others say they are the face of the bodhisattva of compassion named Avalokitesvara or possibly they are supposed to represent both. The temple also has many bas-reliefs that show the history, daily life, and wars fought by the Khmer.

The energy at the Angkor Archaeological Park is serene, calm, and spiritual. It flows in tight bands of high frequency from the exterior of the park to the interior and then back out again. The energy here will enhance your creativity, embolden your spirit, and bring balance to any areas within you that aren't in a state of steady flow. The energy here can also help to quiet your mind so you can easily connect with your higher self and the energy of the divine.

2. AYUTTHAYA–THAILAND

**Categories: Islands/Reefs, Man-Made Sites, Monasteries/
Temples, Ruins/Archeological Sites**

Ayutthaya is located in the Phra Nakhon Si Ayutthaya District of the Phra Nakhon Si Ayutthaya Province of Thailand, approximately fifty-five miles north of Bangkok, in the Ayutthaya Historical Park. It is also known as the Historic City of Ayutthaya—and the history of the city is well documented.

Ayutthaya is located on an island surrounded by the Lopburi River, the Pa Sak River, and the Chao Phraya River. When the tide came in, it created a tidal bore, which is a tidal wave that pushes against the river's current and flows into the river's water. This location is beneficial because the tidal bore protected the city from attack. The island was also approximately the same distance to China, Malaysia, and India, which made it a popular stopping point for people from all of these countries.

Ayutthaya was the second capital of Siam and was founded by King Ramathibodi I in 1350. By 1378 it was an active and vibrant city, until 1767 when the Burmese army invaded and burned it to the ground, destroying the majority of the city, which was made of wood. The city was abandoned instead of being rebuilt because many of the occupants were killed or taken as slaves.

Prior to the Burmese attack, Ayutthaya was an active trading port that brought many merchants from Europe and other countries around the world to the city to conduct commerce and for reasons of global diplomacy. The city contained hundreds of temples and three royal palaces, whose occupants kept detailed records about the city, some of which survived the Burmese fire and are an excellent source of historical information.

Visitors to Ayutthaya weren't allowed to camp inside the city, so there are various sites and settlements outside of the city walls that were created by the Thai-Chinese and people from Portugal, Japan, and the Netherlands.

When visiting Ayutthaya, there are many ancient temples and ruins to see. At Wat Yai Chaya Mongkol Monastery, there are hundreds of Buddha statues, stupas, and Buddhist shrines that are dome-shaped (called chedi), all of which are dressed in yellow scarfs.[21] At Wat Phra Si Sanphet, you can view many stupas, some of which contain the ashes of some of the Kings of Siam. At Wat Mahathat you can see the famous stone head of Buddha enclosed in the roots of a Banyan tree. The head is protected at all times by a guard and is roped off so people can't touch the tree or stone head. It is customary to bow to show respect to this Buddha head. At Viharn Phara Mongkol Bophit, which is a replica of Bangkok's Grand Palace, is the largest Buddha in Thailand. It was once outside, but after a lightning strike in 1706 it was placed inside to protect it. Another large Buddha in a reclining position is at Wat Lokayasutharam.

The energy of Ayutthaya is exciting, happy, and very energetic. It moves in short spurts in an up-and-down motion as if it's skipping around the area. There is a sense of peacefulness and positivity in Ayutthaya that is radiant and vibrant. This energy will energize and motivate you, and it serves as a catalyst for change. Any time you need to get something accomplished, the energy here can keep you in a great mood and give you the calm peacefulness to focus on the task at hand or to make any changes needed in your life so you can accomplish a lot in a short period of time. It is also a protective energy that, if you hold it close, will keep all negativity at bay while you're working on the growth within your own spiritual self.

---

21. Vietnamitas en Madrid, "Ayutthaya: the Historical Park of Ayutthaya," http://en.vietnamitasenmadrid.com/thailand/ayutthaya-historical-park.html.

3. BAALBECK–LEBANON

Categories: Monasteries/Temples, Ruins/Archeological Sites

Baalbeck is located in the Beqaa Valley on the east side of the Litani River in the foothills of the Anti-Lebanon mountain range. It is approximately forty-seven miles north of Damascus and fifty-three miles northeast of Beirut. The ruins at Baalbeck are known as Lebanon's greatest Roman treasure.

The temples of Baalbek were built on an ancient hill. Archaeologists have found evidence of an enclosed court that had an altar in its center, which they believe was built in approximately the first millennium BC. The Greeks formed the city between 333 and 364 BC and named it Heliopolis, which means "City of the Sun," because they worshiped Baalbek, the sun god. The Temple of Jupiter complex was built to worship three gods, which were Jupiter, Venus, and Mercury. The podium was built with some of the largest blocks of stone ever quarried, including the Triathlon, three huge stones located on the west side of the podium that weigh approximately eight hundred tons each.

When the Romans took over the site, they built the Great Court of the Temple of Jupiter over the old court built by the Greeks. The complex was built beginning in the first century BC and completed by the middle of the third century AD. The Hexagonal Court and the Propylaea were the last built during the third century. The Temple of Jupiter had many porticoes, altars, basins, and rooms with seats or benches where people could carry on a conversation.

In 313 AD, Byzantine Emperor Constantine closed down the Baalbek temples after Christianity became the official religion of the Romans. At the end of the fourth century, the altars and the Temple of Jupiter's great court were torn down by Emperor Theodosius who then used the materials to build a basilica in the upper part of the Temple of Jupiter. In later years, after the Arabs took over the temple around 636 AD, it was turned into a fortress.

The Temple of Jupiter was surveyed by the German Archaeological Mission in 1898 and they began restoration work. The French took over these efforts in 1922 and the restoration was continued by the Lebanese Dick Torre, general of antiquities, in later years. Some of the ruins that you can see at the site today are the Temple of Jupiter, the Hexagonal Forecourt, the Great Court, the Propylae.

The energy at the Temple of Jupiter is bright and airy, stern and respectful, and uplifting and inspiring. It flows in a pattern that's reminiscent of a giant S, moving in a snakelike rhythm. The energy reminds you that there is a time and place for everything. There are times when you feel bright and cheerful and as if you're bubbling over with joy, other times you may feel more reserved and contemplative, and there are still other times when not only will you feel inspired and encouraged, but you also have that same effect on other people. The energy at the Temple of Jupiter is one that will stay with you. It will weave its way into your essence in order to be supportive of your endeavors and to help you maintain forward motion in all areas of your life.

4. BAGAN—MYANMAR

Categories: Monasteries/Temples, Ruins/Archeological Sites

Located in the jungle of southwest Mandalay in the central part of the sovereign state of the Republic of the Union of Myanmar (formerly known as Burma) on the plains of the east bank of the Ayeyarwady River is the ancient city of Bagan—also known as the Bagan Archaeological Area—one of the most spectacular archaeological sites in Asia and the world.

It is in this area that you will find the ruins of 2,200 Buddhist temples, pagodas, monuments, and monasteries made out of red brick, but during the height of the kingdom there were over 10,000 of them in Bagan.

When visiting Bagan, you will pay an entrance fee for a ticket that is good for five days. You can return and explore at will instead of trying to take in everything in one day. Some of the pagodas are away from the central part of Bagan so you may encounter fewer people at those. Balloon rides are also available so you can see the area from the air. Visiting the Bagan Archaeological Museum offers more information about the area and you can view the artifacts collected from the region. There is a small entry fee to the museum.

During a visit to Bagan there are some temples that you definitely want to visit. Ananada Pagoda is a Buddhist temple built during the Pagan Dynasty under the rule of King Kyanzittha. The temple was built in 1105 AD. Legend says that eight monks told the king about the vision they had for the temple during their meditations so the king had them build the temple but in order to preserve its uniqueness and to ensure that another one would not be made somewhere else in the world by the monks, he had them all killed. Another version says that they were buried alive to be the guardian spirits of the temple. The Gawdawpalin Temple is the second tallest temple in Bagan and has two stories, four upper terraces and three lower terraces. It was reconstructed after obtaining severe damage during an earthquake in 1975. The Dhammayangyi Temple is the largest of all the temples in Bagan and is a massive pyramid shaped temple. However, it was never completed and a lot of construction debris was found inside the temple. There is some debate as to whether this was done on purpose by the workers because the king was a harsh ruler or if it was simply left over during construction and never removed.

The energy of Bagan is cool, refreshing, and light. It moves in a breezy fashion and takes a triangular pattern throughout the area before overlapping on itself. It is an energy of exploration, wonder, and uncovering the unexpected. Connecting to this energy can help you feel bright and cheerful on dreary days, can make you more spontaneous, and helps you see goodness, light, and the positive within yourself and others. It helps make situations more joyful and something you look forward to instead of a problem you don't want to face. Any time you need help bringing the power of positivity into any situation you find yourself in, call on the energy found in Bagan to help you through.

5. BODH GAYA–INDIA

Categories: Monasteries/Temples, Pilgrimage Sites, Power Places, Shrine/Birth or Burial Sites of Saints

Bodh Gaya is located in northwest India in the Bihar state, approximately sixty-five miles south of Patna, the capital of Bihar, and about seven miles from the city of Gaya in Eastern India. Bodh Gaya is internationally known as the birthplace of Buddhism, specifically in regards to enlightenment. Bodh Gaya is a pilgrimage site for Buddhists, who come from all around the world to this destination, which is very important to their religion and is one of their holiest sites.

The birth of the Buddhist religion happened approximately 2,500 years ago. It is told that it happened like this. Prince Siddhartha Gautama, who was born in 566 BC, lived with five followers on the banks of the Nairanjana River where they practiced austerities, which means they lived in a very strict manner with extreme periods of fasting. After six years, Prince Siddhartha Gautama realized that he was not attaining enlightenment through his current practices, so he stopped doing them, which made his followers desert him. He then traveled to the village of Senani, where a grass cutter gave him some kusa grass so he could make a mat to sit on, and a Brahmin girl name Sujata gave him rice milk to drink. Prince Siddhartha took his gifts and sat, facing east, underneath a pipal tree. He was determined not to move from the spot until he attained the enlightenment that he had been seeking for the past six years. While he meditated under the pipal tree, the Lord of Illusion, named Mara, tried to distract him. Prince Siddhartha placed his hands on the earth and asked it to bear witness to all the different virtuous lifetimes that he had lived in order to reach enlightenment. In response to hearing the truth of his words, the earth shook and Mara unleashed his demons. The wisdom of the prince shattered all of Mara's illusions as the battle between them raged on. The prince showed extreme compassion to his enemies and changed all of the weapons into flowers. Mara and his demons fled and Prince Siddhartha Gautama became the Buddha and the tree became the Bodhi Tree. He remained in this position under the tree for seven days, the following seven days he did a walking meditation, and the seven days after that he contemplated the Bodhi Tree.

The Mahbodhi Temple was built near the place of Buddha's enlightenment in the third century BC by Emperor Asoka. The temple that stands at the site today dates between the fifth and sixth centuries and is built entirely of brick. It is the earliest example of using brick to build a Buddhist temple. The Mahabodhi Temple Complex located at Bodh Gaya contains many sacred sites that are associated with Buddha's enlightenment. There is the Mahabodhi Temple, whose height is 164 feet; the Vajrasana, which is a throne that sits at the foot of the Bodhi Tree at the spot where the Buddha became enlightened that archaeologists believe was built by Emperor Ashoka; the Bodhi Tree itself; and seven other sites where the Buddha received further enlightenment, including the Lotus Pond, which is located outside of the temple complex. The Bodhi Tree that is currently at the site today is believed to be a direct descendant of the Bodhi Tree that was living at the site when the Buddha received enlightenment.

The energy of the Mahabodhi Temple Complex is, as expected, very enlightening. The energy here will help you attain a cosmic understanding of universal laws and the world we live in and a pathway to greater understanding of yourself as a spiritual being. The energy here is beneficial in every area of your life. It can help you quiet your mind, raise your frequency, and allow you to experience thoughts that are part of a higher consciousness in order to grow as a spiritual being. Whether you practice the Buddhist religion or not, you will come away from this site feeling a sense of renewal within your own frequency because it has been boosted by the energy of this sacred site.

6. BOROBUDUR—JAVA INDONESIA

Categories: Islands/Reefs, Monasteries/Temples

Borobudur is located twenty-six miles northwest of Yogyakarta, in the Magelang Regency, and in the Central Java province Java Island in Indonesia. The Borobudur Temple Compounds are in the Kedu Valley, which is at the southern end of Central Java. The Borobudur Temple is the largest Buddhist temple in the world.

The Borobudur Temple was built during the Syailendra Dynasty in the eighth and ninth centuries. It was constructed to look like a lotus flower, Buddha's sacred flower, and built in three levels around a hill. Each level is meant to reflect the spheres of the universe in Buddhism, which are called kamadhatu, rupadhatu, and arupadhatu. The base of the temple represents kamadhatu, the sphere of desires, which is when a person is restricted by their desires. There are five square terraces built on top of the base and on top of each other, each one smaller in size than the one below it, following the pyramid shape. These five terraces are representative of rupadhatu, which is the sphere of forms, when desires are released and no longer hold you back but you're still connected to your name and body. The next layer of the temple has three circular platforms that contain a total of seventy-two stupas in three separate circles, with each stupa being carved out to look like stone latticework, and inside each one sits a three dimensional stone carving of Buddha. These represent arupadhatu, the sphere of formlessness, which is when you're no longer connected to your name or body but are spiritual energy. At the very top and in the center of the temple is an enormous stupa, which is representative of the enlightened mind. As a person walks through the structure, it represents starting out as a basic human connected to the earthly realm to being an enlightened spiritual being connected to the spiritual realm.

At the base of the temple, there are 160 relief sculptures, which were hidden when the builders added stone buttresses for support due to the weight of the structure. The temple contains statues of the Buddha placed at various points for a total of 504 statues. The walls also have 1,460 stone reliefs, which show events of Buddha's past lives, stories from the sutras, the Buddhist scriptures, and Buddha's teachings, which are called the Dharma.

The Borobudur Temple was in constant use as a religious facility from the time it was built until it was abandoned between the tenth and fifteenth centuries. It was rediscovered in the nineteenth century and restored. It was during the restoration that the relief sculptures at the base were discovered and then hidden again by the stone support buttresses. Pictures were taken at the time as documentation of the sculptures.

The energy at Borobudur Temple is connected to the Divine. Its frequency is very high and moves in a circular flow around the temple from the bottom to the top. This energy will help anyone on a spiritual path, regardless of religion, in that it opens the mind to higher thought and helps you release materialistic connections and dependency on emotions that can hold you back from attaining a deeper bond with the spiritual realm and achieving higher consciousness.

7. BUKIT TIMAH FOREST RESERVE–SINGAPORE

Categories: Forests/Trees, Islands/Reefs

The Bukit Timah Forest Reserve, also known as the Bukit Timah Nature Reserve, is located in the Republic of Singapore, which is off of the southern tip of Malaysia in southeast Asia, approximately seven and a half miles from the city. Singapore is categorized as a city, country, and island nation and is the only place in the world with this classification. In addition to the main island, Singapore's territory also includes over sixty other islands and islets. Singapore also creates artificial islands, which adds to the number.

At the highest point of the island, on Bukit Timah Hill, which is 534 feet above sea level and encompasses approximately 402 acres, is where you'll find the Bukit Timah Forest Preserve, which was established in 1883. It was protected by the government from deforestation due to the great biodiversity of flora and fauna located within the reserve, but, by the time the protection was in place, only one third of the forest remained. Attempts at reforestation were made but only achieved limited success. The timber in the remaining area was never harvested as it was in other reserves on the island, which severely depleted them. Between September 2014 and October 2016, the Bukit Timah Forest Reserve was closed to the public or only limited access was allowed, so that restorations could be performed in the area. These included repairs to the main road, the stabilization of slopes through repair, the planting of trees, repairs to the trails, and the addition of boardwalks over swampy areas. Rope handrails were added to some sections of the trails, and anti-slip surfaces were added in wet areas.

The Bukit Timah Forest Reserve is unique in that it is a hill dipterocarp forest, which means that most of the trees in this type of forest are from the Dipterocarpaceae family and usually contain less undergrowth than other type of forests. This means there is less wildlife and more animals who live in the trees, like squirrels, although they often have a great number of bird species. The Bukit Timah Forest Reserve is only about 0.2 percent of the total area of Singapore but it contains 40 percent of the countries native plants and animals. Today there are over ten thousand flowering plant species and five hundred wildlife species. It is also home to two species of freshwater crabs that are only found in Singapore. Between 1830 and 1930 there were many reports of tigers living in the forest and tiger attacks happened frequently, so the people living on the island killed them. Eventually they became extinct on the entire island.[22]

The energy in the Bukit Timah Forest Reserve is tranquil, energizing, and fills you with a sense of peace. It is also revitalizing especially if you're trekking up the steep hills of the forest. This energy can get your mind, body, and spirit activated to higher levels of frequency, which can aid you on your spiritual path. Connecting with the energy here will help you find your center during meditation and will bring about a sense of inner calm and balance. It feels like a brisk breeze flowing over you.

8. DAMBULLA CAVE TEMPLE—SRI LANKA
Categories: Caves, Healing Springs, Islands/Reefs, Monasteries/Temples

Dambulla Cave Temple, also known as the Golden Temple of Dambulla, is located in Sri Lanka, an island country in Asia, approximately forty-four miles from Kandy and ninety-two miles from Colombo, in the approximate center of the country.

The Dambulla Cave Temple is believed to have been built by King Vattagamini sometime between 103 BC and 77 BC. During his reign the country was invaded by the South Indians and the king had to abandon his kingdom. He went into hiding for twelve to fourteen years and during that time the caves provided a safe haven where he could retreat. Eventually he was able to regain the throne and show his gratitude to the cave that he lived in while hiding. At that time it was one large cave under a huge overhang of rock, so he made wall partitions in the cave and had drip ledges made to protect it from rain and seeping water. He constructed the caves named Maharajalena, Paccimalena, and Devarajalena. His immediate successors didn't have any interest in the caves until King Vijayabahu I who ruled between 1055 and 1110 AD. He did renovations to the caves and

22. National Library Singapore, "Tigers in Singapore," 2007, http://eresources.nlb.gov.sg/infopedia/
articles/SIP_1081_2007-01-17.html.

archaeologists believe that Buddhist monks lived in them during this time. It was King Keerthi Sri Nissankamalla who added the seventy-three Buddha images and plated them with gold. Many other kings added to the caves, renovated and restored them over the centuries, and gave them importance as a temple. The walls of the caves inside the temple have a large number of detailed murals of Buddha, Bodhisattvas, and other gods and goddesses separate from the Buddhist religion, which cover almost the entirety of the inside of the cave. It is believed that King Kirti Sri Rajasinha had these murals painted during his reign. Archaeologists also discovered evidence that these caves had been used during prehistoric times as dwellings.

There are a total of five caves within the Dambulla Cave Temple, all underneath a massive overhang of rock. The first cave is called the Cave of the Divine King and has a statue of Buddha, which is almost forty-six feet tall, that was carved out of the rock. There is a carving of Vishnu, who legend says used divine powers to create the cave, near the head of Buddha. At Buddha's feet is a carving of Ananda, his favorite student. The carving of Buddha itself has been painted and repainted throughout history. The second cave is called the Cave of the Great Kings and is the largest of the five caves. Within this cave there are forty seated statues of Buddha, sixteen standing statues of Buddha, as well as statues of the gods Vishnu and Saman, and statues of King Vattagamani and King Nissanka Malla. This cave also has a spring that is thought to have the power to heal. Its water drips from a crack in the ceiling and is caught in a bowl on the floor. There are also thousands of murals on the walls and ceilings of this cave that show the history of the country and scenes from the life of Buddha.

The third cave is called the Great New Monastery, and at its entrance are Dragon Arch designs. It contains a thirty foot reclining Buddha statue carved out of the rock. There are also fifty additional Buddhist statues surrounding the reclining Buddha that are in both standing and seated positions. Behind the reclining Buddha is a mural with four of his assistants. On the roof of this cave there is a mural that contains one thousand seated Buddha images. The fourth cave is called the cave of the Western Temple and it contains ten figures of Buddha, one of which is carved from the rock, and the Buddha is sitting in the position of meditation. The fifth cave, called the Second New Temple, is the newest and it is unclear when it was constructed. It also contains a statue of a reclined Buddha with quite a few seated and standing Buddha images. The difference in this cave from the other four is that the Buddhas are made from brick and plaster instead of carved out of the granite rock.

The energy at the Danbulla Cave Temple is spiritual, cool, and peaceful. It is a high frequency that meanders at a medium to slow pace throughout the five caves. It has a soft sound that is like the tinkling of bells. This energy is helpful when you need to slow down and let go of the stresses of the world. It is warm, calming, and soothing to the soul. It brings about a feeling of rightness within you, of knowing the truth of yourself as a spiritual being and the love that is entwined in the fabric of universal consciousness.

9. ELEPHANTA CAVES—GHARAPURI ISLAND, INDIA
Categories: Caves, Islands/Reefs, Monasteries/Temples, Ruins/Archeological Sites

Elephanta Caves are located on Elephanta Island. The island was originally named Gharapuri, which means "city of caves," and in ancient times the whole island was a place of worship. It was renamed Elephanta Island by the Portuguese because they found a gigantic elephant carved out of stone near the area where they docked their boats and ships. This statue collapsed in 1814 but it was reassembled and is now displayed at the Dr. Bhau Daji Lad Mumbai City Museum. Elephanta Island is located a little over six miles east of Mumbai and the Gateway of India in the Indian state of Maharashtra.

The Elephanta Caves date back to the fifth century AD, when Silhara kings ruled the land. The original structures of the cave were carved into basalt rock, which is volcanic in origin. The carvings of the cave itself are very detailed and intricate. There are inner cells, shrines, porticos, and grand halls, all of which are filled with large statues carved out of the same stone that makes the pillars and columns. Some of the stones in the cave have been polished while others have been left in their natural state. The Elephanta caves can be grouped into two sections. The first group are five Hindu caves, which are the home of Lord Shiva. The second group are Buddhist caves, which are smaller than the Hindu caves. The total size of all seven caves is approximately sixty thousand square feet and there are three different entrances to the cave. Part of the Elephanta Caves includes a historical Shivji Temple, which means that the temple is dedicated to Lord Shiva, the Supreme Being within Shaivism, who has been worshiped since ancient times and is the most venerated god of Hinduism.

The statues, reliefs, and sculptures inside the cave were damaged by the Portuguese soldiers who conquered the area in 1547 because they used them for target practice. The cave walls were painted and contained writing that archaeologists feel probably gave important information about the builders of the statues and of the cave itself. Unfortunately, the Portuguese soldiers also removed the writing from the walls, so archaeologists have no way to determine who actually carved out this phenomenal cave or who built the huge statues of Lord Shiva. The consensus among the local residents is that the caves were built by the gods.

Today the Elephanta Caves are a popular attraction, but they are also used by the Hindu people as a place of worship, for ceremonies, and for festivals, just as they have been for thousands of years.

The energy of the Elephanta Caves is cool, crisp, and revitalizing. It sounds thick and somewhat hollow, as if an echo is imminent. There's a sense of wonderment, of solemn expression, of deep respect, and a rise toward enlightenment. The energy of the Elephanta Caves is one that will ingrain in your memory and become interwoven within the frequency of your own soul. You can draw on this energy when you are working on raising your own frequency or reaching toward your own spiritual enlightenment.

10. HA LONG BAY–QUANG NINH, VIETNAM
Categories: Bodies of Water/Waterfalls/Springs, Caves, Islands/Reefs

Ha Long Bay, which means "descending dragon bay," is located in northeastern Vietnam in the Quang Ninh Province and in the Gulf of Tonkin. Ha Long Bay contains approximately 1,960 islands and islets that are made of limestone that is believed to be 500 million years old. The majority of the islands are uninhabited because they are very steep, rocky structures with lush tropical vegetation, which is relatively untouched by human hands. A lot of the islands are much taller than their width. Some of the islands are large enough to support residents and businesses that cater to tourism. In 2012, Ha Long Bay was named one of the New Seven Wonders of the World by the New Seven Wonders Foundation. A lot of the caves in the bay are open to the public; however, some are closed in order to preserve them. Archaeologists have found evidence that prehistoric man lived in the area.

Legends of the area say that dragons who filled their mouths with jewels and jade were sent by the gods to create Ha Long Bay. As they flew over the water, they allowed the jade and jewels to slowly drop from their mouths. Wherever they landed, an island was formed.

The natural beauty of Ha Long Bay is phenomenal and unsurpassed. The pillars have many interesting features that have happened over time due to erosion. Some have breathtaking arches, some have notches, while others have caves, and many have secluded beaches. They are arranged in a haphazard way and consist of single towers, pillars with conical peaks, or larger islands with a variety of peak heights. There are also smaller islets that look like boulders emerging from the water. Ha Long Bay is unique in that its bio-systems consist of both oceanic, seashore, and tropical evergreen. There are fourteen floral species and sixty faunal species of plants that are widespread throughout the islands. There are 200 species of fish in the bay and 450 mollusk species. The wildlife on the islands include birds, lizards, monkeys, frogs, and antelope. On the island of Cat Ba in the Cat Ba National Park, you'll find the rarest and most endangered mammal in the world, which is the Cat Ba Langur,[23] who can only be found on this island in Ha Long Bay. Their population was down to only fifty-three in 2000 but now their numbers are starting to rise and there are one hundred of them in the park today.

Only a small portion of the islands have been named. Those that are named are usually named based on the shape of the island; for example, there is one that looks like an elephant that is called Voi Island (voi translates to elephant).

The energy at Ha Long Bay is magical, mysterious, soothing, engaging, and exceptional. The frequency of this energy is extremely high and is a connection to the Divine. There is a peacefulness here and a sense of belonging. The bond with the ancientness of the earth is strong and powerful in this gorgeous location. Connecting to the energy of Ha Long Bay will enable you to settle frazzled nerves, release negativity, engage with your higher self, and feel the powerful pulse of the earth that beats like a drum throughout this energy. You can claim this power as your own any time you feel the need for more strength, endurance, and uniqueness.

23. Cat Ba Langur Conservation Project, "The Cat Ba Langur: An Extraordinarily Beautiful Primate," 2014, https://www.catbalangur.org/Langur.htm.

11. ISE JINGU SHRINE—JAPAN

Categories: Forests/Trees, Shrines/Birth or Burial Sites of Saints

The Ise Grand Shrine, also called Ise Jingu, is located in the city of Ise, in the Mie Prefectre (jurisdiction) of Japan, deep within a sacred forest. It is the ancestral shrine of the Japanese emporers. It is unique in that the shrine is completely rebuilt every twenty years.

The property actually contains two shrines, with the inner shrine, called Naiku, being the most important. It is located in the south central part of Ise in the town of Uji-tachi. It is dedicated to the sun goddess and supreme deity Amaterasu Omikami. The shrine was built in 4 BC when Emperor Suinin reigned. The construction is made of cypress wood, is rectangular, and is thirty-three feet tall. It is windowless, uses wooden joints instead of nails, has a gabled roof and veranda, and copies the style of ancient buildings used to store rice. Underneath the flooring is a symbolic pole known as the heart pillar. It is said the shrine contains one of the three sacred treasures of Japan, which is Amaterasu's Sacred Mirror, where it is believed that Amaterasu can manifest or is where she resides. The mirror is kept in a closed cabinet in the shrine's main sanctuary. Typically, it is kept in a box or wrapped in a cloth to keep it protected.

The outer shrine is called Geku and is dedicated to the food goddess named Toyouke Okami, who is the goddess of food and agriculture, clothing, and shelter. She was brought to the Ise Jingu Shrine in order to oversee the sacred food that was offered to Amaterasu. This twice-daily ritual occurs in a building located northeast of the main hall. Sacred fire is used during this ritual and is created by rotating wood on wood. Sacred water from a sacred well is also drawn so that Amaterasu has something to drink.

The Ise Grand Shrine property also includes other smaller shrines dedicated to Shinto spirits and other kami, the Shinto religion's divine beings. Due to the size of the shrine and the intricate and ornate design, it costs millions of dollars to rebuild it and replicate each detail every twenty years. Upon the completion of the new shrine, the land for the next shrine is allocated as its future location. A small hut and a seven foot pole is built on this land. When the twenty years are up, the new shrine is built, the old one is torn down, and a new plot of land is designated for the next one.

This traditional rebuilding every twenty years is a long-held tradition that began in the late 700s. The last time the Ise Grand Shrine was rebuilt was in 2013, which was the sixty-second time it was rebuilt. The next time it will be rebuilt is in 2033. There is also an additional 124 shrines located in the city of Ise that are also rebuilt every twenty years. This costs the Japanese government $500 million to complete.

The guardian of the Ise Grand Shrine is the saishu, a supreme priestess who acts as a liaison between the worshippers and the gods. She has the highest rank at the Shinto shrines and was always an unmarried princess during ancient times. Today, any female members of the imperial family can be the saishu.

The energy at the Ise Grand Shrine is exciting, happy, and a full of laughter. These joyous feelings are wrapped around the energies of respect, love, and worship. The high spiritual frequency of this location is of the Divine. It is an important energy to access when you are trying to become more enlightened on your own path. This energy can awaken your soul and can bring about greater awareness of ideals that you may not have contemplated as of yet or that you have thought about but were unsure of. This energy will bring clarity and help you see that you are more than just a physical human being but that you, too, are part of the Divine.

12. JEJU (CHEJU) ISLAND—SOUTH KOREA

Categories: Caves, Islands/Reefs, Volcanoes/Volcano Cones

Jeju Island, also known as Cheju Island or Jejudo, is located in South Korea in the Jeju Province, approximately eighty miles off the coast of the Korean Peninsula. It lies southwest of South Jeolla within the Korea Strait. Jeju Island is forty miles long and sixteen miles wide. The island was formed by volcanic activity that happened over two million years ago. The now-dormant volcano is currently the tallest mountain in South Korea, at 6,397 feet above sea level, and is called Halla. The Geomunoreum lava tube system is one of the most spectacular lava tube cave systems in the world. When you look at these tubular caves and imagine how much lava was flowing through them at one time, it just simply blows your mind. The sheer size of the lava tubes is the reason that ninety percent of the island surface is basalt volcanic rock. You will see stalactites, stalagmites, columns, helictites, benches, blisters, cave coral, bridges, shelves, striations, rafts, and what looks like rope all of which are made out of lava. One might expect the walls of the lava tubes to be black due to the heat of the lava, however this is not the case. The walls, roofs, and floors are multicolored due to carbonate deposits, which provide a decorative element to the interior of the lava tubes.

Jeju Island is not the only volcano in the area. Surrounding the main volcano are 360 satellite volcanoes throughout the island. The enormous crater at the top of Mount Halla contains a large lake but it is not full of water. There are many waterfalls and lush landscapes, an abundance of animal life including freshwater shrimp, narrow mouth frogs, thirty thousand bats that live in one of the lava tubes, which is the largest confirmed bat colony in South Korea to date, and a wide variety of bird species.

The symbol of Jeju Island is a life-sized grandfather statue carved out of stone and called a dolharubang. The grandfather looks as if he's wearing a hat and he has both of his hands resting on his stomach. The tradition of the statue began in 1774 when the Korean leader demanded that islanders make forty-eight of them. Today forty-five of these statues are still in existence and they are representative of the ancient culture of the island, its legends, and many gods.

Jeju Island also has Korean Mermaids, which are called Haenyo divers. These are women divers, approximately six thousand of them, who go out into the sea every day and catch fish barehanded in the cold water. What makes this so interesting is that the average age of these women is seventy-five years old. These mermaids are unique to Jeju Island.

The exquisite beauty and distinctiveness of Jeju Island was honored when it was selected to be one of the New Seven Natural Wonders of the World in 2012.

The energy at Jeju Island is very laid-back, relaxed, and easy-going. The energy here flows in a forward-drifting motion similar to a butterfly floating through the air. However, there is also a heavier feel to the energy closer to the volcano and lava tubes. Here the energy is thick, heavy, and powerful. It moves with purpose and force and flows rapidly and feels hot. The energy at Jeju Island is multilayered. When you access this energy, it gives the message that while there are times when you need to just kick back and relax; there is always an underflow of power within you. You are driven, know your purpose, and see the way to make things happen in your life. It is often harder for you to relax than it is for you to push ahead. The energy here is telling you that you have to find a balance between the two and take the time to recharge and rejuvenate yourself by letting go and relaxing.

13. KANYAKUMARI—INDIA

Categories: Monasteries/Temples, Pilgrimage Sites, Regions

Kanyakumari is located in the state of Tamil Nadu in the district of Kanyakumari. It is in the southernmost tip of India where the Arabian Sea, the Indian Ocean, and the Bay of Bengal meet.

Kanyakumari is internationally known for the beautiful architectural designs of their temples, which can be found throughout the area. These temples are steeped in legend and the majority were built by South India Kings. Two of the most important temples in the area are the Kumari Amman Temple and the Vivekananda Rock Memorial. There are many other temples in Kanyakumari and in nearby areas.

Of the three temples mentioned, the one that holds the most importance and is the most famous is the three-thousand-year-old Kumari Amman Temple. It is dedicated to the goddess Kumari Amman, the virgin goddess. Legend says that Banusura, the demon king, gained control over the devas and cruelly punished them. The goddess went to the Kumari Temple to do penance in the form of a virgin girl and Lord Shiva fell in love with her. He planned to marry her on a specific day at midnight but she knew that Banusura could only be killed by a virgin. When the Lord Shiva was due to arrive, the goddess took the form of a rooster and crowed as if it was dawn. Lord Shiva thought he had missed the marriage time and returned home disappointed. The goddess decided to remain a virgin and Banusura tried to force her to become his wife so she killed him. The Devas were freed from their punishments and the goddess continued with her penance and remained a virgin. The statue of the goddess wearing a nose ring bejeweled with rubies stands at the temple. It is said that the rubies in her nose ring were so bright they could be seen far into the night and some sailing ships confused the light of the rubies with the lighthouse and wrecked onto shore. Because of this, the eastern gates of the temple where the statute stands are now kept closed. Thousands of people make pilgrimages to this temple every year to worship the goddess and to view the unique architecture of the temple.

The Vivekananda Rock Memorial was built in 1970 as a memorial to Swami Vivekananda. It is just off the mainland and is built on a large rock that can be reached by ferry. The building itself is enormous, with intricate architectural designs and is situated on two contiguous rocks. The site is considered sacred because it is believed that the goddess Devi Kumari, also known as the goddess Kumari Amman, blessed the rock. It is here that Swami Vivekananda meditated for two days and attained enlightenment.

The energy throughout Kanyakumari is engaging, contemplative, and feels very alive. It moves quickly throughout the area and tends to make small circular patterns similar to an infinity sign or figure-eight. Feeling the energy of this place can help you resolve personal issues through introspection and meditation by causing you to truly engage with your own spiritual truths and path. It can lead to a greater sense of enlightenment and of understanding of the Divine, regardless of your individual religious beliefs.

14. KHONGORYN ELS (SINGING DUNES)— BAYANKHONGOR, MONGOLIA

Category: Sandhills/Sand Dunes

Located in Mongolia approximately 110 miles from Dalanzadgad are the Khongoryn Els singing dunes. They are in the Gobi Gurvan Saikhan National Park and at the foot of the Altai Mountain range in the south part of the Gobi Desert.

The dunes are the largest in Mongolia and are beautiful with their pointed peaks that seem to flow across the tops of the dunes. The dunes cover a large area and they can be up to 7.5 miles wide and 110 miles long, but because they are constantly changing, the width and length changes as well. The height of the dunes, which also varies, can be up to 980 feet tall. The largest and tallest dunes are located in the northwestern section.

The dunes are constantly shifting and changing due to the wind in the area. They're called the singing dunes because of the noise made when the sand cascades down in many small avalanches or when the wind blows it from place to place. The sound is caused by a thin layer of slate over each grain of sand that rubs against each other as the wind moves them, and also due to the heat of the desert. The sound can be so loud that it can be confused with the sound of an airplane during takeoff.

While you can walk to the dunes, the recommended way to explore them is to ride a camel. You can rent camels for short rides around the base of the dunes or for a month if you choose to spend that much time going across the Gobi Desert. If you choose to walk up the dunes, it will take approximately an hour to reach the top. You can't ride the camel to the top, but it can walk along with you and carry your stuff up for you. This is not an easy climb. Due to the texture of the sand and the steep incline of the dunes, you'll find yourself sliding backward as much as you're going forward. You will get sandblasted more than once as the wind whips off the top layers of the peaks blowing them to a new location. This will sting but once you reach the top you are rewarded with outstanding views of the dunes themselves and the surrounding area.

The only way to reach the dunes is to be part of a group tour or arrange for a vehicle and driver to take you. Traveling anywhere within the hot, remote areas of the Gobi Desert should not be attempted by those without experience. It's important to hire a guide who is accustomed to driving in the conditions, or who has experience with camels, and who will make sure to include the appropriate amount of food and water necessary for everyone as well as fuel for the vehicle and food for the camel. This is not a location where you can explore on your own.

The energy of the Khongoryn Els singing dunes moves at a very fast vibration, is hot, and swirls, sometimes in multiple directions at the same time. The energy here is invigorating, exciting, and fills you with joy and happiness. It is a connection to unlimited and ever-changing possibilities. It feels as if someone has opened the door to allow all that you want to flow to you. Accessing this energy can help you succeed in your career, in your personal relationships, and on your spiritual path. This energy will leave a song in your heart that you can sing any time you so desire.

15. KLAYAR BEACH—EAST JAVA, INDONESIA

Categories: Geysers/Blowholes, Mountains/Mounds/Cliff Locations, Regions

Klayar Beach is located in Kalak Village in the Donorojo District in Pacitan, East Java. It is often referred to as the Mediterranean Beach of Indonesia due to its rock formations, turquoise water, white sandy beaches, and the way the tide flows into the beach. It is approximately an hour drive from Gong Cave, a popular destination renowned as one of the most beautiful caves in the region.

This beautiful scenic beach seems somewhat private because not many people visit because it's not a good area for swimming due to the abundance of rocks in the water and the strong flow of the ocean that creates very large waves. Some people like to surf in this location but it is important to be aware of the rocks and the ocean current. In the past, some swimmers were pulled out into the ocean due to riptides in the water, so it's safer just to hang out on the beach and surrounding area. There is also very limited public transportation (only available in the mornings) to get to the beach because of the road condition, which is narrow, has hills, some with extreme inclines and declines, lots of bumps, and sharp turns. Even in a private car, the road can seem treacherous. Klayar Beach is popular with the local residents, especially on holidays.

The rocks here are covered in seaweed and form unique geological structures. One even looks like a sphinx. The entire area has a pristine, natural appearance and isn't commercialized. To the west side of the beach there is a hill that you can climb and on the east there is a cliff you can also climb. From either of these spots you can see phenomenal views of the Indian Ocean and the beach area. The best view of the sunset is from the hill to the west.

One of the most inspirational aspects of the beach is the wave geyser, a blowhole where water from the ocean shoots up through a hole in the rocks approximately twenty-three feet into the air. What makes it so awesome is the sound that is created when this happens; it sounds like someone is playing a bamboo flute. With the exception of the sounds made by the wave geyser and the wind, the beach is relatively quiet.

The energy at Klayar Beach is transformational, peaceful, and relaxing. The flow of the waves as they crash to shore is mesmerizing. Sitting on this beach, relaxing on the sand, and feeling the wind blow over you can put you into a meditative state where you are able to commune with the natural setting, connect with your higher self, and feel part of the earth energy flowing all around you. This energy is powerful and can lift you to realms of higher consciousness. It can help you let go of any negativity that you've been holding within while opening your eyes to solutions to problems you're facing. It can also enhance your creativity, and you may get an idea for a new project that will be beneficial to your life. There is a connection to the Divine and universal consciousness at Klayar Beach.

16. KYAIK PUN PAYA–NEAR PEGU, BURMA

Category: Monasteries/Temples

The Kyaik Pun Paya is located in the city of Bago, in the Bago Division of the country of Burma, also known as Myanmar, in Southeast Asia. Bago, also called Pegu, is the ancient capital of Burma. Legend says that two princesses, who traveled to the area from Thaton, formed Bago around 573 AD. Buddha saw two birds sitting on top of each other on a rock that stuck out into the sea. Upon seeing this, he predicted that the country would be formed in the location where Bago is today and that this country would follow the Buddhist religion.

This Buddhist monastery was built in 1476 by the King Dhammazedi, who was ruler of the Mon Kingdom of Hanthawaddy (Pegu). It is designed in a very unique way. Instead of following the traditional monastery designs, it has four statues of Buddhas who have reached enlightenment, or Nirvana. The statues are one hundred feet high and represent four successive Buddhas—Kassapa, Kakusandha, Konagamana, and Gautama—who each face a cardinal direction while sitting with their backs to each other and against an enormous column made of brick. The facial expressions are different on each of the Buddha statues. They all wear golden robes and headdresses but each are adorned differently. The pagoda is surrounded by an open pavilion, which also has some small signs, a pole with a Hintha bird, which is the symbol for Bago, and a statue of King Dhammazedi.

According to legend, four Mon sisters pledged never to marry. Each sister was represented by one of the Buddha statues. It was said that if one of the sisters married, then one of the Buddha statues would collapse. And then one of the sisters did break her promise by marrying, and that is the reason the Kassapa Buddha collapsed during an earthquake in 1930. The Buddha was completely destroyed and only a brick outline remained. It has since been restored, but the facial features are different from the others. At first look, you won't notice that one is different, but if you look closely enough, you can tell which one was damaged and rebuilt. Today the monastery is still in use and worshippers visit daily.

The energy at Kyaik Pun Paya moves at a gentle, fluid pace. It feels bright and clear; its tone sounds like the music of a harp. There is a churning to the energy here as if it is being stirred and separated into each of the directions that the Buddhas face. This is an indication for you to have a deeper perspective about situations you are encountering in your life. It encourages you to consider situations from multiple points of views, and not close yourself off from possibilities because you're not willing to look around you or change your perspective. This energy means to keep an open mind.

17. KUMANO KODO PILGRIM TRAILS—JAPAN

Categories: Mountains/Mounds/Cliff Locations, Pilgrimage Sites

The Kumano Kodo Pilgrimage Trail is located in Tanabe, Wakayama Prefecture, Japan. This is a pilgrimage walk that has been taken for over a thousand years by people ranging from those of the general public to aristocrats and even emperors. This pilgrimage trail takes you through mystical mountains where you will also see sacred shrines.

During the sixth century, Buddha traveled to Japan, and the forest where the Kumano Kodo trail travels through was used for those wishing to train in the Buddhist philosophies. Eventually the area became known as Buddhist Pure Land. During the ninth and tenth centuries the sacred sites that are now part of this pilgrimage walk came into being. Kumano Sanzan is the name used when referring to all three of the shrines at one time. Individually, the shrines are the Kumaro Hayatama Taisha, the Kumao Hongu Taisha, and the Kumano Nachi Taisha. As you travel along the Kumano Kodo you will also come upon Oji Shrines on the sides of the path. At these shrines, offerings are given and religious rights are performed as the person encounters them.

If you added up all the possible individual trails and paths of the Kumano Kodo, you would find that there are 190 miles that you can walk on this pilgrimage route. The shortest is a little over a half of a mile and takes approximately thirty minutes to walk. The longest is thirteen miles and takes between six and a half to seven hours to walk. The paths are also rated between one and five according to its level of difficulty. Some of the walks are extremely easy and only go a short distance. Many of these have paved pathways or trails that are very well maintained, little change in elevations, and go through populated areas. Some of these even have bus stops nearby if you don't feel like walking back to your original starting point. The most difficult walks can take all day to complete; the trails are not well maintained and are in a very natural state. They are in remote areas with little access, and some of the elevation changes are very steep in both the incline and the decline. These trails are for experienced hikers in excellent physical condition. As with any walk, you should be prepared before you head out. Make sure you take plenty of water, and if you're going on a longer walk, take a few snacks, maybe a small first-aid kit, your cell phone, and identification.

While the purpose of walking the Kumano Kodo Pilgrimage Trail is to visit the shrines, there is a deep connection to the energy found along the paths before you ever get to the shrines. In this instance, the journey is as enlightening as the destination.

The energy along the Kumano Kodo feels deep, dark, strong, resilient, and will speak volumes to an open mind. You often become immersed in the essence of the forest, and feel its energy as a living thing. This energy envelops you, embraces you, and makes you become more aware through heightened senses and an increase in your mental processes so that you think as you walk. Accessing the energy along the way can help you make a deeper connection to your own spirituality and beliefs. You may feel the heightening of your intuition from the energy here as well as a more curious nature where you may question what you currently believe and consider other beliefs, which brings about spiritual growth.

18. LUMBINI—WESTERN TARAI, NEPAL

**Categories: Monasteries/Temples, Pilgrimage Sites, Ruins/
Archeological Sites, Shrines/Birth or Burial Sites of Saints**

Lumbini is located in the Lumbini Zone in the Rapandehi District of Western Terai. This is in the foothills of the Himalaya mountain range in the Mayadevi Gardens.

Lumbini is known as the sacred birthplace of Buddha. He was born in 623 BC in southern Nepal on the Terai plains. In 249 BC Emperor Ashoka of Mauryan had a pillar built where Buddha was born and inscribed the information about Buddha's birth on an Ashoka Pillar. This location is the holiest of all the pilgrimage sites in the Buddhist religion.

According to the Buddhist religious texts, Gautama Buddha's father was King Suddhodana, who was part of the Shakya Dynasty and a member of the warrior caste called the Kshatriya. His mother was Queen Mayadevi, who was on her way to visit her parents in Devadaha during the month of May on the day of the full moon, known as Baishakha Purnima. She had stopped to rest in Lumbini when she went into labor. She took a bath in the Sacred Pond and then held on to the branches of a Sal tree to steady herself while she gave birth. After a while Prince Siddhartha was born. In later years, he became the first Buddha. Legend says that Buddha spoke during his birth and said, "This is my final rebirth." He also walked right after being born and took seven steps where seven Lotus flowers then bloomed in his footprints.

People began making pilgrimages to the site during the third century BC and pilgrimages still continue today. Over the years, particularly from the third century BC up until the fifteenth century AD a host of holy buildings such as the Mayadevi Temple, monasteries, pilgrimage centers, statues, shrines, stupas, and viharas were built near Buddha's birthplace. These ancient artifacts give archaeologists a tremendous amount of insight into the pilgrimages of the ancient past. Archaeologists have been working in the area since the Ashoka Pillar was discovered in 1896.

The Lumbini Garden has three zones that are each one square mile for a total area of three square miles and are interconnected by a series of walkways and a canal. There are many places in the garden where you can sit quietly and meditate or view the ruins from the past and think about the reasons they were built, the people who built them, and how you feel seeing them.

The energy at Lumbini will open your awareness so you see more on both the physical level and in the spiritual realm. This energy is known for making people realize that nothing is permanent, including the lives we are living, therefore, it is important that we understand our own spiritual nature, our own frequency, and the truth of our beings and our place in the divine scheme of the universal consciousness. It is with this understanding that we become more enlightened within ourselves and are able to help others experience their own sense of enlightenment through the sharing of experiences. The energy at Lumbini is one of hope, revitalization, and spiritual transformation.

19. LYCIAN ROCK TOMBS—TURKEY
Categories: Burial Sites, Mountains/Mounds/Cliff Locations, Mythological Sites, Ruins/Archeological Sites

Lycia was located in the areas known today as the Antalya Province and the Muğla Province, both of which are located on the southern coast of Turkey. Lycia also extended further inland to what is now known as the Burbur Province. Lycians are mentioned in the history of the Hittite Empire and ancient Egypt. Eventually the Lycian civilization became part of the Achaemenid Empire.

While the Lycians no longer exist, their ruins tell us about their civilization. They were skilled craftsmen as well as artists, based on the ornate designs of their funerary monuments. One of the most interesting aspects of the Lycian culture is how they buried their dead. They believed that a mythical creature similar to a siren with wings would carry them into the afterlife so they buried the deceased high above the ground in elaborately carved tombs built into the rock cliffs and near the coast to make it easier for this creature to take the souls of the dead. The Lycians habitually buried their dead where they lived and worked. These were very ornate and decorative structures, that archaeologists believe resembled their homes, some up to three levels, carved into the face of the rock. While the Lycians weren't the only ancient culture who created rock tombs, an interesting aspect of their burial tradition is that they buried more than one body in a tomb. Archaeologists believe these were families who were buried together. The earliest carbon dating of the Lycia rock tombs goes back to the fifth century BC.

The Lycians also buried their dead in a three-level stone sarcophagus that included a large base, the chamber for the body, and a lid that had a point or wide ridge at the top. These sarcophagi have less decoration than the cliff tombs and date to the age of the Romans, although archaeologists have found a few older ones that are more decorative. Within this type of sarcophagus, the tradition of burying family members together continues as well as buring slaves with the person. When other people were buried with someone, there was a section under the main grave chamber where their bodies were placed.

The least popular and oldest form of burial chamber was the pillar tomb, a monolith that gets narrow at the top and either sits on a base or directly on the ground. The grave chamber is normally at the top of the pillar. These pillar tombs are only found in the western part of Lycia.

The energy that surrounds the tombs of the Lycian people is solid, traditional, and dutiful. There is a serene sense of rightness and of protection that mixes throughout the frequency, which moves at a moderately quick pace. Connecting to the energy here encourages you to embrace the family unit even if there are disagreements between members. This energy means to look ahead and not back, to be supportive not destructive, and to get along with others. It is a reminder that we can choose whether to openly embrace our emotions and the situations we find ourselves involved in or, if we feel the situation is negative and harming us in any way, we can walk away from it. This energy also means to notice the intricacies of life, the ornate and decorative details that fill your life with beauty and inspiration.

20. MOUNT API PINNACLES—SARAWAK, MALAYSIA
Categories: Caves, Mountains/Mounds/Cliff Locations, Rainforests

Mount Api is located in the Gunung Mulu National Park in the Miri District of Sarawak. The Gunung Mulu National Park is best known for its caves, including the Sarawak Cave

Chamber, which is the largest in the world. Mount Api is also known for the pinnacles that are on the side of the mountain. The pinnacles can be up to 164 feet tall, are made of limestone that looks thin and spiky, and are razor sharp. These are called limestone karst formations, which are formed by erosion and often have an underground drainage system like a cave. The pinnacles and the cave systems in the area are approximately five million years old.

The climb up to the Mount Api Pinnacles takes three days and two nights and the hike is difficult and challenging. You must be in good physical condition prior to attempting the hike. The first portion of the hike from the trailhead to Camp 5 is relatively flat and is approximately five and half miles long. From this point forward the trail is very steep as you climb up to the Pinnacles. Toward the end you'll have to climb vertically at times; you'll also climb up metal ladders and use ropes in order to get to the location. After all of your hard work to get there, you will be rewarded with incredible views of the pinnacles. But it's not over yet. The climb down is just as strenuous as the climb up. Sometimes the jungle trails to the pinnacles are very muddy and wet, and you'll find yourself slipping and sliding. It's also necessary to make sure that you wear high socks and that you tuck your pants into them because leeches are everywhere.

While you're at the Mulu National Park, you may also want to check out some of the cave systems or enjoy one of the other jungle hikes offered where you can enjoy the rich biodiversity of the rainforest, or you might enjoy the Mulu Canopy Skywalk where you'll walk along in the tops of the trees. This is the world's largest canopy walk.

The energy at the pinnacles is damp, fresh, and clean. It smells like the forest and the fresh scent of rain. The energy here is motivational, quick moving, and will inspire you. It encourages you to look for your hidden gifts just as the pinnacles are hidden high upon Mount Api. The energy moves upward with quiet strength and feels like it is pushing, pulling, and lifting you along the way. This energy will instigate a strong momentum for whatever task you're undertaking, and it also has the quiet reserve and focus needed when you are trying to discover more about your spiritual self.

21. MOUNT ARARAT—EASTERN TURKEY

Categories: Glaciers, Mountains/Mounds/Cliff Locations, Power Places, Volcanoes/Volcano Cones

Mount Ararat, also known as Agri Dagi, is located in Eastern Turkey and is on the borders of Nakchivan, Armenia, and Iran. According to the Bible, Mount Ararat is known as the resting place of Noah's Ark after the great flood.

Mount Ararat has two peaks, the largest of which is called the Great Ararat, which has an elevation of 16,945 feet above sea level and is located in Turkey. The other peak is called Little Ararat or Lesser Ararat and is 12,782 feet above sea level. Both of the peaks of Mount Ararat were formed by volcanic eruptions. Mount Ararat is considered a dormant stratovolcano and the last known eruption occurred on June 2, 1840. Volcano experts believe that it was most active during the third millennium BC and that both of the Ararat peaks were formed at this time. After the initial construction of the volcanic peaks, there were additional eruptions on the flanks of the volcanoes that formed cinder cones, pyroclastic cones, and lava domes. Mount Ararat lies on the eastern end of a volcanic range that extends to Nemrut Dagi, and on the western side of the mountain, there is a low pass that separates it from the volcanic range. Both the northern and eastern slopes begin on the alluvial plain of the Aras River, which is approximately 3,300 feet above sea level, and on the southwestern portion of the mountain, the slopes rise from a plane that's approximately 5,000 feet above sea level. The very top of Mount Ararat is covered by a glacier and the top one third of the entire mountain is always covered with snow. All along the slopes there are enormous black basalt rock formations and little vegetation.

In order to climb Mount Ararat you have to get permission from the local government. They are wary of foreigners climbing the mountain because of the national military security precautions in place. Once you receive permission it is recommended that you book a local guide and start your trip on the south side of the mountain because it cuts a little less than a mile off of your climbing time. You can drive across the valley from Dogubayazit to the base of Mount Ararat where you can meet your local guide. The trip up the mountain will take between three to four days to complete.

There have been many expeditions up Mount Ararat in search of Noah's Ark. While there have been many alleged sightings of a structure that could be a boat and other anomalies found, there hasn't been absolute archaeological proof that Noah's Ark has been located. That being said, it very well could have come to rest at the top of Mount Ararat but is now currently buried under the ice cap or possibly under lava from the 1840 eruption. Archaeologists also state that there is a probability that the Ark was dismantled and the wood used to build housing or maybe used as firewood. We may never know.

The energy at Mount Ararat is ancient and carries a deep connection to the earth's core. This energy moves at a slow, steady vibration, but it carries a high spiritual frequency. The energy here is connected to building a firm foundation and urges you to create your own foundation not only for your own spiritual self and in your life but also for any projects you decide to undertake in order to ensure that they will be successful. The energy here also spurs new creativity. If you are embarking on a new endeavor, then accessing the energy at Mount Ararat can give you the positivity needed to be successful. Spiritually, this energy can lift you up to great heights.

22. MOUNT EVEREST—NEPAL
Categories: Mountains/Mounds/Cliff Locations, Power Places

Mount Everest is located on the Tibetan Plateau known as Qing Zang Gaoyuan, in the Mahalangur Range, and the Himalayas, on the border between Nepal and Tibet in Asia. The summit of Mount Everest is between Nepal and Tibet. In Tibet it is located in the Xigaze area and in Tingri County, an area that China considers to be part of their autonomous region. In Nepal Mount Everest is located in the Solukumbu District in the Sagarmatha National Park. The Nepal section of Mount Everest is the easiest to access. Mount Everest is the tallest mountain above sea level.

Mount Everest is not of volcanic origin and there is no magma underneath the mountain according to geologists. It was created as part of the Himalayan mountain range when the Indo-Australian and the Eurasian continental plates had a fierce collision approximately sixty million years ago. This collision of plates is still happening at an extremely slow rate, which makes Mount Everest increase in height at approximately one half inch every year. Currently Mount Everest is 29,029 feet at its peak according to the current surveys by Nepal.

The Sherpas are the indigenous people who live around Mount Everest and who often act as guides for those who want to climb the mountain. To the Sherpas, Mount Everest is sacred and hallowed ground. According to their beliefs, it is the Mother Goddess of the World, which is *Chomolungma* in their native language. They believe the Mother Goddess lives inside the mountain. Before they ever step onto the mountain, they conduct a special ceremony where they ask permission from the Mother Goddess to ascend her slopes and for her protection as they make the climb. This ceremony is called Puja and the Sherpas require every climber to participate in the ceremony prior to climbing the mountain. It is a long-standing tradition that designates the official beginning of a Mount Everest expedition. There are others who also believe the mountain to be sacred, including Buddhists and Hindus, and they often visit the area of the mountain for spiritual reasons even if they don't climb to the summit.

If you want to climb Mount Everest, you're going to spend some money. The permit alone from the government of Nepal costs $11,000 per person. You also have to pay fees to have rescue personnel at the ready, for insurance in order to have your body removed if you fall and die, and for hiring a guide or Sherpa, who is a mountaineering expert, especially in the area of Mount Everest. You will spend two months or more at Base Camp, which is at an elevation of 17,600 feet, and is where you will acclimate to the height of the mountain before going further. During that time, you will have to pay for phone access, garbage removal, meals, and even weather forecasts. Then there's the gear, which can run approximately $10,000 per person. On average, the cost to reach the summit of Mount Everest runs approximately $65,000 per person.

The energy at Mount Everest is a connection to the Divine. It is pure, crisp, and can clear your mind so you can focus on your spiritual essence and your own link to the divine. The energy here moves in a circular motion around the mountain from the bottom to the top. Just as the mountain gains in height each year, this energy can lift you up and revitalize you as a spiritual being. It insists that you look within, that you listen to your own higher self and your spiritual voice. Accessing the energy of Mount Everest can help you to attain wonders within your own life while remaining grounded and centered within your spiritual self.

23. MOUNT FUJI—JAPAN

Categories: Earth Chakras (Third Eye), Mountains/Mounds/Cliff Locations, Pilgrimage Sites, Power Places, Volcanoes/Volcano Cones

Mount Fuji, also called Fujisan, is located in central Honshu, in both Shizuoka and Yamanashi Prefectures, near the Pacific Ocean coastline about sixty miles southwest of Tokyo in the Fuji-Hakone-Izu National Park. Typically, volcanoes are not privately owned, however, this is not the case with Mount Fuji. It has been privately owned since 1609 by the Fujisan Hongu Sengentaisha Shrine. It is also surrounded by five lakes.

Mount Fuji is the highest volcano in Japan. Its summit is at 12,388 feet, and there is an extremely large crater at the summit that has eight peaks. It has a conical shape and has two other volcanoes inside of it. The one at the bottom is called Komitake, the one in the middle is called Kofuji, and Mount Fuji is on the top. The older volcanoes at the middle and bottom were active between 10,000 and 100,000 years ago. Approximately 8,000 years ago, large lava flows created an increase in the size of the basaltic edifice, the lava rock cone structure of the volcano. In ancient history, Mount Fuji had explosive eruptions, and during the last 3,000 to 4,500 years, these explosive eruptions happened between lesser eruptions. In the last 2,000 years, most of the eruptions occurred at the summit but there were a lot of flank eruptions that created more than one hundred cones. The last time Mount Fuji erupted was in 1707 when it also produced an 8.4 magnitude earthquake and formed a new crater on the east side of the volcano during its sixteen-day eruption. Mount Fuji is currently classified as restless, meaning there could be an eruption in the future. Japan already has an evacuation plan in place should an eruption occur.

Japan has three holy mountains, which include Mount Fuji, Mount Tate, and Mount Haku. Mount Fuji is especially important to the Shinto religion. Princess Konohanasakuya is the deity of Mount Fuji, according to the Shinto religion. Her symbol is the cherry blossom and she is the symbol of rebirth. There are eight large Shinto shrines and hundreds of small shrines dedicated to her at the base of Mount Fuji. Mount Fuji is believed to bring good luck, so you'll see pictures of Mount Fuji all over Japan. The indigenous Ainu people of Japan and some Buddhist sects also consider it a sacred place.

People regularly make pilgrimages to Mount Fuji and more than 400,000 people climb to the summit every year. The climb to the summit can take between four to eight hours to complete. The majority of the pilgrimages happen in July and August every year when the snow has melted from the peak and the weather is good. Many people walk up the mountain at night in order to see the sunrise from the summit.

The energy at Mount Fuji is brilliant, exciting, and energizing. The energy moves in a column from the center of the volcano and out of the top before arcing far away from the volcano and flowing into the ground around the area of the lakes where it then is absorbed and goes back to the center of the volcano to repeat the action. The energy here feels as if you just received great news, it is happy, harmonious, and joyous. There is also a sense of power rumbling underneath the flow of positivity and the energy here urges you to tap into your own great power and inner light and to let it move through you before erupting into the world for all to see. The energy of Mount Fuji encourages you to share your knowledge and inner self with others because this is a path to spiritual growth.

24. MOUNT KAILASH—TIBET, CHINA

Categories: Bodies of Water/Waterfalls/Springs, earth Chakras (Crown), Mountains/Mounds/Cliff Locations, Pilgrimage Sites, Power Places, Pyramids

Mount Kailash is a four-sided sacred mountain in the Kailas Mountain Range located in both Pulan County and Burang County. Mount Kailash was well known in the ancient world as Mount Meru, the birthplace of the entire world and the way to heaven. It is surrounded by mystery, legends, and a multitude of theories from numerous sources. Some even believe it to be a man-made pyramid that is surrounded by hundreds of smaller pyramids. If that is ever proven to be true, it would rewrite history as we know it. Geologists assure us that it is only a mountain range created at the same time as the Himalayan Mountains, when earth's plates crashed together.

Mount Kailash is internationally known as one of the world's most holiest and spiritual places to many religions including the Buddhist, Hindu, Jain, and Bon. In the Hindu religion, Mount Kailash is the throne of Lord Shiva. To the Jains, it is called Astapada and is where the first Tirthankara, named Rishaba, became liberated. In the Bon religion, it is called Tise and is the sky goddess Sipaimen's throne. To Tibetan Buddhists, Mount Kailash is known as Kang Rimpoche and is where Chakrasamvara lives with his consort, Dorje Phagmo.

People make pilgrimages to Mount Kailash from around the world in order to receive spiritual purification, enlightenment, and levels of higher consciousness from the mountain. This pilgrimage is said to allow you to leave behind the materialistic, egocentricity part of the human condition and move to an understanding that everything and everyone within the Divine is interconnected and that we are all part of the whole fabric of the universe.

Depending on the religion, the route is walked either clockwise or counterclockwise. People take part in the Kailash Parikrama, which is a thirty-two mile walk around the base of Mount Kailash. This pilgrimage is at a high altitude of 14,763 feet, and at one point you have to go through a pass at 19,200 feet, so it is very challenging due to the low oxygen levels at this altitude. It takes three days to complete the route around the mountain but a few more days to actually get to it due to its remote location. There is also a less challenging route that circles Lake Manasarovar, a sacred lake also known as the Lake of Consciousness and Enlightenment, which is near Mount Kailash. Some people will also take a quick dip into this lake to ensure enlightenment even though the water is freezing cold. Some people who walk the Kailash Parikrama will make plans to go to a certain point and then return instead of circling the mountain due to the possibility of altitude sickness or their own physical limitations.

The energy of Mount Kailash is intense, spiritual, and contains surges of power that can be felt all through your own frequency. It is transformative and will take you from being conscious of the issues of your daily life to being hyper aware of the moments you experience. When you access the energy of Mount Kailash, you will only think of putting one foot in front of another, of moving toward your goal one step at a time. Your mind will not wander; you will not be distracted. Mount Kailash's energy makes you appreciate the things you take for granted and encourages you to do small things for others while walking your own path. A little thing to you may be a huge thing for them.

25. MOUNT T'AI SHAN–CHINA

**Categories: Monasteries/Temples, Mountains/Mounds/
Cliff Locations, Power Places**

Mount T'ai, also called T'ai Shan, is located in the central part of the Shandong Province of China in the cities of Tai'an, where the main peak is located, and Jinan. The mountain itself covers almost sixty-two thousand acres and its highest point, called Tianzhu Peak, is at five thousand feet above sea level. Mount T'ai is made up of ancient fault block that has been shattered and that contains crystalline shale, some limestone and granite, all of which are as ancient as the fault block.

This sacred mountain is considered one of the most beautiful locations in China and one of the most significant symbols of ancient Chinese history and of the culture of the Chinese people. For over two thousand years, the sacred mountain was connected with Daoism and was worshipped by the people of China. Mount T'ai was also the place where people held rituals to the spirits who lived on the mountain to ask for protection from natural disasters such as earthquakes and floods, to ask for a good growing season, and to give thanks when the harvesting was completed. They also held festivals of celebration at the mountain.

Mount T'ai has been considered the cradle of the east Asian oriental culture since ancient times and was the site where people held a ceremony called the Fengshan Sacrifice. This ceremony was to worship heaven and earth and was carried out by the current dynasty to ensure its success during ancient times. The offerings to heaven were made at the summit and the offerings to earth were made at the base. This ceremony was held twelve times in recorded history between 206 BC and 725 AD. During one of the ceremonies Emperor Li Longji, who ruled from 712 to 756 AD, carved his address on an entire cliff face in order to show all of his achievements to the gods.

The slopes of Mount T'ai have many religious structures that were constructed over thousands of years. In the main temple on the mountain, the Temple to the God of Taishan, there is a painting made in 1009 AD during the Song Dynasty named *The God of Taishan Making a Journey*, which is considered a Taosist masterpiece. This painting is located in the temple's main sanctuary called Tiankuang Hall and is almost eleven feet wide and 203 feet tall. There are 697 people in the mural, some of them are riding animals and there are detailed images of palaces, bridges, and a forest that the God of Taishan passed through on his journey. The Dai Temple contains more than three hundred ancient stone tablets. There are also several monuments at the summit in the location where Confucius visited. One is a flat stone with the inscription, "Confucius finds the world small" and another is at a platform where Confucius looked at the Chinese kingdom below that says, "The Platform for Viewing Lu Kingdom." Other temples, for example, the Azure Cloud Temple, are used for people to pray for happiness and health while burning incense. There are many more temples you can visit at Mount T'ai.

The energy at Mount T'ai is very open, bright, and spiritual. The energy flow here spirals from the top of the mountain to the base and back up again in an uplifting motion. The energy is warm, loving, and feels as if you've just received a hug. It is happiness and joy surrounded with the lightness of being and feelings of enlightenment. The energy here can help you push aside negativity and strive to bring more positivity, hope, and bliss into your life. You can call on this energy at any time that you're feeling down or overwhelmed.

26. PAGODA FOREST—CHINA

Categories: Burial Sites, Monasteries/Temples

Shaolin Temple, also known as Shaolin Monastery, is located in Dengfeng County in the Henan Province. The temple was founded by Fang Lu-Hao 1,500 years ago. It is located at the base of Shaoshi Mountain, and the Pagoda Forest at Shaolin Temple is located approximately one third of a mile from the temple. It was built in 495 AD as a shelter for a monk from India named Buddhabhadra. The monks of the temple were introduced to Zen Buddhism thirty-two years after the original temple was constructed, when a monk from India named Bodhidharma came to visit and eventually became the first Chinese Zen Buddhist.

In ancient times when a Shaolin monk or abbott passed away he was buried in the ground and a pagoda was built to mark his final resting place. A pagoda forest is a cemetery and the pagodas are the headstones for those buried underneath. The pagoda would be inscribed with information about the monk including his name, his lifetime accomplishments, the contributions he made to society, and anything else about him that was important for others to know after his death. The pagodas were made in a very specific way. The number of tiers always had to be an odd number and there could never be more than seven tiers on the pagoda. Even with the seven tiers it could be no taller than fifty feet high. They were made of either stone or brick and there were a variety of shapes and silhouettes that were popular for the pagodas, including but not limited to octagonal, hexagonal, quadrilateral, conical, parabolic, and cylindrical.[24]

The Pagoda Forest at Shaolin Temple is on three and a half acres and contains 243 pagodas, making it the largest Pagoda Forest in China. The oldest pagoda was built in 791 AD and the most recent was built in 1803 AD. The majority of pagodas are from the Ming Dynasty with the rest being built during the Tang, Song, Yuan, Qing, or Jin Dynasties. The pagodas of Shaolin Temple contain many carvings and inscriptions and every one of them has the exact year of construction engraved into it. There are also some foreign monks who were buried in this Pagoda Forest.

People visit the Shaolin Temple to see the ancient Pagoda Forest but they also visit for another reason as well—kungfu. The Indian monk Bodhidharma created kungfu as an exercise that he could do while he meditated. The other monks followed his lead and soon kungfu was part of the tradition of the Shaolin Temple. Today the monks put

---

24. China Tours, "Pagoda Forest," https://www.chinatours.com/travel-guide/luoyang/pagoda-forest.html.

on kungfu performances at the temple throughout the day beginning at 9:30 a.m. and every hour afterwards until they close. The performance takes thirty minutes, then the performers rest for thirty minutes before repeating the performance. You can also take a Shaolin Kungfu lesson while you're visiting the temple. There are schools and teachers located both inside the temple and in the nearby area.

The energy of the Pagoda Forest at Shaolin Temple is wise, penetrating, and solemn. This energy flows in an upward and outward pattern that encircles the area of the temple in the Pagoda Forest before returning to center, separating, and moving through the pagodas in a side to side motion as many individual streams of energy before combining again as one on the other side before shooting up into the air in a burst of power. There's a deep respect intertwined within the energy here not only for those who have come before but a deep respect for the spiritual self of each and every person on the planet. The energy here will guide you through darkness into the light and will show you patterns within your own spiritual being that can be improved upon so that you can make the most spiritual growth possible. It helps you see others as individuals while understanding that each of us is a powerful part of the whole universal consciousness.

27. PLAIN OF JARS–LAOS

Categories: Megalithic Sites, Rock Formations

The Plain of Jars is located in the Xieng Khouang plain of Phonsavan, in the Xiangkhouang Province, in the northern part of Laos in Asia.

There are a lot of mysteries, legends, and theories surrounding the Plain of Jars since their discovery in the 1930s. The jars are megalithic stones with the center carved out so they look like an enormous jar. There are over three thousand of these giant stone jars spread out across the plains. Archaeologists have dated the jars to between 500 BC and 500 AD. Each jar can be up to ten feet tall, although most are shorter, and weigh several tons. Some of them are made of sandstone while others are made of granite.

The jars are surrounded by local legends. According to one legend, thousands of years ago the king of a race of giants needed somewhere to store his rice wine for an upcoming feast to celebrate his military victories, so the jars were made and filled with wine. People also believe they were made to capture monsoon water.

All of the jars have rims so archaeologists believe that they had lids made out of rattan, wood, or stone sometime in the past. Some stone pieces found at the site look like lids. Archaeologists also believe they may have been created by Indian tribes traveling through the area and used as funerary urns to bury their dead inside. They think the bodies of the dead were placed inside the jar and a lid was placed on it so that the person could distill, or decompose and dry up, so that their remains could then be cremated. Allowing the body to distill has been a common practice in Laos and Thailand history, although using a pit is more common than using a giant stone jar. Archaeologists believe that once the distilling process was complete the body would be burned. It is not clear what would happen at this point since there is some discussion that the ashes were returned to the jar while others believe they would bury the ashes in a sacred area so the jar could be used again to distill someone else's remains. Archaeologists proved this theory because they found some bits of bone, pieces of metal including bronze and iron tools, shells, glass beads, and bracelets inside some of the jars. In 1994, archaeologists also found an image of a human carved into one of the stone jars at the bottom section that was buried in dirt. Close to this jar and about a foot underground, they also found seven flat stones, which served as a lid to a pit underneath. Of the seven pits, six of them contained human bones and teeth. There are sixty fields of jars found to date.

The Plain of Jars is an extremely dangerous place due to the fact there are many unexploded bombs and landmines left in the area from times of war. If you plan on visiting, it is imperative that you stay within the marked areas and not deviate from them for any reason whatsoever.

The energy at the plain of jars is cautious, inquisitive, and has a sense of renewal. The energy here moves in short quick bursts. It seems to bounce around from one place to another. The energy here urges you to be inquisitive and to learn more than what you see in front of you. It means to dig deeper, to uncover secrets, and to make decisions based on your discoveries. The energy here can be transformative, be enlightening, and can renew you by releasing fear which can hold you back from attaining what you truly desire.

28. SOCOTRA ISLAND—REPUBLIC OF YEMEN

Category: Islands/Reefs

Socotra, also spelled Sokotra, is located in the Indian Ocean off of the Horn of Africa. It is an archipelago of four islands. The islands of Socotra are in Southwest Asia, in the Republic of Yemen, and in the province of Aden. Socotra is the largest island of over two hundred islands that are part of Yemen's territory. The island does have a commercial airport.

The environment on Socotra Island is unique and one third of the plants and trees found on the island cannot be found anywhere else on earth. Some of these species of plants are twenty million years old. Socotra has approximately eight hundred rare species of plant and animal life on the island.[25] The island tends to be very hot and dry but they do have their share of monsoons. Some of the well-known plants that grow on Socotra are frankincense, myrrh, the bottle tree, which is also known as the Socotra desert rose and grows nowhere else in the world, and the dragon's blood tree.

This species of dragon's blood tree called *dracaena cinnabari* is only found on the island of Socotra. It should not be confused with other trees of the same name. It is an evergreen tree that has a bright red resin. On Socotra Island, it is found in the Dragon's Blood Forest where it grows in very rocky conditions, typically in granite and limestone. It has an umbrella shape, and some of them look like an umbrella turned inside out, which helps it get moisture from the atmosphere especially during monsoon season. It has become specifically adapted at capturing and transferring the water to its roots. Dragon's blood tree resin has been used for medicinal purposes for thousands of years; even the Romans used it during the first century. It has also been used as varnish. The locals will feed its berries to their livestock in very small amounts, which helps them maintain excellent health, however, eating it in excess will cause illness. The tree is considered vulnerable by the IUCN Red List Threatened Species at this time because of human use and a drier climate at Socotra Island, which is also causing some of the younger trees to not develop the umbrella shape that is typical of the species.[26]

---

25. Abu Taleb Group, "Animals & Species," http://www.atg-world.com/index%2017.7.11/soc/animals.html.

26. Crampton, Linda, "The Strange Dragon Blood Tree of Socotra Island," March 24, 2018, https://owlcation.com/stem/The-Dragon-Blood-Tree-of-Socotra-Island-Dracaena-cinnabari.

There are 180 species of birds on Socotra Island, six of which are endemic to the island. There are 190 species of butterflies, 600 species of insects, and 22 species of reptiles, 19 of which are endemic to the island. The only mammals native to the island are bats and civil cats. Goats, donkeys, and camels have been brought to the island by the people who live here.

The energy at Socotra is hot, dry, yet breezy. It moves from the ocean over the island and then circles around and comes over the island again in the same direction. At times, the energy will switch directions causing a change in flow. Accessing the energy of Socotra Island can give you a direct connection to the Divine and universal consciousness. The energy here is spiritual, calm, and is deeply connected to the earth and water, both of which increase the power of this energy. The frequency here is connected to surviving, to being a survivor, and to accessing the inner part of yourself where the survivor lives in you. It urges you not to forget that you must take care of yourself before you can take care of others.

29. TAKTSANG PALPHUG MONASTERY–PARO, BHUTAN, HIMALAYAS

Categories: Caves, Monasteries/Temples, Mountains/Mounds/Cliff Locations

Taktsang Palphug Monastery, also known as Paro Taktsang and as the Tiger's Nest Temple, is located on the side of a cliff approximately 950 feet above sea level in the upper Paro Valley, on the southern slopes of the Himalayas. During most of its history, Bhutan has never been conquered or occupied by another country. It consistently ranks as one of the happiest countries in the world and as the happiest country in Asia. The Paro Valley is considered the heart of the country and its only airport is located in this valley.

Taktsang Palphug Monastery is a Buddhist temple complex and the most famous destination in Bhutan. It was built in 1692 at a cave. The monastery is in such a remote and isolated location; it is built on the side of a cliff and the only way it can be reached is by following a mountain pathway to the cliff. In 1998, the monastery burned down completely because emergency crews were unable to get to it, and so it was subsequently rebuilt. The monastery also had to be rebuilt after a fire in 1951 for the same reason. The trail to the monastery has three stages. The first two stages are often completed on horseback, with stage two being steeper than stage one. The horses are only allowed to go to the end of stage two because stage three is a long set of stairs that first leads to a bridge and then up to the monastery. Along the trail to the monastery, you will also see gifts left by Buddhist devotees including prayer flags hung on lines and groups of mini stupas, which are made out of clay and small enough to fit in the palm of your hand and placed in large groups at specific spots along the way or sometimes even sitting alone in a niche of rock

Once you finally reach the actual monastery, you will have to leave all cameras and cell phones at the entrance. The monastery is very serious about this, as they absolutely do not want any pictures taken of the interior of the monastery. To make sure this doesn't happen, you will have to go through a metal detector before entering. Any cameras found will be confiscated and returned to you when you leave.

The monastery has four temples and a few homes for the monks. Between each building are steps carved out of the cliff to connect them to each other. Almost every building has a balcony that overlooks the valley below. They also have a prayer wheel that they rotate every morning at four o'clock to indicate the start of the day. There is also a large tiger statue carved into the rock. According to legend, Guru Rinpoche transformed into one of his eight manifestations called Dorje Drolo and his consort changed into a tigress. They flew to the cave to defeat a demon named Singye Samdrup. After the demon was defeated, Guru Rinpoche meditated in the cave for three months and then they built the monastery on the site.

The energy at Taksang Palphug Monastery is gracious, grounded, and unique. There is a sense of discipline and order connected to this energy as well as being courageous, creative, and independent. The energy urges you to take time for yourself, to explore your own spirituality, and to seek knowledge you may not have known you needed in order to become all that you are as a spiritual being. This energy means you don't conform to the expectations everyone else has of you. Instead, you walk your own path, you believe in your own truths, and you have no problem letting others know what that truth is. The energy here indicates you are an old soul who can see through lies to the truth of the matter, and, once you see the truth, you have the grace, acceptance, and ability to handle the situation in a way that enables you to help the person who feels like they need to tell lies instead of telling the truth, while being true to your own core beliefs.

30. THE AJANTA CAVES—INDIA

Categories: Caves, Monasteries/Temples, Mountains/Mounds/Cliff Locations

The Ajanta Caves are located in Lenapur Village in Soyagon Taluka, in the Aurangabad District and the Maharashtra State. The entrance to these rock-cut caves are at a cliff section of rock shaped like a horseshoe overlooking the Waghora River.

Archaeologists believe the caves were occupied during the second and first centuries BC and that the Buddhist monuments were added approximately six hundred years later. The people who made these monuments abandoned the caves and they lay untouched, except by wildlife, for over 1,400 years. The site was discovered by Jon Smith in 1819 while hunting a tiger. There are thirty caves within the Ajanta cave system, each showing work that can be dated to various time frames and are reflective of both the Mahayana and Theravada Buddhist traditions.

The Ajanta caves are considered one of the most beautiful places in India. The inside of the caves are up to 250 feet tall. Indian art paintings that are considered masterpieces are painted on the walls throughout the caves. Some of the artwork has eroded from the walls over time, so when archaeologists first started working there, these paintings were re-created on canvas. Archaeologists believe that the paintings and intricate carvings were done by Buddhist monks who stayed in the caves during the monsoon season, when they were not supposed to travel, and were used as prayer halls and as a monastery. To keep themselves busy, they painted and carved. Before they actually painted the walls, they prepared them with a base construction of earth mixed with grit and sand, some vegetable fibers, grass, and other organic fibrous materials. They then applied another coat of mud and earth mixed with finely ground rocks and sand in an organic fibrous material. They washed these two layers with a coat of lime before they actually began their paintings. Glue was used as a binding agent in the paint.

The monks also built Buddhist stupas and places of worship, created pillars with detailed carvings, and made sculptures to enhance the look of the cave in alignment with the Buddhist beliefs. Many of the carvings were done in such a way as to imitate wooden construction even though they were made out of stone. While some of the paintings are of important figures in the Buddhist religion, others depict scenes that portray everyday life.

Of the thirty caves at the site, five of them are halls that hold the stupa monuments and are also called chaityagrihas. The remaining caves are called vhiharas and were used as residences where the monks lived. Archaeologists believe that the caves were made during two specific times in history, the Satavahana period and the Vakataka period, based on the styles of sculpture and other information found within the caves.

The energy at the Ajanta caves is firm and solid and yet vivacious and bright. The energy is filled with passion, determination, and high levels of creativity. This energy flows gently and softly and meanders throughout the caves similar to a stream flowing around rock. Accessing the energy of the Ajanta caves can help you boost your own levels of creativity, can keep you firmly grounded in the present, and encourages you to be bold, persistent, and vivacious in all that you do.

31. THE DEAD SEA—JORDAN/ISRAEL/ WEST BANK, SOUTHWESTERN ASIA

Category: Bodies of Water/Waterfalls/Springs

The Dead Sea is located between the countries of Jordan, who owns the eastern shore, and Israel, who owns the southern half of the western shore, and the Israeli occupied West Bank, who owns the northern half of the western shore in Southwestern Asia. The Dead Sea receives almost all of its water from the River Jordan that flows in from the north, but water does not flow out. The Dead Sea is well known for its significance in Judaism and Christianity and among other religions.

The Dead Sea is actually a hypersaline lake that is over three million years old and not a sea at all. It has the distinction of being the lowest body of water on land. Its current elevation is 1,385 feet below sea level. At one point, the Dead Sea was fifty miles long and eleven miles wide but the water level has been dropping because the water flow of the River Jordan was diverted in order to be used in the cities and for commercial activity in the area. In the past, the shape of the bottom was similar to a typical swimming pool in that the northern basin was much deeper, around 1,300 feet, and the southern basin was very shallow at only about ten feet deep. In recent history, with the reduction in the water levels of the Dead Sea, there is now a strip of land visibly separating the northern basin from the southern basin.

The Dead Sea received its name due to the high salt content of the water, which means the only things that can live in it are some forms of bacteria. This includes the shoreline as well. The only plants able to grow along the shore are ones who prefer alkaline and salty soil. The salt content is also the reason that people who bathe in the Dead Sea do not sink.

According to the Bible, King David sought refuge at the Dead Sea and Herod the Great used it as a health resort in ancient times. Minerals and salts from the Dead Sea have been used for a wide range of things for thousands of years. The Egyptians used it in their mummification process, it has been used for fertilizer, and it is also been used to improve health in the form of baths or spa treatments. The one thing you cannot do is eat the salt from the Dead Sea. People travel to the Dead Sea to soak in its salty water to cure what ails them, including conditions like dandruff, hives, cellulite, psoriasis, acne, and dry skin. It is also helpful for muscle aches and pains.

The energy at the Dead Sea is rejuvenating, healing, and buoyant. It encourages you to dig deep within yourself and examine your emotions, beliefs, and inner truths to better understand yourself. The energy here is cleansing and purifying both on a physical and spiritual level. It can help you cleanse your aura, add protection for your spiritual being, and transform anything that you feel you need to change within yourself or about your personality. You can call on the energy of the Dead Sea any time you feel that you are transitioning from one level to another on your spiritual path or during times of change. The energy here will make transitions easier and will open your mind to new possibilities.

32. THE LAKE OF HEAVEN—TIBET, CHINA
**Categories: Bodies of Water/Waterfalls/Springs, Mountains/
Mounds/Cliff Locations, Volcanoes/Volcano Cones**

The Lake of Heaven, also known as Sky Lake, Cheonji, Heaven Lake, and several other names, depending on the language used when referring to it, is located on the northeast border between China and North Korea and fills up the caldera at the summit of Paektu Mountain, which is part of both the Changbai Mountain Range and the Baekdudaegan Mountain Range. The Lake of Heaven's water comes from precipitation, may also possibly be spring fed, and is covered in ice in the winter.

Paektu Mountain is an ancient and very large stratovolcano that is also known by the names Changbaishan or Baitoushan. Its last eruption happened between 949 and 989 AD. It was the largest and most explosive eruption that has occurred in the world over the past ten thousand years and it is known by volcanic experts as the Baitoushan eruption. China has fourteen active volcanoes and this one is considered the most dangerous of them all. It is currently classified as restless, which means there is a possibility of eruption sometime over the next few decades.

The Lake of Heaven is surrounded by mystery and people say some type of ancient monster lives in the lake. The lake monster is called the Lake Tianchi Monster and it was first sighted in 1903 and again in 2007. Other legends say there are dragons, unidentified monsters, and beasts that live underneath the frigid waters of the lake.

According to Korean legend, a mean dragon blocked the water routes and dried up the land. A man named Baekjangsu ("white warrior") was helped by a princess to become the mightiest warrior in the world, and together, they defeated the dragon. Using the restored water, they created the crater lake on top of Mount Baekdu and called it Cheonji. A flood made the lake overflow and everyone died except a mother and her son, who was born after the death of his father. The mother died of starvation and the great-granddaughter of Yeogwassi came to earth from heaven and carved out a stone needle from the mountain and used it to sew Cheonji so that the lake would be contained, which brought peace to the world. The granddaughter stayed on earth and married the son, and soon the people came back to live around the mountain. There are several versions of this legend in both North Korea and China and variations depend upon the religion affiliated with the story. Another legend about the lake is that is believed to be the birthplace of Tangun, who was the founder of the Korean nation.

The people of the area believe the volcano, including the Lake of Heaven, is a sacred place that gives life and provides sacred medicine that will cure people. They believe the lake brings luck to those who visit it and it is customary for those who are in love to throw coins into the deep waters of the lake as a token of their undying love for one another.

The energy of the Lake of Heaven is pristine, pure, refreshing, and inspirational. The sheer beauty of the crystal clear water feels like a direct connection not only to the high-frequency that surrounds the summit of this volcano but also to its deep, power-ful, and primeval energy. Connecting with this energy will benefit you in two ways—it will ground you to the earth so you benefit from its powerful energy, but it will also inspire you to do great things. With your feet firmly balanced on a strong foundation, you can reach out with purity of heart to make a difference, one that only you can make, to refresh and revitalize the world around you.

33. THE SOMAPURA MAHAVIHARA–BANGLADESH
Categories: Monasteries/Temples, Relic Sites, Ruins/Archeological Sites

Somapura Mahavihara, also known as the Great Monastery and the Ruins of the Buddhist Vihara at Paharpur, is located in the Naogaon Subdivision of the Rajshahi District in Paharpur, in the northwest region of Bangladesh. It is one of the most well known Buddhist monasteries from the Pala period in ancient Bengal and Magadha and one of the largest in the Indian subcontinent. Archeologists discovered a clay seal within the monastery that said it was built by the King of Varendri-Magadha named Dharmapala Vikramshila who ruled between 770 and 810 AD. The monastery remained an important religious center for the Buddhist religion until the twelfth century.

According to historians and researchers, the Somapura Mahavihara monastery was so famous between the ninth and twelfth centuries that many Buddhist monks from other countries, especially Tibet, would journey to the monastery and often stayed for many years. This was the case for the famous eleventh century Tibetan Buddhist scholar, Atish Dipanka Srijnan who lived there for twelve years before returning to India. There are three religions represented at Somapura Mahavihara—Buddhism, Hinduism, and Jainism—and deities from all three are found in carvings, structures, and artwork throughout the ruins.

The site is situated on twenty-seven acres. The monastery itself is a 920-foot-square quadrangle with 177 cells in the outer walls. It is built in a cruciform shape and has two enormous terraced courtyards surrounding the main structure and a massive stupa at its top that sits upon a central brick shaft. The main shrine is in the middle of the courtyard and the highly structured, elaborate, and fortified main entrance faces north. The monastery contains four main chapels, which are surrounded by a walking path so you could travel between the chapels, the kitchen, and dining hall. Archaeologists discovered over sixty stone sculptures that represent the deities from the Hindu religion at the base of the shrine. During its peak, the Sompura Mahavihara worked together with four other monasteries, called the five great mahaviharas, to exist together and coordinate their events.

The Somapura Mahavihara was eventually abandoned during the twelfth century after being attacked repeatedly and nearly burned to the ground. Even though it was repaired, interest in the monastery began to dwindle when the area came under the rule of Muslim practicing leaders. Over time, the Somapura Mahavihara became completely covered with grass and lay forgotten and decaying. In the 1920s the site began to be excavated by archeologists and today is a protected UNESCO World Heritage Site. There is a small museum at the ruins that displays relics recovered from the site. Some of these are statues of gods and goddesses, some made of stone, and some of clay, other clay objects, coins, pottery, ornamental bricks, terracotta plaques, and various inscriptions.

The energy at Somapura Mahavihara is peaceful, quiet, and somewhat lonely. It feels warm, still, and otherworldly. The energy here moves in a wave over the monastery and you will feel it as a breeze moving through you, not just over you. Connecting to this energy will help you during times of spiritual growth by giving you the focused inner reflection needed to accurately analyze how you feel, what your beliefs are, and how you want to move forward on your path. This is especially helpful during trying times, as the quiet peacefulness of this energy will help to settle you and allow your mind to focus.

34. YAZILIKAYA—TURKEY
Categories: Fertility Sites, Rock Formations, Ruins/Archeological Sites

Yazilikaya, also known as the Hittite Rock Sanctuary of Yazilikaya, is located in Turkey, which is located in both Asia (95 percent) and Europe (5 percent). Yazilikaya is located in the Asia section of Turkey almost a mile north of the ruins of Hattuša, the capital of the Hittite Empire between 3300 and 1200 BC, which is known as the Bronze Age. Hattuša is located near the modern day city of Boğazkale.

The Hittite Rock Sanctuary of Yazilikaya is an open-air sanctuary located in an area of a natural spring. This spring has long since run dry, but the rock formations will be here for many years to come. The term *yazilikaya* means "inscribed rock," and the village was named Yazilikaya because of a rock inscribed with a reference to Mida, which was incorrectly translated as Midas. Some researchers believe it refers to the famed King Midas who turned everything he touched into gold, while others believe it is a reference to the surname of the Phrygian mother goddess named Cybele, who was said to be the mother of the gods. There is an area of rock at Yazilikaya that is thought to be the tomb of King Midas or a sanctuary dedicated to the goddess Cybele because there is a niche where a statue of the goddess would have been placed during a religious ceremony.[27]

Archeologists discovered that the village was first settled in the eighth century BC by the Phrygians, who were really Thracian Brygians that had crossed Hellespont and then moved into Anatolia where they decided to live, and often refer to the Yazilikaya as the Midas Monument or the City of Midas (Midas Kenti). They believe that the Hittite Rock Sanctuary was a place of prayer for the Hittites, where they would come to worship their gods through prayer.

The rock formations at Yazilikaya are huge and have many rock-cut reliefs and chambers. The ruins contain an inscription of the Phrygian alphabet, an acropolis where one could view the city, and a necropolis to the south where the dead were buried in rock-cut tombs. There is an open-air sanctuary with two large alcoves that show the gods and goddesses in a parade with all of the gods on one side and the goddesses on the other side of a center open aisle so that both can be seen as a person walks through the area. There is concern that erosion is wearing away at the relief sculptures quite quickly, even though they are made of stone, and that the site should be covered in some way, although this would be quite the undertaking, to save these ancient sculptures.

The energy at Yazilikaya is hot, intense, and feels as if it's moving around you in quick strides. At times, it also feels cool and distant as if it's standing back and waiting for you to make a decision. The energy here is connected to fertility, generosity, and abundance. There is a sense of community associated with the energy of Yazilikaya, of coming together for a common cause, and of joining with others to accomplish a goal. This energy will be beneficial to you whenever you have to work with someone else to achieve a specific goal or when you're part of a team. This energy will bring rewards to you after you've worked hard to attain your goals.

---

27. Epifanes, Horus Neo Ikon, "In Hittite Lands: Yazilikaya and Alaca Hoyuk," August 20, 2012, http://unchartedruins.blogspot.com/2012/08/in-hittite-lands-yazilikaya-and-alaca.html.

35. YUNGANG CAVE SHRINES—CHINA

**Categories: Caves, Monasteries/Temples, Mountains/Mounds/
Cliff Locations, Relic Sites, Shrines/Birth or Burial Sites of Saints**

The Yungang Cave Shrines, also known as the Yungang Grottoes, are located in the northern Shanxi Province about ten miles west of the city of Datong in the People's Republic of China at the base of the Wuzhou Shan Mountain Range in the Shi Li River Valley. The Yungang Grottoes occupy a space about one half of a mile long and between thirty to sixty feet high, and are carved into a ridge of soft sandstone. At the top of the cliff, where the caves were cut out, there is a fort built during the Ming Dynasty.

Between 446 and 452 AD the followers of Buddhism were often persecuted. In order to appease the gods of the religion and to make amends of the violent actions taken against the Buddhists by the previous emperor, named Emperor Wencheng, who reigned over the Northern Wei Dynasty, the people chose this location to create a phenomenal complex of caves to honor the Buddhists and their religion. Some researchers believe that a monk named Tan Yao may have been the person who had the grottoes built with the help of forty thousand Buddhists.

The Yungang Grottoes consists of 53 major caves, 1,100 minor caves, and 51,000 niches, with each niche containing a statue of Buddha. The grottoes vary in purpose, some serve as chapels and others contain enormous carvings of Buddha that are up to fifty-five feet tall and there are also tiny statues of Buddha that are only a few inches tall.[28] The walls of the caves are painted and still retain their vibrant colors after all of the time that has passed since their creation. Some of the images depict figures playing musical instruments, others are wearing crowns and dancing. There are carvings of Buddha that are calm, joyful, and peaceful and others where Buddha looks like a fierce warrior. The interior of the caves are artistic with intricately carved detail.

In the past people have cut out pieces of the cave to take home with them, invading forces cut off the heads of some of the Buddha statues, and erosion has caused further damage to the paintings and carvings. Sandstorms have affected the grottoes due to deforestation in the area and some of the stone began to crack. In an effort to restore and protect the site, the cracks were filled with grout and trees were planted to reduce the erosive effects of the sandstorms. At this time only forty-five of the caves are open

---

28. Hays, Jeffrey, "SHANXI PROVINCE (Datong, Yungang Grottoes, Pingyao)," 2009, http://
factsanddetails.com/china/cat15/sub103/item447.html.

to the public in order to help preserve the site and its temple relics, which are an ancient tribute to the history, culture, oriental sculpture art, and architecture of Eastern cultures and the Chinese people.

The energy at the Yungang Cave Shrines is joyful, engaging, and wondrous. The energy flows at a steady pace within and throughout the caves before lifting upwards over the top of the cliff and then moving slowly back around on its path. Connecting to the energy here will fill you with purpose, with the ability to remain focused and steady within yourself, while experiencing the joy and happiness of the past and living in the present. This energy urges you not to let go of your own past but to appreciate the people, emotions, and situations you've experienced in your life with positivity while opening yourself up to the incredible opportunities that are waiting for you and the joy that these new experiences will bring into your life.

Chapter 6
AUSTRALIA, THE PACIFIC ISLANDS, AND OCEANIA

Australia is filled with amazing places that formed millions of years ago and have a tremendous amount of earth frequency today. There are places like Uluru (Ayers Rock), an island rock that extends three and a half miles into the earth, the Bungle Bungles, which were created by sand formations beginning 360 million years ago, and Kata Tjuta (the Olgas), which archeologists believe were formed by sand and stone deposits that were compressed 500 million years ago when the area was covered by a shallow sea. What we see today in these locations is a result of millions of years of change and erosion.

Other places in the Pacific Islands and Oceania that are interesting and filled with earth's frequency are the Great Barrier Reef off the Australian coastline, Huka Falls in New Zealand, Nan Madol in Micronesia, and the Cook Islands in Oceania. In Palau, Oceania, there is Jellyfish Lake where you can actually swim with the jellyfish. The region of Australia, the Pacific Islands, and Oceania is a wonderful and exciting place to explore and search for energy connections that helps us raise our own frequency and become more in tune with the higher self within us all. Our souls are as ancient as the earth and these locations will enable us to reach the spiritual part of ourselves that always exists throughout time.

Map key

1. Alofa'aga Blowholes (Taga Blowholes)—Palauli, Samoa
2. Ayers Rock (Uluru)—Northern Territory, Australia
3. Bagana Volcano—Papua New Guinea, Bougainville Autonomous Region
4. Bridal Veil Falls—New Zealand
5. Bungle Bungles—The Kimberley, Australia
6. Cape Tribulation—Queensland, Australia
7. Carnarvon Gorge—Queensland, Australia
8. Cook Islands—Oceania
9. Devils Marbles—Northern Territory, Australia
10. Fraser Island—Queensland, Australia
11. Freycinet Peninsula—Tasmania, Australia
12. Gabarnmung Rock Shelter—Northern Territory, Australia
13. Goanna Headland—New South Wales, Australia
14. Gondwana Rainforests—Queensland/New South Wales, Australia
15. Great Barrier Reef—Queensland, Australia
16. Great Ocean Road—Victoria, Australia
17. Ha'amonga 'a Maui —Tonga, Oceania
18. Huka Falls—New Zealand
19. Jellyfish Lake (Ongeim'l Tketau)—Palau, Oceania
20. Kata Tjuta (The Olgas)—Northern Territory, Australia
21. Lake Mungo—New South Wales, Australia
22. Mount Wollumbin—New South Wales, Australia
23. Nakauvadra Standing Stones and Narara Caves—Fiji
24. Nan Madol—Micronesia
25. Nourlangie Rock—Northern Territory, Australia
26. One Tree Hill—New Zealand
27. Ra'iatea—Society Islands, Oceania
28. Rotorua—New Zealand
29. The Blue Mountains and Lilianfels (Three Sisters and Echo Point Lookout)—New South Wales, Australia
30. The Pinnacles—Western Australia
31. The Tiwi Islands: Bathurst and Melville—Northern Territory, Australia
32. Ubirr—Northern Territory, Australia
33. Wairakei Terraces—New Zealand
34. Walpole-Nornalup—Western Australia
35. Wet Tropics of Queensland—Queensland, Australia
36. Wilpena Pound—Outback, South Australia

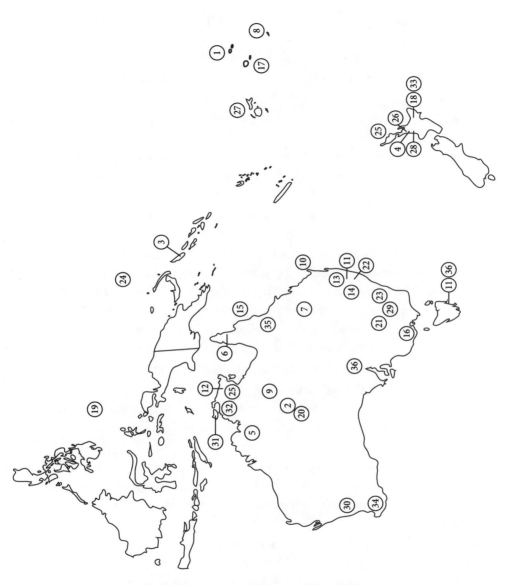

Map of Australia, the Pacific Islands, and Oceania

1. ALOFA'AGA BLOWHOLES (TAGA BLOWHOLES)— PALAULI, SAMOA

Categories: Caves, Geysers/Blowholes, Islands/Reefs

Located in the Pacific Ocean and on the southwest coast of the island Savai'i, are the Alofa'aga Blowholes, also known as the Taga Blowholes (because they are near the village of Taga), which are some of the most powerful and impressive blowholes in the world.

When the Samoa Islands were formed, lava flow also created underwater sea caves. Over time, tunnels formed from cracks in the lava, which eventually became tubes or tunnels with one end that opened to the land above or into caverns that are above sea level. When the ocean waves break against the seaward side of the tunnels, the water is projected through the tunnel and erupts out of the other end onto land. The Alofa'aga blowholes can spout sixty-five to ninety-eight feet into the air due to the strength of the ocean as it pushes the water through the tunnels and straight up with a powerful force.

On the Samoan Islands, it is customary for the land to be owned by communities of indigenous people, who are then charged with taking care of that land. The people in Taga administer the land where the blowholes are located, so prior to visiting you'd pay an entrance fee in the village of Taga. If you also pay a local person, they will place a coconut into the hole before the water erupts, the coconut will go even higher than one hundred feet, which is a sight many visitors enjoy seeing. If you watch the coconut closely, you'll see the force of the water is so strong it will cause it to disintegrate before your eyes. The best time to visit to see the largest and highest bursts of water is during high tide.

A short distance from the Taga Blowholes is the Pa Sopo'ia Cave, which also has blowholes. Legend has it that the spirits of deceased Samoans would travel on their way to Cape Mulinu'u, which was the last gathering place of souls before entering Pulotu, the spiritual realm.

The energy at the Taga blowholes is dynamic, majestic, and vibrant. The sheer force of the energy required to propel the water through these blowholes and into the air will fill you with a sense of wonder, awe, and happiness. As you walk along the black lava rock around the blowholes, you can't help but feel a connection to the ancientness of the earth. When the water surges through the holes into the air, the wind turns a lot of it into a mist that sprays across the lava stone. Imagine this mist washing over you, feel the power of the ocean and water as it shoots high into the sky, and allow its power to move through you, helping you to embrace your own inner power while releasing any negativity you've been holding inside your spiritual essence. Not only are the Alofa'aga Blowholes an amazing spectacle of nature to watch, but the energy of this place can have incredibly astounding results within you at a spiritual level.

2. AYERS ROCK (ULURU)– NORTHERN TERRITORY, AUSTRALIA

Categories: Earth Chakras (Solar Plexus), Power Places, Rock Formations

Located in the Northern Territory of Australia within the Uluru-Kata Tjuta National Park is a large magnetic mound called Uluru, which is its true Anangu Aboriginal name, but it is also known as Ayers Rock. A surveyor named William Gosse, to honor Henry Ayers, who was the Chief Secretary of South Australia in 1873, named it Ayers Rock. In 1993 it was renamed Ayers Rock/Uluru, but in 2002 the names were reversed.

For years, the Anangu Aboriginal people placed a sign at the bottom of Uluru that simply said, "please don't climb." While the government has allowed climbing, Uluru will be off-limits to climbers beginning in October 2019. This decision was made because climbing the rock violated the wishes of the Anangu Aboriginal people who own the rock, and for whom it is a sacred spiritual site and climbing it is considered very disrespectful. People who removed rocks from Uluru as keepsakes of their visit often return them along with letters about tragic events that happened to them. People say the rocks they removed from the sacred site are cursed and the ranger's office has received a package of returned rocks nearly every day since 1970. So if you visit, only take memories and pictures home with you.

Uluru is a sandstone inselberg (island mountain) formation that geologists believe is the top portion of an enormous rock that extends deep into the earth, possibly as far down as three and a half miles. Uluru was originally created by sand that blew there from the south and west as part of an alluvial fan, which is a deposit of sand, silt, and gravel created by flowing water from higher elevations such as mountains. Normally Uluru is a dark dusty red, due to oxidation, but when the sun hits the arkosic sandstone, which has reflective properties, it appears to glow bright red, orange, or purple (the colors depend upon the time of the year) at sunrise and sunset.

Approximately ten thousand years ago, the first aboriginal settlers arrived at Uluru. They believe that Uluru was created by their ancestors at the beginning of time, which they refer to as Dreamtime. They believe that they can call upon the spirits of their ancestors to request blessings or to communicate with them simply by touching the rock. The route to the summit is also the route that their ancestors traveled during the creation of Uluru. It has a plethora of shallow caves at the base where the aboriginal ancestors created wall art with water-based paints. These paintings are delicate in nature. Several aboriginal tribes still live in the area and continue the practice of painting on the walls of the caves for their sacred rituals. They often paint over the old paintings with new ones. The history and importance of Uluru is still passed on to the younger generations through song and during ceremonies that initiate the youth into adulthood.

The energy at Uluru is transformative and healing. There is a feeling of universal oneness, grounding, and freedom within the soul. The frequency is light and vibrates rapidly but yet it has a depth within which represents the earth connection. Sitting near Uluru, taking in its beauty and uniqueness, you'll feel overwhelmed by a sense of wonder, love, and being as timeless as the massive stone before you. Embracing the energy of Uluru will allow you to let go of negativity and pain and to experience both personal and spiritual growth that you will carry with you throughout your life.

3. BAGANA VOLCANO—PAPUA NEW GUINEA, BOUGAINVILLE AUTONOMOUS REGION

Categories: Islands/Reefs, Volcanoes/Volcano Cones

Located between the southwestern Pacific Ocean and the Solomon Sea is Bougainville Island, which, along with several island groups including Buka Island, form the Autonomous Region of Bougainville. Bougainville is the largest of the Solomon Island chain and is home to seven volcanoes that were active in the past ten thousand years. It is also home to Benua, one of the world's largest caves and two other volcanoes—Balbi, which is considered dormant but did show some activity in the 1980s, and Billy Mitchell, which last erupted around 1580 AD.

The majority of Bougainville is a thick, heavy jungle. Bagana volcano is located almost in the center of the island within the jungle. Geologists classify it as a lava cone because it is made of accumulated lava flow. The lava is typed as viscous andesitic, which tends to be more blocky than other types of lava. Bagana is one of the youngest volcanoes on the island but it has proven to be the most active. In 1842, Bagana erupted for the first time and has erupted many times since then. Geologists believe that the current height and width of Bagana could have built up over the past three hundred years based on the amount of lava that it currently produces in a year. Since 1972, it has been in "near-continuous activity" according to Volcano Discovery, who tracks volcanic activity. About half of the time, it has major explosive eruptions that produce huge ash clouds and pyroclastic lava flows, which means that the lava moves down the volcano very quickly. The rest of the time it has non-explosive eruptions where lava flows slowly and steadily from the volcano, which builds up the size of the lava cone as it makes its way toward the ground.

If you're up to a challenge, it would take you about a week to hike to all three volcanoes if you make your base camp at the village of Wakunai. However, this is a very strenuous hike and you should be in very good physical shape if you're considering this adventure. If this trek is too difficult for you, there are other hiking trails outside of the towns. It's recommended that you take a local guide with you on any hiking expeditions. If hiking isn't your idea of fun, you can visit some of the other islands that are close by, swim in the clear water with white beaches, relax in the sun, go snorkeling, diving, bird watching, or learn about the culture of the island. Just be aware that there are saltwater crocodiles in the area.

The energy at Bagana volcano is pure, strong, and in constant movement with occasional bursts of even higher frequency (like what happens during a volcanic eruption). It vibrates at a high frequency that feels deep and churning, hot and quick-moving, but also steady and powerful. Think about your emotional status at this time. Are you holding onto negative feelings about people or situations until you erupt? Volcanoes are often symbolic of looking deep inside to understand yourself better. Sometimes you might experience the destruction of the old in order to create something new, just as a lava flow destroys everything in its path yet volcanoes create islands where there was once only water. Connecting to the energy of Bagana will enable you to experience transformation, renewal, cleansing, and growth.

4. BRIDAL VEIL FALLS—NEW ZEALAND

**Categories: Bodies of Water/Waterfalls/Springs,
Mountains/Mounds/Cliff Locations**

Located in the South Pacific on the northern island of New Zealand in the Waikato Region and between the beachside town of Raglan and the town of Te Uku is Bridal Veil Falls, also known as Govett's Leap, which is called Waireinga by the Maori people who live in New Zealand. The Maori name means "water of the underworld" or "leaping waters," depending on the translation. This fits because the water appears to leap from the edge of the cliff out into the air before plummeting into the amphitheater-shaped pool below. Someone who thought it resembled a bride's wedding veil gave the name Bridal Veil Falls to this beautiful waterfall.

Bridal Veil Falls is approximately one hundred and eighty feet high. The rock at the top of the waterfall is basalt, which formed from volcanic lava from a volcano that is about a mile away. The water comes from the Pokoka River, which flows through the 540 acres of the Waireinga Scenic Reserve, where the forests are primarily made up of the Beilschmiedia tawa, a common New Zealand tree with broad leaves, and various species of rata, which are flowering vines with different types and colors of blooms. The vines themselves can be very thick and ropelike. The Waireinga Scenic Reserve also has a number of orchid species.

To view Bridal Veil Falls, you'll park your vehicle in the lot on Kawhia Road and walk about ten minutes to reach the top of the waterfall. At the top, there are two viewing platforms where you can see the falls from above. The top viewing platforms are also accessible by wheelchairs—or strollers if you're taking young children to see the falls. There are also steps leading down to the bottom of the falls with another viewing platform about halfway down and a fourth platform at the bottom. It will take you about fifteen minutes to walk down to the base of the falls, more if you stop to take photographs at the middle viewing platform. It's also a good spot to rest a bit before continuing to the ground level viewing platform. The steps are steep so you may decide to only go halfway and then head back up.

Swimming is prohibited because of the poor water quality within the pool at the bottom of the falls, which makes it unsafe for swimmers. There is also an enormous boulder under the water in the center of the pool that can't be seen from the surface.

Rock climbing is also prohibited due to the presence of an endangered spider orchid that could be damaged by rock climbing.

The energy at Bridal Veil Falls is buoyant, light, and moves at a high frequency, just as the water that plummets from the cliff and free falls to the earth below. It is serene and connects you to a quiet calmness within you. If you've been feeling stressed or emotionally overwhelmed within your daily life, encountering this energy will quiet your mind and allow you to feel more settled and secure within your own spiritual essence. This high frequency can elevate your own energy, lifting you up to feel a deeper spiritual connection to the Divine. The energy here encourages you to let go of the things that are holding you down so that you can rise above negativity and embrace the positives in your life with the unique strength of the spiritual energy within you.

5. BUNGLE BUNGLES—THE KIMBERLEY, AUSTRALIA
**Categories: Burial Sites, Petroglyph/Rock Art Sites,
Power Places, Rock Formations**

The Bungle Bungles are located in the northwestern part of Australia, in the eastern section of the Kimberly region, and in the remote area of the Purnululu National Park. Aboriginal people have inhabited the area for more than forty thousand years, but the Bungle Bungles were only "discovered" by a documentary film group flying overhead in 1983. They promoted its existence in the media, and in 1987, the area was established as a national park to protect the Bungle Bungles.

What makes the Bungle Bungles so unique is the fact that they look like massive beehives spreading out across the land. They are orange- and black-striped domes made of sandstone that are over 984 feet tall. Starting about 360 million years ago, sand was deposited by rivers that flowed through the area. Winds caused the formation of sand dunes. Gravel was also deposited in the area as the mountain ranges eroded. The two compacted together until it was almost four and a half miles deep. Sixty million years ago, the rocks under the earth lifted and tilted, which raised the deposits to a higher elevation. The Bungle Bungles range is what remains of those deposits after millions of years of erosion. The dark bands contain a type of blue-green algae, which provides a protective coating, and the orange bands contain iron oxide that coats the sandstone, which makes it look rusty.[29]

---

29. UNESCO, Purnululu National Park, https://whc.unesco.org/en/list/1094.

The quickest way to reach the Bungle Bungles is to take a helicopter flight from Kununurra for a day trip. The views as you fly toward the site, and the site itself, are amazing from the air. There are also land tours that will guide you through these unique and inspiring geographical structures. Two-wheel drive vehicles are not permitted in the park, so if you're driving you must have four-wheel drive. The drive is sixty-two miles of paved road then another thirty-three miles along a dirt road. The drive itself can take three or more hours because the roads are steep climbs with sharp corners and you'll have to drive very slowly. Once you arrive at the site you can explore the area on foot. There are also hidden gorges, caves, and long narrow crevasse's to explore between the domed structures.

To get the most out of the experience, it is suggested to book a tour with an Aboriginal guide who will tell you stories of their culture and can show you some of the ancient burial sites and rock art located within the Bungle Bungles.

The energy of the Bungle Bungles is vibrant, strong, energizing, and inspiring. Connecting to this energy will help you recharge your spiritual self, raise your frequency, and inspire you to greater creativity. It enables you to see deeper inside yourself, to see your true spiritual colors, and to allow your light to shine, just as the color of the Bungle Bungles adds depth of character to the area. You will connect to the truth of your own character while visiting this sacred site and find the strength to make any changes you desire in your own life.

6. CAPE TRIBULATION—QUEENSLAND, AUSTRALIA

Categories: Rainforests, Regions

Cape Tribulation is located in northern Queensland in the Shire of Douglas of Daintree National Park in the Wet Tropics World Heritage area. Lieutenant James Cook named the area Cape Tribulation after he ran his ship into the Endeavor Reef and he believed it was where all of his troubles began.

Cape Tribulation is famous for its beautiful scenery, tropical climate, the Daintree National Park rainforest, and its remote beaches. The valley looks like a huge amphitheater enclosed by Mount Sorrow and Mount Hemmant. There are three main areas of Cape Tribulation to visit: the beautiful white sandy beaches, the intriguing rainforest, and the Great Barrier Reef.

The main beach is on the northern side of the Cape Tribulation headland. The area is slightly offshore and is excellent for snorkeling—or from the beach, you might choose to take a boat out to investigate the Great Barrier Reef or a sea kayak to explore the coastline or the nearby islands.

If you enjoy hiking, you'll enjoy a day in the rainforest. You could choose a guided tour to learn about the over forty-thousand-year-old indigenous culture, take a short walk on your own, or take a Daintree River cruise to view the native crocodiles. There are also private property tours where you can see local flora and fauna that you might have missed on your own. In some areas, you can walk out of the rainforest right onto the beach. There are a lot of shells and driftwood to enjoy. There are also opportunities to go horseback riding on the beach or trail riding through the rainforest.

The Great Barrier Reef is considered one of the original eight wonders of the world. It was the first coral reef to obtain world heritage status, is enormous (about the same size as either Germany or Japan), and is over 1,400 miles long. It can easily be accessed from a number of places in and around Daintree. If you go diving or snorkeling at the reef, you'll find a plethora of different species of fish, sharks, rays, whales, and both hard and soft coral. The Great Barrier Reef is home to one fourth of the world's sea-grass species and one third of the world's coral species. The current reef is believed to be about 8,000 years old, but scientists believe it was created on multiple layers of algae and coral that are over 500,000 years old.

The energy in the Cape Tribulation area is three-fold. At the beach, you'll feel the warmth of the sun, the movement of the wind, and settled and relaxed. The energy here is light and airy, moves at a high frequency, and is especially good for meditation and feeling connected to your inner essence. The energy of the rainforest feels tranquil, cool, and has a depth that connects you to the primal essence of the earth. Its calmness is soothing and helps you to work though emotions, make decisions, and feel an overall sense of peace within yourself. The Great Barrier Reef has a deep, pulsing frequency that is attuned to the ancientness of the universe and the earth. Covering this frequency is a smooth back and forth fluidity of energy. It is brilliant in color, reflecting the individual energies of the animal and plant life beneath the water, and connects you to a higher level of spiritual enlightenment.

7. CARNARVON GORGE–QUEENSLAND, AUSTRALIA

Categories: Canyons/Gorges, Caves, Mountains/
Mounds/Cliff Locations, Regions

Carnarvon Gorge is in central Queensland and in the Sandstone Wilderness of Carnarvon National Park in the Southern Brigalow Belt bioregion. It is between the towns of Emerald and Roma. The Carnarvon Gorge is usually inaccessible during the rainy season due to the rapidly rising waters of Carnarvon Creek that make it impossible to travel the roads. Even during the dry season, a four-wheel drive vehicle is necessary because Carnarvon Creek is always flowing due to rain from the mountains and cliffs that moves down into the gorge.

The area is made of sandstone with high, white cliffs forming the steep walls of the gorge. Boulders are found throughout the gorge and Carnarvon Creek meanders around them. Carnarvon Gorge is home to a wide variety of animals, including many bird species, possums, bush stone-curlews, turtles, frogs, and platypus to name a few.

Scientists believe that the Bidjara and the Karingbal Aboriginal people have lived in this area for 19,500 years with evidence of humans being in the gorge for approximately 3,650 years. Archeologists believe that the Aboriginal people didn't live in the gorge but visited it for short periods of time. There are many Dreamtime stories of these Aboriginal people that explained the creation of humans, the earth, and the plant and animal life. One of these stories explains how the gorge was created. Before creation of the Carnarvon Gorge, the people lived on flat land. As a rainbow serpent named Goorialla appeared and moved across the flat land, his body made mountains and gorges, including Carnarvon Gorge, and the water made rivers, which gave an abundance of life to the earth. Since there are many different Aboriginal tribes throughout Australia, each one has a slightly different version of this creation story.

All along the rocks throughout Carnarvon National Park, specifically in Baloon Cave, Kookaburra Cave, Cathedral Cave, and along the Maranoa River, is the ancient artwork created by the people. One side branch of the gorge is home to the Art Gallery Site, an enormous sandstone wall that contains over two thousand different examples of ochre stencil art, engravings, and freehand paintings of people's feet, animal tracks, axes, boomerangs, shields, nets, and hands. The hand stencils are fascinating because you can see where one person lost half of their pinky, another had a broken middle finger, and some appear to be of older people with arthritis while others are young looking, thin, and appear strong. The hands themselves give an instant look into the lives of these people simply based on their shape. Scientists believe that this artwork also represents some of the religious ceremonies held by these ancient people, and that they were created to store educational information, to show emotional events, and to tell of times of mourning.

The energy in Carnarvon Gorge moves in a spiraling yet straight motion around the upper edges of the gorge all of the way down to the land and creek below. It flows steadily, in a left to right motion. From the top it vibrates at a light, fast moving frequency that is connected with universal consciousness and at the bottom it vibrates at a slower rate but one that is just as powerful because it's connected to the earth's energy. As these two energies move and blend together, you get a tremendous energy that is very powerful, stable, and creative. Connecting to this energy on a spiritual level is extremely beneficial in all areas of your life. It can help you become more resourceful, more balanced, have clearer sight for your future, and allows you to see and plan your future path in harmony with your spiritual self.

8. COOK ISLANDS—OCEANIA

Categories: Caves, Islands/Reefs

Located midway between New Zealand and Hawaii are fifteen islands in the center of the Pacific Ocean known as the Cook Islands. The main islands to visit consist of Rarotonga, Aitutaki, Atiu, and the Outer Islands. You can arrive at the Cook Islands by airplane or by boat. The islands were named by the Russians in honor of Captain James Cook who sighted the islands in 1773. While the weather in the Cook Islands is warm and sunny year-round, the drier months are from April to November and the more humid months are from December to March.

Aitutaki is the island most people visit even though it's not the largest of the Cook Islands. The draw of Aitutaki is that it is promoted as a romantic, relaxing, and secluded island of incredible beauty. It's all of those things and more. Water activities are a highlight of visiting Aitutaki. You can take a day cruise or charter a boat, swim, or go snorkeling at any of the three other islands surrounding Aitutaki Lagoon with One Foot Island being a must see.

Atiu is the third largest island and is eight million years old. This island is home to many birds; it has dense rain forests and a cave system that can be explored through cave tours. You can go fishing in the lagoon or take a day trip from the island to go deep-sea fishing. There are many diving opportunities as well.

Rarotonga is considered the hub of the Cook Islands because it is the largest island of the group. It is unique in that the coral reef that circles the island is a bright orange color, which contrasts with the brilliant blue of the water and the white sandy beaches. There are many activities to enjoy and things to see. Some people say the whole island is like one huge resort. Scuba diving and snorkeling are popular activities and so is hiking in the mountainous areas or visiting the night market where you can buy a delicious dinner.

The Outer Islands consist of six islands in the southern group and six islands in the northern group, including Mangaia, the oldest of all of the Cook Islands, which is believed to be eighteen million years old. All of these islands are accessible by boat and a few are accessible by local flights. These outer islands are undeveloped and are purposely kept as close as possible to their natural state. Some of the islands are known for the massive amounts of wild flowers that fill the island, others are known for their subterranean limestone pools within caves, and still others have mountains and underground caverns and many of the outer islands have amazingly beautiful lagoons. One of the islands, Suwarrow, is typically uninhabited by people. Between April and November each year, caretakers stay on the island because yachts may stop by while making their way across the South Pacific Ocean. This is primarily done for the protection of the animal and plant life, not as an amenity for the visitors.

Regardless of which of the Cook Islands you decide to visit, the energy that surrounds and flows through all of these tropical islands is one of vibrancy, joy, and positivity. The energy moves and flows around you like the waves and the wind. It moves through you, lifting you up to higher levels of consciousness and helping you release negativity. The water greatly amplifies the rejuvenating effects of the powerful, sacred energy that lives within the area of the Cook Islands.

9. DEVILS MARBLES—NORTHERN TERRITORY, AUSTRALIA
Categories: Power Places, Rock Formations

The Devils Marbles Conservation Reserve is between Alice Springs and Katherine off of the Stuart Highway, which goes through the middle of the reserve. You'll see the two most famous Devils Marbles, also called Karlu Karlu by the Warumungu Aboriginals, from your car. These two are sitting one atop the other and look as if they may fall at any given moment. To truly appreciate the beauty of the place, stop for a moment and get out of your car to take in the phenomenal view of the multitude of Devils Marbles that fill the area. You might even enjoy spending a night under the stars in the campground so you can experience the energy of the marbles at sunset and sunrise when the sun's light makes the stones look like they are glowing and changing colors. It's a truly wondrous experience. While there aren't guided tours of the Devils Marbles, there are clearly worn paths where visitors have walked among the structures.

The Devils Marbles are enormous granite boulders that are spread across the area. The marbles started out 1,700 million years ago when molten magma was deposited beneath sandstone and, as it cooled, formed granite. Over time this giant slab of granite cracked both horizontally and vertically and eroded, which smoothed down the edges, making them a variety of shapes, some of which are completely round. Due to the way the erosion occurred, the rounded boulders sit on top of other boulders. Some of the base boulders are larger than the top ones but others sit on top of small bases, which make them look as if they'll topple off at any moment.

Most of the Devils Marble Conservation Reserve is protected as a sacred site under the Northern Territory Aboriginal Sacred Sites Act, due to the spiritual importance of the area to several of the Aboriginal tribes who live there. This area also has many Dreamtime stories associated with it, many of which are not shared with people outside of the tribes. Here's one that is shared by the Alyawarre people about how the marbles were made:

While traveling through the area, an ancient Aboriginal ancestor named Arrange the Devil Man stopped to make an adornment worn only by initiated Aboriginal men called a hair-string belt. While twisting the hair to make the strings for the belt, he dropped clumps of hair on the ground. This hair turned into the red boulders that populate the land. Arrange returned home to a hill named Ayleparrarntenhe where he still lives today. On the way home he spat on the ground which created more boulders across the valley. Ayleparrarntenhe is the Aboriginal name for this area and for the hill with two peaks on the eastern side of the reserve, where Arrange is believed to live today.

The energy at Devils Marbles vibrates at a medium fast rate and is pure, electric, and ancient. Just as the boulders balance one upon the other in precarious positions, the energy here can help you find balance within your life. It centers you, makes you dig deeper into yourself to find areas that are out of balance, and then guides you to equilibrium within yourself. As you walk through this magnificent and powerful area, you'll feel changes within your body as you connect with the energy. You may feel a bit heavy and grounded to the earth or you may also feel a profound sense of peace. Even in the heat of the day you may feel chills or get goosebumps on your arms as you feel the oneness of your spiritual self and the fluidity of being one with universal consciousness in this sacred site.

10. FRASER ISLAND–QUEENSLAND, AUSTRALIA
Categories: Islands/Reefs, Rainforests, Sandhills/Sand Dunes

Fraser Island, also known as K'gari, is located off of the coast about 186 miles north of Brisbane and adjacent to Hervey Bay. Fraser Island has the distinction of being the largest sand island in the world. It is seventy-seven miles long and at the widest point it is thirteen miles across. Fraser Island is over 800,000 years old and the Butchulla people have lived on the island for approximately 20,000 years. The island has a distinct smell of sand, sea, and eucalyptus trees, which are overly abundant on the island. The center of Fraser Island contains what is left of an ancient tall rainforest atop high sand dunes. You can also find rainbow-colored sand, which was created through erosion.

Watch out for dingoes during your explorations. There are twenty-five to thirty packs of dingoes that live on Fraser Island, with each pack containing approximately twelve dingoes. The wildlife service urges visitors not to feed the dingoes or their pups because they need to remain wild animals and not become dependent on humans for food. Some of the other animals on the island that you might see are wallabies, turtles, snakes, possums (including flying possums), echidnas, and over 325 species of birds.

The best way to view Fraser Island is with a four-wheel drive vehicle but still stay to the hardened routes so you don't get stuck. The 75 Mile Beach on Fraser Island is a nationally registered highway, even though it's made out of sand.

There are many things to do on Fraser Island. You can rent cabins during your stay but don't leave garbage outside because the dingoes will prowl around at night. Each year many humpback whales go to Fraser Island to calve out and to rest. Viewing them from the beach is an exciting spectacle as you experience the energy of the mothers and their young. When you're out exploring during the day you'll want to visit the sand dunes at Waddy Point, go beach fishing, and explore the Maheno Shipwreck, which happened in 1935 when a cyclone off Fraser Coast caused the ship to wreck into the island.

The beach is gorgeous and you'll want to get your toes wet, but be aware that sharks are often sighted around Fraser Island and surfing or swimming in the ocean isn't permitted because of them—and due to the strong undertow and dangerous, unpredictable, water conditions—so it's better to connect to the ocean's energy from the beach instead. You can also choose to swim in one of the one hundred inland freshwater lakes, float down Eli Creek, or swim in the champagne pools to feel the energy of the water on the island. While camping is allowed on most of the beach unless otherwise posted, you can't have open campfires unless you're at one of the communal fire rings located at the Dundubara and Waddy Point campgrounds.[30]

Walking in this beautiful setting is a given. There are several tracks you can explore; some are short and take less than ten minutes to complete, or if you have several days, you can take the Forest Lakes Hiking Trail, which will take you three to five days to walk. The Queensland Parks and Wildlife Service has this trail set up so you can either walk the entire track straight through or you can be picked up and returned to set points along the trail in order to walk shorter distances over more days.

The energy of Fraser Island is exciting, adventurous, and vibrant. It gets you moving, elevates your mood, and ignites your own energy. It moves at a high frequency and an escalating motion, slipping around you and lifting you up in joy and delight. It moves like the wind, caressing with gentle guidance, and in gale force when you're not paying attention to your path in order to get you back where you're supposed to be. Connecting with the energy of Fraser Island will keep you motivated, inspired, and on track.

11. FREYCINET PENINSULA–TASMANIA, AUSTRALIA
Categories: Islands/Reefs, Mountains/Mounds/Cliff Locations, Regions
Freycinet Peninsula is located on the east coast of Tasmania off of the Great Eastern Drive north of Schouten Island. It is part of the Freycinet National Park, Tasmania's oldest national park, and takes up a majority of the park's land. The Pydairrerme people, who are also known as the Aboriginal Oyster Bay Tribe, have lived in the

---

30. Just Because, Top Ten Things to do on Fraser Island, November 6, 2017, https://www.youtube.com/watch?v=CmV-S77pPrU.

Freycinet Peninsula for more than thirty thousand years. The park is known for the beautiful pink granite mountains, white sandy beaches, and crystal blue waters. In fact, the Hazards, and the Mount Graham and Mount Freycinet sections of the peninsula are just giant blocks of granite connected by a sand isthmus.

There is a wide variety of things to do at Freycineet Peninsula and in the Freycinet National Park. You may enjoy bird watching, beach strolls, swimming, watching wildlife, taking a flight over the park, or simply sitting back and relaxing while taking in the natural beauty all around you. If you enjoy hiking, you can hike up into the Hazards to the lookout point for breathtaking views of the world famous curved beach of Wineglass Bay, which consistently ranks as one of the world's best beaches. The hike will take about forty-five to ninety minutes (depending on your walking speed) from the car park to the lookout and another twenty-minute walk down to Wineglass Bay along a steep descent. There are other hiking options available as well. You can walk seven miles from Wineglass Bay to Hazards Beach, which takes you across the park at the isthmus, or if you're feeling adventurous, there is a four-day guided walk from one end of the Freycinet Peninsula to the other that goes through remote places like Bryans Beach and Cooks Beach. Depending on the tour you select, you could walk up to ten miles each day. Spend the time during your hike taking in and communing with nature and the energy flowing all around you in this pristine setting. At Wineglass Bay, you can view many different types of wildlife, including penguins, seals, whales, and dolphins.

If you're a food connoisseur, then the Freycinet Peninsula will feed your appetite. It is internationally known for its fresh seafood like scallops, freshly shucked oysters, and crayfish—its grass-fed beef, game meats, and wide variety of produce and fruits.

Campers will enjoy the various campgrounds throughout the Freycinet National Park. One that is a favorite is the small campground at the end of the beach in Wineglass Bay. It is popular with newlywed couples and those who want the experience of waking up in this gorgeous location.

The energy at Wineglass Bay is powerful, pristine, and clear, even though it had a sordid past in the 1800s when whalers used the bay and made the water turn red from the whale's blood, thus the name, Wineglass Bay. The frequency is high but the energy doesn't move around a lot. It is instead settled and grounded around the bay. It feels magical and wondrous and will fill you with a sense of awe. It enables you to look beyond the difficulties of the past and into the future with hope. The energy throughout the rest of the Freycinet Peninsula and the national park is active and moves in a strong undulating motion from one end to the other and back again. This energy is motivating, energizing, and captivating. It helps you see the small things in nature and will help you see the things you're taking for granted in your life. Once seen, they can be appreciated.

12. GABARNMUNG ROCK SHELTER– NORTHERN TERRITORY, AUSTRALIA

Categories: Mythological Sites, Petroglyph/Rock Art Sites

Located in Jawoyn Country in the southwestern Arnhem Land of Australia's Northern Territory is the Gabarnmung Rock Shelter, also known as Nawarla Gabarnmang, which is owned by the Aboriginal Jawoyn clan Buyhmi, who are direct descendants of the people who lived in the area and created the ancient artwork for which the site is known. Gabarnmung Rock Shelter contains the oldest Aboriginal rock art in Australia and the Oceanic Art zone. Carbon dating placed the charcoal drawing's creation at approximately 26,000 BC and the bottom layers of the site have been carbon dated at 48,000 years old. Archaeologists also found the world's oldest stone axe at the Garbarnmung Rock Shelter.

The shelter itself is composed of an enormous slab of rock supported by thirty-six sandstone columns, many of which were created through natural erosion of water in the area. Humans, to make it into a comfortable living area, purposefully altered it. It is a very large space with interconnected caverns, which provided a balance between the space, air flow, and insulation from the outside elements for the ancient people.[31]

There are thousands of ancient paintings on the ceiling of the rock slab and down the sandstone columns. Because of the age of the drawings, many are superimposed upon one another. These drawings primarily used ochre or a mulberry pigment. They show things the Jawoyn people would have experienced as part of their daily life like barramundi, turtles, crocodiles, lizards, kangaroos, wallabies, and snakes. Some of the animal drawings show the internal organs of the animal and are referred to as an x-ray drawing. Other drawings show the sacred rituals of the people including spiritual deities from their creation mythology. Many of the people in the drawings are wearing

---

31. Numerous Authors, The Archaeology of Rock Art in Western Arnhem Land, Australia, http://press-files.anu.edu.au/downloads/press/n3991/html/ch10.xhtml.

headdresses, have long limbs, and are drawn in a way that make them look elegant, graceful, and refined.

The Jawoyn people used the Garbarnmung Rock Shelter as a living space, which is evident by the purposeful enlargement of the living area by removing stones. Archeologists were able to prove this by moving some of the rocks back to their original location. It is a monument to the Jawoyn people as a cultural structure with beautiful artistry. Garbarnmung Rock Shelter was a central place for the people to participate in religious ceremonies, to socialize with one another, and to create artistry that lasted for thousands of years, much longer than they ever imagined possible when they drew the pictures.

The energy of the Gabarnmung Rock Shelter is one of peaceful contentment. There is a sense of well-being within this area. It feels vibrant, happy, and as if the spirits of the ancient people still move about the space. Connecting to the energy here will help you find peace within your home life, will give you an appreciation of the simpler things in life, and encourage you to find the beauty in everyday situations. This energy will help you become more creative, will open your mind to new possibilities, and help you see situations from a new perspective.

13. GOANNA HEADLAND—NEW SOUTH WALES, AUSTRALIA
Categories: Caves, Ceremonial Sites, Mountains/Mounds/Cliff Locations, Mythological Sites, UFO/Extraterrestrial/Paranormal Sites

Goanna Headland is located in the Bundjalung National Park, in the northeast part of New South Wales along the Coral Sea, which is also part of the south Pacific Ocean. The town of Evans Head, known to the locals as Hevans Head, is also part of the Goanna Headland, and it is one of the most easterly points of Australia. A goanna is one of several species of monitor lizards in Australia.

For thousands of years, the Goanna Headland has been considered a sacred place for the Aboriginal Bundjalung Nation, who called it the Dirawong. According to their Dreamtime creation mythology, the Dirawong is the Creator Being that appeared in the form of a goanna and taught the Bundjalung people their traditions, customs, and culture. Another story about the Goanna Headland is that back during the time of creation, a wise Bundjalung man named Nimbin asked a goanna to stop Rainbow Snake from harassing a bird. The goanna chased the snake to Evans Head and bit it on the tail.

The snake bit the goanna on the head and then it had to retreat and recover. The snake started to return the way it came and created Snake Island before it realized the goanna was back. The snake escaped out to sea and disguised itself as an island while the goanna laid down to wait on the shore for it to return. Goanna Headland is the body of the goanna. Its head is to the north near the Red Hill coast with its right front foot formed by the rocks to the south of Red Hill beach. Snapper Rock forms its tail and Chinaman's beach forms the right side of its chest and belly. Because of the massacre of hundreds of Bundjalung people by Europeans in the 1840s, they believe that their ghosts wander the headland and that you can hear them screaming if you walk the beach at dusk.

There are two caves on the headland that are important sacred sites for the Bundajalung people. The first is Rain Cave, where the tribal elders would go to sing for rain. Only elders are allowed in the cave and it is said that if anyone other than an elder enters the cave, there would be massive flooding. The second is Snake Cave, which is at the cliffs at sea level. At this cave you can hear the goanna thump his tail and the snake hiss in response whenever the wind is strong and the ocean waves high. The Bundajalung people believe that this place is still filled with the power of the Dreamtime because so many rock fishing accidents happen near the cave.

To date archeologists have discovered twenty-four archeological sites south of Evans Head Village on the Goanna Headland. There are many secret, sacred, and ceremonial sites throughout Goanna Headland, some of which are still used today by the Bundjalung people who are the official custodians of the land.

Stunning views abound in this quiet and peaceful environment. You can walk along the coastline, swim, surf, go snorkeling, fishing, crabbing, or take a boat or canoe trip down the Evans River. You might enjoy visiting one of the four national parks in the area or go out to sea for the day to do some deep-sea fishing.

The energy at Goanna Headland is deep and powerful yet energizing and calm. Connecting to this energy will enable you to expand your intuitive abilities, especially your abilities as an empath or medium, clairvoyance, and clairaudience. The energy can also feel unsettling because there is a stillness here that makes you want to look over your shoulder even though it feels peaceful and calm. It can help you tune into the subtle nuances both within yourself and the energy of the place to gain clarity about yourself and your beliefs. If you've never experienced a paranormal event before, you might just have your first one while connecting with the energy of Goanna Headland.

14. GONDWANA RAINFORESTS–
QUEENSLAND/NEW SOUTH WALES, AUSTRALIA

Categories: Rainforests, Volcanoes/Volcano Cones

The Gondwana Rainforests are located in southeast Queensland and northeast New South Wales, Australia, and have gone through several name changes over the years. The Gondwana Rainforests are along Australia's Great Escarpment on the east coast. The Great Escarpment wasn't simply formed by erosion, which was a factor, but was primarily created due to global tectonics, continental rifting, and earth lifting.

In history, Gondwana was a supercontinent that split apart approximately 180 million years ago. This continent was filled with rainforests during the Jurassic period and the Gondwana Rainforests that are in Australia today are what are left from this ancient time. Within the Gondwana Rainforests, there are four volcanic shield craters with the Tweed Shield caldera being the most preserved caldera in the world. It is home to almost all of the Antarctic Beech cool temperate rainforest, which contains a specific species of beech trees, and has only one dense canopy layer, unlike tropical rainforests that have several canopy layers, and if it's not raining, there is often mist in the air.

The Gondwana Rainforests are home to many species of plants and animals that are considered rare or threatened and that represent various stages in the earth's development. These plants and animals have changed very little since ancient times. For example, there are ferns, conifers and other primitive plants that are directly connected to events from one hundred million years ago when flowering species began. Many of the flora and fauna are separated into specific locations within the rainforest, which is a type of natural isolation that encourages the evolution of new species. Australia's rainforests contain half of all plant species and about a third of the mammal and bird species in the country.

There are four national parks within the Gondwana Rainforests—Mount Barney, Lamington, Springbrook, and the Main Range, which makes it easy for people to visit this phenomenal specimen of nature at its finest. The different areas of the rainforest can be warm, subtropical, cool, or dry. All of these parks offer camping and extended walks that take you by some of the more well-known sites.

The energy of the Gondwana Rainforests moves in a slow rhythm that is in tune with its ancient roots. As you walk through any part of the rainforest, you can imagine that you're millions of years in the past, seeing the world as the dinosaurs and ancient people saw it. The energy here is soothing and will quiet your mind. As you pass through, you may feel power spots where the energy is more intense and feel as if you're connected to the ancient power of the volcanoes that erupted here long ago. This power will affect you in a positive way as you embrace the energy and make it part of your inner self. You may begin to think of yourself in a more naturally spiritual way, as part of the whole, as being a timeless, ancient spirit as you walk among life that is ancient itself. The energy here will stay with you, reminding you that it only takes a moment to calm your mind and see yourself back in the rainforest that had such a powerful effect on you.

15. GREAT BARRIER REEF— QUEENSLAND, AUSTRALIA

Category: Islands/Reefs

The Great Barrier Reef, one of the Seven Wonders of the World, is located off of Australia's northeastern coast in the Coral Sea, which is part of the South Pacific Ocean. It begins at Cape York Peninsula in the north and extends to the south to Bundaberg. Because it is so large (1,800 miles), it is divided into the northern, central, and southern sections. It is between nine and ninety-three miles from Australia's coastline. Its sheer size makes it visible from space and is the world's largest living organism with the most biodiversity because it contains over 3,000 individual reef systems plus numerous continental slopes, deep ocean troughs, coral cays, mangrove estuaries, sponge gardens, and continental islands.

Containing over 400 different species of coral gives the Great Barrier Reef the distinction of being home to the world's greatest collection of corals. It is also home to over 2,000 species of fish, numerous species of rays, dolphins, sponges, and over 5,000 species of molluscs including giant clams, oysters, squid, and triton shells that some of the soft-bodied molluscs live inside. It is also home to a large number of sea grasses and over 2,200 native plant species, over 800 echinoderm species, the world's largest population of dugong (which is similar to a manatee/sea cow), six turtle species, and it is a breeding ground for many whale species including the humpback whale.

Between March and November of 2016, as much as one third of the Great Barrier Reef underwent massive amounts of coral bleaching and eventually coral death. Marine biologists are calling it a devastating die-off unlike any that has ever been seen before in the reef. Some of the coral affected were hundreds of years old. The coral loss is blamed on the rising temperatures of the ocean, to which coral is very sensitive. Marine biologists, scientists, and reef managers are now working together to find the best way to try to save the reef systems around the world, including the Great Barrier Reef.

The Great Barrier Reef is one of the most desired destinations in the world. Many people want to see the reef before it completely dies off but others aren't aware that it is in jeopardy. Some tour guides will inform the public that the neon colors of the coral aren't natural but indicate that they are undergoing stress. They educate the public about the reef and things they are doing to help it survive. Some reefs have survived bleaching and have even appeared dead for many years, but then were revived by the arrival of coral larvae from other reef systems. So there is still hope for the Great Barrier Reef. Only time will tell.

The energy here is hopeful, sturdy, and flows in strong waves. It vibrates at a high frequency and is bright, energetic, and alive. There is a sense of renewal, change, and the brilliance of living life to the fullest while you can. It is invigorating and inspiring. Connecting to the energy of the Great Barrier Reef will enable you to know deep within yourself that you can do anything you set out to do if you'll only believe in the infinite possibilities within yourself and that are happening all around you.

16. GREAT OCEAN ROAD—VICTORIA, AUSTRALIA
**Categories: Canyons/Gorges, Mountains/Mounds/
Cliff Locations, Rainforests, Regions**

The Great Ocean Road is located on the southeast coast of Australia between the town of Allansford and the town of Torquay. It is 186 miles long and known for having some of the most incredible scenic coastal views. Traveling the Great Ocean Road is on many people's bucket lists and it is known as one of the best road trips in the world. There are many sites to see along the way so, let's go over a few of the highlights on this phenomenal drive.

In Port Campbell National Park, there are several sights to see. The Twelve Apostles located within this park are considered one of the sites that should never be missed on the Great Ocean Road trip. Twenty million years ago, as the sea eroded the limestone cliffs, large chunks of land were left standing in the ocean, forming the Twelve Apostles. Of the twelve, only eight remain today. The other four eroded so much that they fell into the ocean. The best time to see the Twelve Apostles is at sunrise when the sun's light causes the rock to change color and it seems to glow. You may choose to visit at sunset where the fading light leaves the Twelve Apostles as dark silhouettes against the sky, which is also incredibly beautiful. To get a close-up view of the Twelve Apostles, walk down the Gibson steps to the beach where the Twelve Apostles sit in the ocean while the land that they came from appears like a high wall on the other side of the sandy beach. You'll also want to visit Lock Ard Gorge, which has a pristine beach and glorious views. It is like a little inlet with its own private beach hidden behind walls of stone. Nearby, London Arch, which used to be called London Bridge before the collapse of the area closest to the mainland, still looks like a bridge although you can no longer walk out to the end. Then there's the Grotto, a large sinkhole filled with ocean water. The views from behind the arch covering the sinkhole to the ocean are gorgeous. Further south on the Great Ocean Road, you'll find the Bay of Martyrs and the Bay of Islands, which are similar in structure to the Twelve Apostles.

Otways National Park offers a different type of adventure. This park is within a cool temperate rainforest that has high amounts of rainfall, which keeps the waterfalls within the park in a state of constant flow. Here you can walk on your own or take guided tours among the ancient trees within Beech Forest, along the tops of cliffs, and on the ocean beaches. There are also four different Aboriginal tribes that are represented in this national park where their culture, spirituality, and connection to the earth are still celebrated.

As you tour the Great Ocean Road, you will encounter many types of energy. The energy along the ocean is calming, introspective, and invigorating. The energy in the forested areas is peaceful, deep, and makes you feel part of universal consciousness. In any of these places, you will feel a sense of belonging, of being uplifted, and of a deeper sense of who you are in spirit. Taking the time to stop and become one with these different energies will help you grow on your own spiritual path and realize that you are more than just a physical being.

17. HA'AMONGA 'A MAUI–TONGA, OCEANIA

Categories: Islands/Reefs, Megalithic Sites, Power Places

The Tonga Islands are located in the southern Pacific Ocean in Oceania. There are 176 individual islands that make up the Tonga Islands and only a fourth of them are inhabited. Archeologists believe that Tongatapu was the first island settled on, approximately 1500

BC based on carbon dating done at sites on the island, although the exact year of occupation is uncertain. This island is where the megalithic trilithon called the Ha'amonga 'a Maui is located. These first inhabitants were the Lapita people, a pre-historic culture that pre-dated the Polynesians.

The oral history of the area was passed down through the ages and is now an official recorded history of the area. This history states that around the year 950 AD the Tu'i Tonga Empire was formed and the capital of the empire was located on Tongatapu Island in the village of Toloa. The capital was relocated to the eastern part of the island in the tenth century and was named after the Polynesian god Maui. The Tu'i Tonga (king) named Tu'itatui, who ruled around 1200 AD, built the Ha'amonga 'a Maui as the grand entrance into his royal compound, which was called Heketa. Today the area is known as the Ha'amonga 'a Maui Historic Park and is near the village of Niutoua, which is where the first capital was originally located. There is some discussion among scientists and historians as to whether the trilithon was built in 1200 AD or if it was actually built in an even earlier time in history since it is built in the same manner as other prehistoric trilithons.

The Ha'amonga 'a Maui is a stone gateway with two vertical pillars on either side and a lintel across the top. The lintel sits inside mortises, two vertically carved rectangular spaces that were cut out of the pillar stones. The two pillars honored Tu'itatui's sons and the lintel represented the bonds of their brotherhood and the royal families unity. Legend says that the demigod Maui brought the stones used to build Ha'amonga 'a Maui to the island in a large canoe. He had supernatural powers, which gave him the ability to move stones of that size and weight. Other legends say that it is where the dead chiefs of the villages were cremated.

Each of the three sections are constructed of coral limestone and the visible parts weigh between thirty-three and forty-four tons. Scientists think the stones go down to the bedrock layer of the earth. The stones are porous and have been carved to be relatively flat with straight edges but they don't match exactly in size. A short distance from the trilithon is a tall slab known as the king's throne, which may have been for protection as well. It is where he would sit to deliver his speeches to his people. The stone still has indentations where a person's body would fit if they were sitting against it.

The energy at Ha'amonga 'a Maui feels laid back, restful, and relaxing. You may feel contemplative as you walk around the trilithon, more secure within yourself, as a feeling of peace and well-being surrounds you. This energy is of a high, stable frequency; one that when you're experiencing it will make you feel that all is right within the world and within yourself. It feels like a warm breeze, the mist coming off of the ocean waves, and the high pitched song of a bird in flight. It will inspire you to be true to your beliefs and spiritual purpose.

18. HUKA FALLS—NEW ZEALAND

Category: Bodies of Water/Waterfalls/Springs

Huka Falls is part of the Waikato River, which is the longest river in New Zealand, and is located in the Bay of Plenty region of the North Island, specifically within the Wairakei Tourist Park, which is approximately a ten-minute car drive north of Lake Taupo off of state highway SH5 north.

Huka Falls is called a horizontal waterfall because there is only a thirty-six foot change in elevation from the top to the bottom. The change in the water flow from that of a peaceful river to thundering rapids occurs because of the natural bottlenecking of the riverbanks and a volcanic rock ravine right before the falls, which increases the speed of the water's flow down the thirty-six foot descent known as Huka Falls. The river is normally a little over 326 feet wide, but in the area of the falls it's only forty-nine feet wide. Over 58,000 gallons of water are propelled through Huka Falls every second. The water moves through the falls at such a great speed it looks pale blue and white due to the water reflecting blue light and the air bubbles causing the white foam, especially at the thirty-six foot drop where the water shoots out approximately twenty-six feet into the basin pool.

There are several ways to view Huka Falls. There is a wide concrete walkway called the Spa Park Walk that goes from Taupo to the end of the falls. This walk gives you phenomenal views of the river and the falls. On the side of the falls, there are large viewing areas. If you start in Taupo, expect to spend about two hours walking round-trip if you do the entire circuit. Cycling isn't allowed on this walk so you'll have to rely on your own leg power. There is also a pedestrian bridge across the falls where you can get a close-up, mesmerizing view of the water as it moves beneath you. Once you cross the bridge, there are viewing points on the other side. If you're up for an adventure, you can join a jet boat ride in the section of Waikato River below Huka Falls, where at one point you'll come extremely close to the thundering water in the fall's basin pool. But don't worry, the drivers of the boats don't take you close enough to get pulled into the strong undertow at the base. If that's a little bit too exciting for you, then a leisurely river cruise might be more to your liking. There are bus trips from Taupo to sites including Huka Falls that you can enjoy.

There are two different types of energy to experience at Huka Falls. The first is the tranquil, easy flow in the area of the river before you reach Huka Falls. This energy is deep and vibrates at a strong, slower rate. This type of energy grounds you, brings balance at a spiritual level, and helps you see situations clearly. The other type of energy is found at Huka Falls where the water cascades with force through the narrow volcanic opening. The energy here is powerful and vibrates at a very high frequency. It is spectacular, motivational, and inspirational. It is the kind of energy that encourages you to make changes in your life, gives you the courage to surge forward toward your desires, and enables you to enjoy the success you will achieve when reaching your goals.

19. JELLYFISH LAKE (ONGEIM'L TKETAU)– PALAU, OCEANIA

Categories: Bodies of Water/Waterfalls/Springs, Islands/Reefs

Jellyfish Lake, a marine lake also known as Ongeim'l Tketau, which means fifth lake, is located in Eil Malk within the Rock Islands of Koror. Marine lakes are close to the sea and have a combination of rainwater and seawater, which gets into the lake from tunnels or cracks in the earth. There are three types of marine lakes: holomictic (that are closer to the coast, have direct connections to the ocean, and are where the seawater and rainwater mix), meromictic (stratified lakes further inland with indirect connections to the ocean where the seawater and rainwater don't mix and have anoxic bottoms filled with poisonous hydrogen sulfide), and transitional lakes (shallow lakes that change from holomictic or meromictic, depending on the weather).

Palau has fifty-seven marine lakes, five of which are home to the golden jellyfish, but only one, Jellyfish Lake, is surrounded by mangrove trees and open to the public. It is a meromictic lake made up of three layers. The first layer is mixed and is where the jellyfish live. The second layer is a pink bacterial layer and the third is the poisonous layer without light or oxygen.[32]

---

32. Coral Reef Research Foundation, Types of Marine Lakes, http://coralreefpalau.org/research/marine-lakes/types-of-marine-lakes/.

The jellyfish that live in Jellyfish Lake are a subspecies of the golden jellyfish found in the other lakes on Palau and their entire population of approximately five million is contained within Jellyfish Lake. These jellyfish can't be found anywhere else on the entire planet and are unique in that they have symbiotic algae that live inside their tissues. The algae give the jellyfish nutrients and energy through photosynthesis and the jellyfish swims around the lake so that the algae get enough sunlight for photosynthesis. It's a win-win for both species. Some of the jellyfish also feed on zooplankton in the lake using their stinging cells. If they sting you it's so mild you probably will not even feel it and it's harmless to people. Like most jellyfish they have a medusa and polyp life stage. The polyps live at a depth of about thirty-two feet and the medusas live in the top layers of the lake and are the golden jellyfish that you see swimming around. Every day they migrate around the lake by swimming in a specific pattern that follows the sun. They're always in the sunlit portions of the lake and avoid the shadowed edges where their predator, the sea anemone, lies in wait. They avoid being eaten by staying out of the shadows.

Tourists are allowed to dive in the top portion of jellyfish lake and experience swimming with the millions of jellyfish but there are specific rules that must be followed to avoid contaminating the lake and to protect the jellyfish. You must not create bubbles, wear sunscreen, stir up sediments, never lift a jellyfish out of the water, and never ever dive into the poisonous layer because the hydrogen sulfide will enter through your skin and poison you. You must be clean before going in the water, wear clean fins, move slowly, and be quiet and gentle so as to not disturb the jellyfish.

The energy of Jellyfish Lake is surreal, unique, and ancient. It vibrates at a steady, pulsing rate and flows in a circular motion. It is invigorating, calm, and pure with a hint of danger. After swimming in this lake you will feel grounded and connected to the ancient vibrations of the universe, more alive and unique within your spiritual essence.

20. KATA TJUTA (THE OLGAS)– NORTHERN TERRITORY, AUSTRALIA

Categories: Canyons/Gorges, Power Places, Rock Formations

Located in the Northern Territory of Australia within the Uluru-Kata Tjuta National Park approximately twenty-two miles from Uluru (Ayers Rock) is Kata Tjuta, which is also known as the Olgas. The National Park was named for both Uluru and Kata

Tjuta because they both lie within its borders and are the most prominent monoliths in the park. Kata Tjuta is about sixteen miles from Uluru so both can be visited within the same day if you so choose.

Kata Tjuta is composed of thirty-six different formations. It formed around 500 million years ago by boulders, pebbles, and cobblestone, which together created conglomerate, a course-grained sedimentary rock. During the time of formation, the area was covered by a shallow sea. The sea deposits compressed, and 300 to 400 million years ago during the Alice Springs Orogeny, the land fractured and folded, raising the region. The Kata Tjuta turned between 15 to 20 degrees to their current position. Geologists believe that, like Urulu, Kata Tjuta is also an inselberg, the tip of a gigantic rock that could possibly extend almost four miles into the earth. Mount Olga is the tallest formation and is 3,497 feet above sea level and 656 feet taller than Uluru.

Since Kata Tjuta has eroded into separated formations, there are pathways, some of which are wheelchair accessible, so you can walk through them. The popular and easy Walpa Gorge walk is a little over a mile and a half while the Valley of the Winds walk is a bit more difficult and about four and a half miles. On both of these walks, you'll move between the rock formations and experience breathtaking views, especially at sunrise and sunset when the Olgas seem to change color and glow in the same manner that Uluru does. If you don't want to walk, you can always check out the Olgas from the dune viewpoint where you can park your car and walk a short distance to the viewing area.

Kata Tjuta is also a sacred site for the Anangu Aboriginal people and is prominent in the Dreaming, which is their viewpoint on creation. Kata Tjuta is a site that belongs to the male Anangu (whereas Uluru is known as belonging to the females of the culture), and many of the legends associated with it are only revealed to the aboriginal men. One legend that is well known to everyone is that they believe the giant serpent king named Wanambi, also called the Rainbow serpent and other names, lives on the summit in a large hole filled with water during the rainy season and it moves into the gorge during the dry season, living in the caves found within the rock formations. Other rocks form shapes that the Aboriginal people call the mice women, a kangaroo man, a lizard woman, and the Pungalunga (giant cannibals). Today the Anangu Aboriginal people hold sacred ceremonies at Kata Tjuta but women are not allowed.

The energy at Kata Tjuta is powerful and resonates deep within the earth. As you take in the beauty of the Olgas, you will feel the energy as a deep vibration within the ground that rises up into you through your feet. You may feel as if you want to just stop and observe, to feel this energy flow through you. It is very grounding, which can enable you to become more centered and balanced. There is a deeper resonance to the energy here, which helps you to connect to the ancient parts of your soul, to your higher self, and to grow within your own spirituality. It can be healing and put you back into forward motion, especially if you've been feeling out of sorts or as if your life isn't on the right track.

21. LAKE MUNGO–NEW SOUTH WALES, AUSTRALIA

Categories: Bodies of Water/Waterfalls/Springs, Burial Sites, Footprints

Lake Mungo is located in Mungo National Park, which is in New South Wales in eastern Australia. The park is always open unless there is danger from weather or fire. Lake Mungo is home to both Mungo Man and Mungo Lady. Lake Mungo is part of the Willandra Lakes World Heritage Area, which consists of seventeen lakes which have been dry for the past twenty thousand years. The area has been compared to the surface of the moon due to the wrinkled and grooved ridges in the earth, the pinnacles that rise up into the air, the small waves created by wind in the sand, and the sparse vegetation.

The lake area is protected by three local Aboriginal tribes and the National Parks and Wildlife Service of Australia in order to preserve it. For the Aboriginal people, the land is a significant part of their heritage and culture and there are over 65,000 Aboriginal sites in New South Wales including Lake Mungo. Many of these sites are part of the Dreaming stories and the Dreamtime creation and their cultural activities and ceremonies. Burial sites are considered sacred areas. If you visit Lake Mungo, it is important to know that any archaeological evidence that shifts to the surface must not be touched or disturbed in any way but instead reported to the Aboriginal caretakers or park officials as per New South Wales law.

There have been many archeological finds in and around Lake Mungo that date back to the ancient Willandra people. They found extinct animals such as giant kangaroos that had short faces, Tasmanian tigers, and the zygomaturus, which was an animal similar to an oxen. Numerous discoveries were found that detailed the lives of the people, including but not limited to, fireplaces, stone tools, fire baked sediments, food preparation waste, and most significantly, burial sites.

The discovery of Mungo Lady and Mungo Man changed the history of Australia and what was known about the origin and history of Homo sapiens. Geologist Jim Bowler discovered the first remains in 1968 embedded in a lunette, which is an eroded dune with sedimentary layers. He marked the find and came back the following year with additional archeologists to excavate the site. These remains turned out to be a female, which they named Mungo Lady. She had been cremated, her bones crushed and then burned again, and then buried inside the lunette. Five years later, Bowler discovered more bones, the skeleton known as Mungo Man whose remains have been carbon dated to be at least 42,000 years old. Other analysis determined that he was around fifty years old at his death. He was buried on his back with his hands crossed in his lap and red ochre sprinkled over his body. The way both Mungo Lady and Mungo Man were buried gave a great deal of insight into the culture of the ancient Willandra people.

Archeologists discovered 460 ancient footprints in 2003 embedded in the clay around the lake. They dated to twenty thousand years old and are the oldest ones known in existence anywhere in the world.

The energy of Lake Mungo is cool, dry, and moves with what feels like a wispy breath of wind. It is focused, bright, and deep. Connecting to the energy of Lake Mungo will settle you but also instill in you a sense of awe and a spiritual bond to the ancientness of the area. The strength of the positive energy of Lake Mungo and the people who lived there in the past is humbling and will help you see that time means nothing in the relative scheme of things, which can help you to find balance in your daily life and to set your priorities.

22. MOUNT WOLLUMBIN—NEW SOUTH WALES, AUSTRALIA
**Categories: Mountains/Mounds/Cliff Locations,
Rainforests, Volcanoes/Volcano Cones**

Located in the Northern Rivers region, New South Wales, Australia, in the Wollumbin National Park, formerly known as Mount Warning National Park, is the mountain known as Mount Warning, or Wollumbin to the Aboriginal people who live in the area. It is near the borders of Queensland and New South Wales and part of it is in the Tweed Valley area. It received the name Mount Warning from Lieutenant James Cook, who saw the mountain from his ship out at sea and thought it served as a warning to other sailors about the reefs in the area. Mount Wollumbin is the remains of a shield volcano that erupted approximately twenty-three million years ago. The caldera is still visible at the summit and is considered one of the best remnants of an erosion caldera worldwide.

Mount Wollumbin is sacred to the Aboriginal people in the area, specifically those descended from the ancient Bird Tribes like the Bundjalung People, the Ngarakbal, and Githabal tribes who believe they were created on this land during the Dreaming, it is where the birds gave them the land, their language and their cultural lore. In the Aboriginal legends Wollumbin is the turkey who was wounded in the neck and that's why the mountain has a bend to it.

At Wollumbin National Park you can view the central vent of Mount Wollumbin from several different vantage points within the caldera. There are several other national parks within the caldera because it is so vast. There are two walking tracks in Wollumbin National Park. The first is the summit track, which takes you to the top of Mount Wollumbin. Because this is a sacred place, visitors must adhere to the requests of the tribal Elders who care for the place. The second is the Lyrebird track, which is a short walk into the subtropical rainforest to a lookout point. Hiking along either of these trails you may see some of the animal life in the park, such as the koala, which lives high in the tall eucalypts and gum trees; the Lace Monitor, which is one of Australia's largest lizards that are usually dark blue with white spots; and the Australian brush turkey (scrub turkey) who live in the rainforests and have a bright red head making them easy to identify, just to name a few. You might choose to visit during the spring when the birds display their plumage in their mating dances, the flowers are in full bloom, and the colors of the rainforest are in brilliant display, or during the summer when thunderstorms fill the afternoon making for great photo opportunities. Whenever you decide to visit, there will be plenty for you to see and experience.

The energy of Mount Wollumbin is energizing, is forward in momentum, and is representative of understanding and embracing your pure spiritual essence and giving yourself the permission and power to grow into the truth of your soul. There is vibrancy in the air here, born from the ancient roots that reach to the heart of the earth and lift upwards high into the sky above. This energy will empower you and guide you on your path, making it easier to fulfill both your spiritual and life purpose and to attain all that you desire in life.

23. NAKAUVADRA STANDING STONES
AND NARARA CAVES—FIJI

Categories: Burial Sites, Caves, Islands/Reefs, Megalithic Sites, Mountains/Mounds/Cliff Locations, Mythological Sites, Petroglyph/Rock Art Sites, Power Places

Located in the Pacific Islands near the village of Narara, which is deep in the jungles of western Fiji and Viti Levu (Greater Fiji), at the top of the Nakauvadra mountain range are thirteen enormous monoliths, called the Nakauvadra Standing Stones with Narara Cave below them. The standing stones overlook several caves, one of which is the Narara Cave, which was discovered by four tribal men who were out hunting for wild boar and accidentally stumbled upon it. This cave is unique because it is the only one with ancient petroglyphs on the walls.

Getting to these sites is difficult because of the altitude and you have to walk about six hours up the mountainside through the thick, nearly impenetrable, plant life of the jungle. When you reach the mountain that the stones sit atop of, the climb up is very steep. Due to the jungle environment, they are also covered with green lichen.

The stones are arranged in a circle with twelve of the stones being the same size and the thirteenth one being a bit longer than the others. The twelve stones represent twelve months, the rising of twelve moons, and the thirteenth represents rebirth so that the circular movement of the twelve months could continue, which may explain why it is longer than the other stones. It is believed that the stones were used to worship nature. Their location at the top of the mountain with an eastern view is in relation to their belief that the birth of each day and each night happened in the east because that is where they saw the sun and moon rise. Archaeologists have carbon dated cremated human remains from the Nakauvadra Standing Stones site to 3000 BC and believe it was used as a burial center.

The people of Fiji have a creation myth regarding the Nakavadra Mountain Range. It is said that the snake god, Degei, lived with a hawk named Turukawa in the beginning of time. Turukawa disappeared so Degei went looking for her but only found her nest with two eggs. He took them home with him and when they hatched there were two tiny humans inside. Degei raised them and taught them about nature. A lot of time passed and the humans had children of their own and those children had children. Degei took all the humans and traveled to Lautoka where he created the village of

Viseisei, the island of Viti Levu and the other 332 smaller islands in the area. He left the humans there to live their lives and he moved to the Nakavadra Mountain Range where he still lives today. When someone in Fiji dies, their soul has to pass through Degei's cave and he determines if they go to paradise or are banished into a lake where they will await their punishment.

The energy at the Nakauvadra Standing Stones is of a high frequency that feels like a breath of fresh air, as if you have experienced a great relief of some kind or a wait that is finally over. The energy here is connected to the higher consciousness of the universe, is deep, pure, and embraces love for the natural world that we live in. The energy of Narara Cave is more subdued, relaxing, and feels safe and secure from outside dangers. Becoming one with this energy will enable you to take more time for yourself and for making sure that you are taking care of your spiritual essence.

24. NAN MADOL–MICRONESIA

**Categories: Burial Sites, Islands/Reefs, Monasteries/
Temples, Ruins/Archeological Sites**

Located off of the southeast coast of Pohnpei on the southern side of the Federated States of Micronesia in the South Pacific Islands is Nan Madol, an ancient city that was built on the coral reef in the lagoon of a small island named Temwen. It includes over one hundred man-made islets, which earned it the name the Venice of the Pacific. Nan Madol is the only ancient city ever built on top of a coral reef and the Smithsonian refers to it as "an engineering marvel" because the Saudeleur people who built it didn't have access to anything like levers or pulleys to help them move the heavy black rocks.

The city was constructed by placing volcanic rock, specifically columnar basalt, on top of the coral reef in a crisscross pattern. Like monoliths found around the world that were constructed during the same period of time, some of these columns weigh up to 100,000 pounds, and the oral history of the area didn't include how they were able to move these massive pieces. Legend says they had magical abilities that allowed them to fly the rocks to their current locations. Around Nandauwas, the spiritual temple of the Saudeleur people and royal burial complex, they built walls that are up to twenty-five feet high that surround the tomb area. Other islets also have high walls surrounding tombs with basalt columns that weight up to fifty tons each but they aren't as tall as the royal burial area.

Nan Madol was considered both the political and spiritual center for the Saudeleur people between 1300 to 1700 AD. Legend has it that two Saudeleur brothers, who were sorcerers with magical abilities given to them by the gods, were the first to come to Pohnpei around 1000 AD and they built Nan Madol with their magic. After this feat, they were allowed to marry into the Pohnpei tribes. One of the brothers died and the other self-appointed himself as king, and by 1300 AD, Saudeleurs ruled the area. Archeologists believe that Nan Madol was built between 1000 to 1500 AD. Historians believe that approximately one thousand people lived on the islets during this time and it served to isolate the rulers from the rest of the population. The oral history of the Saudeleur paints them as cruel, dictatorial, and oppressive people who were very religious and whose legends are still feared through superstition by the Pohnpeian people who live in the area today. The Saudeleur people didn't leave much behind. There isn't any art, writing, or carvings to be found that could give some insight into these people and how they lived.

Today you can tour the area by boat through the tidal canals between the islets. The majority of the buildings on the islets are still standing. The area is now protected by the Nan Madol Foundation in order to limit tourism, and take care of the overgrowth of vegetation that threatens the walls built by the Saudeleur people.

The energy of Nan Madol is cool, crisp, and flows at a medium pace encompassing all of the islets. It is bright and clear and has a deep feeling of purpose and strong will that will fill you with confidence and motivate you. The energy of Nan Madol is empowering, a connection to ancient power and to the positively flowing energy of the sea. It is fluid and you'll feel as if it wraps around you, embracing you to become more than you are and all that you strive to become.

25. NOURLANGIE ROCK–
NORTHERN TERRITORY, AUSTRALIA

Categories: Mythological Sites, Petroglyph/Rock Art Sites

Nourlangie Rock is located in the Northern Territory of Australia, which is about three hours east of the capital city of Darwin, in the Kakadu National Park. Nourlangie Rock is divided into two sections by the local Aboriginal people. The upper sections at the higher elevations are known as Burrunggui while the lower sections are called Anbangbang. Nourlangie Rock is one of the most famous locations worldwide for people to view ancient rock art and is known for having more rock art sites within its borders than any other national park in the world.

The park contains over five thousand Aboriginal art sites and dwelling shelters used by the ancient Aboriginal people who lived in the area. Some of the paintings in Kakadu National Park are over twenty thousand years old. The Aboriginal people use rock art as a way to express their culture, religious ceremonies, and their connection to the natural world. Today Aboriginal artists also use bark, paper, and fabric as the medium for their paintings. At Nourlangie Rock, the art reflects changes in the social structure of the people and changes in the environment. The art shows the animals people hunted at the time, stories from their creation myths, religious ceremonies, tools, things they saw, and their life experiences. They also painted prophecies about the future and how people would live their lives, which was considered sorcery.

The descriptions of the art at some of the sites are incomplete on purpose. It is said that each painting contains six layers. Only the Aboriginal people at the highest levels within the tribe know the full meaning of the story and most of this information is not meant to be shared with people outside of their own culture. Even within their culture, the various layers of these painted stories are only shared with other Aboriginal people based upon their status within their tribe. The more importance you hold, the more layers of the story you're allowed to know.

Visiting Kakadu National Park is an adventure where you can view the native animals and plants. This national park has over 10,000 different species of insects, 280 species of birds, 60 species of mammals, 53 species of fish, 117 species of reptiles, and more than 1,700 species of plants. Some of these species are endangered and rare, while others can't be found anywhere else in the world. There are many waterways in the park including South Alligator River, but is highly recommended that you do not swim at this park because the water is home to saltwater crocodiles. An interesting fact is that the person who named South Alligator River didn't know the difference between a crocodile and an alligator and the name was never changed.

The energy at Nourlangie Rock is empowering and contains an echo of vibration from times long past. Its frequency is a mid-range tone that feels like it bounces around you, and has a slight sizzle that feels like electrical surges powering through it. This energy encourages you to get back to your roots, to embrace your higher self, and to take the time to examine your current path and make any changes that are needed. The frequency of Nourlangie Rock will both ground you and elevate you at the same time.

It indicates a time of change, a time of looking back and letting go, and a time to look forward with purpose and joy. This is the time to paint your own story and to seek out that which you desire most.

26. ONE TREE HILL–NEW ZEALAND

Categories: Mountains/Mounds/Cliff Locations, Pilgrimage Sites, Volcanoes/Volcano Cones

Located in Auckland is a volcanic cone in the center of four hundred acres known as One Tree Hill or Maungakiekie, which is the name the Maori people gave to the volcano. Cornwall Park is also part of the four hundred acres, which together with One Tree Hill makes up the Recreation Park of Auckland. Cornwall Park was once farmland owned and worked by Sir John Logan Campbell, who gave the property to the people of New Zealand by making it a private park that is open to the public. He is buried at the summit of One Tree Hill beneath a huge obelisk. In his will, he left five thousand British pounds with instructions to have the obelisk built as a memorial to the Maori. There are also three large craters, which serve as natural amphitheaters at the top of One Tree Hill.

The volcano at One Tree Hill is believed to have erupted 67,000 years ago. There are many craters in the area because the land formed from the lava flow at the time of eruption. It was named One Tree Hill because there was a pohutukawa tree that was the only tree on the hill until 1852 when someone chopped it down for firewood. It was replaced with a Monterey pine tree. In 1994, a Maori activist tried to cut down the tree with a chainsaw. It survived this attack, but five years later it had to be cut down after vandals damaged it so much that it couldn't be saved. At the time of its death, the tree was 120 years old. To date, it hasn't been replaced. There is some debate among historians as to whether the "one tree" that was originally located at the top of the volcanic cone was a pohutukawa or a totara tree.

From the summit of One Tree Hill, you can see some spectacular panoramic views of the city of Auckland and its harbor. It is Auckland's highest natural point. There are walking trails to explore and you'll feel like you're out in the country even though you're in the middle of the city. If you visit at night be sure to check out the Stardome Observatory, which is also open during the day. One Tree Hill is a sacred place to the Maori people. At one point, it housed the largest settlement of Maori in the area and contained three hill fort sites. Today the Maori make pilgrimages to the site to honor the spiritual home of their ancestors. It also draws people from other religions due to the high frequency and the power of the place. They visit to celebrate the solstice and to perform other ceremonies, often using the natural amphitheaters for these ceremonies because of the way the drums and other music sounds from within them. The energy here is vibrant and alive, joyous and exhilarating, and will bring a smile to your face as it wraps you within its warmth. There is a feeling of love that flows through this area, of rejoicing, and of celebration.

27. RA'IATEA–SOCIETY ISLANDS, OCEANIA

**Categories: Bodies of Water/Waterfalls/Springs,
Islands/Reefs, Monasteries/Temples**

Located in French Polynesia of the Pacific Islands are the Society Islands, among which is Ra'iatea, the second largest of all the Society Islands that is a forty-five minute flight from Tahiti, the largest. Ra'iatea shares a lagoon with Taha'a, is home to Mount Temehani and Taputapuatea Marae, and is known as the cradle of the Polynesian culture.

The island has several deep bays, many gorgeous waterfalls, and about thirty-one endemic plants including the odorous flowering plant called Tiare Apetahi, which only blooms at dawn and grows only on Mount Temehani and nowhere else in the world, even though people have tried to get it to grow in other places. Legend says that a girl who was in love with the king saw his empty canoe on the ocean and knew he died in battle. She was overcome with grief, so instead of waiting for confirmation of his death, she thrust her arm into the side of the mountain and broke it off so if the king did return he would smell her in the air and know that the white flower represented her hand. Then she jumped into the chasm of Apo'o hihi ura to her death.

Ra'iatea, originally named Havai'i, is known as the sacred island to the Polynesian people because it is the first island their ancestors settled before branching out to Hawaii and New Zealand. It has the only traversable river in French Polynesia, which legend says was the departure point for those who traveled to other islands.

Marae were focal points of the Maori culture and places where they would meet for spiritual reasons, ceremonies, and celebrations. In ancient times Taputapuatea Marae, located on Ra'iatea, was the political and religious meeting place for all of the Society Islands and other islands in the South Pacific. Priests, heads of tribes and other spiritual and political leaders would all travel to Taputapuatea Marae for international meetings. Taputapuatea Marae is the most sacred temple in French Polynesia and the largest marae on Ra'iatea. When visitors would arrive, the lagoon acted as the holding area before they came ashore. It is located on the end of a peninsula that extends out into the lagoon.

Archeologists believe that Taputapuatea Marae was built around 1000 AD and was also used as a funerary center. Legend says it is where the god 'Oro was born and lived. There are temples built to honor the world of the living people, their ancestors and origin, and the gods they worshipped. There are also stones in the marae that were used for human sacrifice and other altars.

The energy of Ra'iatea is solemn, quiet, and reserved. There is a feeling of peacefulness in the energy but there is also a sense of unease. The energy here draws you in and makes you feel contemplative, so that you find yourself considering different aspects of life and feeling appreciative for your way of life and the people you are close too. It encourages you to be thankful for the little things that are often taken for granted and motivates you to be true to your beliefs and ideals. It moves through you, shaking you up so that you look deeper into your own motives, intentions, and purpose in life.

28. ROTORUA—NEW ZEALAND

Categories: Bodies of Water/Waterfalls/Springs, Geysers/Blowholes, Regions

Rotorua is a district located on the North Island of New Zealand that consists of the town of Rotorua and over 647 thousand acres including eighteen lakes, three rivers, farmland, forests, and is globally recognized for its seven geothermal fields and Maori cultural experiences.

The town sits in an ancient volcanic caldera, which has amazing floral displays in beautiful gardens that are both privately and publicly owned. The town is kept exceptionally clean and manicured. There is no litter and the buildings receive regular maintenance to keep them in pristine condition. There is a competition called Keep New Zealand Beautiful, which has been in existence for eleven years. Because of all of the attention and care given to the town by the residents, it was chosen for this high honor for six of the eleven years. The beauty of Rotorua isn't limited to the town but expands to the surrounding district with its volcanic landscape.

Rotorua contains a Maori village where the Te Arawa people, one of the largest Maori tribes, live traditionally today. They invite people to visit and learn about their culture, traditions, and way of life. You can also experience the New Zealand Maori Arts and Crafts Institute, which has schools to teach weaving and traditional Maori wood carving techniques.

The geothermal fields are one of the primary draws for the area's 3.3 million people who visit the area each year. They cause the air to have a mild sulphur smell. There are mud pools that are always bubbling in Whakarewarewa Valley and the Pohutu Geyser, which erupts quite a few times daily. The most active geothermal park is called Hell's Gate. There are many spas where you can soak in a thermal hot pool after a day of adventuring.

If you like adventure then you'll love visiting Tutea Falls which is in the Rotorua district about thirty minutes from the city. It holds the honor of being the most "commercially rafted waterfall" in the world. If you aren't up for wild water rafting, then the Rotorua Canopy Tours might be just your thing. It's the only native tree-top forest zipline tour in New Zealand and includes a network of ziplines with bridges, platforms, and trails that are up to 148 feet above the forest floor. Sometimes you're walking along these pathways and other times you're flying through the treetops from one station to the next. This tour takes about three hours to complete but is one of the things that is recommended as a must do when in Rotorua. There is also a guided tour through Whirinaki Forest, which is a podocarp forest, also called a dinosaur forest because it looks today the way it would have looked when dinosaurs roamed the earth.

Other adventurous activities include rolling downhill in a giant orb, riding in a suspended aerodynamic racing pod, riding a luge that is part toboggan and part go-cart, going off-roading in a four-wheel drive vehicle, jet boating, or monster trucking. While there are many exciting things to do and see in the Rotorua district, the energy here moves in a slow, suspended manner. It taps deeply into the ancientness of the earth, to the core of the planet's being. As it moves upwards from the earth into the area, it is cleansing, purifying, and energetic and will affect you in the same way. Connecting to this energy will allow you to release any negativity you've been holding onto and purify your soul, which gives you more positive energy both physically, emotionally, and spiritually.

29. THE BLUE MOUNTAINS AND LILIANFELS
(THREE SISTERS AND ECHO POINT LOOKOUT)–
NEW SOUTH WALES, AUSTRALIA

Category: Mountains/Mounds/Cliff Locations

Located in New South Wales, Australia, the Blue Mountains is a mountain range owned by the Dharung, Wiradjuri, Tharawal, Wanaruah, Gundungurra, and Darkinjung Aboriginal Nations and is in the Blue Mountains National Park. The mountain range gets its name from the blue haze created by the small drops of oil released by the trees in the eucalypt forests. The oil mixes with water vapor in the air and when the sun hits it, a blue color is produced. Eucalypt forests include over nine hundred different species of trees in the genus Eucalyptus, Angophora, and Corymbia. Most of the trees in a eucalypt forest are evergreen and burn easily due to the oils but they also regrow quickly if burned by fire.

One of the most popular places to stay in the region is at the Lilianfels Resort and Spa because it is located in the middle of the Blue Mountains National Park and convenient to some of the most visited sites in the area. There are many different ways to visit the attractions in this national park. If you prefer guided tours you can go on a trolley, explorer bus or Segway tour or take a guided bushwalk, or an adventure tour, which includes activities such as mountain biking, abseiling (rappelling), rock climbing, and canyoning.

Three Sisters is an internationally-known landmark in the Blue Mountains and are located at Echo Point lookout. It is a rock formation with three separate sections that look like thick pinnacles reaching toward the sky. Their appearance changes during the day depending on how the sun is hitting them but they always seem to be exploding in beautiful colors. The site is lit up at night and looks like glittering gold. Sometimes they appear crisp and clear and other times they look like they're glowing. They sit side-by-side and were formed by erosion of the land. You can get up close to these unique rock formations by walking the Giants Stairway down to a bridge that will take you over to the site. Aboriginal legend says three sisters fell in love with three brothers from a nearby tribe. The girls weren't allowed to marry outside of their tribe so the brothers decided to kidnap them and marry them anyway. A battle broke out and many people died during the kidnapping attempt, so an old witchdoctor cast a spell on them to turn them to stone to keep them safe. The witchdoctor was killed during the battle and was unable to reverse the spell, so they stand today, looking out over the valley that was their home, unable to return.

Other places to experience in the Blue Mountains includes the Scenic Railway, which is the steepest railway in the world that allows passengers. It goes up a fifty-two degree incline but the seats in the cars are adjustable and you can choose to increase your individual incline up to sixty-four degrees. There is also the Blue Mountains Cultural Center where you can learn about the history, culture, and environment of the area; the Waradah Aboriginal Center where you can learn about the Aboriginal culture, a museum, wildlife park; and the Mount Tomah Botantic Garden.

The energy of the Blue Mountains is passive, laid back, and very spiritual. The energy here is connected to universal consciousness and is transformative. It moves is waves, dipping into the valleys and soaring high above the mountaintops. It is pure, focused, and in forward motion. Experiencing this energy will help you stay true to your spiritual path and enables a deeper connection to your higher self. It enhances your intuition, especially clairvoyance, mediumistic, and empathic abilities. It encourages you to be true to your spiritual essence and gifts.

30. THE PINNACLES—WESTERN AUSTRALIA
Categories: Rock Formations, Sandhills/Sand Dunes

The Pinnacles, also known as the Pinnacles Desert and nicknamed "Rock Stars" in the Outback, are located in Cervantes in the Nambung National Park approximately 155 miles from Perth. The closest towns are Cervantes, Leeman, and Jurian Bay. Nambung National Park borders the Indian Ocean.

The pinnacles are eroded limestone spires found in the middle of the sand dunes. When you first look out across the desert it may feel as if you're looking at some alien planet, or the headstones in a vast burial ground, or sculptures that an artist has created in the desert, because there are thousands of pinnacles scattered throughout the yellow sand. The pinnacles can be as small as a large rock or up to twelve feet tall, with all sizes in between. Some are rounded at the top, some look like mushrooms, others are pointed, some have holes in the top that you can look through, others appear somewhat flat, and each one is completely unique. There are several theories in regards to the formation of the Pinnacles: they are thought to be remnants of the Tamala Limestone that runs along the coast of Western Australia, or they were formed from tree or root casts.

The Pinnacles are believed to be twenty thousand to thirty thousand years old and were created when the waves of the Indian Ocean brought sand to the shore. The sand is mostly made of calcite, which is broken pieces of shells. The pinnacles show cross beds, which indicate they were created by wind-blown sand dunes instead of dunes created by water.

When visiting the pinnacles in the spring, you will discover there are many different species of wildflowers. That being said, it is also illegal to pick the wildflowers. The fine is two thousand Australian dollars for those who pick them. Instead, take pictures. There is a paved road that goes through the Pinnacles Desert and you can drive your car through the area as long as you stay on the road, or you can park the car and walk through the area, which takes about an hour. If you want to go off-roading in the sand with a vehicle then visit the Lancelin sand dunes, which are off the Indian Ocean Drive on the way back to Perth, where you can ride a dune buggy or four-wheel drive along the dunes.

At the Pinnacles, you may see wild emus or grey kangaroos walking around throughout the spires. Other animals also live in the area such as bobtail lizards, carpet pythons, white tailed black cockatoos, and the black shouldered kite to name a few.

The energy at the Pinnacles is somewhat jarring and bright. It moves in bursts in both a spiral and up and down motion. It is like a catalyst that invigorates you, making you feel as if you're ready to change things up in your life and get things done. If you've been putting off work or making a decision, the energy at the Pinnacles will inspire you and urge you into action.

31. THE TIWI ISLANDS: BATHURST AND MELVILLE—NORTHERN TERRITORY, AUSTRALIA

Category: Islands/Reefs

The Tiwi Islands are located off the coast of northern Australia approximately sixty-two miles north of Darwin, the capital city of Australia's Northern Territory, where the Timor Sea and the Arafura Sea meet. The Tiwi Islands consist of two larger islands, Melville and Bathurst, and nine uninhabited smaller islands. Of all Australia's islands, Tasmania is the largest and Melville Island comes in second. It is a two-hour ferry ride to get to the islands.

Legend says the islands were created when an old woman named Mudungkala rose out of the earth carrying three children, two sisters and a brother. As she walked, water filled the area behind her separating the islands from the mainland. These children were believed to be the ancestors of all the people who live on the island, and they traveled all through the land. The aboriginal people celebrate their journeys with over five hundred different songs. Researchers believe that the land settled in that area around 9,650 years ago which brought the ocean inland and made the islands.

Bathurst Island is home to about 2,500 people and is more populated than Melville Island where approximately 700 people live. World renowned for their carvings and brightly designed fabrics, the work of Tiwi artists are sought after by collectors. There are several art centers operated by the Tiwi artists who display and create their work, which include wood carvings of birds and animals that, once completed, are also painted. A screen printing shop prints the designs on clothing, other fabrics, and tea towels, and there are painters who paint with natural colors on paper, bark, canvas, and boards using a wooden comb and ceramics, bronze sculptures, and glasswork. Traditionally the men and women work in separate sections to create their artwork.

The aboriginal people of the Tiwi Islands believe that they are different from the aboriginal tribes on the mainland because they have kept their culture alive while adapting to living with people of other nationalities. They have distinct traditions that differ from other aboriginal tribes and a unique language. They prefer walking but enjoy technology such as mobile phones and tablets. They hunt regularly and fish using wooden spears with three prongs, nets, and fishing lines.

While visiting the Tiwi Islands, you can immerse yourself in the energy of the culture by participating in a cultural tour during which you can create your own artwork in the style of the Aboriginal people or you can just support the culture and buy the piece of artwork they've already created. Australian football is extremely popular on the islands; they even have their own league, so you can catch a football game almost anytime.

The energy of the Tiwi Islands is energizing, exciting, and joyous. It flows in an uplifting movement. It is highly motivational, inspires a deep appreciation of all that is in the connectivity between the people, the land, and the sea. Connecting to this energy will make you smile and see the ease of living a simple life filled with hope, aspirations, and creativity. The energy of the Tiwi Islands will stay with you for a lifetime. It is the joy in a moment, the gift of a smile, and the passion of living life to the fullest.

32. UBIRR—NORTHERN TERRITORY, AUSTRALIA

Categories: Mythological Sites, Petroglyph/Rock Art Sites, Power Places, Rock Formations

Located in the East Alligator region of Kakadu National Park is Ubirr Lookout and Rock Shelter. The area of Ubirr is in the Nadab floodplain with natural rock shelters located around the edge. It is underneath these rocks that the Aboriginal people lived and painted the rock art that the area is known for today.

The rock art at Ubirr is believed to be more than twenty thousand years old. There are a variety of styles that the ancient Aboriginal people used to show how they lived in their environment. Some of the paintings at Ubirr show x-ray art where they draw the insides of the animals that they ate. Some of the animals drawn were wallabies, mussels, fish, water birds, and lizards. In the main gallery, there is a painting of a Tasmanian tiger that went extinct about three thousand years ago. There is also contact art in the main gallery at Ubirr that shows a white man the people came into contact with who was wearing boots, a shirt and had his hands in the pockets of his pants. It is believed that this painting was created during the 1880s.

The Dreamtime creation myths are also prevalent in the rock art. There is a painting of the Rainbow Serpent, which legend says is a self-portrait that she painted of herself as she traveled through Ubirr to remind people about her.

From the parking lot, it takes about an hour to walk the track to Ubirr. To get to the top of the lookout takes another half hour. From the top of the lookout, you'll experience amazing 360-degree views of the Nadab floodplain. There are three separate sites of rock art available to view. The rangers provide Ubirr Rock Art Talks where they will tell you about the rock art, the history of the place, and the people who lived there. This service is only provided during the dry season. During the wet season, access to Ubirr is often restricted due to the amount of flooding in the region making some of the roads impassable. You can still reach Ubirr during the wet season by taking a Guluyambi boat cruise along Magela Creek, which always floods during that time of year.

In order to help preserve the paintings during your visit, do not touch them or the silicon drip lines. It's important to stay behind the barriers and fencing set up by the park service and to stay out of prohibited areas. In order to respect the wishes of the Aboriginal people who look after Ubirr, which are the Bunitj, Mandjurlgunj, and Manilagarr tribes, alcohol is not allowed at Ubirr.

The energy of Ubirr is smooth, clear, and bright. It radiates a warmth from within its frequency, which reminds you of growth and progression. This energy, when applied to both your personal and spiritual life, will help you experience your own inner growth. The brightness of the energy of this place will help illuminate your path, and also clears away any darkness that you may be feeling within yourself.

33. WAIRAKEI TERRACES—NEW ZEALAND
Categories: Bodies of Water/Waterfalls/Springs, Geysers/Blowholes, Healing Springs, Power Places

The Wairakei Terraces are located in Taupo, which is in the Bay of Plenty Region of the North Island and the Waiora Valley. There is a large amount of geothermal activity on both the North and South Islands of New Zealand because the land is situated where two of the earth's tectonic plates meet.

The Maori people came to the area of the Wairakei Terraces approximately one thousand years ago. There was an abundance of food in the area and hot water for bathing. The thermal activity was the major reason for settlement. The Maori believed the waters in the hot springs could heal diseases like arthritis and were often used to ease the aches and pains of sore joints and muscles. The mineral-rich waters helped skin conditions as well. When the Maori first settled the area it was very raw in its power with areas where steam poured out of the earth, the mud bubbled from the heat, geysers erupted frequently and the ground often shook from the movement of the tectonic plates.

The water at the Wairakei Terraces contains many different minerals, which make the water feel silky to the touch and appear blue in color. Some of the minerals in the water include, but are not limited to: manganese, which helps convert sugar to energy and maintains healthy heart rhythms, muscle tissue, and hormonal levels; potassium, which helps the heart and can reduce high blood pressure, eliminates toxins from the body, and helps heal skin ailments; silica, which helps the body make collagen and makes the skin look younger, strengthens the skeletal and nervous system, aids in healthy hair and nails, and helps eliminate acne; sodium, which helps alleviate the symptoms of arthritis; sulfate, which is anti-inflammatory; chloride, which helps the muscular system; and iron, which helps reduce stress and fatigue and promotes increased health of the blood and skin. With all of these types of health benefits, it's no wonder that so many people visit the Wairakei Terraces to soak in the water and take time for rest, relaxation, and rejuvenation.

Today the area has been developed to take advantage of the geothermal power in the area but there are still places where you can experience the same types of healing that drew the Maori here all those years ago. In the past one hundred years, people from all around the world would travel to the Waiora Valley and the Wairakei Terraces to see the amazing spectacle of nature's power or to seek healing from the hot pools, springs, and mud. This is still a draw for those looking for a mind, body, and spiritual retreat, and are interested in natural practices that can give them better health and well-being. At the Wairakei Terraces, you can participate in hot mud treatments, a variety of relaxing baths in the hot pools, or even get a massage.

The energy of Wairakei Terraces is rejuvenating, invigorating, and healing. It moves in an upward motion from the center of the earth to the surface, bringing with it an ancient power that will affect you at a soul level. Even if you don't get in the water or mud, you'll still feel this energy and benefit from its ability to heal mind, body, and spirit. You'll find yourself relaxing and letting go of negative energy as the purity of the energy of this place fills you. It is inspiring and brings clarity of being to all of your senses.

34. WALPOLE-NORNALUP–WESTERN AUSTRALIA
Categories: Forests/Trees, Mountains/Mounds/Cliff Locations

Walpole-Nornalup National Park is located in the southwest region of Western Australia approximately 220 miles south of the capital city of Perth. The Walpole-Nornalup National Park is one of seven national parks in the middle of the remote Walpole Wilderness and includes karri and tingle forests, wetlands, granite peaks, inlets, coastal cliffs, and rivers in a natural landscape. The Wagyl Kaip people are the traditional custodians of Walpole Nornalup National Park.

The tingle forest is one of the biggest draws of this national park and the Valley of the Giants walk is set up in a way so people can enjoy these massive trees but their shallow root systems are protected from people walking over them. There are several species of trees in the tingle forest including the red tingle, yellow tingle, and marri and karri trees. The red tingle is the largest of the tingles in the Valley of the Giants and can only be found between the Deep River and the Bow River within six miles from the coastline. When the red tingle is around thirty years old it starts producing white flowers every four years for its lifetime of approximately four hundred years. The base of the red tingle can be almost sixty-six feet across and they have the largest girth of any eucalypt tree in the world and can grow up to 230 feet tall while karri trees can grow up to 265 feet tall. A unique feature of the red tingle tree is that the base of the tree is hollowed out. The tree's root system is shallow and they do not have a taproot. As they grow older and taller, the trunk will create buttress roots on the sides to provide more stability and allow them to absorb more moisture from the soil. The Giant Tingle Tree in the park is the site of an enormous fire-hollowed red tingle, which is the oldest living eucalypt in the world. Yellow tingles do not buttress like the red tingles.

There are other engaging activities that you can participate in at the park in addition to viewing the trees, all of which allow you to experience variations of the earth frequency in this location. You can go fishing in the inlets, rivers, on the beach or from the rocks. You can go bush walking on several different walking tracks, some of which also allow biking. There's also boating, surfing, sailing, snorkeling, camping, or four wheeling. There are wilderness communities where you can learn about the people and listen to their stories about their culture and the area.

While visiting the Walpole-Nornalup National Park, because it is located in such a remote location, officials suggest that you travel in groups of three or more in case there is an injury so that someone can go for help without leaving the injured person alone. It is important to be careful around the rocks on the coast and aware of the weather forecasts, which can change quickly. Diving or jumping into the inlets isn't allowed because of the danger involved.

The energy of Walpole-Nornalup and the Walpole Wilderness is soft, still, and prominent. It feels supportive, endearing, and gives you a sense of inner peace. You will feel awe-inspired, uplifted and moved by the wonder that surrounds you in this natural setting. The energy here flows in an up and down motion, swooping down from high above to connect with the earth and then moves is a snakelike motion along the forest floor before rising back up into the sky. It will take you back in time, make you think about your past and your future, and feel safe and serene in your plans for yourself. It embodies universal truth, which will make you feel a part of the wonder of the planet and all that exists in creation.

35. WET TROPICS OF QUEENSLAND— QUEENSLAND, AUSTRALIA

Categories: Canyons/Gorges, Mountains/Mounds/ Cliff Locations, Mythological Sites, Rainforests

The Wet Tropics of Queensland is a rainforest located on the northeast coast of Australia that is approximately 280 miles long. It is the oldest tropical rainforest in the world and is over eighty million years older than the Amazon rainforest. It is located between Cooktown in the northern part of Australia all the way down to Townsville in the southern part of the country. The Wet Tropics has over thirty national parks and two other world heritage sites (the Wet Tropics itself is also a world heritage site) located within it, all of which offer something unique and special to see. The area contains natural beauty in the form of mountain ranges, gorges, rivers, numerous waterfalls, volcanic lakes, and craters.

The area has a rich biodiversity. Scientists consider the Wet Tropics of Queensland a source for understanding the earth's evolution because they can trace almost every major stage during the past 200 million years through discoveries in the Wet Tropics. It has survived many weather and earth changes during that time. Within the Wet Tropics there are nine sub-regions, each with its own unique features and landscapes that are different from the other areas.

The Wet Tropics is home to many rare, endemic, and endangered animals and plants. For example, there is the Southern Cassowary, an endangered bird with only 4,500 remaining in the wild. It is the world's second heaviest bird and can run thirty-one miles per hour. Thirty percent of Australia's marsupial species live in the Wet Tropics including the musky rat kangaroo, which is the most primitive kangaroo species left on earth and also the smallest of the kangaroo species. It is the only surviving species, of four similar species, that lived in the area some twenty million years ago. It retains the same characteristics as its ancient ancestors, which includes a prehensile tail, opposable thumbs on its back feet, and unique digestive tract, teeth, and diet, and has twins or triplets instead of a single offspring. The oldest animal species that lives here is the carnivorous Velvet Worm, which is approximately 500 million years old. There are more than 3,000 unique plant species in the Wet Tropics, including many of the world's most primitive flowering plants, with 380 species considered rare or threatened.

People have lived in the Wet Tropics for over five thousand years. At one point over eighteen different Aboriginal tribes, which constituted over twenty thousand people who spoke six different languages, lived here. They lived on the land and learned how to prepare even toxic plants so they were edible through techniques such as fermenting and sun drying. Today you can learn about these cultures and their Dreamtime myths by participating in a Dreamtime Gorge Walk led by the local Indigenous people at the Mossman Gorge Center.

The energy of the Wet Tropics feels like a low deep vibration. It is ancient, a solid foundation that builds layer upon layer to a lighter, breezy feeling at the highest point. It is grounding yet freeing, firm yet light, and radiates a buoyant positivity of growth and slow forward movement. It is long lasting and will stay with you, guiding and urging you to paths that will bring about positive growth in all that you set out to do. Feeling this energy as a grounding presence deep within your spiritual essence will bring about progressive, although slow at times, change.

36. WILPENA POUND–OUTBACK, SOUTH AUSTRALIA
**Categories: Mountains/Mounds/Cliff Locations,
Petroglyph/Rock Art Sites, Power Places, Rock Formations**

Wilpena Pound, also known as Ikara, which means "meeting place," is located in South Australia's outback in the northern part of Ikara-Flinders Ranges National Park approximately 267 miles north of Adelaide and between the towns of Blinman in the north and Hawker in the south. Wilpena Pound looks as if a meteor crashed into the earth but in actuality, it is a natural amphitheater that forms a bowl shape, with the edges higher than the valley inside. It is ten miles long, almost five miles wide and the valley floor is 656 feet taller than the land that surrounds the high walls surrounding the valley. The highest point of the edges is at St. Mary's Peak at nearly four thousand feet above sea level. It is an impressive site that will get your imagination going as to how it was formed.

According to geologists, Wilpena Pound is part of the Adelaide Rift Complex, also known as the Adelaide Geosyncline, which were rifts in the earth that occurred about 514 million years ago and caused changes to the continents. The mountainous edges of Wilpena Pound eroded slower than the center part, which is made of softer rock that eroded faster, which gives Wilpena Pound its bowl like amphitheater appearance today.

The Adnyamathanha people hold Wilpena Pound as one of their sacred sites and their ancestors lived in this area for 15,000 years. According to their Dreamtime stories, Wilpena Pound formed when two giant serpents, one male and one female, each about twelve miles long, surrounded a large number of people who had gathered to have an initiation ceremony. A huge battle occurred and the people killed the snakes. Their bodies turned into stone and created the walls of Wilpena Pound with the head of the male at St. Mary's Peak and the female's at Beatrice Hill. Other legends say that the snakes followed an old man to the ceremony and ate all of the people in attendance and they were so full they laid down and willed themselves to die, their bodies creating the walls of Wilpena Pound.

If you plan to visit Wilpena Pound, in person, you'll do a lot of bushwalking; there are thirteen different walks located within the Pound to see it from the inside. You can also participate in the Arkabab Walk, which lasts for four days and is classified as one of Australia's eight Great Walks. There are several sites to see on the inside as well as several different walking trails that cross the valley. Some of these sites are Wangara Lookout, where you can see the entire amphitheatre from the top, after a steep climb up the side. You can also walk to Arkaroo Rock where you'll find ancient Aboriginal rock art. Climbing to St. Mary's Peak is a strenuous walk that takes between six and seven hours to complete but you'll experience the view of the entire Pound from its highest point. Or if you don't want to walk that much you can take a flight over Wilpena Pound in a small plane or helicopter.

The locals say Wilpena Pound will speak to you but that you have to be inside it to truly experience its voice. This references the energy of this place, which will move you with its strong and deep flow. It feels thick and warm, moving slowly around you and through your spiritual essence. It affects you deeply in its power to affect you spiritually, emotionally, and embrace you with its strength. Wilpena Pound will speak to the truth of your soul if you'll only listen.

Chapter 7
UNITED STATES AND CANADA

As part of North America, both the United States and Canada are home to some interesting and beautiful locations that speak to the soul, bring feelings of peace and serenity to troubled minds, and make us question if there is more to our world than what we know as fact.

In the United States, the area of Sedona, Arizona, is known for its vortex energy that can heal what ails you. In Asheville and the Western North Carolina region, there is a feeling of coming home when you interact with the vortex energy there, healing and soothing to the spirit.

At the Martyr's Shrine and Healing Spring in Ontario, Canada, there are many instances of physical healing in addition to spiritual healing. Dreamer's Rock on Manitoulin Island in Canada can assist you in healing from within and becoming one with your spiritual self. Step back in time at Petroglyphs Park in Ontario, Canada, to see drawings that were made by ancient people who walked the land. There's also the Valley of the Ten Peaks in the Canadian Rockies where beauty is unsurpassed and the earth frequency is strong and pure.

Just when you think you've seen it all, take a visit to Texas where the Marfa Lights Vortex is located to watch the strange lights that appear or to Mount Shasta in California, a highly spiritual energy location where the elusive Bigfoot has been sited multiple times. There are many vortex areas in the United States and Canada where you can not only experience earth's frequency but you can gain a new respect for your own spirituality and experience spiritual growth.

Map key

1. Airport Mesa—Sedona, Arizona, USA
2. America's Stonehenge Mystery Hill—Salem, New Hampshire, USA
3. Antelope Canyon—Arizona, USA
4. Asheville and Western North Carolina Region—North Carolina, USA
5. Assateague Island—Maryland, Virginia, USA
6. Badlands National Park—South Dakota, USA
7. Bell Rock—Sedona, Arizona, USA
8. Big Sur—California, USA
9. Bighorn Medicine Wheel—Bighorn National Forest, Wyoming, USA
10. Boynton Canyon—Sedona, Arizona, USA
11. Bryce Canyon National Park—Utah, USA
12. Carmanah Walbran—Vancouver Island, Canada
13. Cathedral Rock—Sedona, Arizona, USA
14. Chaco Canyon—New Mexico, USA
15. Coral Castle—Florida, USA
16. Crater Lake—Medford, Oregon, USA
17. Devils Tower—Crook County, Wyoming, USA
18. Dreamer's Rock—Manitoulin Island, Ontario, Canada
19. Giant Springs—Great Falls, Montana, USA
20. Great Sandhills and Athabasca Sand Dunes—Saskatchewan, Canada
21. Haleakala Crater—Maui, Hawaii, USA
22. Lac Sainte Anne—Lake Saint Anne, Alberta, Canada
23. Lake of the Woods—Minnesota, USA/Ontario, Canada
24. Mabry's Mill—Blue Ridge Parkway, Virginia, USA
25. Marfa Lights Vortex—Texas, USA
26. Martyr's Shrine and Healing Spring—Ontario, Canada
27. Mount Shasta—Mount Shasta, California, USA
28. Petroglyphs Park—Woodview, Ontario, Canada
29. Serpent Mound—Ohio, USA
30. Spiro Mounds—Oklahoma, USA
31. Sproat Lake—British Columbia, Canada
32. The Grand Canyon—Arizona, USA
33. Valley of the Ten Peaks—Canadian Rockies, Calgary, Alberta, Canada
34. Wanuskewin—Saskatchewan, Canada
35. White Sands—New Mexico, USA
36. Wind Cave National Park—South Dakota, USA

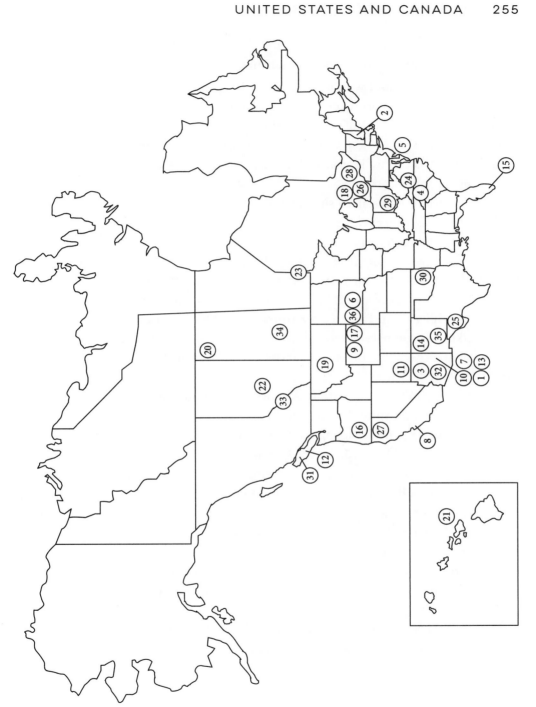

Map of United States & Canada

1. AIRPORT MESA–SEDONA, ARIZONA, USA

Categories: Power Places, Rock Formations, Vortexes

A mesa is a piece of land with a flat top and steep sides. Airport Mesa is so named because it is a popular vortex spot on a 4,500 foot elevation mini-mesa located beside the Sedona airport. It is one of the four red rock formations in Sedona that are believed to be power vortexes. You can experience the grandeur of Airport Mesa by driving up to the viewing area and walking around to take in the exceptional beauty of the red rock vistas, canyon, and vortex sites.

Airport Mesa is a well-liked site to physically visit because you can view the sunrise and sunset and see other vortex areas like Bell Rock, Courthouse Butte, and Cathedral Rock in the distance. Sunrise is an especially good time to meditate and connect with the vortex energy radiating from the mesa because there will be fewer people around, which makes it easier to find a spot where you can sit, connect with the vortex energy, and meditate. Sunset can be packed with people and meditation may be difficult due to both the ability to find an area for yourself and because of the noise level of other visitors talking. If you're remotely connecting with Airport Mesa, make sure to include pictures and videos of the sunset and sunrise in your viewing library to have an in depth experience with the vortex energy.

If you enjoy hiking, the Sedona Airport Mesa Loop Trail will provide you with exceptional views. As you hike through the red dirt, pay attention to the pine trees, the cacti, and other plant life along the trail. You may even come across agave or yucca plants, which are used for medicinal or spiritual purposes.

When connecting with Airport Mesa, you can feel the vortex energy as a tingling throughout your body as a tightening sensation moving across your skin or it may feel as if you've been touched by someone's hand. You may feel the vortex energy move across your shoulder blades, along the nape of your neck, or it may cause goose bumps along your arms. You can feel the vibration within the ground and feel the energy move upward into your body, often following the chakra system from the root to the crown as it moves from your feet to the top of your head. The energy feels smooth, balanced, and alive with strength and empowerment.

In the summer, the air in the area is very dry and warm as you wander around to find the perfect spot where the energy feels as if it's meant specifically for you. Along the trail are areas of shade where you can take a breather and simply sit for a while and experience the energy of the area. Take notice of the cloud formations, too. They vary widely at different times of the year.

In the winter, there can be snow or ice in the area, which gives it a pristine and noble feeling. The awe-inspiring views, the earth frequency emitted from the vortexes, and the beauty of the sunrises and sunsets can leave you with feelings of calmness and connectedness to the earth, all of which grounds you. At Airport Mesa, you can find balance and oneness of being that can truly be transformational.

2. AMERICA'S STONEHENGE MYSTERY HILL– SALEM, NEW HAMPSHIRE, USA

Categories: Astronomical Observatories, Megalithic Sites, Power Places, Vortexes

America's Stonehenge is thought to possibly be the oldest megalithic site in the United States. It was originally called Mystery Hill by William Goodwin, who purchased the area in 1936. The name was changed in the 1960s after a news article called it America's Stonehenge, but there is no cultural connection between the two locations. The area was changed significantly by Goodwin because he believed it was an ancient site where Irish monks had lived prior to the arrival of Christopher Columbus, and he moved some of the rocks around to support his idea.

The site consists of large standing stones, walls, chambers, a sacrificial altar, and an astronomical observatory used to follow solar, lunar, and star events. The stones within the site align with more than forty-five different stars and geographical points (one points true south) and more than two hundred astronomical alignments with the moon. Some of the structures are similar in design to the European Neolithic structures. Another similarity is that it is located on an old fault line, as are other European megalithic locations. Some of the stones have what appears to be ancient writing on them.

There is some controversy surrounding the area. Some archaeologists believe that there was evidence of tool manufacturing similar to that of Native Americans and that, in its original state, it could have been a sacred site to the population. Others believe local farmers arranged the stones during the eighteenth and nineteenth centuries in order to extract lye from wood ashes so they could manufacture soap. However, carbon dating of the charcoal pits in the area found them to be dated between 2000 BC and 173

BC. One of the stones was locked in the stump of a tree that started growing in 1769. A previous owner of the land, Jonathan Pattee, was believed to use the stone structures as part of the Underground Railroad to hide slaves. It is said that he built his home directly over many of the stones and also sold a lot of them.

Even though the exact origins of this location are uncertain, the energy has a positive and reflective quality about it, which makes it a popular power place to visit during solstices and equinoxes. The air in the area is said to feel charged with an electrical type of energy, which indicates that it is quite possibly located on an energy vortex. There are 105 acres of trails where you can participate in both daytime and candlelight snowshoeing during the winter. As you walk through the pristine snow on a self-guided tour of the facility, you can feel the positive, electric energy of the earth as it radiates through the serenity of the quiet, snow-covered environment. During the summer, you can hike the trails while listening to the sound of the birds and other animals. Take a moment to meditate as you walk the trails or while sitting quietly on one of the stone structures within the facility. As you feel the energy move through you, consider the world as it was four thousand years ago when the rocks were placed. Think about the people who lived back then and the significance that the energy of this place held for them.

3. ANTELOPE CANYON—ARIZONA, USA

Categories: Canyons / Gorges, Power Places

If you're visiting land in the Navajo Nation near Page, Arizona, Antelope Canyon is a must see. Located outside of the Glen Canyon National Recreation Area, it is the most visited slot canyon, which means it is narrow and deep, in the southwestern part of the United States. While slot canyons can be formed in any type of rock, they're more frequently found in sandstone or limestone. During formation, water rushes through the rock to create interesting sculptures within the rock, which displays beautiful patterns of color. From an aerial view, the canyon looks like a large fissure in the land.

When visiting Antelope Canyon, you have the choice of visiting the Upper Canyon (which is also known as Corkscrew Canyon) or the Lower Canyon. Each part of Antelope Canyon has a unique energy of its own. In the Upper Canyon, specifically between ten o'clock and noon, the sun illuminates the canyon in a mystical way, forming beautiful light beams that pierce the darkness of the canyon's interior. This time frame can change based on the seasons of the year, so it's always a good idea to call ahead to check on the best time to visit, especially if you're going to take pictures of the light beams from within the canyon.

The energy inside is grounding and uplifting and it swirls together to create a feeling of magnificent power. As you walk along the sandy floor through narrow, dark passageways (in some areas you can't see at all and must feel your way around the walls) and view the various sculptured forms, you can feel the positive energy moving with you. It propels you forward to see what is around the next curve, which may lead into a wide open area filled with light creating changing patterns of brightness and shadow against the canyon's walls. The energy of the Upper Canyon also makes itself known in the pouring sands that can unexpectedly be blown down into the canyon by the wind from the land high above you. Guides will also throw sand into the light beams for photographers to capture intriguing images, which can result in the same pouring sand effect on a lesser scale. Upper Antelope Canyon can become crowded with people but it is easier to walk through it.

The Lower Canyon is deeper, more physically challenging, and can only be navigated with a guide, due to the risk of flash flooding, after a tragic event in 1997 where eleven people lost their lives during a flash flood. To take the guided tour of the Lower Canyon, you must be able to climb and descend stairs and ladders and not be claustrophobic because there are some narrow spaces that you'll have to maneuver through. The energy here seems filled with a hovering anticipation of the unexpected. It's positive, empowering, and can help you connect with your basic instincts of survival and your core spiritual essence. You'll still experience the shafts of light in the Lower Canyon but they aren't as numerous as they are in the Upper Canyon.

Whether you decide to visit the Upper Canyon, Lower Canyon, or both areas during your expedition to Antelope Canyon, the energy of the area will give you a deep appreciation for the art created beneath the surface of our planet. It encourages you to find the artist within you.

4. ASHEVILLE AND WESTERN NORTH CAROLINA REGION—NORTH CAROLINA, USA

**Categories: Mountains / Mounds / Cliff Locations,
Power Places, Regions, Vortexes**

Asheville is located in the western Blue Ridge Mountains. There are more than twenty-four known active energy vortexes in Asheville and the surrounding western North Carolina area. This region is thought to be where several ley lines converge over crystal formations deep within the mountains and create an energy vortex strong enough to affect the entire vicinity. Other locations such as Mt. Pisgah, Linville Falls, and Black Mountain have a distinct energy and vortexes of their own, which adds to the strength and power of the entire area's earth frequency.

There is a feeling of peacefulness and of being *home* that you feel when visiting Asheville. People are often drawn back to this region time and time again for this simple feeling of belonging that it invokes within them, as though you are part of something greater than our human existence, an integral part of the vastness of the universal consciousness. The beauty of the Blue Ridge Mountains is unsurpassed here. You may choose to hike up to the top of Max Patch, a bald mountain (it was cleared for herd grazing) about forty miles from the city, and experience the wind as it whips across the top of the mountain, lifting your energy so that it soars in the air while you quietly mediate and take in the phenomenal view of the mountain range.

As you explore the Blue Ridge Parkway, you'll want to make sure you visit one of the natural waterfalls in the area. Or you might choose to make a day of it and drive a loop from Asheville to Linville Falls, Crabtree Falls, and Graveyard Fields. This has always been one of my favorite routes in the area. Make sure to map it out before you go because there are several other waterfalls you can see by taking small detours of a couple of miles. The waterfalls of western North Carolina radiate a serene, calm energy. Absorb it in as you watch the movement of the water cascading down from above. And if you're close enough, feel the mist across your face and arms, imagine it cleansing you of any negativity and absorb its strength. Let the energy of the mountains and the water that flows through them, speak to your core spiritual essence. Become one with its energy and positive effects.

Another way you can connect to the energy of this area is to take a self-guided float trip from Bent Creek through the Biltmore Estate property or from Hominy Creek through the River Arts District. Both are enjoyable scenic seven-mile routes where you can feel the energy of the river as you float along it.

Asheville's frequency is strong, pure, and will increase your spiritual growth, personal power, and can bring about feelings of inner peace, contentment, and happiness. Its energy is often compared to the Sedona area of Arizona, Mount Shasta in California, and the Great Pyramids of Giza, Egypt. It is known for its ability to heal the mind, body, and spirit. Let the frequency of Asheville heal what ails you.

5. ASSATEAGUE ISLAND—MARYLAND, VIRGINIA, USA

Category: Islands / Reefs

Off of the coast of Virginia and Maryland lies Assateague Island, a thirty-eight–mile wildlife sanctuary barrier island that protects the mainland from storms and erosion. At the southern end of Assateague Island is the Chincoteague National Wildlife Refuge, which protects Chincoteague Island and is connected to Assateague Island by a bridge. The northern section of Assateague Island is owned by Maryland and the southern part, including the Chincoteague National Wildlife Refuge, is owned by Virginia.

Chincoteague Island and Assateague Island are both well known for the wild ponies that live on the islands. The heritage of these wild ponies was traced back to a Spanish galleon that wrecked off of the coast of Assateague and some believe they are also descendants of horses released by early settlers to the area. To manage the herd size of 150 ponies, 50 are kept on Chincoteague Island where the public can view them but the remainder live on other parts of the islands. Every year on Pony Penning Day, the northern herd is rounded up and they swim to Chincoteague Island where some of the ponies are auctioned off at the end of July. The annual swim is a huge event that many spectators come to watch. The ponies of Chincoteague and Assateague Island were made popular in 1947 by children's author, Marguerite Henry, who wrote Misty of Chincoteague and many other books about the ponies of Chincoteague and Assateague.

If you'd like more things to do in the area, there are boat tours where you can ride through the marshlands and bays, which will also enable you to see the wild ponies in their natural oceanside habitat. If you prefer walking over boating, there are many nature trails in the Chincoteague National Wildlife Refuge where you can see native animals such as heron, egrets, and other wading birds, waterfowl, or songbirds. You can even walk to the Assateague Lighthouse, which was built in 1867. Assateague Island is commonly used by migrating birds as a pit stop where they can rest.

The energy of Assateague is crisp and clear. In this natural setting, you can commune with the energy of the ocean, the plant life, the animal life, the sand and the wind. The waves and wind coming off of the ocean can help ground and center you in your spirituality. Take a day to just sit out on the beach at Chincoteague, feeling the waves roll against the shore and the salty wind against your face. Think about the energy of the water, the power of the ocean, the heat of the sun on the sand, and let these elements of nature flow though you. Feel its power engaging your spirit, letting you become one with its positivity. As you look around, the energy of the animals, birds, deer, and ponies, fills you with even more positive energy.

6. BADLANDS NATIONAL PARK–SOUTH DAKOTA, USA
Categories: Caves, Regions, Rock Formations

Southwestern South Dakota is home to a number of national and state parks. The largest are the Badlands National Park and the Black Hills National Forest, which also contains Wind Cave National Park, Custer State Park, and Mount Rushmore National Memorial Park. The parks are within a short distance of one another, so if you're in the area you might like to visit both.

Geologically, badlands are areas of land that have little vegetation, cannot be cultivated, and have been extensively eroded by the wind and water. The Badlands in South Dakota were called *Mako Sica* by the Lakota, which means "bad land." The weather has created very unique formations of buttes, gorges, pinnacles, and spires in this area. Among these formations is a large mixed grass prairie, where you can see a wide diversity of wildlife including bison, coyotes, eagles, and prairie dogs.

In the Badlands, there are many fossils of both sea creatures and land animals. This is because there was a shallow sea that covered the Great Plains region about 75 million years ago. Park officials are still uncovering prehistoric fossils, bones, and plant life. Since that time, the weather has eroded the area so that today there are many sedimentary layers visible to the naked eye. The colors range from the volcanic ash layer, which is white, to a red and orange layer of iron oxides, to the tan and gray colored sand and gravel layer, to the yellow and purple shale layer. A grayish black layer is where the bottom of the sea was and where most of the fossils are found.

The energy feels ancient in the Badlands, as if you're connecting to the beginning of the planet's existence. It has a power that seems to resonate from earth's core, yet is as vibrant as the colors that beautify the landscape. Dramatic, desolate, and colorful, the area can bring feelings of a peaceful knowing to a vastness of universal connection. In the evening and early morning the sunlight caresses the land, bringing to life colors that spark inspiration and calmness within you.

There are many things you can do in the Badlands to connect to its awe-inspiring energy. The Badlands National Park allows visitors access to the entire park; there aren't any restricted spaces that you can't enter. If you enjoy spending time in nature, you can hike one of the numerous trails. Carry a GPS unit with you in case you happen upon a fossil. The park has a system where you can enter the specific coordinates so park officials can follow up on the site. If you don't want to get out into nature, you can take a scenic drive along Highway 240, also known as the Badlands Loop Road, and stop at some of the lookouts to view the spectacular landscape. As you stand there, looking out over the vastness of the region, the vibrancy of the color schemes, and the birds flying in the sky, absorb the energy that radiates from this ancient space; let it ground you to the earth, to your own spirituality, and to the universal consciousness of being. The energy is very strong and healing in the Badlands National Park.

7. BELL ROCK–SEDONA, ARIZONA, USA

Categories: Power Places, Rock Formations, UFO/Extraterrestrial/Paranormal Sites, Vortexes

Bell Rock is another of the four red rock formations in Sedona that are believed to be power vortexes. Its name comes from its bell shape, which makes it easy to find when you're looking out across the landscape. Bell Rock is north of the Village of Oak Creek on Highway 179. The Bell Rock formation is known as a butte, which means it is an isolated hill with steep sides and a flat top. A butte is smaller than a mesa, which is smaller than a plateau. Bell Rock is made up of horizontally layered sedimentary red rock. The area can be rocky and rough so if you plan to hike up Bell Rock make sure you wear some good hiking boots or shoes. On the west side of Bell Rock is an observation area that isn't accessible by road.

The Sedona region drew many people in the New Age movement due to the high levels of energy in the area, especially around places such as Bell Rock. In 1987, during the Harmonic Convergence, thousands of people gathered to wait for Bell Rock's top to open and reveal a spaceship, which didn't happen, but a lot of UFO enthusiasts visit the area on a regular basis.

The energy at Bell Rock is so strong that it can be felt as soon as you get out of your vehicle. If you hike to the structure, the energy gets even stronger and makes you feel revitalized, refreshed, and energized. The twisting of the Juniper trees is said to be an indication of a vortex, but it must be noted that Juniper trees can live hundreds and even thousands of years and, for some unknown reason, as they age, the trunks twist. I guess it's like wrinkles on a human face. It adds character to the tree. So don't automatically assume that the vortex is causing the trunks to twist when you might just be looking at a two-thousand-year-old Juniper tree.

In addition to hiking, you can also go horseback riding through the area or you can take a bike ride. Just make sure that before you head out you're well hydrated and have plenty of water with you. It's also a good idea to stick to the trails with a degree of difficulty you can easily handle instead of choosing one that is too difficult. Once you're on your way, take the extra time to stop for a few minutes and just absorb the energy around you. It will feel different as you travel from one area to another. Some places may feel shimmery and cool while others feel bubbly and hot. The energy can feel like a small vibration that moves along your skin or a heavy drumming sound that thumps inside of you like the beat of a bass drum.

Connecting to the energy at Bell Rock helps you to understand your own being at a deeper level. It is believed to have a balance of feminine and masculine energy. This can help you in finding balance within your core essential being.

8. BIG SUR—CALIFORNIA, USA

Categories: Bodies of Water/Waterfalls/Springs, Mountains/Mounds/Cliff Locations, Regions

Untamed ruggedness, exceptional beauty, and windy, winding roads make up the part of the California coastline known as Big Sur. The section of the Pacific Coast Highway (Highway 1) that runs through Big Sur is a narrow two-lane, eighty-five-mile road along the edge of the coast between Carmel and San Simeon. This section of road took eighteen years to complete and there are often closures due to mudslides, so it's important to check out the conditions prior to traveling there. With the Santa Lucia Mountains to the east and the Pacific Ocean to the west, the scenic beauty of the ocean pounding into the ragged cliffs, which is often misty or foggy, draws visitors from all over the world, so you may encounter a lot of traffic and people at stops along the way.

As you drive along, you'll find yourself wanting to pull over just to enjoy the magnificent views. If you stop in one of the lookouts, notice the strong pull of the energy of the ocean and the powerful inspirational energy of the mountains that surround you. The rocky cliffs and sandy beaches bring balance, while the color of the water gives a feeling of peacefulness and awe. Notice the smell of the ocean, the scent of sage, and the animals. Let the energy seep into your being. If there is fog or mist in the air, it will add a feeling of mystery to the area. Take a moment to just absorb the energy of the elements of Big Sur, to let yourself become one with the land and sea. These feelings will be with you always, and you can tap into them whenever you want to feel balanced, calm, or inspired.

In addition to the scenic drive there are quite a few things you can do along the Big Sur to experience its wide variety of energies. The drive over Bixby Bridge makes you feel at one with the sky because it is 280 feet in the air and 714 feet long, the arch of the bridge provides you with dramatic views that you can lose yourself in (as long as you're not the one driving!). Pfeiffer Beach is a popular stopping point because of the distinctive beach with its purple sand, which is caused by the manganese garnet deposits from the surrounding rocks. It also has intriguing rock formations including the famous Keyhole rock arch.

You can go hiking through the redwood groves and experience the solemn, enduring frequency of these ancient trees that are over 2,500 years old in the Julia Pfeiffer Burns State Park. This park is also home to McWay Falls, where you absorb the energy of the eighty-foot freshwater waterfall as it flows into the ocean. Other points of interest where you can connect with the energy of Big Sur are Sand Dollar beach, the largest beach in the area; Ventana Wilderness, where you can go camping and hiking; and the Big Sur Village beaches, where you can search for jade stones.

As you make your way along Big Sur try to take your time, explore a little, and experience the grounding and uplifting energy that flows all along Big Sur.

9. BIGHORN MEDICINE WHEEL–
BIGHORN NATIONAL FOREST, WYOMING, USA

**Categories: Ceremonial Sites, Medicine Wheels,
Mountains/Mound/Cliff Locations**

Medicine Mountain is located almost thirty-three miles east of Lovell, Wyoming, in the Bighorn Mountain Range and within the Bighorn National Forest. It has an elevation of 9,642 feet and at the very top is where you'll find the Bighorn Medicine Wheel. The Medicine Wheel area is only open for viewing between the end of June and September because it is covered in deep snow during the remainder of the year. To get to the Medicine Wheel, you'll have to walk the last mile and a half because motorized vehicles aren't allowed.

The Medicine Wheel and Medicine Mountain were registered as National Historic Landmarks in 1969. This ancient Native American construction is in the shape of a wheel made up of stacked stones that form a central cairn (stones stacked by humans). There are a total of seven large cairns at the Medicine Wheel—one in the center and six around the circumference of the circle. All are large enough to sit inside. In North America, the Bighorn Medicine Wheel and surrounding area is one of the most well preserved Native American sacred site complexes.

Native Americans have placed sacred and symbolic items along with prayer cloths on the protective wire fence with wooden posts that surrounds the Medicine Wheel. Sometimes you'll see these offerings within the cairns as well. These items aren't to be disturbed by visitors but are to be respected as part of the Native American culture at the Medicine Wheel. The Native Americans still use more contemporary structures in the area surrounding the Medicine Wheel for vision quests, sweat lodge sites, and ceremonial staging areas. It is believed that the Medicine Wheel was built by the Plains Indians between 300 and 1,500 years ago.

The Medicine Wheel also has astronomical significance. Of the six outer cairns, four of them line up with the sunrise and sunset on the summer solstice, the longest day of the year. Three of the cairns line up with the heliacal rising of the stars Aldebaran, Rigel, and Sirius when they are visible for a brief moment just before sunrise on the eastern horizon.

Medicine wheels are believed to act as a mirror that reflects back what is within you. It is used to help one see if you're on the right path and the things within you that need additional work in order to help you fulfill your life purpose and fullest potential. The energy at the Bighorn Medicine Wheel is healing, reflective, and powerful. There is a sense of calmness that surrounds the wheel; it feels balanced, peaceful, and uplifting. It can make you feel as if anything is possible if you reach inside yourself and tap into your inner strength. You may feel as if a weight has lifted from you when visiting the Medicine Wheel. There may be a tingling sensation throughout your body due to the energy in the area or you may experience a desire to breathe more deeply of the mountain air to clear and cleanse the physical body as you clear and cleanse the spiritual body.

10. BOYNTON CANYON—SEDONA, ARIZONA, USA

**Categories: Canyons / Gorges, Mountains/
Mounds/Cliff Locations, Power Places, Vortexes**

Boynton Canyon is one of the four main vortex sites in Sedona. This canyon is called a box canyon because it has a flat bottom and vertical walls. It is located on Dry Creek Road about three miles from the junction of highways 89A and 179 in Red Rock State Park. To reach the vortex, you'll park at the entrance of the Boynton Canyon Trail and then walk the trail until you see a sign for Vista Trail. Further along Vista Trail you'll come to a high knoll (about thirty feet), which is the masculine vortex, and you'll also see the feminine vortex, Kachina Woman, to the east. In this area, the energy feels balanced, which helps to strengthen both the masculine and feminine (yin/yang) energies within you.

The trail through Boynton Canyon is easily accessible and not too hard to navigate. The trail itself is about three miles long one way so plan to hike for almost six miles, take plenty of water to keep yourself hydrated and a light snack to fuel your energy during the trek. The trail is popular because of the incredible views of Sinagua cliff dwellings that date back to the fourteenth and fifteenth centuries, the natural rock formations, wildlife, plant life, its proximity to a luxury resort, and being an easy trail to walk. If you're going in the summer months, get an early start at first light in order to enjoy the sunrise and beat the afternoon heat. When you reach the end of the Boynton Canyon trail, there's an area where you can sit and rest for a while, eat your snack, and meditate to purposefully connect your frequency to the energy of the area and rejuvenate your energy before you start the hike back.

The energy at Boynton Canyon is believed to be sacred, balanced, and mysterious. It is said that a powerful feminine spirit lives in Boynton Canyon and many native tribes still perform private sacred ceremonies within the area.

As you walk along the Boynton Canyon Trail, you can enjoy the quiet peacefulness of its energy. If you feel like you are drawn to a specific place while you're walking, then go to it, sit quietly, and open your mind, heart, and spirit to the energy of the earth. You can meditate if you like but you don't have too. You can just sit there, with your defenses down, your mind clear and open, and allow the energy of the vortex to move through you. Notice how it feels. Does it make your mind more alert, does it pull you into yourself so you can connect with your higher self, or does it open your spiritual self to the vastness of universal consciousness? Even if all you feel is grounded to the earth, an integral part of the natural world you're sitting in, then that's the message. You can also participate in a walking meditation during your hike on the trail.

11. BRYCE CANYON NATIONAL PARK—UTAH, USA

Category: Canyons / Gorges

Bryce Canyon National Park is in Southwestern Utah. Theoretically, Bryce Canyon is not a canyon but instead a series of amphitheaters on the eastern side of Paunsaugunt Plateau. When canyons are formed it is from erosion that is initiated from a central stream. In Bryce Canyon, erosion was caused by water and ice in a mechanical weathering process called frost-wedging when water freezes, expands, then thaws, instead of erosion by a central stream or river. After repeated cycles of frost-wedging in the cracks or pores of the rocks, it causes them to turn into huge fissures which eventually breaks the rock. It took millions of years for this type of erosion to create the unique red, white, and orange hoodoos, thin spires of tall rock that can be up to 200 feet high, located in Bryce Canyon. The colors are dependent upon the type of mineral deposits in the rock.

In the 1850s, Mormon pioneers settled the area, and Ebenezer Bryce homesteaded there in 1874. According to the National Park Service, in the Pioneer History section of their website, he built a logging road through the largest amphitheater. Locals refer to this road as Bryce's Canyon, thus the name. Due to the harsh environment of the area, most people didn't stay there for long periods of time. Archaeological discoveries show that people have been in Bryce Canyon for about ten thousand years.

Bryce Canyon is filled with diversity in the plant and animal life. Fox, coyotes, mountain lions, bears, elk, bobcats, badgers, squirrels, marmots, chipmunks, porcupines, rattlesnakes, lizards, salamanders, a multitude of birds, insects, butterflies, and moths all call Bryce Canyon home.

When visiting Bryce Canyon if you decide to stay after dark, the stargazing is phenomenal due to the distance from any other light sources. The stars shine brightly and the darkness is intense. There are two campgrounds and two hotels if you decide to stay overnight. Driving through the area, you'll find thirteen overlooks where you can view the colorful, rugged landscape. Sometimes you can see for more than one hundred miles. If you want a more intimate experience to connect with the energy of the amphitheaters, there are eight hiking trails you can travel by foot. Or if you enjoy horses, there are horseback tours during the summer months. There are many other programs available at the park that offer a wide variety of experiences during your stay.

When connecting to the energy of Bryce Canyon, there is a sense of being part of the beginning of time and the timeless beauty of the earth. The energy feels strong, pure, and grounding. There is a sense of extreme power, yet unlimited peace. The hoodoo formations radiate a positive energy that humbles and balances your spiritual being. Walking along the trails, you may experience a feeling of smallness and of being a speck within the grand scheme of universal energy. Bryce Canyon pulses with ancient power that feels as if it radiates from the core of the earth into you. This energy can give you strength of purpose, clarity of being, and help you focus on your path in life.

12. CARMANAH WALBRAN— VANCOUVER ISLAND, CANADA

Categories: Canyon/Gorges, Forests/Trees, Islands/Reefs

Carmanah Walbran Provincial Park is a protected ancient, old-growth forest that is part of a rainforest in the wilderness area on Vancouver Island. It is difficult to access and the trails are often muddy. There is active logging going on in the area, so you have to be aware that you could encounter huge logging trucks at any time. A lot of bears live here, so you'll need to be attentive to the fact that you're traveling in their territory and know what to do if you encounter one.

Hiking in the Carmanah Walbran is an experience you'll never forget. You'll encounter nature at its finest, from slippery, moss-laden green logs and roots to mud pits, western red cedar, and Sitka spruce trees that are a thousand years old. As you look up into the trees you'll notice ferns and fungi growing on the tree trunks. The scent of pine is strong in the air and it can feel heavy with rain at times, which can cause fog and mist throughout the area. The ground cover is just as impressive as the trees. You'll see a wide variety of plants and animals, impressive amounts of moss, and many different kinds of insects. Prepare yourself for the mosquitoes, which are abundant, before you start your hike.

Within the park in the Carmanah Creek canyon is the Carmanah Giant, the world's tallest Sitka spruce tree. Being in the presence of this enormous Sitka spruce will give you a feeling of awe and inspiration. Think of all of the changes that have happened, all of the inventions that have occurred, and how the world has evolved since this tree came into existence. Now consider how this tree has grown and survived year after year. It will make you look at life differently, will make you consider this undisturbed forest with a sense of wonder, and will make a profound, and life-long, lasting impression on you that will remain long after you've gone home and left the forest behind. Losing yourself in this natural setting for a while will affect your energy on a deep spiritual level. It's an experience that, if you allow yourself to become one with the energy of the place, can ground, balance, rejuvenate and impact you with its strength and power.

The energy here is pristine, striking, and humbling. Being in the energy of the Carmanah Walbran forest feels like you're being hugged by nature. You're totally enclosed within its energy, which awakens all of your senses including your intuition. It is intense, vibrant, and spiritually enlightening as you move through this sacred space. As you connect to the energy of the forest, you're connecting to the energy of the universe, of time, and of the ancient world.

13. CATHEDRAL ROCK–SEDONA, ARIZONA, USA
Categories: Power Places, Rock Formations, Vortexes

Cathedral Rock is located in the Coconino National Forest in Red Rock State Park and is one of the four main vortex points in Sedona, Arizona. It is a popular destination because it is close to the highway. Due to the convenient location and the unique formations of saddles (gaps) between the tall spires, Cathedral Rock is one of the most photographed of the redbed sandstone formations in the area. The vortex is at the top of Cathedral Rock but you can also feel the energy of the vortex if you hike the Red Rock Crossing, which runs along Oak Creek. Photos of Cathedral Rock with water in the foreground are taken along the Red Rock Crossing hike. This is an easy mile-long hike that is popular for families with small children or those who want to experience an easy hike to view Cathedral Rock.

For those hikers who like a more strenuous adventure there is the Cathedral Rock Trail Number 170. The first half mile of this trail is an easy walk with a moderate slope up to a flat ledge area that has amazing views. This is a good location to connect to the energy of Cathedral Rock through meditation or through sharing your frequency with the earth frequency of the vortex located above you between the spires. Take time to reflect upon issues that have been concerning you and you'll find that it seems as if the solution just flows to you. This part of the trail is known as an upflow vortex, which means that the energy here is inspirational, serene, and helps you to spiritually align yourself for positive forward movement.

The remainder of this trail is very difficult and involves a lot of climbing. Some of the rocks you'll climb over are slick and bald and even have toeholds that have been cut into them to help you with the ascent, which is very steep because you're climbing almost straight up the six hundred foot increase in elevation to the saddle. This trail isn't for the faint of heart. For those with balance issues, if you're out of shape, or if you have other health issues, you may want to experience the energy along the first half of the trail. If you do continue on, you may feel energized due to the intense energy from the vortex, but you will have to exert yourself during this rigorous climb. Make sure you wear good hiking boots if you want to tackle Trail 170.

Once you reach the top, saddled between two of the spires is a small rock formation called the Grandmother Rock. This is where the vortex is located. The energy here is warm, calming, and embraces you with positivity. It strengthens the feminine side of you, which means it enhances the positive characteristics of goodness, kindness, and compassion. It helps you be more patient, to think before you speak or take action, and to be considerate and aware of the feelings of others. The energy here feels like you've just been wrapped in a loving embrace.

14. CHACO CANYON—NEW MEXICO, USA
Category: Canyons/Gorges, Ceremonial Sites, Petroglyph/Rock Art Sites, Ruins/Archeological Sites

Located in the remote northwestern deserts of New Mexico is Chaco Canyon and the extensive ruins of an ancient Pueblo civilization, which consists of fifteen major complexes of huge, multi-storied buildings, which have orientations to view the sun, moon, and stars.[33]

Chaco Canyon is well known as one of the best stargazing locations in America. It became the newest international Dark Sky Park on August 19, 2013. It observes protection of the dark night skies for the protection of the natural environment, to maintain the natural nocturnal ecosystems, the day-to-night cycles that the plant and animal life

33. NM True TV, Chaco Canyon & Aztec Ruins, January 25, 2016, https://www.youtube.com/ watch?time_continue=7&v=KzmLnsljAKo.

depend on for survival, and for the star-gazing enthusiasts. To achieve this, there is no permanent lighting in 99 percent of the park.

There are four hiking trails that will take you to some of the more remote locations within the park. Gallo Campground offers tent camping but it sometimes fills up so the park recommends that you have alternative places to stay. While the campground can't accommodate RV's or trailers, car camping is allowed. The campground is surrounded by a cliff dwelling, a high desert landscape, petroglyphs, and inscriptions, but there isn't any shade and campsites are available by reservation only.

The ancient Pueblo people who lived in Chaco Canyon built what was the center for trade of the prehistoric Four Corners area a thousand years ago and it was the main ceremonial and social center for their culture. The term *Anasazi*, a Navaho word meaning "the ancient ones," is how modern culture refers to the people of the time. Artifacts from these ruins are stored in the Chaco Museum Collection.

The area of the ruins is surrounded in mystery. Walking through these remarkable one-thousand-year-old walls of a once flourishing culture, you'll feel the power of the people, the steadfastness of the structures and the sacredness of the energy that flows through and around the structures. It is extremely well preserved, so walking through the ruins feels like you're walking back in time, which gives you a new perspective on your own spirituality, a unique experience in that you're standing where many people worked together to build structures that have stood the test of time.

The energy in the Chaco Canyon moves like a ripple. It is strong and pure in the center where the ruins are located but it moves like a wave outward for miles away from the center. Sitting within the ruins, meditating, and feeling the ancient energy of the old ones all around you, as the earth energy moves from the ground and through you, empowers you to achieve what you want in life. As you feel this ancient energy, allow your spiritual self to receive the positivity and motivational upsurge as it pulses through you, boosting your desire to fulfill your spiritual purpose while on the earthly plane of existence.

15. CORAL CASTLE—FLORIDA, USA

Category: Power Places, Vortexes

Coral Castle is located in Homestead, Florida, off of South Dixie Highway. It is an amazing structure built out of Florida oolite limestone, which is also known as coral stone, that is found near the surface of the land. Coral stone is highly porous and permeable and is made of fossiliferous limestone, aquatic sediment, quartz sand, and coral, mollusk, and bryozoan fossils. Coral stone is a popular building material in South Florida, and you'll find it everywhere in both interior and exterior construction.

Coral Castle has long been shrouded in mystery. It was built by Edward Leedskalnin, who was born in Riga, Latvia, in 1887. While still living in Riga at age twenty-six, he was engaged to sixteen-year-old Agnes Scuffs, the love of his life, whom he referred to as his Sweet Sixteen. However, Agnes called off the wedding the day before the ceremony was to take place. Devastated, Ed moved to Florida City in the United States and lived there until 1936. It was at this location that he started carving the coral stone but he moved to Homestead in 1936 and took the carvings with him.

At the Homestead location he continued the work as a testimony to his undying love for Agnes and ultimately created Coral Castle, moving the stone himself and using hand tools to carve the stone. He often worked at night and it took twenty-eight years to complete. Leedskalnin was only five feet tall and weighed about one hundred pounds, so it seemed impossible that he could move such large stones by himself. According to the Coral Castle Museum, when asked how he moved the rocks Ed would reply that he "understood the laws of weight and leverage well."[34]

Some of the coral stone structures within Coral Castle are a five thousand pound table in the shape of a heart, a table in the shape of Florida with a water basin that represents Lake Okeechobee, a rocking chair that can be moved with just one finger, a sundial that is calibrated to the summer and winter solstice and is accurate within two minutes, a sun couch, moon fountain, bathtub, BBQ, Ed's bedroom, a throne room and a twenty-five foot telescope aligned to the North Star, a forty foot obelisk weighing 57,000 pounds and a series of circular coral stones that represent the solar system. The engineering and construction of Coral Castle has been compared to Stonehenge and the Great Pyramids of Egypt.

The energy of Coral Castle is very intense, especially if you're empathic, intuitive, or highly sensitive, or if you are able to do psychometry. Coral Castle is built where nine ley lines converge, which is one of the reasons the energy is so strong here. You'll feel it as a living thing. It feels as if your frequency is pulled tight, stretched thin, and as if it's beating to a deep, heavy pulse. You may experience a headache, tightness around your

---

34. Coral Castle Museum, Who's Ed, 2018, https://coralcastle.com/whos-ed/

eyes, or a feeling of exhilaration while you're there and you'll probably be a little tired when you leave. Visiting Coral Castle is a joyful experience that will keep you wondering about its mysteries.

16. CRATER LAKE–MEDFORD, OREGON, USA

Categories: Bodies of Water/Waterfalls/Springs, Islands/Reefs, Power Places, Volcanoes/Volcano Cones

In southern Oregon, about a hundred miles east of the Pacific Ocean in Crater Lake National Park, is the deepest lake in the United States. Crater Lake is 1,943 feet deep, a little over six miles at its widest point, and its water comes from the melted winter snow in the area instead of streams or creeks like most lakes. Because of the lack of inlets and outlets and the large amount of sun penetration into the lake, the water always appears very blue and clear. In most lakes finding clarity at one hundred feet is rare, but at Crater Lake clarity is typically around 120 feet, and in 1997 it was measured at 142 feet according to the National Park Service statistics.[35]

Crater Lake was formed 7,700 years ago when Mount Mazama, an active volcano, erupted and collapsed, creating a volcanic basin. Mount Mazama had additional, smaller eruptions, which created Wizard Island, a small volcanic cinder cone with a small crater at the top, on the west side of the lake. Steep rock walls surround Crater Lake and black volcanic lava blocks make up Wizard Island.

Another very intriguing feature of Crater Lake is the Old Man of the Lake. This thirty-foot hemlock log is thought to be a minimum of 450 years old and has been floating upright in Crater Lake for at least the past 120 years. The Old Man moves all around the lake as the wind blows. It is upright because of the higher density of the submerged part of the tree beneath the clear cold water, which preserves it.

There are many ways to experience the energy of Crater Lake. In the summer you can drive around the thirty-three-mile rim, take a boat tour on the lake, or hike through the forests or down to the water. You can go swimming at the end of Cleetwood Cove Trail or go fishing. The lake was stocked with six different species of fish between 1888 and 1941 and today only the Rainbow Trout and Kokanee Salmon have survived. Since fish aren't native to the lake you don't have to have a fishing license and there is no

---

35. National Park Service, Crater Lake, 2002, https://www.nps.gov/crla/planyourvisit/upload/
    Introduction-to-Crater-Lake-508.pdf

limit to how many fish you can catch, but you must use artificial bait. Winter activities include snowshoeing walks led by a park ranger or cross country skiing along the many trails.

The energy of Crater Lake will inspire you and fill you with a sense of wonder and admiration for its sheer breathtaking beauty. When you first look across the lake, its magnificence will take your breath away and cause you to stop in your tracks. The energy of the lake is vibrant, powerful, and ancient. There is a sense of timelessness, of enchantment, and of being part of a universal power bigger than you can imagine. Crater Lake's energy will awaken your spiritual self, attune you to the Divine, and bring about clarity of being. Taking some time just to sit alone on the rim and stare out across this peaceful, powerful, and sacred place will stir your soul. It will inspire you and humble you, and its energy will recharge and activate your own spirituality or vision quest.

17. DEVILS TOWER—CROOK COUNTY, WYOMING, USA
Categories: Power Places, Rock Formations

Devils Tower was named America's first national monument on September 24, 1906, by President Theodore Roosevelt. Located in Crook County, Wyoming, Devils Tower is a laccolithic butte of igneous rock. It formed during an igneous intrusion when magma pushed the igneous rock within the earth's crust upwards, which made a dome shape with a flat base on the surface of the earth. Over thousands of years, erosion has eaten away at the intrusion until all that is left is what we know as Devils Tower. Eventually, thousands of years from now, the tower will wear down and disappear altogether.

This grand structure wasn't always called Devils Tower. Native Americans who have always considered it a sacred place originally called it Bear's Lodge. Due to an error in translation, it became known as Devils Tower. American Indians also call it Bear's Tipi, Tree Rock, Grizzly Bear's Lodge, and Bear Lodge Butte. Devils Tower is culturally important to many Native America tribes today, who still hold religious ceremonies there. Individually it is used as a place of worship or vision quests and you'll often find prayer cloths tied in the area.

For the past one hundred years, rock climbers have frequented Devils Tower to climb the hundreds of parallel cracks that divide it into hexagonal columns, which is considered an acceptable recreation. However, June is the most sacred month to many tribes, so there is a voluntary climbing closure in place during the entire month where rock climbers are asked to refrain from climbing on Devils Tower or over the boulders surrounding the base out of respect for the cultural and spiritual respect to these tribes. Climbing the structure is dangerous and you must take the necessary precautions, especially when rappelling down the tower, which is when most of the accidents and deaths have occurred. Helmets are recommended due to the amount of rocks that fall from the structure.

The energy surrounding Devils Tower is like a deep rumble of constant vibration. It is an ancient, positive, and transformational frequency. It is drawing, which means it pulls you to it, making you feel as if you must visit or find out more about the site. Once you've experienced the energy you will feel it resonate within your spiritual self. Its frequency has the ability to reconnect you to your true spiritual essence through the energy of earth's beginning. As you feel the power of the tower move through you, think back to when it formed, when the earth was new; a time when mountain ranges were created. As you feel the power of creation flowing around you, think about what you can create with your life, how you can form and shape yourself to become all you want to be while on the earthly plane. Feel it, own it, and accomplish it. You may even decide to participate in your own vision quest while focusing on the energy of Devils Tower. Let the energy lead you and guide you to what you need to know.

18. DREAMER'S ROCK—
MANITOULIN ISLAND, ONTARIO, CANADA

Categories: Bodies of Water/Waterfalls/Springs, Ceremonial Sites, Islands/Reefs, Power Places, Power Stones, Rock Formations

Dreamer's Rock is made of solid white quartzite. It is located on Birch Island in the District of Manitoulin in the northern part of Lake Huron. It gets its name from the Anishinabek Nation because of its use as a vision quest and dream visitation site by the First Nations Aboriginal people, who believe the rock is a gift from the Creator where they could seek guidance through life. Today it is used, as it was in the past, for vision and dream quests. In the fall of the year, sweat lodge ceremonies are held there, which is a time of cleansing for the First Nations people. It is a spiritual place that was also used as a sacred ceremonial and rite-of-passage site, a place to seek spiritual healing, inspiration, and clarity of mind. In the past, when First Nation boys reached adolescence, they would go on a vision quest to Dreamer's Rock without their parents or any kind of food. With only a blanket and some water, they would lie in a depression within the rock where they prayed and fasted until they met their lifetime spirit guide who would then advise them on their path in life and true purpose. This practice is commemorated with a plaque near the rock, which also states that after the arrival of the Europeans, the rock wasn't used as much, and today it is no longer used for rites of passage ceremonies.

To visit Dreamer's Rock, you'll have to ask permission from the Whitefish River First Nation's office out of respect for their culture. Since it is a spiritual place, photos aren't allowed. Once permission is received, it's a short walk to the site. The views from Dreamer's Rock are spectacular. As you turn you'll see the lake, island, and the La Cloche Mountains on the mainland. These mountains are also formed from quartzite stones and you can see the light from the sun reflecting off of them. As you take in the view, you can't help but to feel connected to the strong essence of the mountains, the calmness of the lake, and the vibrancy of the sun reflecting off of the quartzite. The area is primeval, which makes you feel introspective and in awe of its connection to the Divine.

The energy at Dreamer's Rock is prophetic and can often enhance or trigger intuitive abilities. After visiting Dreamer's Rock, you may have dreams that come true, your intuition becomes stronger and more accurate, and you feel a deeper connection not only to the earth but to your own inner spiritual being as well. The energy in this sacred place enhances the connection to your higher self and to your spirit guides, making it easier to connect with them and receive their messages. You don't have to sleep on Dreamer's Rock to become one with the energy of the area. At the top, you can simply lie on the rock, run your hands across its smoothness, and feel the power of the earth frequency flow from the rock into your mind, body, and spirit.

19. GIANT SPRINGS—GREAT FALLS, MONTANA, USA
Categories: Bodies of Water/Waterfalls/Springs, Power Places, Vortexes

Giant Springs is the world's most abundant natural freshwater spring. Lewis and Clark recorded it in 1805. The Blackfeet Indians called it Black Eagle Spring and revered it as a sacred site for hundreds of years prior to the arrival of Lewis and Clark. The outflow of water from Giant Springs is an astonishing 150 to 190 million gallons of water per day; it has an average temperature of fifty-four degrees Fahrenheit; and the spring has been carbon dated to be about three thousand years old. The water of the springs begins in the Little Belt Mountains and takes fifty years to travel from that area to the surface of Giant

Springs, which is sixty miles away. That is a long time, which is an indication that some things take time, and you can't rush them. If you're feeling rushed into making a decision about something, a visit to Giant Springs, even if it's in the pages of a book, can help you gain clarity of mind so you can slow down and make a well thought out and logical, not emotional, decision.

The water of Giant Springs bubbles up into a large pool that is surrounded by lush plant life. It then overflows into the Roe River, the shortest river in the world at only 201 feet in length, before flowing into the Yellowstone River, a tributary of the Missouri River. Nearby are two of the waterfalls that the Lewis and Clark expedition originally noted, Rainbow Falls and Crooked Falls. You can also explore other nearby points of interest like the fish hatchery and the Lewis and Clark Overlook and Trailhead.

Native Americans noticed that some of the fish in the Missouri River used the springs to lay eggs because it was the right temperature for the young fish to thrive. In 1928, a man-made hatchery was built with water flow to the hatchery from Giant Springs at the rate of about seven hundred gallons per minute. Since the water is from a deep aquifer and is rich in nitrogen, it is pumped through packed columns to add more oxygen into the water, which is better for the hatchling fish.

Giant Springs State Park borders the banks of the Missouri River. Spend some time in the presence of the massive amount of energy being expelled from the earth through the water at Giant Springs. The energy here is mighty, strong, and overflowing. You may notice spiraling sections within the spring that look like little vortexes. The energy at Giant Springs is stimulating on a spiritual level. Springs are generally thought of as cleansing, pure, spiritual sites. Feel the energy of abundance, rejuvenation, and inspiration that Giant Springs creates within you as it lifts you up, creates changes, and motivates you along your path.

20. GREAT SANDHILLS AND ATHABASCA SAND DUNES— SASKATCHEWAN, CANADA

Categories: Bodies of Water/Waterfalls/Springs, Sandhills / Sand Dunes

You wouldn't expect to find sand dunes located in the middle of Canada, but that's exactly what you'll discover in the province of Saskatchewan. The most famous sand dunes are in the southern and northern part of the province.

If you're in the southern part of Saskatchewan within the protected area of the Great Sandhills Ecological Reserve, you'll find one of the largest sandhill complexes in Canada. This easily accessible 1,900 square mile tract of land is called the Great Sandhills. When you hear the name, you might think that the whole area is one large sandhill but it is a large native grassland region with sections of sandhills within it. Looking at the area in an aerial view, you can see the contrast between the dunes and the grass. As the dunes move, grass covers the area where they were previously located. While visiting the Great Sandhills, you can hike across the top of a dune or take a toboggan ride down the side of one. The energy here is radiant, fun, and engaging. The wind and sand give the energy in this area lightness and high frequency. It's a great place to visit when you're feeling like you're in a rut and need an energy boost to get yourself moving in a new direction.

Now let's travel to the northwest corner of Saskatchewan to Lake Athabasca, which is home to the world's most northerly active sand dunes. Along the south shore of Lake Athabasca you'll find the Athabasca Sand Dunes. This very remote location can only be reached by boat or plane. There is evidence that Native Americans used the area eight thousand years ago. The dunes here are nearly one hundred feet high. There are six areas designated for camping but you have to bring everything you need with you and are expected to leave no evidence of your stay behind. Ecologically, the area of the Athabasca Sand Dunes is considered delicate and fragile so it's important not to disturb it when you visit. The area has many sand blasted structures and surfaces covered with pebbles. You'll see rare plant species as well when you hike the area. The energy at the Athabasca Sand Dunes feels profound and alive. The combination of wind, sand, and water touches a place deep within you, a connection to the Divine. As you stand atop the sand, looking out over the lake, with a strong wind blowing against you, there is the energy of knowing, of being at the beginning, of starting over, of moving with the flow, and of progressing along your path. The energy here can bring about a spiritual rebirth; it can settle your soul and give you the strength of rejuvenation for your spirit.

Both the Great Sandhills and the Athabasca Sand Dunes are continually moving, which means the landscape is always different and unique whenever you visit. Since there is constant movement, the energy is also in a state of movement and flow. If you need to get yourself moving forward or if you need to turn your energy inward and connect with your soul essence, then visit Saskatchewan's beautiful sand dunes.

21. HALEAKALA CRATER—MAUI, HAWAII, USA

Categories: Islands/Reefs, Volcanoes/Volcano Cones

Haleakala is a dormant volcano located in Haleakala National Park on the island of Maui in Hawaii. Haleakala has erupted more than six times during the past one thousand years. *Haleakala* means "house of the sun." The volcanic crater got this name because legend has it that the demigod Maui imprisoned the sun at Haleakala to make the days longer. It is the highest peak in Maui at 10,023 feet above sea level. Native Hawaiians call it the wilderness of the gods and would visit the summit of Haleakala to honor the gods, hunt for food, or to get rocks that they could fashion into tools. The summit of Haleakala has always been thought of as a sacred place, where one could communicate with the Divine, the deceased, and find peace within oneself.

You can enjoy a wide variety of activities such as backcountry camping, horseback riding, hiking, and swimming, or you can take a commercial tour of the area. The summit of Haleakala is a popular destination that more than 1.45 million people visit each year. Most people drive up a winding road to reach the summit, but some enjoy riding their bikes along this same road. Because of the elevation at the summit, the weather can turn on a dime. It's important to be prepared because there aren't any amenities in the park. The temperature is colder at the summit and it can be very windy. So gas up, bring food and water; clothing for hot, cold, and wet weather; and sun protection, and wear good walking shoes or boots. There are many rare and endangered species of plants and animals in the park that you may encounter if you hike within the nineteen square miles of the crater floor, where you'll also find a lake, meadow, forested areas, and a desert area among the cinder deposits formed from previous eruptions.

From the summit of Haleakala, as you look out across the vast crater to the blue skies and white clouds beyond, it is an impressive sight to behold. There really aren't any words that can do it justice. It will catch your breath, inspire, and humble you with its sacred beauty. Sunrise and sunset are popular times to visit the summit and it can get crowded. It's a bit strange to look down at the clouds instead of looking up at them, but it's at this vantage point that you can truly connect to the powerful energy of Haleakala. The terrain has rich colors and unique formations. When you really think about it, you're standing in a place that once ran red with the powerful energy from the center of the earth. The strength and high frequency of the lava flow can still be felt through the soles of your feet if you take a moment to form a connection with it.

On Haleakala you can let your intuition run free, let your soul soar, and feel the true timelessness of the ancient volcano. It can be a catalyst to remembering the ancientness of your true spiritual self.

22. LAC SAINTE ANNE—
LAKE SAINT ANNE, ALBERTA, CANADA

Categories: Bodies of Water/Waterfalls/Springs, Pilgrimage Sites

Lac Sainte Anne is located forty-eight miles northwest of Edmonton. Saint Anne is known as the mother of the Virgin Mary, grandmother of Jesus. In 1876 Pope Pius IX named her the Patroness of Canada. She is known for working miracles and curing thousands of ailments.

For centuries before the Roman Catholic Reverend Thibault named the lake Lac Sainte Anne, First Nation tribes called the lake Big Medicine Lake, Spirit Lake, God's Lake, and Holy Lake due to the ability of the water to heal both animals and people. These various tribes would often camp out at the lake to partake of its healing powers. The aboriginal tribes use the area today as a spiritual and sacred place to gather. For the aboriginal people, the grandmother figure is traditionally important in their beliefs.

In the late 1890s a severe drought occurred in Alberta that lasted for several years. A Roman Catholic missionary went to the holy lake of the First Nation tribes to pray. While at the lake, he noticed that birds and other animals seemed to be healed after drinking from the lake or getting into the water. He told other priests about what he'd seen and they all decided to go to the lake to pray for rain. After five days and nights of continuous prayers, it rained enough to end the drought. Since that time, Roman Catholic's have conducted pilgrimages every July to Lac Sainte Anne to pray for miracles and to be healed from ailments. A permanent mission was built on the site in 1844. Today the pilgrimage is a two-day event that is attended by 40,000 people who wade into the holy waters and are blessed by a priest in the name of Saint Anne. It is always held during the week of July 26, which is the feast day of Sainte Anne. The pilgrimage site is a cleared flat portion of land near a small church, confessional building, and rectory, and includes a 328-foot half circle of the lake in front of the cleared land.

There are many stories of not only physical healing but also mental healing that have occurred after people have participated in the Lac Sainte Anne pilgrimage. The energy of Lac Sainte Anne is very strong and powerful, especially in its healing energy.

The frequency of the area is very high and attuned with the Divine. As you stand in the cool water and look out across the lake, feel the energy of the water as it spirals around your legs and moves upward through your body, removing blocks, and freeing your frequency so that it elevates even higher. The energy is pure and bright with white light and radiates with positivity. Lac Sainte Anne can clear your mind and heart from negative emotions that are holding you back from achieving all you desire in life. Its healing essence can touch and heal you even from afar.

23. LAKE OF THE WOODS— MINNESOTA, USA/ONTARIO, CANADA

Categories: Bodies of Water/Waterfalls/Springs, Islands/Reefs, Mountains/Mounds/Cliff Locations

Lake of the Woods is located in Minnesota in the United States as well as the Ontario and Manitoba provinces of Canada. The lake is huge and has 65,000 miles of shoreline if you include the shorelines of the 14,522 islands within the lake. It is 85 miles long, 56 miles wide, and 310 feet at its deepest point at Whitefish Bay.

The rocks and cliffs surrounding Lake of the Woods have many sites where you can find pictographs believed to be five thousand years old. These locations are only accessible by boat and it is traditional to show your respect by leaving some kind of offering if you visit them. The energy at these sites flows with intense positivity and light. It is a step back in time, to the frequency of the area when people led a simple life in tune with nature. The pictograph sites have always been sacred to the Ojibwe tribes and they prefer that they aren't photographed.

At the lake, you can participate in outdoor activities all year long. In the summer months you can go hiking, take guided fishing tours, rent a boat and go out on the lake by yourself, or ride ATVs along designated trails. During the winter months, you can go ice fishing, snowmobiling, or cross-country skiing. Lake of the Woods is known as the Walleye Capital of the World due to the abundance of walleye fish. The musky (muskellunge) fish is the second most abundant fish in the lake, and it is full of many other species such as northern pike, perch, bass, lake trout, and lake sturgeon, to name just a few.

While the world-class fishing creates the largest draw of people visiting the lake, you can go to have a spiritual experience as well. Even if you don't like to fish, renting a boat for the day and losing yourself among the thousands of islands, breathing in the clean air, and feeling the connection to the earth, lake, and sky is invigorating, refreshing, and helps you to attune to the inner essence within you. During the winter, you can walk in the snow while looking over the lake to connect to the purity of the world around you. Visiting Lake of the Woods offers many unique opportunities to reflect on your life, settle your emotions, and make plans for positive change. Seeing the vast amount of animal life, from bald eagles to loons, deer, river otters, and beavers, gives you the ability to practice animal frequency and receive messages from the animals you encounter.

Stargazing at Lake of the Woods is phenomenal due to the lack of light pollution from towns and cities. Bring a blanket or reclining lawn chair and just stare at the night sky. Look for shooting stars and at the northern lights for a real treat.

Whether you visit in the winter or summer, each experience at the Lake of the Woods will be unique spiritually as well as in the activities you participate in and the natural encounters you make. Its breathtaking beauty will make you want to return for additional visits.

24. MABRY'S MILL—BLUE RIDGE PARKWAY, VIRGINIA, USA
Categories: Mountains/Mounds/Cliff Locations, Power Places, Vortexes

As you're riding along the Blue Ridge Parkway in Floyd County, Virginia, now about a mile north of Meadows of Dan, you'll arrive at Milepost 176 and there, on the side of the road, is an old water powered mill made out of wood. Welcome to Mabry's Mill, one of the most photographed places on the Blue Ridge Parkway.

Ed Mabry began work on the mill when he moved back to the area after working as a blacksmith in West Virginia in 1903. Previously he'd used a water-turned lathe to make chairs so he decided to build a water powered mill. Once the mill was constructed, Mabry and his wife, Lizzie, ran the mill as a blacksmith shop, then a wheelwright shop, then as a sawmill, and finally a gristmill for grinding grain. In 1914 Mabry purchased land bordering what he already owned to get access to more water to run the mill. Mabry also built a wooden aqueduct system built several feet off of the ground that transported water to the mill. In its time the mill was a place where locals would come to have work done but also to visit with their neighbors.

Park naturalists restored the buildings and during the summer they offer many demonstrations to teach visitors about the mountain industry in the early 1900s at the mill and the surrounding buildings. The people who work there dress up in local period clothing from the time when the mill was in full operation, usually bib overalls, flannel shirts, and some kind of hat. You can watch a miller grind corn in the gristmill and see how they cut logs in the saw mill. Around the mill is a trail that goes past several historical exhibits, including Matthews Cabin, which shows how homes were built in the mountains during Mabry's lifetime. At the cabin there are demonstrations about tanning and making shoes. There's also a working blacksmith shop where you can watch how they made shoes for the horses and tools. You'll also walk by a whiskey still and a sorghum mill.

If you visit Mabry's Mill in the summer, they offer live musical performances every Sunday. It's a way to create the same sense of community that Mabry's Mill was known for in the past. At the restaurant and gift shop, you can have breakfast all day, lunch and dinner (the cobbler is delicious), or pick up some souvenirs.

The energy at Mabry's Mill is peaceful and pure. It flows with positivity and is very calming and healing. As you walk through the area, listening to the water flowing through the aqueducts, some of it splashing out of the sides, or stop for a moment to look out over the pond by the mill, you'll feel a sense of comfort, of tranquility, as if everything is right with the world. It will take you back to your own beginnings and make you think about life in a unique perspective. Enjoying the energy at Mabry's Mill is relaxing, rejuvenating, and refreshing.

25. MARFA LIGHTS VORTEX—TEXAS, USA

Categories: Power Places, UFO/Extraterrestrial/Paranormal Sites, Vortexes

Nine miles east of Marfa, Texas, on Highway 90 going toward Alpine, you'll find the official Marfa Lights Viewing Area, which is basically a wide shoulder off of the road where you can pull over and watch for the lights. The Marfa lights are usually viewed near Route 67, which can be seen from the viewing area on Mitchell Flat.

The Marfa lights are an unexplained phenomenon that happens year round. They are also called the Marfa ghost lights and are thought to be some type of paranormal event, ghosts, will-o'-wisps, or UFOs. Scientists conducted experiments with people in the viewing area and others driving along the road, parking, and flashing their car headlights while on Route 67. They concluded that most of the Marfa lights seen by the people in the viewing area corresponded with car headlights and campfires. However, there were several reports of the lights in the late 1880s through the early 1900s where cowboys saw the lights while herding cattle but couldn't determine the source of the lights. Today these encounters are primarily classified as folklore. Other scientists believe that they are a mirage caused between layers of warm and cold air.

The Marfa lights are described as orbs of light that appear below the darkness of the Chinati Mountains but above the foliage of the desert. They act in a wide variety of manners that makes you take note of them as different from car headlights or the motionless lights of ranch houses. Some appear to be stationary and their light just pulses with varying intensity. Others blink on and off, some appear out of nowhere, and others move rapidly across the terrain as if they are flying. Some have even been said to chase cars. Some seem to merge with other lights while others seem to divide in half creating two lights out of one. Some are dim and others extremely bright. There are also a wide variety of colors associated with the Marfa lights including red, green, blue, orange, and yellow.

The energy at the location of the Marfa lights sightings feels like a deep humming sound reverberating through you. The dryness of the air, the darkness of the night, the twinkling of the stars overhead, all add to the overall energy. As you connect with the energy of the place while waiting for the lights to appear, you'll feel a sense of anticipation, of urgency, as if you need to make plans to do something and get it finished right away. This energy can help you achieve your goals, motivate you, and urge you to finish what you started. When the Marfa lights appear, their energy adds to this to let you know that there are mysteries that aren't always explainable. Tap into this portion of the energy of the lights to become more mysterious or to keep secrets that are important to keep to yourself so you can achieve what you desire in life. Sometimes the best forward movement happens when you keep your plans shrouded in secrecy until they come to fruition.

26. MARTYR'S SHRINE AND HEALING SPRING—
ONTARIO, CANADA

**Categories: Healing Springs, Pilgrimage Sites, Relic Sites,
Shrines/Birth or Burial Sites of Saints**

Located off Highway 12, two miles east of Midland, Ontario, the Martyr's Shrine and healing spring honors eight Jesuit saints who came to Ontario from France to spread the Catholic faith. They built the first Catholic church in Ontario and converted many of the local people to their religion. Housed within the national shrine are the relics of St. Charles Garnier, St. Gabriel Lalemant, and Saint Jean de Brebeuf. The other martyrs of the shrine are Saint Antoine Daniel, Saint Noël Chabanel, Saint Isaac Jogues, Saint René Goupil, and Saint Jean de Lalande. The building has a stone facing, which gives it immense presence when you approach it. The interior has beautiful stained glass windows, unique architecture, and there is a sense of reverence within. The grounds have many grottoes and statures and you can look out across Georgian Bay at the observation structure.

It is said that the relics have healing powers. There have been many people who have experienced physical healing by touching the relics kept at the shrine. It is well known as a holy place where people can spend time worshipping, praying, and seeking answers to their problems. In the past the healings were made public knowledge but now they are kept private. According to the shrine's archivist, Steve Catlin, as posted on the shine's website, the shrine has received thousands of letters from those who have visited and were cured or granted favors by the martyrs.

Each year there is a weeklong pilgrimage of nearly seventy-eight miles that begins at Saint Patrick's Church in Wildfield, Ontario and ends at the Martyr's Shrine. During the pilgrimage, people celebrate mass in the morning and then they pray and chant all day as they travel, then when they stop for the night they light a bonfire. Each year the pilgrimage has grown. Now there are more than 100,000 pilgrims from many different cultural backgrounds who visit the shrine of the Jesuit saints each year. Since the shrine is a place for anyone who needs help from the martyrs, anyone from any cultural background is welcome to visit. There are also some pilgrimages that are shorter and happen over the weekends where different ethnic groups will attend to spend time in prayer on the seventy-five acres at the shrine. Today many people make pilgrimages to the shrine by driving their cars, taking a bus, or participating in a structured walking pilgrimage.

The energy at the shrine is positive, holy, healing, and uplifting. It is powerful and pure, a link to the Divine. Whether you connect with this energy inside the cathedral of the shrine or on the grounds surrounded by nature, it can be transformative on many levels. It can help you to become one with your own spirituality, let go of negativity, embrace new paths and ideals, and give you the positive reinforcement and motivation needed to achieve your dreams.

27. MOUNT SHASTA—MOUNT SHASTA, CALIFORNIA, USA
Categories: Ceremonial Sites, Earth Chakras (Root), Glaciers, Healing Springs, Mountains/Mountain Ranges/Mounds/ Cliffs, Power Places, Volcanoes/Volcano Cones, Vortexes

In Siskiyou County of northern California along the Cascade Range, Mount Shasta sits alone at an elevation of 14,162 feet. You can see this beautiful snowcapped cascade volcano from several hundred miles away. It is considered a spiritual place by many people due to the energy surrounding it. Geologists classify Mount Shasta as an active volcano because it has erupted once every eight hundred years for the past ten thousand years.

The summit of Mount Shasta is made up of four overlapping volcanic cones, which includes the main summit, Shastina, Misery Hill, and the Hotlum Cone, which is the section that has had the most eruptions. Mount Shasta also has seven named glaciers. It is also famously known for its lenticular clouds that form around the summit. The volcano's sheer height aids in the formation of these unique clouds. Around the base of the volcano there are large rocky fields, some areas of grassy tundra, and the glaciers. The tree line on Mount Shasta ends at about eight thousand feet. Its sides are made up of hardened lava flow and lahars (mudflows), some of which extend twenty-five miles from the volcano into the valleys. The last known eruption was in 1786 when a French explorer named La Perouse saw the eruption from the coast.

Mount Shasta has long been considered a spiritual site by many of the Native American tribes who used the volcano for healing, guidance, vision quests, training of medicine men/women, and ceremonial use. Many people of all cultural traditions, and from around the world, also consider Mount Shasta to be a sacred site for healing because of the energy vortex associated with the site. As previously discussed, it is also considered one of earth's chakras and is a place of powerful rejuvenating and healing frequencies.

There is an abundance of animal life that live in the protected wilderness surrounding Mount Shasta including coyote, deer, bears, eagles, squirrels, owls, and many others, including sightings of the mysterious and elusive Bigfoot. Encountering any of these animals while visiting Mount Shasta often means they are trying to deliver a spiritual message to help you with problems you are encountering or that will advance you along your spiritual path. There are many springs on the volcano that are considered sacred. The forest surrounding the volcano feels like the vibration of a tuning fork, high in pitch and frequency. It feels calming yet invigorating, peaceful yet stimulating, and as if your spirit is connecting to universal energy.

Mount Shasta has the power to draw you to it, especially when you have a lesson to learn from the energy of the vortex located there. It is a place where ceremonies are held within the sacred boundaries of Mount Shasta and of spiritual practices by people of all beliefs.

28. PETROGLYPHS PARK—WOODVIEW, ONTARIO, CANADA
Categories: Bodies of Water/Waterfalls/Springs, Petroglyph/Rock Art Sites

Petroglyphs Park is located on Northey's Bay Road. It is famous for its Aboriginal petroglyphs, which are rock carvings often called the Teaching Rocks.

On the hiking trails you can meander through the forest that goes by McGinnis Lake, one of the few meromictic lakes in Canada, where the layers of water don't mix together, or you can climb steep hills into the uplands. One trail even goes across rock outcroppings after crossing a wetland area. In the park you will encounter a wide variety of plant and animal life. Some of the trees are white birch, sugar maples, and red oaks, and you also encounter chipmunks, squirrels, beaver, whitetail deer, and occasionally you'll see bald eagles during the winter.

The petroglyphs are considered sacred. Petroglyphs Park has the largest known concentration of these aboriginal rock carvings in all of Canada. The petroglyphs show pictures of humans, snakes, birds, turtles, boats with oars, and other beings. When the petroglyphs were discovered, there were also thirty-one hammerstones discovered in the crevices of the large marble stone that the petroglyphs are carved into. It is believed that these hammerstones were used to create the petroglyphs.

When you look at the petroglyphs, you may be surprised to find that the pictures are much larger than you may have imagined. While some are easy for us to recognize others are somewhat unrecognizable. The petroglyphs give us a look into ancient man's daily life and the things they encountered.

The energy at the petroglyphs site is stoic, strong, and flows forward with purpose and strength. Viewing the petroglyphs, you may feel wonderment and awe, or a sense of connecting to those who came before us through their art. If you're going through a time of confusion in your own life, visiting Petroglyphs Park is a good way to come back to center and find yourself while looking at the drawings of those who came before. Taking a walk through the forest surrounding the petroglyph site you'll also feel the ancientness of the land. The wind that rustles through the trees, the sound of the lake waters lapping against the shore, and the gentle breeze that flows all around you; these will make you feel grounded, serene, and one with the world. The energy here is in forward motion, even though it looks to the past, and it will help you take charge of changes you want to make in your life in the future.

29. SERPENT MOUND—OHIO, USA
Categories: Burial Sites, Man-Made Mounds/Mountains

In northern Adams County in the village of Peebles, Ohio, running along the top of a ridge off of State Road 73, is Serpent Mound, which is believed to have been constructed in 321 BC based on radiocarbon analysis. This site, which is a national historic landmark, is known as an effigy mound because it is constructed in the shape of an animal, specifically a snake. It is made of a layer of clay and ash with stones placed on top. Today, grass covers the stones. Iridium, a rare element, is found in large quantities at Serpent Mound, which leads to the belief that it may have been built by aliens although it is probably due to the natural shifting of the earth's crust. There have also been reports of bright lights in the sky over Serpent Mound, which adds to the theory that it was constructed by aliens. Another theory is that it was built by giants. Archeologists think Serpent Mound was built by the Adena culture who lived in the area around 800 BC due to the discovery of two of their burial mounds nearby. While there are several thoughts on the origin of Serpent Mound, no one knows for sure who built it or what purpose it served.

Serpent Mound is a quarter of a mile long, has three coils in its tail, and its head faces the sunset. The head has a 120 foot oval inside. This oval is thought to represent the snake's eye, the sun, possibly an egg, or maybe venomous glands. It is also theorized that it could be the holding spot of a tall rock used to attract lightning strikes and create energy. The body of the snake slithers over the ridge in seven arcs. These curves in the snake's body are thought to represent the seven steps to spiritual enlightenment necessary to become a medicine person according to the Shawnee Chief Frank Wilson.[36] In the 1880s additional earthwork was done to the mound to reconstruct it to its original state.

Visiting Serpent Mound is best done either early in the morning or late in the afternoon when deep shadows are cast. The energy during these times of day is more powerful, clearer, and is easier to feel. That doesn't mean you can't feel and connect to the energy at any time of day, it's just stronger in the morning and late afternoon. The energy of the snake means renewal and rebirth. Because the snake has the ability to shed its skin as it grows, snakes indicate purification at a soul level because as you grow and shed the thinking of old ways then you are able to experience rejuvenation and rebirth.

The snake also signifies balance and transformation. Just as a snake sheds its skin, when a snake appears it means that it is a time to shed the old and find balance in the new, transforming your life into what you want it to be and to align to your true purpose. The energy at Serpent Mound can help you during times of transformation by bringing balance to your emotional self and your spiritual self and by working through emotions you are struggling to understand or that are holding you back.

30. SPIRO MOUNDS—OKLAHOMA, USA

Categories: Burial Sites, Man-Made Mounds/Mountains

In Le Flore County, seven miles outside of Spiro, Oklahoma lies Spiro Mounds. The site was once a small farming village but grew to a hub for the Caddoan-speaking people, who were part of the Mississippian Culture that had trading complexes from the Gulf Coast of Florida to the Great Lakes and from the Rocky Mountains to the Virginia coastline between 1850 and 1450 AD.

The Spiro Mounds are a complex of twelve mounds. There are nine house mounds and two temple mounds. The site's only burial mound is called Craig Mound. The site is internationally known due to the 600 burials and artifacts that were found inside Craig Mound. In 1933 the Pocola Mining Company was awarded the lease for Craig

---

36. CERHAS—University of Cincinnati, 2017, http://www.ancientohiotrail.org/index.php/sites/serpent-mound

Mound, which they excavated. Unfortunately, the excavation wasn't done in a precise archaeological method. Instead one third of the mound was destroyed by disorganized and random digging. They discovered thousands of artifacts that were made out of copper, fabric, stone, and shells, which they sold all around the world. Ancient basketry was also discovered. Some of the artifacts were very elaborate and sophisticated and showed an artistic design. In 1935 legislation was passed to shut down the mining company and preserve the site. The University of Oklahoma began scientific excavation of the remaining part of the mounds in 1936.

Today, 150 acres are preserved around the mounds by the Spiro Mounds Archaeological Center. There are trails you can access to tour the grounds and a gift shop for souvenirs. The culture of the Caddoan people is still wrapped in a lot of mystery, however, and the artifacts that were discovered indicate they had political beliefs, economic ties with other people from across the land, and they were religious. It is believed the area of the mounds was used for elaborate ceremonies, that it was a central area where people visited, traded, and lived. It is still unknown why the area was eventually abandoned but it is known from the artifacts found that over sixty different tribes shared a writing system, ceremonies, horticulture, and mound building during the time.

The energy at Spiro mounds is steady, grounded, and moves in a circular motion. The energy feels as if it is coming from the center of the mounds, but you can also feel the energy as it spirals throughout the surrounding area. Spiro Mounds is a good place to visit if you would like to get back to your center. The energy here is very balanced, and it can fill you with a sense of purpose, and a sense of forward motion surrounded with a bit of mystery. Connecting to the energy of these prehistoric people, and considering the artifacts they created by hand, can help you to get back to your own spiritual roots and enhance your creativity. It can help you connect to the energy of the place and the people who made Spiro Mound their home.

31. SPROAT LAKE—BRITISH COLUMBIA, CANADA

Categories: Bodies of Water/Waterfalls/Springs, Ceremonial Sites, Islands/Reefs, Petroglyph/Rock Art Sites, Rainforests

Sproat Lake Provincial Park is on the north shore of Sproat Lake off of Highway 4, about eight miles northwest of Port Alberni in Vancouver Island. In 1860 Gilbert Malcom

Sproat arrived on Vancouver Island from Scotland and established a sawmill at the beginning of the Alberni Canal. The lake was named after him.

Sproat Lake is best known for its petroglyphs of sea creatures. A petroglyph is called K'ak'awin by the First Nation people. The ancestors of the Nootka or the Hupacasath tribe of the First Nation people are thought to be the creators of the petroglyphs due to comparison to other petroglyphs and the way the carving was done by other known tribes. It is unclear if the petroglyphs are depicting ancient sea monsters that lived in the lake or if it was part of a ceremonial center since there are also carvings of mammals and some creatures included that can't be named by modern standards. The biggest mystery is the age of the petroglyphs because it is unknown. The rock that the petroglyphs are carved on is partially in the water and faces the lake. To view them you have to walk out on a small dock or you can go out on a boat to view them.

The energy at Sproat Lake is rejuvenating, relaxing, and spiritually replenishing. Whether you're trying to get away for some rest and relaxation or are trying to enhance your spiritual growth, spending time at Sproat Lake can help you make the connection within your spiritual essence. There are also many homes people will rent to visitors for meditation retreats; some of which have docks that venture out into the lake. If you choose to stay in one of these homes, you could spend your early mornings sitting on the end of the dock meditating as you watch the sunrise. Spending time at Sproat Lake can help you grow spiritually as you connect with nature and the energy surrounding the lake and its petroglyphs.

32. THE GRAND CANYON—ARIZONA, USA

Categories: Canyons/Gorges, Earth Chakras (Root), Power Places

The state of Arizona is home to one of the most inspirational sites in the United States. The Grand Canyon is located entirely within the state's borders. Its sheer size will fill you with awe and make you feel small in comparison. The Grand Canyon is eighteen miles wide and a mile deep and is measured in river miles of which there are 277.

While no one really knows for sure exactly how the Grand Canyon formed, there are theories that over twenty million years ago, what is now known as the Colorado River began eroding the land in the area. There are other theories that the earth shifting due to the continental drift also caused changes in the lay of the land and aided in the formation of the Grand Canyon. Erosion by water, ice, and wind are responsible for the majority of the canyon's creation.

The Grand Canyon National Park is divided into the South Rim and the North Rim. The South Rim is open all year round and is the location where the majority of the five million visitors per year to the park will view the canyon. Only 10 percent of the visitors to the Grand Canyon go to the North Rim of the park because it is in such a remote location. In order to reach the North Rim, you must drive 220 miles around the canyon or hike 21 miles across the canyon through the North and South Kaibab Trails. The North Rim is only open from May to October.

The inner part of the canyon is a desert. The environment is very harsh, there's almost no shade, and in the summer the temperatures can go well over 100 degrees Fahrenheit. Even still, there are many people who like to hike or backpack through the canyon. Some people enjoy taking mule rides to Phantom Ranch or take a river trip through the Grand Canyon on the Colorado River. These trips last from several days up to three weeks.

When you stand on the South Rim and look across the magnificent expanse of the Grand Canyon, the energy feels ancient and grounded but at the same time feels light and airy. The expanse of the canyon itself feels like the connection to universal consciousness, to the beginning of time, and all that is. As you're standing along the canyon's rim, observe the layers of striated rock that form the canyon walls and their unique shapes that were carved out over millions of years. Feel the slow, warm, movement of energy that has been flowing through this canyon since the world was young.

As you begin your adventures at the Grand Canyon, experience the energy of each part of this amazing place during your visit. If you go down to the river, feel the energy of the water that has flowed through here for millions of years. Notice the changes of the rock, feel the ground beneath your feet, and see how the air moves in different parts of the Grand Canyon. All of these things affect the energy flow and are what make the Grand Canyon a sacred place.

33. VALLEY OF THE TEN PEAKS–
CANADIAN ROCKIES, CALGARY, ALBERTA, CANADA

**Categories: Bodies of Water/Waterfalls/Springs,
Glaciers, Mountains/Mounds/Cliff Locations**

Banff National Park, located in Alberta, Canada, is home to the Valley of the Ten Peaks, which are ten snowy capped mountains that overlook Moraine Lake. This section of the Canadian Rockies is approximately 112 miles west of Calgary. Beside the lake is a pile of boulders and rocks that were formed by the Wenkchemna Glacier that is also situated beside the lake. This type of formation is called a moraine, and that is how the lake got its name. Moraine Lake is at an elevation of 6,300 feet and one of the mountains that towers over it is Temple Mountain, which is the third highest peak in Banff National Park.

Upon viewing the reflection of the peaks in Moraine Lake, you will feel a sense of calm peacefulness from the energy in this area. Not only is it a photographer's dream but it is also an excellent location to connect to the energy of the pristine blue waters offset by the brilliance of the white snowcapped mountains. The nearby hanging glaciers add to the surreal quality. The blue color of the water is caused by tiny particles of rock the size of silt reflecting light in the water. This is called glacial flour or rock flour, which happens when bedrock is ground down during glacial erosion, and is the reason that all glacial lakes are so blue.

Many people choose to visit Valley of the Ten Peaks because it is considered a once-in-a-lifetime experience, one that affects you on both a personal and spiritual level. There are many fun things to do in this unique environment. Valley of the Ten Peaks is at a high elevation so the road to get to it by car is only open from June to September. If you'd like to visit in the winter you have to ski to the site, which takes about two hours, because snowmobiles are not allowed in any of Canada's national parks. While it may get crowded during the summer, you can still enjoy taking a canoe rental across the crystal blue waters of Moraine Lake, spending time enjoying the scenery and the energy of the lake, and looking inward with your thoughts. You may decide to go sightseeing in nature by walking around the lake or utilizing one of several hiking trails. As you enjoy the uniqueness of the Valley of the Ten Peaks make sure you are aware that wolves, bears, cougars, weasels, coyotes, wolverines, moose, river otters, elk, caribou, snakes, beavers, and many other wild animals make this area their home.

Visiting the Valley of the Ten Peaks will speak to at on a spiritual level. This smooth, steady energy in this pristine location can help you to find stability within yourself as you connect to the truth of your core spiritual essence.

34. WANUSKEWIN—SASKATCHEWAN, CANADA
Categories: Medicine Wheels, Regions

The Wanuskewin Heritage Park is located near Saskatoon in the southern part of Saskatchewan Province of Canada. This area is linked to the First Nations people's past in many ways and is considered a sacred place, which has been occupied for over six thousand years. Wanuskewin represents the Northern Plains Indigenous peoples' sacred relationship with the land. There are 360 acres in the park along with a tipi village where you can help build a tipi, buffalo jumps (cliffs where the bison were herded over to hunt several at a time for food), and a medicine wheel.

The Wanuskewin Heritage Park contains some archaeological finds that are older than the pyramids. Currently there are nineteen pre-contact archaeological sites within the area. The Opimihaw Creek Valley is a location where almost all of the ancient peoples visited. The archaeological finds from the valley are very complete and show many different aspects of how these ancient people hunted, gathered their food, their daily life, and information about the spiritual beliefs. These artifacts allow us a look back in time to understand how the people of these plains cultures lived. They visited the area every year as they followed the bison and other animals they hunted for food. By understanding their lives, it helps us to gain a better understanding of the human race.

During a visit to the Wanuskewin Heritage Park, you have the opportunity to watch exhibitions which show how the First Nations people lived in ancient times. You can also dine on site to experience some of the traditional First Nations cuisine. If you'd like to spend the night, call ahead and you can arrange for a tipi sleepover. This will enable you to connect to the energy even more as you sit around a fire listening to First Nation stories and sleep under the stars in a traditional tipi.

The positive energy in this area feels welcoming, grounded, and tranquil. You will feel a sense of relaxation as you immerse yourself in the energy and history of this area. As you experience the natural beauty and learn about the First Nations people you will feel as if you've entered another world, or stepped into the past. The energy here can help you consider your life from a different, more simplistic point of view. As you look across the prairie and savannah you can almost hear the thundering hooves of the bison, imagine the song and dance of the First Nations people as they prepared for the hunt. The energy of survival, of spirituality, of being part of the land, is very strong here. Becoming one with it, even if only for a short while, can empower and inspire you.

35. WHITE SANDS—NEW MEXICO, USA

Category: Sandhills/Sand Dunes

White Sands National Monument is located in New Mexico off of Highway 70 fifteen miles south of Alamogordo and fifty-two miles north of Las Cruces between mile markers 199 and 200. Because the national monument is located at the White Sands Missile Range, there are times when missile tests are being conducted. These tests can take up to three hours and the dunes are closed during that time. The visitor centers will remain open so you can view the museum exhibits while waiting to go out onto the dunes. Upcoming closures are posted on the NPS.gov website.

The sand dunes are white because they are made of gypsum. About 280 million years ago the Pangaea Sea covered parts of the current state of New Mexico. Gypsum was what made up the seabed. Over the next several million years many changes took place that affected the location of the gypsum. After the Ice Age the area of New Mexico became a desert and the wind picked up the particle chips and blew them to their current location where the gypsum dunes were formed.

When you visit the gypsum dunes at White Sands you can drive your car into the center of the dune field along Dunes Drive. If you want to stop to slide down the dunes you can use creative visualization to connect to the energy of the gypsum material and the feeling of strength and power that is held within it.

The energy at White Sands National Monument feels prehistoric. The gypsum has been in this location for millions of years. As you walk across the dunes just imagine that you are walking on the floor of an ancient sea. Take off your shoes and allow your toes to curl into the gypsum. Feel its coolness, its uniqueness, and think about the unusual nature of a seabed becoming dunes. The energy of the dunes is reminiscent of change. Just as the dunes change with the wind, the energy here can help you make changes in your life. Take a few moments to stand on the top of a dune, feel the wind blowing against your body, and connect with yourself on a deep spiritual level. Now is the time to let go of negativity, to shift your way of thinking, and to vow to move forward with purpose, positivity, and acceptance of the changes that will come your way.

36. WIND CAVE NATIONAL PARK–SOUTH DAKOTA, USA
Category: Caves

Wind Cave National Park, one of the oldest national parks in the United States, is located in Hot Springs, South Dakota, southeast of the Black Hills National Forest and south of the Mount Rushmore National Memorial. At first look you'll notice the grassland of the prairie where wildlife roams the open fields. However, what you might not realize is that underneath the beautiful grasslands filled with grazing bison, pronghorn, and elk is Wind Cave, one of the world's most complex cave systems. It is also considered one of the most beautiful caves in the world.

Wind Cave is named for the wind effect that occurs at the cave's natural entrance. At times the wind is blowing out of the entrance and at other times air is being sucked into the cave. It has long been a sacred place for many tribes of Native Americans. In 1903 it became a national park when President Theodore Roosevelt signed the bill in order to protect the cave. It was the eighth national park created in the United States.

It has been determined that the use of the land above affects the cave below. It is an ongoing project to continually explore the cave and to prevent any type of work being done to the land above that will alter the water flow into the cave or that will adversely affect the cave in any way. Each year, a few miles of cave are surveyed. There are currently 143.16 miles of cave that have been discovered, which makes it the seventh longest cave in the world and the third longest in the United States.

In addition to the wind flow at the cave's entrance, the other distinguishing factor that makes Wind Cave so unique is the boxwork inside, which are thin plates of calcite that create box shapes. The boxwork in Wind Cave is the largest in the world and usually measures fifteen centimeters wide and thirty centimeters deep per boxed section. Inside the cave there are also designs called frostwork and popcorn which are made of calcite and often frostwork will grow on top of other structures.

The energy at Wind Cave National Park is twofold. Above the ground the energy is free flowing and moves with a gentle force throughout the grasslands. Underneath the ground inside Wind Cave, the energy strums with the gentle beat of the earth's pulse. It is confined, specific, and can be accessed to help you become balanced and centered at your core. Just as the cave has created miles and miles of intricate pathways and awe-inspiring designs within its interior, you too can unravel the complexities of your spirit, of your purpose, and of the lessons you are striving to learn on the earthly plane of existence through exploration and an understanding that the deeper you look the more you will find.

Chapter 8
MEXICO AND
CENTRAL AMERICA

The mystery of the Mayans, the temples and pyramids created by ancient people who lived in the regions in times past can connect you with earth's energy in these locations by experiencing that which they left behind. You can visit Actun Tunichil Muknal in Belize, a difficult to reach cave that contains the skeletons of ancient Mayans who were sacrificed to Chichén Itzá, and the Temple of Kukulkan, where you can watch the Descent of Kukulkan, the Mayan feathered serpent god, which happens when the sun creates a shadow that slowly moves down the side of the temple. The energy here can help you reach great heights on your spiritual journey. While many places are connected with the Mayan culture and contain ancient ruins there are also places such as Coiba Island, which was once used as a prison and is now one of the best preserved rainforests in the world. In Nicaragua, there is Volcan Masaya, an active volcano with an intermittently viewable lava lake where you can connect to the core of the earth's energy. At Lighthouse Reef in Belize, the Great Blue Hole offers a connection to earth frequency with the amplification of the ocean water that can settle, soothe, and bring back into balance an unbalanced spiritual frequency. Mexico and Central America offer a wide range of landscapes from rainforests and mountains to deserts that offer exceptional opportunities to become one with the frequency of the power places and sacred sites located here.

Map key

1. Actun Tunichil Muknal—Belize
2. Altan Ha—Belize
3. Capacha—Colima, Mexico
4. Carocol—Belize
5. Cenote Sagrado—Yucatán Peninsula, Mexico
6. Chichén Itzá—Mexico
7. Coiba Island—Panama
8. Copan—Honduras
9. Cuetzalán—Puebla, Mexico
10. Dzibilchaltun—Yucatán, Mexico
11. El Tajin—Veracruz, Mexico
12. Great Pyramid of Cholula—Puebla, Mexico
13. Huellas de Acahualinca—Managua, Nicaragua
14. Izapa—Chiapas, Mexico
15. Joya de Cerén—El Salvador
16. Kaminal Juyú—Guatemala
17. La Basilicia de Nuestra Señora de los Angeles—Costa Rica
18. Lake Atitlán—Guatemala
19. Los Naranjos Eco-Archeological Park—Western Honduras
20. Mask Temple—Lamanai, Belize
21. Palenque—Chiapas Region, Southern Mexico
22. Popocatépetl—Morelos/Puebla, Mexico
23. Pyramid of the Magician—Uxmal, Mexico
24. Quiriguá—Guatemala
25. Río Plátano Biosphere Reserve—Honduras
26. Sendero Los Quetzales and the Highlands—Panama
27. Stone Spheres—Delta of the Térraba River, Costa Rica
28. Talamanca Range-La Amistad Reserves—Panama
29. Tarascan Ruins at Tzintzuntzan—Michoacán, Mexico
30. Tazumal—El Salvador
31. Teotihuacan—Mexico
32. The Great Blue Hole—Lighthouse Reef, Belize
33. Tikal's Maya Temples—Guatemala
34. Tula—Mexico
35. Volcan Masaya—Nicaragua

Map of Mexico and Central America

1. ACTUN TUNICHIL MUKNAL—BELIZE

Categories: Caves, Mountains/Mounds/Cliff Locations, Relic Sites

Located in Tea Kettle Village, Belize, Actun Tunichil Muknal (ATM) is a remote cave in the Mountain Tapir Reserve filled with Mayan relics. It is a historical and cultural site. It was originally thought to be the entrance to the Mayan underworld and the locals called it Xibalba. The National Geographic Society named Actun Tunichil Muknal the most sacred cave in the world.

Getting to this cave is quite an adventure in itself and you must book a tour with a touring company. Due to the delicate nature of the relics inside of the cave no photographic equipment or personal belongings of any kind are allowed. This is a memory only location. You are only allowed to wear your clothes, which should be something that will dry quickly and make sure you have closed-toe water shoes like you would wear at the ocean, and the helmet with a light on it that the tour guide will give you.

To get to the cave you must drive along an unpaved road with your tour guide. You will get wet on this trip because you have to swim across a river three times to get to the cave, then you'll hike through the jungle a short distance, and there is water inside the cave. Once you arrive at the entrance you will swim into the cave and then you are hiking through water, climbing over rocks, and wading through large chamber rooms. About forty-five minutes later, you'll arrive at a ledge and will be asked to take off your shoes. This is because the guides want you to be very conscious of where your stepping due to the huge amount of Mayan artifacts in this archaeological part of the cave. As you're walking through this area it's important to realize that archaeologists have never excavated this area. What you see is exactly as the Mayans left it. This is where the Mayans made ritual sacrifices to the rain gods approximately one thousand years ago between 700 and 900 AD. There were fourteen skeletons found in this back portion of the cave, one being a well-preserved, full-bodied skeleton of a sixteen-year-old boy.

The ages of the skeletons have been determined to be between one year old to forty-five years old. The younger skeletons show signs of skull shaping, which is when they would tightly wrap the skull or place some type of device on the head to reshape the skull so that it looks elongated. It was determined that all of the people in the cave were sacrificed by blunt trauma to the head. The most famous of these skeletons is that of an eighteen-year-old girl. She is known as "The Crystal Maiden" because her skeleton has been there for so long that is completely calcified, which makes her bones look plump and as if they are sparkling.

The energy within this cave reverberates with a deep hum that you can feel throughout your own frequency. It is an energy that can both motivate and ground you. There's a feeling of chaos, fear, and frenzy within the upper chamber where the sacrifices occurred. Those who are intuitive quite often pick up on this energy and the link to the deaths of the past. Refocusing and applying the positive energy over the negative will enable you to bring a bit of the Mayan civilization back with you in the form of a spiritual energy connection.

2. ALTAN HA—BELIZE

Categories: Ceremonial Sites, Monasteries/Temples, Power Places, Pyramids, Relic Sites, Ruins/Archeological Sites

Altun Ha, also known as Rockstone Pond, is located off of Old Northern Highway, thirty-one miles north of Belize City. Once you pass Sandhill Village you'll drive for about a half hour before you see Rockstone Pond Road on the left. The site is two miles down this road. The name Rockstone Pond comes from the Mayan built water reservoir there, which is lined with yellow clay. This reservoir is also home to crocodiles. Due to the jungle location, a wide variety of wildlife live in the area around the ruins. Because of its proximity to Belize City it is a popular destination for those who want to immerse themselves in the energy of the Mayan ruins.

Altun Ha is close to the Caribbean Sea and, based on the relics found in the tombs, the people were wealthy and participated in the exchanging of exotic goods such as jade and obsidian and it was a major center for trade. Altun Ha was also a ceremonial center that included thirteen structures. Today many of the structures are still covered with jungle vegetation while others have been cleared for the public to view.

Archeologists consider Altun Ha a religious and spiritual center because jade was found there. In the Mayan culture only those who were leaders of great importance were allowed to wear jade or to use it in any way. The area was settled in approximately 200 BC and was at its peak of power during the third century AD and again in 900 AD. Looting of some of the tombs occurred and it is theorized that this could have happened due to revolt against the site's leaders. After this event the area did not grow anymore and the population dwindled over the next hundred years. During the twelfth century AD, the population increased for a while but eventually it became an agricultural village.

The site consists of two large plazas with medium-sized pyramids with steps going to the top. The largest pyramid is the Temple of the Masonry Altars and it is also known as the Temple of the Sun God. This Temple was enlarged many times by building on top of the previous temple. Seven tombs were found at Altun Ha and in the oldest tomb they discovered a ten pound solid jade carved head of the Mayan Sun God Kinich Ahau. The replica of this relic is at the Museum of Belize, but the real relic is in a bank vault in Belize City.

The energy at Altun Ha is tranquil, quiet, and serene. There is a deep sense of spirituality and of connection to the Divine. The overall feeling is one of happiness and joy and the frequency is light and lively. This is one of the smaller Mayan ruin sites but as you stand at the top of one of the pyramids or in the center of the plazas you can connect to times past and feel a sense of community in this area. This can help you to spread the joy in your own life to those who may need your assistance in your community.

3. CAPACHA–COLIMA, MEXICO

Categories: Burial Sites, Relic Sites

Capacha is located in Colima, about four miles northeast of the Colima Municipality in western Mexico. Capacha is an archaeological site of ancient shaft tombs.

Shaft tombs are part of the Mexican Shaft Tomb Culture, which existed from 300 BC to 300 AD in the areas of Colima, Jalisco, and Nayarit, Mexico. A shaft tomb is when the people would dig straight down into the earth (this is the shaft) and then at the end of that shaft they would dig out a room under the ground where they would bury their dead. The shaft lengths varied but could be up to fifteen feet deep. Pre-Hispanic cultures built shaft tombs approximately two thousand years before the Spanish arrived in Mexico.

While we don't know what specific group of people created the shaft tombs, we can tell a lot about their life from the relics that were found in the tombs. Due to illegal looting, archaeologists didn't find an unlooted shaft tomb until 1993. Almost all of the artifacts and relics that have surfaced came from illegal looting of the sites. Collectors around the world, especially the Hollywood elite and highly artistic collectors, often purchased these artifacts during the 1930s and 1940s. Archeologists say that looters must have robbed thousands of tombs during this period in order to produce the amount of true relics that have surfaced. Archaeologists did excavate the looted sites in order to salvage any artifacts that the tomb robbers might have missed. The amount of looting that happened destroyed any chance archaeologists had to learn more about these cultures.

A lot of pottery was found buried in the tombs with the person. Some of the items that were found were bowls, obsidian shards, and lots of figurines. These figurines give us a glimpse into the daily life of these people. Most of the figurines depict people in the sitting position who often have multiple nose rings and ear spools. Many times, there are couples depicted with the man's arm over the woman's shoulders, animals, and scenes of events. Relics found in the ancient shaft tombs include people dancing in the Village Plaza, people dancing in a circle, and warriors. Some of the most highly desired relics among collectors are the ones from Colima that portray small dogs. Overall the relics show how the people lived, how they dressed, and how they adorned themselves, which gives us a greater understanding of how they lived. Archaeologists determined that the art found in the tomb indicates that there was a political or social hierarchy and that these people participated in shamanistic rituals.

The energy of Capacha in Colima is, on the surface, disruptive, however if you reach out and search deeper using your own frequency, you will feel the energy of belonging, of family and home, and of bonding with those you love. Connecting to this energy can help you resolve any issues you have at home or within your family. It means to look deeper than the disruption at the surface in order to find the gems underneath.

4. CAROCOL–BELIZE

Categories: Monasteries/Temples, Relic Sites, Ruins/Archeological Sites

Caracol, also known as El Caracol, is located in the Cayo District of Belize. It is in the western part of Belize near the Guatemala border south of Xunantunich and San Ignacio and is in the Chiquibil Forest Reserve. It was buried under the jungle canopy until 1937 when a logger found it completely by accident.

Caracol is Belize's largest Mayan site. The main area covers fifteen square miles and was one of the largest sites of the ancient Mayans with a total area of seventy-five square miles. While some of the ruins are cleared there are many that are still under the cover of the jungle and uncleared.

Archaeologists and researchers have determined that Caracol began between 900 and 600 BC and its royal dynasty formed in 331 BC. Over the next several hundred years Caracol was a powerful city who participated in wars and rose in power due to its success after defeating the cities of Tikal and Naranjo. The last date found on any of the buildings in Caracol was 859 AD. The city was eventually abandoned around 1050 AD. It is thought that at one point 140,000 people lived in Caracol. It was a well-developed city that was elaborately planned. It was larger than Belize City is today and may have been even larger than Tikal.

In addition to being the largest Mayan site, Caracol is home to the largest Mayan pyramid and the largest man-made building in Belize. Named Caana, which means Sky Palace, it is 141 feet tall. It consists of three temples and four palaces, which had white stucco walls with red paint. There are over one hundred tombs, a variety of relics, and hieroglyphic inscriptions found within Caana.

Mayans believed that everything in the world was sacred and they use the words *K'uh* and *K'uhul* to describe the sacredness, spirituality, and the Divine in everything. This reminds me of frequency and the energy within all that is and how it is connected to our own sacredness and the Divine within each of us. Just as we speak of how our frequency is our connection to our divine spirituality, the Mayan's held a similar belief. To the Mayans astronomy, rituals, and the natural world were all part of their religious philosophies. Today many people can relate to the same beliefs even though we give them modern names. The energy at Caracol is very powerful, is linked to the Divine, and to spirituality. It is a warrior type of energy that makes you want to stand up for yourself, to take on the battles of others, and to win at everything you attempt to do. Connecting to the energy of Caracol can help you in any area where you are struggling. It is a reminder to be a warrior, but to be a spiritual warrior, so that you are connecting to your greater soul purpose as you stand up for what you believe in and reach for your goals.

5. CENOTE SAGRADO—YUCATÁN PENINSULA, MEXICO

Categories: Healing Springs, Mountains/Mounds/
Cliff Locations, Power Places, Relic Sites

Cenote Sagrado, also known as Chen Ku, is located within walking distance of the Chichén Itzá archaeological site in Mexico's Yucatán Peninsula. It is a healing spring that is also known as the Well of Sacrifice.

A cenote is a sinkhole that forms due to the collapse of the limestone bedrock underneath and then fills with groundwater. The clear waters of cenotes are fresh and naturally filtered, which makes them pure and rich in vitamins and minerals, and are often said to have healing qualities. *Cenote* means "well" and the Mayans would build villages around these water sources, which were life sustaining for them. The Mayans that lived in the Yucatán Peninsula also believed that cenotes were places where you communicated with the gods. Because sinkholes can happen anywhere, the cenotes often occurred in remote locations deep in the jungle or within caves. Cenotes in the area were categorized by the Mayans depending on their use. Some were for drinking, others for bathing, and some for crop water. Others were considered sacred and were where they made sacrificial offerings to the water god Chaac.

Cenote Sagrado is one of the largest cenotes in the area. It is almost 197 feet wide. It has sheer cliffs that rise eighty-eight and a half feet above the water. The water at Cenote Sagrado isn't as clear as other cenotes in the area and its water visibility is very low due to the amount of algae that grows within it.

At Cenote Sagrado the Mayans worshiped the rain god, Chaac, by sacrificing people during droughts and giving other ritual offerings in order to appease the god so that he would send the rains and their crops would grow, which enabled the population to thrive. One theory is that the Mayans believed that when they sacrificed a person to the cenote that the person didn't die but was taken directly to the underworld. Diving is allowed but only with a special permit issued by the local government. Many dives have been made at Cenote Sagrado over the years and the skeletal remains of over 127 men, women, and children were found at the bottom of this cenote but it is believed that there were many more sacrificial victims. Some of the other relics that were found in the cenote were jade, gold, obsidian, shells, wooden items that were preserved, rings, gold bells, pottery, flint, rubber, stones, and cloth. Many of the items found weren't native to the area but brought from other places.

While many cenotes allow swimming, today it is prohibited at Cenote Sagrado due to the nature of this sacred cenote and its importance of providing insights into the Mayan way of life. The energy at Cenote Sagrado is solemn, concerning, yet grounded and enlightening. Just as the Mayans sacrificed their prized possessions, and people, in order to achieve specific goals, the energy here can help you as you consider situations in your life that concern you or that have you upset. It can lead you through murky waters of confusion to the clarity of enlightenment. You may have to sacrifice, or let go of, something in your life in order to gain what you desire.

6. CHICHÉN ITZÁ–MEXICO

Categories: Astronomical Observatories, Ceremonial Sites, Monasteries/Temples, Ruins/Archeological Sites

Chichén Itzá archaeological site is located in Tinum, Yucatán, Mexico. It was named one of the New Seven Wonders of the World in 2007. Chichén Itzá was an important pre-Hispanic trade city and religious and ceremonial site between the years 750 to 1200 AD. The Mayan-Toltec civilization combined elements from Mexico along with the Mayan construction to create the city that is there today. It is considered the most important archaeological ruin site for the Mayan-Toltec civilization in the Yucatán area. The structures built within Chichén Itzá were considered sacred to the Mayan civilization so let's take a look at some of them. The Mayan people who lived in Chichén Itzá were quite concerned with watching the skies and using the layout of the stars and planets to determine their planting seasons, their calendars, and other important days of the year such as the equinox or solstice. In order to see the skies the people had to build structures that would be high above the tree canopy due to the thickness of the jungle in the Yucatán.

The Chichén Itzá Great Ball Court is the largest ball court found to date and is 554 feet long by 231 feet wide. It has steps, that doubled as seats, built into the sides so people could look down into the ball court to watch the competitions. The winners of the competition received the honor of being a sacrifice to the gods. Other historians say that the losers were sacrificed.

The cenotes in the area were the water supply for the people who lived in the city. However, they were also used to sacrifice people to the Mayan rain god that lived under the water at the bottom of the cenote during times of drought. Bones, jewelry, and other objects were found by archeologists who excavated the cenotes that substantiate this theory.

El Caracol is sometimes referred to as "the observatory" due to the rounded part of the structure on top of a large platform. This rounded part looks like what we might use to house a large telescope today. Archaeologists and historians have discovered evidence that Mayans used this structure to watch the skies. From its position, there are clear unobstructed views of the sky in all directions. It also seems to have been aligned specifically with the movement of Venus. The grand staircase on the front of the building matches the extreme northern position of Venus. The building's corners, specifically the southwest and northeast ones, align with the summer solstice sunrise and winter solstice sunset.

The Temple of Kukulkan is ninety-eight feet tall and the public is no longer allowed to climb to the top due to safety reasons. This four-sided pyramid is the biggest within the location, has ninety-one steps on each side with the Temple on top of the pyramid being an additional step. This totals 365 steps on the pyramid with each one representing a day in the Mayan calendar. The pyramid has nine stages, which represent the eighteen months of the Mayan calendar year. The Temple also creates the Descent of Kukulkan, which is when the feathered serpent god, Kukulkan, returns to earth to be with his worshipers on the equinox. Beginning at the top, the sun produces a shadow that moves its way down the pyramid creating a snakelike shadow.

There are other buildings on site including the Temple of the Warriors, House of Eagles, the Jaguar Temple and the group of the Thousand Columns, the Market, and the Tomb of the High Priest.

The energy at Chichén Itzá radiates upward and spirals from the right to the left throughout the city. It is a serene, positive, and uplifting energy. It makes you feel contemplative and inspired. Connecting to the energy here can help you to reach great heights in both your spiritual life and other endeavors. It is harnessing the power of the earth and sky in a creative way.

7. COIBA ISLAND–PANAMA

Categories: Islands/Reefs, Rainforests

Coiba Island is located in the Gulf of Chiriqui off the Pacific coast of Panama. It is part of the Coiba National Park system, which protects Coiba Island and thirty-eight smaller islands. The water around the islands are an animal refuge within the Gulf of Chiriqui. The islands in Coiba National Park are volcanic islands that have become tropical forests. This area is well known for having the best diving experiences in the world where you can see a wide range of different and unique types of ocean animals and fish. The area also has the second largest coral reef in the eastern Pacific Ocean, which makes it of interest to oceanographers and the scientific community as a whole.

Coiba Island was once a penitentiary that had up to three thousand prisoners. There are some small buildings on the northern part of the island but they were not for the prisoners, instead, the guards lived in these buildings. Coiba Island was where they sent the most dangerous criminals in Panama and for some it was a death sentence. On Coiba Island prisoners lived in one of the thirty makeshift camps and they were free to roam anywhere on the island. They had to learn to survive in their natural surroundings and to get along with the other prisoners who might try to kill them. If they tried to escape, it was pretty much a guarantee they wouldn't make it due to the sharks who made their homes in the waters surrounding the island and the crocodiles who lived on the island. It was a very dangerous environment and many of the prisoners did not survive. However, there is always a balance of energy and on Coiba Island the jungle flourished because people stayed away out of fear of the dangerous criminals who were sent there. The prison closed in 2004 and at that time the majority of the island and forest was in its natural state and is today one of the best-preserved rainforests in the world.

The island itself is a nature preserve and is uninhabited except for the ranger station where you can stay overnight. The island is still thought of as a deadly and dangerous place to those who live on the mainland. Researchers and scientists have very different thoughts though. The carnivorous species found on the Panamanian mainland are not found on Coiba Island but many rare species can be found on the island.

The energy of Coiba Island is quiet, reserved, and strong. There is a sense of isolation and intense awareness. Becoming one with the energy of this island can deepen your own spiritual truth, allow you to explore your own divine nature, and allow you to grow in your own spirituality.

8. COPAN–HONDURAS

Categories: Power Places, Pyramids, Relic Sites, Ruins/Archeological Sites, Vortexes

Copan Ruinas, most commonly known as Copan, is located in western Honduras in the Copan Department close to the border of Guatemala. It is on the west side of the Copan River.

Copan was discovered in 1570 by Diego Garcia de Palacio and archaeologists say Copan Valley was first populated in 1500 BC. In 427 AD the Mayan named Yax Kuk Mo arrived in Copan from Tikal. His reign began what would be a sixteen ruler dynasty that transformed Copan into one of the greatest Mayan cities of the time. Archaeologists discovered, through the ruins and relics, that Copan achieved many cultural advancements in writing (hieroglyphics), math, and astronomy. Copan reached its height earlier in the ninth century and as many as twenty thousand people lived there. By 1200 AD the site was abandoned due to extreme droughts and the inability to grow food.

The site of the Copan Mayan ruins is on approximately 250 acres. The main complex is on fifty-four acres and contains five plazas, large stairways, a ball court, a stadium opening, altars, pyramids, and sculpted figures of Jaguars that archaeologists believe were originally covered with black obsidian. Another interesting feature found at the site is the hieroglyphic stairway, which contains the largest amount of Mayan text in the region. The Mayan ruins of Copan are known for their intricate stone sculptures and hieroglyphics. There are two different areas of buildings and over 4,500 structures; the first is called the principal group and the second is known as Las Sepulturas. The primary group is at the Copan main site and consists of the Acropolis, the Great Plaza, Stelaes (carved monuments depicting the history of the site), the Hieroglyphic Stairway, the Tunnels, and is thought to have been where the nobles and rulers lived. The smaller site at Las Sepulturas is where the general population lived.

The energy at Copan is regal, upbeat, and positive in nature. The energy here spirals and is a vortex energy that drew people to it in the past and still draws people to it today. It enables you to see beyond what is holding you back from achieving your desires, and to find ways to break free from fears of success. The spiraling vortex of energy also brings a sense of peace and well-being, a deeper connection to the natural world, and helps you release feelings of grandiose or superiority that you may feel. In other words, the energy here can put you in your place so that you don't live with your head in the clouds and are able to connect with your own reality. The energy at Copen can help you awaken to your own inner truth and can guide you in a new direction. Don't be surprised if you get visions of future events when connecting to the energy at Copen. It can be inspirational and life-changing.

9. CUETZALÁN–PUEBLA, MEXICO

Categories: Caves, Man-Made Sites

Cuetzalán is a remote village east of Mexico City in the Sierra Norte region in the Mexican state of Puebla. It is an old-world town with sloping cobblestone streets and quaint buildings with white stucco. The town began in 1475 and has pre-Hispanic origins. During its history, it changed names several times and was named Cuetzalán in 1863. In 1986 it became a city and in 2002 it became part of the Pueblos Magicos program and now attracts a lot of tourists to the area. It has modernized to accommodate the tourists, because tourism and coffee sales are the town's primary source of income. They also built restaurants, nightclubs, and bars.

The region still celebrates its old Mesoamerican heritage that began during Mayan times of worshipping deities and nature through the Dance of the Quetzals and the Dance of the Flyers. In the Dance of the Quetzals, the performers wear elaborate headdresses that were once made from feathers of the Quetzal. During the dance they play flutes, sing, and dance.[37] The Dance of the Flyers is a different tradition altogether. During this dance, five men climb to the top of a very high pole with ropes secured to each side of four pieces of wood that form an open square. One man sits on each side and one man stays at the top and the other four fall off of the square and swing upside down around the pole until eventually they reach the ground. It is believed that this dance was done during times of drought in order to appease the gods. It's quite the spectacle to watch and you can see videos of it online. In Cuetzalán, one man is often dressed in a bird outfit and he dances on top of the large wooden post before falling to the side and spiraling to the ground.[38]

---

37. Sanchez, Miza, "Danza de los Quetzales," 2010, https://www.youtube.com/watch?v=ySAFZt-DXAU

38. Carpe Viam, "Danza de los Voladores (Dance of the Flyers)," 2014, https://www.youtube.com/watch?v=C9gO9qAT7MM

The city itself is like stepping back in time. The energy here is calm, content, and has an old-world feel to it. Steeped in culture, legends, and surrounded by forest, waterfalls, and caves, it is easy to lose yourself in its charm. Connecting to the energy of Cuetzalán can help you release stress, and connect to your inner spirituality. Watching either of the traditional dances fills you with a sense of awe and inspiration. They can empower you to do anything that you set out to achieve.

Cuetzalán is also known for its cave system called Grutas de Cuetzalán. It could possibly be the largest cave system in Latin America. Since the 1970s, sixty-two miles of caves have been discovered with the longest being almost twenty-two miles. The most popular cave that most tourists visit is Grutas Aventura de Cuetzalán. Visitors follow the cave for a quarter of a mile and reach depths of approximately 260 feet during the tour. This cave has large rooms with high ceilings but there are also some smaller places too. You will get wet during this cave adventure.

The energy in the Grutas Aventura cave is positive and flows in forward motion. It feels as if it wraps around you, embracing you in love and splendor. It fills you with a sense of awe and inspiration, is empowering, and connects you with the energy of the earth.

10. DZIBILCHALTUN–YUCATÁN, MEXICO
**Categories: Burial Sites, Monasteries/Temples,
Relic Sites, Ruins/Archeological Sites**

Located near the city of Merida in the Yucatán is an ancient city named Dzibilchaltun, which means "writing in the stones" according to the carved gravestones found at the site. The area was once an important Mayan trade center. Archaeologists believe that at one time between twenty thousand to forty thousand people lived in Dzibilchaltun and there were more than 8,400 buildings here throughout its history. While eight thousand have been identified by archeologists, there are still more to be discovered under the growth of vegetation. Archeologists are still studying the site today. They believe it was occupied for over three thousand years prior to the arrival of the Spanish, which makes it the longest occupied city of the Mayans. It is close to the gulf coast and the people made tools from snail shells, ate food from the sea, and made salt.

When the Spanish arrived during the 1500s, there were still people living in Dzibilchaltun. The Mayan people moved out when the Spanish arrived. The Spanish continued to build as shown by the Franciscan chapel, known as the Open Chapel, which stands in ruins among the Mayan ruins. It is one of the only Mayan sites that incorporates both Mayan and Spanish ruins.

The Temple of the Seven Dolls was discovered in the 1950s underneath the ruins of a larger pyramid. As archeologists removed rubble of the larger pyramid it revealed the temple underneath. It is a quadrangular substructure of the larger pyramid and has a pyramid base with a square building on top of it that has a small pyramid like structure on top of its roof. It was built so the sun's rays pass through the doorways of the temple during the spring and autumn equinoxes. The temple also has a stelae in front. It was named Temple of the Seven Dolls because seven small effigies were found inside the temple. These dolls, along with other artifacts found at Dzibilchaltun, are in the museum located at the entrance to the site. Some of these artifacts include swords and other weapons, carved stone tablets, maps, Spanish armor, and old textile machinery to name a few. Artifacts from the area date between 700 and 800 AD.

Dzibilchaltun was built around Cenote Xlakah. Archeologists believe that this source of clean drinking water was the reason for building the settlement here. It is also thought to have religious significance due to the relics found at the bottom of this cenote. Today it is used for swimming by visitors and people who live in the area and has numerous lily pads in the water.

The energy at Dzibilchaltun is peaceful and calm. The energy that flows from Cenote Xlakah around the area is a wavelike circular motion. It is light, airy, and feels subtle in its strength. There is power here that can be tapped into to help ground you and find balance within yourself. As you stand atop one of the ruins, imagine the positive energy that helped the area thrive for thousands of years. Feel it move upwards from your feet and through your body, energizing and empowering your frequency. Sometimes it feels like a buzzing or prickly sensation. Letting the energy of this place connect with your own frequency can be uplifting and bring about a sense of purpose.

11. EL TAJIN–VERACRUZ, MEXICO

Categories: Ceremonial Sites, Power Places, Pyramids, Ruins/Archeological Sites

El Tajin is located north of the city of Veracruz just outside of the town of Papantla. *El Tajin* means "thunderstorm" in Toltec, and it is believed that this name came from the

Totonac rain gods, which were twelve old men (called Tajin) that lived in the city and were the Lords of Thunderstorms.

El Tajin is a large complex with over 150 buildings, twenty of which were excavated and restored. The remainder is still covered by the jungle's vegetation. El Tajin features a large main plaza surrounded by a variety of styles of pyramids, seventeen ball courts, and palaces. It displays both Mayan and Oaxacan influence and was an important Mesoamerican center. Archaeologists state that this center reached its height between the ninth and twelfth centuries AD. After 1200 AD El Tajin was abandoned when the Aztec empire took power. Archeologists found some indications that fire may have destroyed it.

Archaeologists have also discovered, through imaging techniques, that there are many more ball courts that are still underground, which suggest that games and ceremonies were important events at this location. Archaeologists also believe that they made human sacrifices at the site. One of the carvings in the southern ball court (Juego de Pelota Sur) depicts a contestant being sacrificed. The carvings, niches, decorations, wall paintings, and reliefs all show how people lived in El Tajin and the rituals that they participated in, which gives us more understanding about their beliefs.

The most significant structure at El Tajin is the Pyramid of Niches. This sixty-foot-high pyramid structure has 365 niches built into the building. Each of the niches was painted red on the inside with the outer frames painted in blue. Archaeologists believe that these niches were somehow used to measure time. Also on the pyramid are relief carvings and paintings of the rulers of El Tajin as well as ceremonial scenes. There is also a stela of a leader or ruler of the city on the outside of the pyramid, which is a Mayan influence. Inside the pyramid is a smaller stela.

Another section of El Tajin is Tajin Chico, which is believed to have been constructed during the ninth and tenth centuries AD, and was where the city's aristocrats lived. In Tajin Chico there are smaller ball courts at the four corners of the area and a Mayan arch at the southern entrance. One building, which archaeologists have labeled Building A, has more decorations, key patterns, and relief carvings, than any other building in El Tajin.

The energy at El Tajin is extremely powerful and can create a tremendous amount of spiritual awakening at a soul level when you connect with it. If you're going through a time when you need to call on your own physical, mental, emotional, and spiritual reserves, then connecting with the power of El Tajin will give you a boost, the focus needed, and the transformational ability to handle whatever situations, both positive and negative, that you encounter.

12. GREAT PYRAMID OF CHOLULA–PUEBLA, MEXICO
Categories: Monasteries/Temples, Power Places, Pyramids

Cholula is located in the state of Puebla approximately two hours from Mexico City and twenty minutes from Puebla City. Cholula is home to the largest man-made ancient structure in the world, even larger in volume than the Egyptian pyramids. It is known as both the Great Pyramid of Tepanapa and the Great Pyramid of Cholula, although technically a temple, the people built this pyramid beginning in 200 BC until the Spanish arrival in 1519 AD.

The building of the Great Pyramid of Cholula to its current size happened in stages by whatever culture was ruling the city at the time. The main area around the pyramid is ten acres, which includes many sacrificial altars. Human sacrifice, including that of children by beheading, was a religious ritual for the ancient people of Cholula, especially during times of drought when they appealed to the God of rain. At the Altar con Ofrenda, archeologists discovered two skeletons of decapitated children with deformed skulls that confirm this theory.[39]

It is unclear as to whether the pyramid became overgrown naturally over thousands of years or if the Aztecs purposely buried the pyramid to save a piece of their culture when they learned that the Spanish were in the area and overtaking cities. When the Spanish arrived in 1519, they only saw the grass-covered hill so they built a church called La Iglesia de los Remedios on top of the pyramid, which stands there today.

There is a saying that eventually all things come to light and it is the same with the Great Pyramid of Cholula. Over time the earth fell away, revealing the secret hidden pyramid underneath. This was a great find for archaeologists who to date have excavated over five miles of tunnels inside of the structure. There've excavated the pyramid's stairways, altars, and platforms as well as altars outside of the pyramid itself. Today you can walk through the tunnels and see two famous murals inside. The first is called Los Bebedores and shows people drinking, and the other is Chapulines, which shows grasshoppers surrounding a black skull. You can also see the pyramids primary staircases, which are nine floors tall.

---

39. AztecHistory.com"Cholula Pyramid," http://www.aztec-history.com/cholula-pyramid.html

The energy at Cholula and the Great Pyramid of Cholula is uplifting, sacrificial, and is one of growth. Just as the Great Pyramid of Cholula was built in stages one upon the other, connecting to the energy here can help you grow on your own spiritual path. Just as this temple wasn't built over night, you too must build your knowledge one step at a time and in stages. If an idea for metaphysical thought doesn't feel right to you at this point in time then let it pass by. When you are ready, and when you have grown to the level where you require this information to grow further, it will come back around to you. Connecting with the energy of the site can help you with that growth. This energy is also important in realizing that sometimes you have to sacrifice something by letting it go in order to experience spiritual growth.

13. HUELLAS DE ACAHUALINCA—MANAGUA, NICARAGUA
Categories: Bodies of Water/Waterfalls/Springs, Footprints, Relic Sites

Located in Managua, Nicaragua, at the border of Lake Managua are the Huellas de Acahualinca, which translates to the Footprints of Acahualinca.

Miners discovered these prehistoric footprints in 1874. They are the fossilized footprints of approximately ten to fifteen people including men, women, and children, as well as deer, raccoons, and birds who walked across the mud along the shores of Lake Managua. The animal prints were made separately and the animals were not with the people because their tracks intersect with those of the people.

Archaeologists have determined that these footprints are approximately six thousand years old and were preserved when a layer of volcanic ash covered the mud. These preserved steps are the oldest human footprints found to date. Forensics experts report that the people were Paleolithic Indians between 4.75 and 5.24 feet tall who were probably walking around collecting food or water. Originally it was thought that the people were running from volcanic activity, however the forensic reports eliminate that theory because the distance between the footprints is too short to indicate that they were running.

The footprints are currently maintained by the Acahualinca Footprints Museum, under a covered area. Taxis are highly recommended when visiting this area because, unfortunately, the town around the museum is not very safe. The museum is difficult to find because an earthquake destroyed Managua in 1972 and the city was never rebuilt, which makes it hard to navigate. Also, make sure you call before you go to verify that they are open because they often close due to flooding. The museum also is home to other relics found in Nicaragua such as a mammoth's footprint, a skull from the ruins of Leon Viejo, and pre-Columbian tools. If you don't speak or read Spanish, it is also highly recommended that you hire a guide.

All of the energy surrounding the area is scattered and unfocused but when you actually get to see the mummified footprints in stone, the energy changes. It is purposeful, driven, and in forward motion just as the steps of an ancient people who moved forward as they traveled. The energy here can propel you to step out of your comfort zone. Although these prints are set in stone, you don't have to be. If you find yourself struggling in a deep muck, you can pull your feet out of the mud so that you can step forward, one foot at a time, and keep moving to discover what it is you are searching for.

14. IZAPA–CHIAPAS, MEXICO
Categories: Mythological Sites, Ruins/Archeological Site

Izapa is located in the region of Soconusco on the Izapa River at the foothills of the sixth tallest mountain in Mexico, the Tacaná volcano. Surrounded by cocoa fields and coffee plantations, Izapa is a pre-Columbian archaeological site containing ruins of buildings that date back to 600 BC and are part of the Formative Era. Izapa had platforms that were approximately 72 feet tall and the largest pyramid is 197 feet tall. There are two ball courts, 89 stelae carved with religious depictions, and 252 stone monuments. One stelae stands out among the rest and is the most famous. It is stelae Number 5, called the Tree of Life. In this carving, it shows the creation of the universe by a deity that includes earth, fire, and water. It is considered to be both a religious and mythical stelae. To protect it, they removed it from the site and now have it on display in Tapachula at the Archaeological Museum of Soconusco.[40]

Izapa was originally started by the Mize-zoque people. It is theorized that this area was selected to start the settlement because of the climate. The soil was fertile and the area has a high degree of humidity, which is necessary to produce agriculture. Due to being able to grow enough food for the people who lived in the area, plus an abundance of extra food, Izapa became an important trade center of the time. In addition to the food trade they also traded cocoa, rubber, jade, quetzal feathers, and obsidian. The site is also known for a massive monolith carved like a huge jaguar with his jaws opened as he eats a man. The people of Izapa abandoned the site in 1200 AD.

---

40. Mundo Maya, "Izapa," http://mundomaya.travel/en/arqueologia/top-10/item/izapa.html#descubrelo.

During excavations, archaeologists found a lot of astronomical references which led them to believe that Izapa had an important part in creating the Mayan calendar. Some of the stone monuments around the site seem to depict things in the solar system. The Mayan calendar system combined a 365-day solar calendar with a 260-day cycle calendar, which, when combined, created a fifty-two year period known as the Calendar Round. The primary purpose of this calendar was to track the planet Venus, because it held a high place in their belief system about the creation of the world.

Today you can visit the group of restored buildings known as Group F, which consists of stone sculptures, stelae, and buildings. The rest of the buildings located to the south of Group F are known as Groups A and B. These groups contain many stelae but vegetation covers the whole area.

The energy at Izapa is robust, mystical, and connected to the universe. It is creative, in forward motion, and related to the concept of time. If you were to apply the energy here in your own life, it would serve to boost your creativity and to get you out of a rut and into forward motion. It will also give you the ability to pull ideas from the universal consciousness that will enable you to make a difference not only in your own life but in the lives of others as well, should you so choose. This energy can help you see when time is of the essence and you need to move quickly or when you can slow down and take more time to accomplish your tasks.

15. JOYA DE CERÉN—EL SALVADOR

Category: Ruins/Archeological Sites

Joya de Cerén is located in the Department of La Libertad in El Salvador outside of San Salvador at the Canton Joya de Cerén in Central America. The site is a pre-Hispanic farming community that was buried in 590 AD when the Laguna Caldera volcano erupted.

In 500 AD the eruption of the Ilopango volcano covered the area with volcanic ash and was responsible for what is known as the Classic Period Hiatus when the Mayans stopped building stelae and global cooling happened over an eighteen-month period between 535 and 536 AD that resulted in famines and crop failures. After the ground became fertile again, the people returned to the area and built Joya de Cerén.

The eruption of Laguna Caldera in 590 AD is similar to the eruption that buried Pompeii and Herculaneum in Italy. In Joya de Cerén it is believed the earthquakes that happened prior to the actual eruption gave the people in Joya de Cerén time to evacuate. The sudden abandonment meant that they left everything behind as it was and ran for their lives. When the volcano erupted, it covered everything in sixteen to twenty-two feet of volcanic ash which preserved everything underneath it.

Today, this archeological site gives us one of the best-preserved examples of a Mesoamerica pre-Hispanic village in the world. So far, eighteen structures have been located within the area, and of those, twelve have been excavated in whole or in part. The structures were made of earth with thatch roofs, which were also preserved, as well as other organic materials such as sleeping mats, animal remains, bean filled pots, garden tools, and religious items. Several fields containing maize plants at various stages of growth, a garden of herbs and agave, and guava and cacao trees have also been discovered.

It is thought that about two hundred people lived in Joya de Cerén. Since there are no human remains at the site, it is believed they all escaped the village and, hopefully, they traveled far enough away that they survived the eruption. The buildings are grouped together in compounds. There are buildings that were used for storage, another for cooking, one for making handicrafts, and one for sleeping. There is also a sweat house and communal building that were used by a healer or shaman.

Even though the area experienced two traumatic events in the form of volcanic explosions, the energy here is relatively calm and quiet, peaceful, and happy. Viewing the homes of people who lived here thousands of years ago gives you a deep connection to the past and the present. Connecting to this energy can help you simplify your life, get back to basics instead of rushing to and fro with too many things to do every day, and will enable you to find joy and happiness within yourself. Sometimes we have to strip away all of the things weighing us down to get to the core of ourselves, to simplify and regain our joy, just as tons of volcanic ash had to be stripped away to find Joya de Cerén.

16. KAMINAL JUYÚ–GUATEMALA

Category: Ruins/Archeological Sites

Located beneath the western third of modern Guatemala City are the ruins of another city, Kaminal Juyú (*Kaminaljuyú*), which means "place of the ancestors," and is a pre-Columbian Mayan city.

Kaminal Juyú was built in 1200 BC in Guatemala's highland central valley where water was abundant, the soil rich, and the land fertile. It was occupied for two thousand years and during that time was a prosperous trade center. It was abandoned in 900 AD due to drought.

A large portion of the extended site was destroyed due to real estate development in the area. One portion of the city is preserved as the Kaminal Juyú Archaeological Park so people can visit it. Since the buildings were constructed of hardened adobe they are more fragile and perishable than the limestone structures at other sites.

During the late preclassic ceramic phase, the people built a huge amount of pottery. Archaeologists have discovered over fifteen million ceramic pottery fragments at the site of Kaminal Juyú, which equates to 500,000 pieces of completed pottery.[41] During this time, the people who lived in Kaminal Juyú created giant masks that they placed on edifices and they painted beautiful colorful murals on the walls. There are also monuments of animals that included bats, toads, jaguars, owls, and bird deities.

This archaeological site has been of interest to many scholars throughout the years and quite a few have conducted digs, which resulted in new data that gives us a look at these people's lives and how they interacted socially with one another. An important discovery was of extremely large stelae, which were determined to be parts of enormous thrones, and had many carvings in the stone of events that happened in the city and how people lived. For example, the carvings on Monument 65 depict three rulers sitting on their thrones. Beside each ruler kneeling on either side of the throne are two captives. Some of the stones are thought to be ascension stones because the carvings show the death of one king and the next king coming into power.

Archaeologists believe the people who lived in Kaminal Juyú were the most literate of all the Mayans due to the amount of writing they found at the site, which appears to be a combination of Mayan and Olmec writing and glyph drawings.

Today you can visit the covered area of the completed excavations of Kaminal Juyú and you can walk over the mounds within the site. The energy here is the epitome of strength and power. It feels controlling and can be somewhat overwhelming. That being said, the energy in this place can help you recognize areas in your life where you are trying to control or overpower someone else. Recognizing this energy will help you

41. Atwood, Roger, "Maya Metropolis," February 16, 2016, https://www.archaeology.org/issues/209-1603/letter-from/4152-maya-metropolis-kaminaljuyu-guatemala-kaminaljuyu.

balance it and realize that you can live a happy, prosperous life without having to be in control of every little thing around you. Sometimes by letting go you have more control than if you hang on too tightly.

17. LA BASILICIA DE NUESTRA SEÑORA DE LOS ANGELES–COSTA RICA

Categories: Marian Apparition/Miracle Sites, Pilgrimage Sites

Located in the city of Cartago in Costa Rica is the La Basilicia de Nuestra Señora de Los Ángeles, which means "Our Lady of the Angels Basilica." The basilica is Roman Catholic affiliated and is built in a Byzantine architectural style. It was originally built in 1639 but a part of it was destroyed in an earthquake. Afterwards it was rebuilt to the structure you see today. The interior of the basilica is beautiful and has many golden archways leading to the altar. There are lots of small arched windows around the top of the structure and some stained-glass windows as well. The interior has wooden pews and the tile floor has a circular pattern with the circles creating straight lines.

The basilica is a pilgrimage site because it is believed that healings and miracles happened at the basilica. Every year on the evening of August 2, people from all over Costa Rica and throughout Central America walk from their homes to the basilica to give thanks or to ask for favors from the Virgin of Los Ángeles, also known as La Negrita. This walk or pilgrimage is called romería. According to legend, the Virgin Mary appeared at the location of the basilica in 1635 to a woman named Juana Pereira, who lived in the area. She found a small statue of a woman holding a baby in her arms. She took the statue home but in the morning it was gone. She went back out to the place she found it in the woods and found the statue there again so she took it home again. And it vanished. Again she found it in the woods so this time she told the town's priest what had happened. He declared that it was a message from the Virgin Mary and that a church should be built on the spot where the statue had appeared. The doll is believed to be a representation of La Negrita and is currently kept near the altar on a gold platform. During the pilgrimage, most people wear shoes but some who want to show that they are devout in their faith will make the walk barefooted or on their knees.

The energy at the basilica is uplifting, positive, and touches your spiritual core. It enables you to feel the divine connection between universal consciousness and your spiritual self. It feels like a heavy silence that forces you to look deep inside yourself, to understand all that you are as a spiritual being, and to feel that you are part of something greater than what you can see with your eyes and that you must feel it inside your soul. The energy here is transformative and once experienced on a soul level, you will carry it with you always.

18. LAKE ATITLÁN—GUATEMALA

Categories: Bodies of Water/Waterfalls/Springs, Power Places, Volcanoes/Volcano Cones, Vortexes

Located in the Solola Department of southwestern Guatemala, in the area called the Western Highlands of the Sierra Madre mountain range, Lake Atitlán is a volcanic crater lake of exceptional beauty surrounded by mountains and pointed volcanoes. The lake is halfway between Guatemala City and Antiqua and takes approximately two and a half hours to drive there from either city. Lake Atitlán, at a depth of 1,049 feet and twelve miles by six miles wide is the deepest lake in Central America.

Around eleven to twelve million years ago volcanic activity began in the area. Today you can still see three volcanoes, Atitlán, Tolimán, and San Pedro, on the southern end of the lake. The volcano that once existed in the space that the lake is at had a major eruption approximately 85,000 years ago. As the volcano caved in upon itself in a caldera, it created Lake Atitlán. It is an endorheic lake, which means that its waters do not feed into the ocean, but instead it drains into two rivers that are nearby.

Along the shores of Lake Atitlán are a variety of villages and towns. One of the most popular towns is Panajachel, which caters to tourists, and many refer to as the best shopping place in Guatemala along Calle Santander. Another popular town is Santa Cruz, a traditional Mayan town built along the hillside, where diving is a popular activity. You might enjoy the small town of Jaibalito, which is very quiet and serene. Backpacking is a common activity in San Pedro La Laguna. Here you can climb the San Pedro volcano or experience the nightlife that the town has to offer. Santiago is the largest town on the lake and is famous for its church and marketplace. This is just a small sampling of some of the towns in the area. Each one offers different types of energy connections that add to the overall frequency of the lake.

The energy at Lake Atitlán is healing, peaceful, and is an energy vortex. Many people visit the lake to swim in its healing waters or for spiritual cleansing. The way the mountains and volcanoes surround the lake makes it feel enclosed while the earth energy spins from the edges around the shore, slowly moving inward until it reaches the center of the lake. The energy here is positive and can be clarifying to you on many levels. If you tune into your intuition while connecting with the energy of the lake you can also feel the energy of the volcano that was previously located here. This may make the energy feel a bit unsettling or dark, or as if there is a presence lurking beneath the waters, but it is just the powerful energy left behind by the volcano. Your heightened intuition allows you to feel the high-frequency energy of the volcanic eruption that created the lake. In other words, there is no dangerous, menacing presence that is going to come up from the lake and grab you. Connecting to the energy here is very helpful when you need to cleanse yourself from things that are keeping you in a rut or holding you back.

19. LOS NARANJOS ECO-ARCHEOLOGICAL PARK– WESTERN HONDURAS

Categories: Bodies of Water/Waterfalls/Springs, Ruins/ Archeological Sites

Located in western Honduras, the Department of Cortés, and the municipality of Santa Cruz de Tojoa, on the northern shore of Lake Yojoa, lies the Eco-Archeological Park of Los Naranjos. The site dates from 1300 BC and is a small Lenca site that has a few mounds. Because the ruins are made out of clay, the majority of them have not survived. Of those that have, most were not excavated due to the damage it would cause to the ruins. A small museum near the Lencan ruins houses some of the pottery artifacts found at the site.

The Lenca civilization dates back to 700 BC and currently there are 612 Lenca communities in Honduras today. They typically live in remote mountain areas that do not have roads to their villages. Today they make their living by selling woven handicrafts, pottery, and coffee beans.

While the ruins don't compare with other archaeological sites, this area offers many miles of raised boardwalks where you can walk over the protected marshland. From these boardwalks there are amazing views of the lake and national park. The area is popular among people who enjoy walks in nature and for those who are avid birdwatchers. The area has a plethora of species of birds including, but not limited to, various species of parrots, wrens, flycatchers, ducks, geese, curassows, chachalacas, quail, guans, flamingos, storm-petrels, storks, grebes, blue-footed boobies, and cormorants just to name a few.

Many of the hiking trails in Honduras are strenuous because you're climbing up and down mountains so these flat trails are a welcome deviation from the norm. If you decide to visit this area, be aware that at times the boardwalk is in a state of disrepair. Even if you only walk half of the trails before turning back due to a damaged boardwalk, you will still be able to enjoy the peacefulness of this location. There are several areas where you will be walking out in the sun over the marsh and other areas where you'll walk in the shade from the canopy of the trees. Some of the trails go right by the river and people will often swim in the water while they have a picnic on the shore.

The energy at Los Naranjos Eco-Archeological Park is filled with positivity, peacefulness, and is meditative. In this quiet surrounding with only the sound of the water and the birds, it is easy to get into a meditative state of mind as you are walking. Letting yourself settle into this calmness of earth's energy in this place can help you resolve issues in your mind or consider changes you've been contemplating making in your life and to come to a resolution. It can also help you relieve stress via tuning you to the transformative energy of the natural surroundings. Creativity will be sparked here and you may just come up with a fantastic new idea.

20. MASK TEMPLE–LAMANAI, BELIZE

**Categories: Burial Sites, Ceremonial Sites, Monasteries/
Temples, Power Places, Pyramids, Ruins/Archeological Sites**

The Mask Temple is located in the Lamanai Archaeological Reserve on the edge of the New River Lagoon, in the Orange Walk District in the northern part of Belize, in Central America. In this archaeological reserve are the ruins of an ancient Mayan city that was continuously occupied from 500 BC until 1675 AD.

The complex at Lamanai has three pyramids, a small ball court, eight large plazas, and numerous stelae. It was a trade center as well as a ceremonial facility. Lamanai survived through the Postclassic period when many of the Mayan cities were abandoned, although the reason why it survived is unknown to us today. The ball court is unique in that there is only one at the site and it is smaller than most of the ball courts found at other ruin sites, but it has the largest ball court marker found to date. Under the marker's circular stone, archaeologists found a vessel that had a lid, which held miniature pots, jade, and other items inside, and was filled with liquid mercury.

When the Spanish arrived they built two sixteenth century Spanish Roman Catholic churches near the Mayan city and attempted to convert the Mayan people to Christianity. In 1640 they revolted against the Spanish and burned the churches down because one of the churches had been built upon a Mayan temple. Soon after this revolt the Mayans also abandoned the city.

The word *lamanai* in the Yucatec Maya language translates to "submerged crocodile" and it is believed that the crocodile was an important part of the Mayan culture at this location. Even today the New River Lagoon is filled with crocodiles. There are also many carvings depicting images of crocodiles in the Lamanai ruins.

The High Temple is the largest of the three pyramids at the site at 108 feet high. It is believed that it was originally constructed in 100 BC to its full height and renovations were made to it in later years. The second largest pyramid is called Structure N10-9, also known as the Jaguar Temple, because archaeologists found a jaguar mask inside. It was built around 500 AD and is approximately twelve feet shorter than the High Temple but a large part of this pyramid is underground. The smallest of the three temples is the Mask Temple, which was built beginning in 200 BC. The temple gets its name from the two large masks found on the temple. One mask is exposed on the outer part of the building and the second is hidden beside the stairs. Both of the masks represent a person's face adorned with a headdress that is supposed to represent a crocodile. Beneath the temple is another preclassic temple that also contained a plaster mask. It is believed that even after the city was abandoned the Mayan people would return and leave offerings at this temple. It was also the burial site for a man and a woman, who were possibly the city's rulers.

The energy at Lamanai is dynamic, uplifting, and empowering. There is a sense of strength, as seen through the connection with the crocodile, and purpose in the energy at the site, which can enable you to become purposeful, strong, and inspired to reach all that you want to achieve.

21. PALENQUE—CHIAPAS REGION, SOUTHERN MEXICO

**Categories: Monasteries/Temples, Mountains/
Mounds/Cliff Locations, Ruins/Archeological Sites**

The Palenque Pre-Hispanic City and National Park of Palenque is located in the Chiapas region of southern Mexico in the Carretera a Palenque-Zona Archaeologica. The site is located in the Tumbalá mountainside so that it overlooks the jungle. The location is a unique balance of buildings constructed in harmony with nature, as mahogany, sapodilla, and cedar trees surround it. There are two entrances to the site, the first being the main entrance by the museum, and the second is a little higher up the mountain.

Palenque was built around 226 BC. It rose to power during the seventh century under the ruler Pakal. It has 1,400 buildings on the site but only ten percent of those have been excavated including the palace and observation tower. The remaining buildings are still covered with jungle vegetation.

The architecture, relief carvings, and sculptures are some of the most comprehensive found at any of the Mayan ruins. The detail on the monuments and the abundance of hieroglyphic inscriptions has enabled archaeologists to learn a lot about the history of the rulers, the people, and what life was like for the Mayans at Palenque when the city was thriving. Archaeologists also found the tomb of K'inich Janaab Pakal, also known as Pakal the Great, inside the Temple of the Inscriptions. This pyramid is the largest one in Palenque and was specifically built as the ruler's tomb. The Temple of the Inscriptions also contains the second longest text in glyph form from the Mayans. It details approximately 180 years of the history of the city. In the building called Temple XIII, also known as the Tomb of the Red Queen, a woman's remains were found covered in cinnabar, a bright red powder and it is thought that this noble woman was the wife of the ruler Pakal.

Some of the other structures within the city include the Temple of the Cross complex, which consists of three separate step pyramid structures. These are the Temple of the Sun, the Temple of the Cross, and the Temple of the Foliated Cross. The Temple of the Beautiful Relief, which is also known as the Temple of the Jaguar, has a carving of the king, in the form of a jaguar, seated on a throne. There are many more temples with their own unique carvings located within Palenque.

The energy at Palenque is very tranquil, spiritual, and relaxing. It will leave an enduring impression upon you and the transformational properties of the energy in this location will also last a lifetime. Once you connect with the energy at Palenque, you will feel inspired to achieve greatness. It allows you to form a deep and long lasting connection between your spiritual self and the connection to the Divine found in the energy at Palenque. The frequency here feels pure, loving, and inspires a sense of awe and childlike wonder within. The energy at Palenque can take you wherever you want to be on the spiritual plane or in the earthly realm.

22. POPOCATÉPETL–MORELOS/PUEBLA, MEXICO
Categories: Glaciers, Mythological Sites, Volcanoes/Volcano Cones

Popocatépetl is located in the eastern part of the Trans-Mexican volcanic belt in the states of Morelos in Central Mexico and Puebla, Mexico and is forty-five miles from Mexico City. Since 1345 AD it has erupted at irregular intervals and is one of the country's most active volcanoes. It was dormant for approximately fifty years until it erupted in 1994 and has been erupting on and off since that time. Popocatépetl's elevation is over 17,800 feet and is snow capped all of the time with glaciers at the summit.

The legend surrounding Popocatépetl includes the nearby volcano Iztaccihuatl. In the Nahuatl language *Popocatépetl* means "smoking mountain" and *Iztaccihuatl* means "white woman." According to Aztec mythology, the volcanoes represent the Princess Iztaccihuatl and the warrior Popocatépetl. When Popocatépetl asked to marry Iztaccihuatl, the princess's father, a tribal king, said that he would allow the marriage if Popocatépetl fought their enemies and brought back the leader's head as proof that he had been victorious in battle. Popocatépetl won the battle but another man who wanted to wed Iztaccihuatl sent word to Izataccihuatl's father that he died in battle. Iztaccihuatl was devastated and died from a broken heart. When Popocatépetl returned home and discovered that Iztaccihuatl had died he carried her body to the mountains and built a funeral pyre where he laid her body in a position where it looked like she was sleeping and then burned her body and killed himself on the same pyre so they would be together. Some versions of the legend say he didn't build a funeral fire but sat by her until he was frozen and they were both covered in snow. The gods turned them into mountains with Popocatépetl being taller so that he could watch over Iztaccihuatl. Legend says that when he thinks of her his heart beats faster and, to remind others that he is always watching over his beloved, Popocatépetl will spew smoke and ash while Iztaccihuatl continues to sleep.

Today Popocatépetl is very active while Iztaccihuatl is considered an extinct volcano. Both volcanoes are sacred to the Aztec culture and religious shrines were found on the sides of both volcanoes when archeologists climbed them in 1889. Looking at Iztaccihuatl's summit today, you can imagine the shape of a sleeping lady. Throughout history, volcanoes were thought by Aztec religions to produce signs from the god Xiuhtecuti, who was their god of heat and fire that also embodied the concept of life after death.

The energy of Popocatépetl is love, power, and protectiveness. It means watching over those you love by offering unconditional and undying support. Connecting to the energy of Popocatépetl can empower you to become more consciously aware of those you care about instead of taking them for granted. It can enable you to deepen your ability to love without conditions, helps you to see through smokescreens that others might put up around them, and helps you to reach out and care for others even when they might think they don't need help.

23. PYRAMID OF THE MAGICIAN—UXMAL, MEXICO
Categories: Power Places, Pyramids, Ruins/Archeological Sites

The Pyramid of the Magician, also known as the Pyramid of the Soothsayer and the Pyramid of the Dwarf, is located in the city of Uxmal in the Puuc region of Yucatán in the northern Maya Lowland of Mexico. The name comes from a Mayan legend of the god Itzamna, a magician, who built the pyramid in one night. Another version of the legend says that a magical dwarf, assisted by his witch mother, built it in one night and then the dwarf became ruler.

The city was built and occupied by 25,000 people between 700 and 1000 AD. The central part of the ruins occupies 150 acres but the residential section surrounding the central part includes many more. The Pyramid of the Magician is the tallest of the Uxmal ruins at 115 feet. It was built in five phases between 600 and 1000 AD with one phase being built over the previous one. These different phases can be seen today in the different architectural styles within three distinct sections that are evident as you climb to the top of the pyramid. It has two large staircases, one on the eastern side and one on the western side. The western stairway faces the setting sun during the summer solstice and the whole city is aligned to the position of the planets particularly the rising and setting of Venus. The pyramid is built primarily in the Puuc style, which used limestone as the primary element of the construction, but they also used a stucco finish to give the walls a smooth surface. They built in horizontal lines, and added masks of the rain god Chaac to the structure.

The site at Uxmal also has other buildings including a ball court, the Governor's Palace, the House of the Tortoises, and the Quadrangle of the Nuns. The nunnery was so named by the Spaniards because its shape reminded them of their convents. It is made of four rectangular buildings and has seventy-four rooms. It is believed that this was a dormitory for students or priests who were studying the sacred arts and was used as a training center for priests, healers, shamans, mathematicians and astronomers. It is also theorized that soldiers may have stayed in the building at some point. The whole central part of the ruins is thought to have been involved in sacred ceremonies; and the study of sacred practices, particularly astronomy, was a primary purpose of this city. The city was abandoned in 1450 AD.

The energy at the Uxmal and the Pyramid of the Magician is one of contentment, of being connected to universal flow. It is vibrant, dynamic, and feels alive with spirituality. Connecting to this energy can help you when you are undertaking new areas of study especially those concerning spiritual and metaphysical topics. It will help you find the knowledge you need to know at this point in your spiritual growth and guide you to new ideals that you are ready to discover. Guided by the universal consciousness, this energy will empower you and expand your consciousness through knowledge.

24. QUIRIGUÁ–GUATEMALA

Categories: Mythological Sites, Ruins/Archeological Sites

Quiriguá is located in the Department of Izabal, in southeast Guatemala in the valley along the Motagua River in the Archaeological Park and Ruins of Quiriguá. The site was occupied around 200 AD, but some historians and archeologists believe it could have been settled around 1500 BC due to its location. Construction on the Acropolis began around 550 AD and construction on other buildings continued until 850 AD, at which time all new construction stopped. By 900 AD the city was abandoned. The reasons are unclear as to why the people left the city but it is theorized that it could have been due to war, a decline in natural resources that were required to live, or, because it is in a seismic zone, an earthquake may have caused the people to leave.

Quiriguá is known for its sculptures, specifically the stelae and zoomorphs, which have been dated between 426 AD and 810 AD. Zoomorphs are when a large boulder was carved to look like an animal and then additional glyphs and figures were added. Some of these boulders are enormous. The carvings in Quiriguá differ from other Mayan sites because they are carved out of sandstone instead of limestone. There are a total of twenty-two such sculptures in Quiriguá, which archeologists say are the best examples of Mayan stone carvings that are still in existence. The tallest stela ever found was discovered in Quiriguá and it stands thirty-five feet tall and weighs sixty-five tons. The stelae at Quiriguá contain a wide variety of information including social events, Mayan mythology, their rulers, astronomical events, calendar events, and stories.

There was a close connection between Quiriguá and Copan and it is believed that it was once under the rule of Copan. But the leader that the king of Copan placed in charge of Quiriguá, K'ak' Tiliw Chan Yopaat, soon decided that he didn't want to be under Copan's rule and proclaimed himself the holy lord of the city. This led to war, which is thought to have begun the city's demise.

The area of Quiriguá is small in comparison to other Mayan sites but it contains one of the largest plazas, called the Great Plaza, of all of the other sites in the area. Set in the valley with the Sierra de las Minas on one side and the Montana Espiritu Santo on the other and surrounded by banana plantations and kapoks trees, the energy in Quiriguá is calm, quiet, and peaceful. The setting is tranquil and there are a lot of birds that live in the area. As you look at the carved sculptures in the area, consider the creation of the art. Patience, focused attention to detail, and the ability to create exquisite art out of a natural stone or boulder are important here. Connecting to the same energetic qualities can enable you to create something amazing in your own life, to have the patience, a calm attitude, and the peace of mind to know that you will be successful in the end.

25. RÍO PLÁTANO BIOSPHERE RESERVE—HONDURAS
Categories: Mountains/Mounds/Cliff Locations, Regions

Located in northeastern Honduras, in the Mosquitia Hondureña region, the Río Plátano Biosphere Reserve is a protected area that goes from the headwaters of the Río Plátano River, which are located in the mountains, to the river mouth at the Caribbean coast. This entire area is what remains of a tropical rain forest. It is comprised of nearly 865,000 acres.

The Río Plátano Biosphere Reserve includes mountains, lowlands, and a plethora of plants and animals. The land was named to the world heritage list in 1982, but it was set aside in 1964 for protection. There are over two hundred archaeological sites within the reserve, including the landing point of Christopher Columbus, ruined settlements, ancient buildings, and roads. Local traditions say that La Ciudad Blanca is located within the reserve. La Ciudad Blanca, which means The White City, is a legendary city that people have reported seeing from aerial views but which cannot be found on land. It is a mystery that has yet to be solved.

The diversity within this biosphere reserve is tremendous. To date, over 721 different species of vertebrates have been reported. This number includes more than half of Honduras's different types of mammals. Also documented are over 411 species of birds, 108 species of reptiles and amphibians, 4 species of marine turtles, and numerous species of freshwater fish. In addition to the animal life, over 586 different species of vascular plants in the low lands were documented. There are many endangered species, which currently live in the Río Plátano Biosphere Reserve.

While the government has set aside these acres in order to protect the forest and the animals and plants that live in the area, in recent history it appears that many illegal activities are happening within the central part of the reserve including illegal fishing and hunting, clearing land without permission in order to graze cattle, and even drug smuggling. Future conservation plans are ongoing in order to protect the area. The people who live within the preserve have maintained their indigenous way of life, but now feel threatened by the illegal activities. The area is still safe for tourists to visit. Due to its remote location, it is recommended that you visit in a group tour instead of going alone.

The energy here is pure, strong, and raw. There is an underlying darkness and sense of danger, due to the remoteness and the unknown possibilities, which exist within the area. The energy here will serve you well when you have to be strong in the face of adversity, when you need to be pure of heart, and when you need the inner strength to move forward through difficult times. In addition, the energy is light, hopeful, beautiful, and filled with love. It is a divine connection to creation and an appreciation for all that is.

26. SENDERO LOS QUETZALES AND
THE HIGHLANDS—PANAMA

Categories: Forests/Trees, Regions

The Sendero Los Quetzales, also known as The Quetzales Trail, is located in the Highlands of Panama between Cerro Punta and Boquete. It is located in the cloud forest within Volcan Baru National Park, which is also the native habitat of the Resplendent Quetzal bird, after which the trail is named. There are more than three hundred pairs of quetzals that live in the park and the species is currently on the threatened list and is in danger of extinction.

The Sendero Los Quetzales are Central America's most gorgeous trails, according to numerous sources, and is home to the Resplendent Quetzal. The Resplendent Quetzal bird has really long tail feathers which were important to many ancient Mayan communities and were often used in headdresses, were sold or traded. While you're hiking, keep a look out for these birds who live high up in the trees.

You can hike the trail in either direction, however, Cerro Punta is higher in elevation so if you'd like an easier hike then start at Cerro Punta and hike down to Boquete. If you'd like a more difficult hike, start at Boquete and hike up to Cerro Punta. The rating of the trail is moderate and some sections are steep. You will be hiking across rivers, most of which have bridges, around big boulders, through dense vegetation, and some of the areas can be very slippery because you're walking through a cloud forest. The people who maintain the trail have put log stumps along the way so you can walk over them instead of traipsing through the mud. A lot of people who enjoy bird watching frequent this trail, not only for the Resplendent Quetzal bird, but for viewing many of the other birds that are native to this area. Other animals live here including howler monkeys, many insects, bugs, reptiles, and amphibians.

The hike itself will take anywhere between four and eight hours to complete. While you do not need a guide to hike the trail, it is recommended because some people have gotten lost along the way. There is a spot approximately three miles from both trailheads where you can camp overnight and finish the hike the following day.

The energy along the Sendero Los Quetzales trail is vibrant, full of vigor, and dynamic. It is a positive force that can propel you forward with an optimistic point of view. As you take part of the energy in this natural world you can't help but feel a sense of excitement and joyfulness. This connection can make you feel more self-assured, and gives you a new sense of respect for nature, of which we are part. You can take this vibrant energy with you whenever you need to be braver, or as you embark on a new endeavor on your life path.

27. STONE SPHERES–
DELTA OF THE TÉRRABA RIVER, COSTA RICA

Categories: Mythological Sites, Power Stones

Beginning in the 1930s the stone spheres of Costa Rica have been an archaeological mystery. They were first discovered in the delta of the Térraba River, which is also known as the Diquis River, the Sierpe River, and the Genergal River, near the southern Caribbean. Since their discovery more than three hundred of these strange spheres have been found all over the country. They have been found as far south as the mouth of the Coto Colorado River and as far north as the Estrella Valley. These spheres are man-made and were found in a variety of sizes. Some are six and a half feet in diameter and weigh sixteen tons and others are only a few centimeters wide and weigh ounces. When they were discovered they were usually found in groups, with the largest one including twenty spheres found together. Today only a few of the balls are still in their original location. They are considered endangered because treasure hunters blew them up to see if gold was inside; some were destroyed when farmers ran over them with equipment, not realizing they were there; and people moved them from place to place.

For some reason the stone spheres have been coveted as a lawn decorations and moved all over the country. There are even two balls on display in the United States at the National Geographic Society Museum and at the Peabody Museum of Archeology and Ethnography.

The balls are made of granodiorite and a few are made from coquina. They have also been found in other archaeological sites in the burial chambers. Archaeologists think that they can be dated between 200 BC and 1000 AD. The age of the stones places them in a period when they would have been made by using other stone tools.

While their original use is unknown, there are a few different theories on the topic. One of the theories is that they were somehow used in the creation of pottery vessels during ancient times. Another theory, based on some of the alignments the balls were in when discovered, (which included straight, curved, triangular, and parallelograms) is that they had some navigational purpose or had something to do with astrological alignments. Some think they were laid out in specific ways to be some type of compass. We will never know for sure because people moved them so much.

There are many myths that are associated with these stone spheres. Some say they come from Atlantis; others believe that the people who lived during that time had a magic potion that made the rock soft and easy to make into a sphere; and other legends say that the center of the stones holds a single coffee bean or gold.

The energy surrounding the stone spheres is solid, strong, powerful and is a reminder to be firm and long-standing in your beliefs. The energy moves in a circular motion without beginning or end, it lifts from the earth toward the sky, with a stone in the center of each spiral of energy. Imagine yourself touching or holding one of the stone spheres. Feel the energy from inside it as it circles around you lifting you up and filling you with positivity, mindful awareness, and clarity of spirit.

28. TALAMANCA RANGE-LA AMISTAD RESERVES—PANAMA
Categories: Forests/Trees, Glaciers, Mountains/Mounds/Cliff Locations

On the border of Panama and Costa Rica is the Talamanca Range-La Amistad Reserves in La Amistad National Park. The Talamanca Mountains contain one of the last segments of natural forests in Central America. One of the unique features of this mountain range is it is the only one in the area that contains lakes and valleys shaped by glaciers, called quaternary glaciation. This process created deep U-shaped valleys where the glacier was previously located. These mountains also have high-altitude grasslands, which provide spectacular views. Many rivers and creeks run throughout the area. La Amistad International Peace Park is a total of 479,000 acres. Other protected areas surround it so getting to this remote location must be accomplished on foot after you go through one of the entrance stations.

The wildlife and plant life in this area is very diverse and wide reaching. It is home to over 1,000 fern species, 900 lichen species, over 10,000 flowering plants, and 4,000 nonvascular plants. There are over 215 species of mammals, 600 species of birds, 250 species of reptiles and amphibians and over 115 species of freshwater fish. Researchers believe that over two thirds of the total species found in Costa Rica live within La Amistad International Park. This park, more than any other place in Central America, contains the largest amount of jaguars.

Most people visit the park to hike and view the animals and vegetation. Some choose to camp overnight or spend several days in the forest, however, make sure that you check out and read reviews of the area of the park where you plan to stay prior to making the arrangements. There are also opportunities where you can actually stay in the village of the indigenous people of Amistad Park.

The energy at Talamanca Range-La Amistad Reserves and National Park is inspirational, spiritual, and a connection to the Divine. Connecting with the energy of this park can make you more contemplative of your life path and can lead you to be more introspective as you experience the energy of nature surrounding you. The vastness and beauty of the region feels sacred and can boost your own sense of intuition and spiritual awareness. Infused with the lightness of being, the strength of its ancient existence and the beauty that can bring about enlightenment, this energy will support and strengthen you in all areas of your life.

29. TARASCAN RUINS AT TZINTZUNTZAN—MICHOACÁN, MEXICO

Categories: Bodies of Water/Waterfalls/Springs, Monasteries/Temples, Power Places, Pyramids, Relic Sites, Ruins/Archeological Sites

Tzintzuntzan is located in the state of Michoacán, Mexico on the eastern coast of Lake Pátzcuaro. The Tarascan ruins are situated on a cut out section of a hill above the town. The name *Tzintzuntzan* means "place of hummingbirds."

The Purépecha civilization, which was named for their language and is also known as the Tarascan civilization, were a powerful force in the post-classic period of Mesoamerica. The Tarascans thrived between 1000 and 1530 AD. Tzintzuntzan was their capital city, spiritual and religious center, and where the rulers lived. The Tarascans reigned over a vast amount of land, over 18,530,000 acres which is almost 29,000 square miles. They often conquered people who could produce, mine, or obtain through agricultural means, items that they liked including gold, copper, salt, honey, feathers, and cotton. They then required the people to give a certain amount of their products to the Tarascan leaders. The Tarascan also created tremendous armies to accomplish their goals. They had 1,500,000 people under their control during the height of their power.

The Tarascan and the Aztec were sworn enemies. The Aztec tried to take over the Tarascans many times but were never successful in their attempts because the Tarascan armies far outnumbered the Aztec armies. In 1519 the Spanish arrived and in 1521 they overtook the Aztec capital in a horrific battle. The Aztecs knew they were coming and sent some of their people to ask the Tarascans for help but they sacrificed them instead. In 1522 the Spanish overtook the Tarascan capital of Tzintzuntzan and the king, instead of fighting, surrendered. After his surrender, all of the villages and towns under his rule also surrendered peacefully to the Spanish.

Archeologists have discovered many relics that tell the story of the Tarascan people. They didn't keep records of their history like many other groups of people but when the Spanish came, they wrote down some of the history, which is how we know more about them today.

The ruins at Tzintzuntzan consists of five yacatas, which are semi-circular basalt slabs, that were used as the foundation for wooden pyramids and temples that the Tarascans built on top of the yacatas. The five yacatas face Lake Pátzcuaro and from them you can look out over the town and the lake. The yacatas are part of the Grand Platform, which is a large rectangular, flat surface on which the yacatas were built. Behind the rounded front of the yacatas are stepped structures that link them all together. Excavations at the site have revealed more traditionally styled pyramid structures underneath the yacatas.

The energy of Tzintzuntzan is one of strength, nobility, and is stoic in nature. It is a determined power of forward motion that shows an intense inner strength which gives you the ability to take action when needed or to take a step back if necessary. The energy here flows forward to the mountains on the other side of the lake and back again in undulating lines. It expands and grows and then comes back into itself. This energy can help you to find balance as you grow along your own spiritual path, to know when you're moving in the right direction and helps you act with directness and conviction and also helps you know when you need to pause and consider other options.

30. TAZUMAL—EL SALVADOR

Categories: Ceremonial Sites, Power Places, Pyramids, Relic Sites, Ruins/Archeological Sites

El Tazumal, also known as Tazumal, is located at Calle Tazumal, Chalchuapa, in the department of Santa Ana, El Salvador. It is about forty-five minutes from San Salvador-within an area where there are a lot of Mayan ruins sites including those at Trapiche,

Casa Blanca, and Las Victorias. Of all of these sites in the region, Tazumal is the best preserved and has been extensively restored, and because of this, it is the area's most famous archeological ruin site and a source of pride for the people of El Salvador. The site is even featured on the country's currency and stamps.

The name Tazumal means "the place where people are burnt," which makes you wonder what happened at this location and if there were human sacrifices by burning. The city dates from 100 to 1200 AD but archeologists believe that the area was inhabited beginning in the fifth century BC. The site covers an area of six square miles. Tazumal was a prosperous ceremonial center. The site contains pyramids, palaces, tombs, a ball court, and a water drainage system. The main pyramid at the site is seventy-five and a half feet tall. The way the buildings are constructed and the sculptures and other relics found at the site suggest that the city was influenced by Copan in Honduras and was tied to Kamina Juyú in Guatemala and Teotihuacan in Mexico. It was a major city for trade between the Mayan civilizations and Mesoamerican civilizations. Jade, metal and other relics and artifacts were found at Tazumal as well as a life-size sculpture of the Aztec god Xipo-Totec. It is believed that this statue was traded from Mexico and that it wasn't created in Tazumal. It currently resides in the Dr. David J. Guzman National Museum of Anthropology in San Salvador. Three gold ornaments were also found at the site, which makes them some of the earliest reported metal artifacts from the Mesoamerican world.

Today if you visit the ruins at Tazumal, you'll notice that the sides of the main pyramid are no longer straight but look as if they were pushed up some in the middle, which also caused cracks in the structure that have been repaired with concrete. This is due to the earthquakes in the area that caused damage to the building. Because it is a city layered upon another city, Tazumal is still being excavated today by archeologists in the hopes of discovering more about this city and the people who lived there.[42]

The energy at Tazumal is calm yet feels alive with anticipation. It is energetic, productive, and feels like a heartbeat. It moves like a pulse that comes up from the earth in a straight line and moves upward into the atmosphere. Imagine a beam of light pulsing upward into the air. The energy at Tazumal can help you be more productive, be successful in business, and keep you in forward motion.

---

42. Hoffmann, David, Davidsbeenhere, "Tazumal 'Mayan Ruins' El Salvador," January 7, 2013, https://www.youtube.com/watch?v=lUz46OwwXFk.

31. TEOTIHUACAN—MEXICO

Categories: Burial Sites, Caves, Monasteries/Temples, Ruins/Archeological Sites

Teotihuacan is located in the municipalities of San Martin De Las Piramides and Teotihuacan De Artista approximately thirty-one miles northeast of Mexico City. Before the 1400s it was the largest city in the entire Western Hemisphere. It was built between 100 BC and 650 AD and covered eight square miles. It is unclear how many people lived in the city during its height of power but some sources say 25,000, others say 100,000, and still others say 200,000. Teotihuacan was considered a holy city. The original names for the city and the buildings in it are not known but the Aztecs named the city Teotihuacan, which means "the place where the gods were created." The city is well known for the painted murals on the walls of the buildings, the majority of which are found in the apartment complexes, palaces, and even the temples.

The city is unique because it contains a central road through it that is more than two miles long, which is called the Avenue of the Dead. Along this road there are three pyramid complexes. Beginning at the north is the Pyramid of the Moon. This began as a small size platform between the years of 1 AD and 350 AD. The people added more and more layers until it became the size it is today, which is 150 feet high with a base of 550 feet x 490 feet. It is believed that the Pyramid of the Moon was used for important rituals that could be easily watched by the people who were standing on the ground. Based on the artifacts found within associated tombs, archaeologists believe that these rituals included both human and animal sacrifice.

Less than a half mile south on the Avenue of the Dead, is the Pyramid of the Sun. This pyramid is over 200 feet tall and the base is 730 feet on each side. The Pyramid of the Sun is the largest structure created in the pre-Columbian world. It is believed to have been completed around 200 AD. Archaeologists discovered a tunnel that went to a cloverleaf-shaped cave underneath the pyramid that may have been used for some type of ritual.

Further south along the Avenue of the Dead is the third Temple complex, which is called the Temple of the Feathered Serpent, also known as the Temple of Quetzalcoatl. This is a six-step pyramid, smaller than the other two, which was completed in the third century AD. This pyramid contains carvings of the feathered serpent god, Quetzalcoatl and what is thought to be the ancient storm god, Tlaloc. Near this Temple are apartment compounds and burial sites for two hundred warriors who appear to have been sacrificed. There are also thousands of residential compounds outside of the central part of the city.

The energy at Teotihuacan is one of feeling in control; powerful, and confident. Imagine yourself at the top of the Pyramid of the Sun looking out across the land with the mountains in the distance and thousands of people looking up at you with the other structures of the city behind them. Now imagine yourself during the time when the city was prosperous and thriving. Feel the energy from that time, and the people, as it is imprinted on this place. There is happiness, a sense of true loyalty, and the energy of knowing what is expected of you. This energy is also transformative in that it can allow you to move past expectations that may be holding you back and allow you to grow and become more than you are today and be all that you can be tomorrow.

32. THE GREAT BLUE HOLE–LIGHTHOUSE REEF, BELIZE
Categories: Caves, Sink Hole

At the center of the atoll named Lighthouse Reef off of the coast of Belize in Central America is The Great Blue Hole, a large underwater sinkhole that has a rich blue color. It is approximately forty-three miles from the mainland. The Great Blue Hole is the largest sea hole in the world. It is in the shape of a circle, is 984 feet across, 410 feet deep and is part of the Belize Barrier Reef System.

Scientists believe that during the last ice age, the sinkhole began forming as a limestone cave underneath a glacier. As the glaciers receded, the waters of the ocean filled the sinkhole. If you were to dive into the sinkhole today, which is a very popular thing to do, at approximately 132 feet deep you would see huge stalagmites and stalactites that are between thirty to forty feet long and that developed when the area was dry land hundreds of thousands of years ago.

You can enjoy the Great Blue Hole in two different ways. If you are a scuba diver, you could choose to dive with the group into the sinkhole. This is a different type of dive than you would experience just diving around a colorful coral reef. It is important to remember this was a cave system before it became a sinkhole so don't be disappointed at the lack of color. While there are some colorful coral at the top, once you begin to dive deeper you'll see limestone walls, stalactites, stalagmites, and other formations that you would typically find in a cave. The deeper you are able to dive, the more complex these formations become. If you are not a diver, you can still enjoy visiting the Great Blue Hole while remaining on the boat or doing some snorkeling around the edge of the reef where you can view the coral and a few species of fish.

The energy around The Great Blue Hole is very relaxing, meditative, yet filled with a sense of mystery and wonder. The energy here feels warm, smooth, and moves at a slow and harmonious rate. It is stable yet fluid. Connecting to the energy at The Great Blue Hole can help you find a sense of peace within you. It can allow you to look at where you've been and consider where you're going and determine if the path you're walking is the one you want to continue to walk. If you decide it's not, then now is the time to make changes that will put you in forward motion in a different direction to walk the path you choose. Always remember the choice is yours, not someone else's, and you must live your life according to your own true soul purpose and not what another expects or wants you to do. The energy here makes the decision making process, regardless of the decision you need to make, easier, more simplified, and less dramatic than it would be if you had not connected to this energy while making your decision.

33. TIKAL'S MAYA TEMPLES—GUATEMALA

Categories: Monasteries/Temples, Power Places, Pyramids, Relic Sites, Ruins/Archeological Sites

Tikal's Maya Temples are located in the Tikal National Park in northern Guatemala, in the Department of El Petén. Tikal is a two-hour drive from the Belizean border. It is located deep within the Maya Forest. Tikal is the largest classic era Mayan city ever built.

Tikal is thought to have been one of the major superpowers of the Mayan Empire. The city was at its height between 300 and 850 AD. The city was believed to be the capital of the Mayan cities in Mesoamerica. A royal dynasty of at least thirty-three kings ruled Tikal for over eight hundred years. The city was powerful when it came to trade, political importance, and military presence. At the pinnacle of its power it is believed that 100,000 to 200,000 people lived in the city and surrounding areas and the rulers also used approximately seventy-eight square miles of property around the central part of the city.[43]

---

43. CyArk, "Tikal," 2006, http://archive.cyark.org/tikal-info.

Only a small part of Tikal has been excavated. So far approximately three thousand of the sites within Tikal have been uncovered, which leaves approximately ten thousand more buildings to be unearthed. The nucleus of the city covers six square miles. In the middle of the site is the Great Plaza, to the north is the North Acropolis, to the south is the Central Acropolis, Temple I is to the east and Temple II is to the west. To the far West is Temple IV, which has an elevation of 230 feet with its summit rising high above the forest canopy.

The ruins at Tikal are popular because of the sheer size of the pyramids located at the site, the great number of ruins, and both the excavated and unexcavated potential discoveries that are contained at this location. It is known that the people who lived in the city were artistic in nature due to the extraordinary carvings in the buildings and stelae. The ceramic relics found at the site were of excellent quality in their artistic expression.

By the end of the tenth century, Tikal was abandoned. However, even after it was abandoned, the Mayan people would visit the structures, often times with religious reasons in mind. Archaeologists believed that people lived in the city into the eighteenth century. Tikal is a popular tourist attraction in Guatemala today. Many people who visit western Belize will also take a day trip over to the Tikal ruins. Due to its large size, the site never feels crowded. You are in the middle of the jungle so prepare for mosquitoes, rain, and heat prior to your visit.

The energy at this impressive city feels regal, active, and organized. It flows in a side to side, rising and falling manner that also dips and curves around the buildings into the sky and back again toward the ground. You can imagine it is a snake moving its way through the city. The positivity of this energy will lift you up. There are no doubts, no confusion, no what if's, when you're connected to the energy at Tikal. There is only a surety of action, positivity of success, and the kick-starting kind of power that will catapult you to where you want to be.

34. TULA—MEXICO

Categories: Monasteries/Temples, Power Places, Pyramids, Ruins/Archeological Sites

Tula is located in Tula de Allende, Hidalgo, Mexico. Its name means "place of the reeds." The city was founded in approximately 750 AD, which coincides with the decline of the Teotihuacan empire. Tula reached its pinnacle of power between 900 and 1100 AD and occupied approximately five square miles for the central part of the city. It is believed that up to sixty thousand people lived in Tula and that it was the capital of the Toltec civilization, known as Tollán. The city sits on a long hilltop and today there is an onsite museum as well.

Legend says that Tula was begun by the Plumed Serpent Quetzalcoatl, who the people believed to be the god of Venus. The archeological site at Tula is smaller in size when compared to other Mayan ruin sites but it has features that sets it apart and makes it unique. It is known for the Atlantes of Tula, also known as the Giants of Tula. These "giants" are telamons—structural supports that portray human figures. These four columns are carved as warriors and are over seventeen feet tall, located on the top of a five-stepped pyramid temple, called pyramid B, and that faces east. Additional uncarved columns are also on the top of the temple, all of which are thought to be support columns for the roof.

The site also contains two additional temple pyramids, a palace complex, a civic center, and two ball courts. The carvings at Tula are very detailed and are found everywhere. For example, the carvings on the warrior columns have detailed feathered headdresses that cover their ears, breastplates, spears, spear throwers, shields in the shape of the sun on their backs, what looks like braided leather belts, and boots that come up to their knees, which appear exposed. There are also sculptured friezes that depict scenes of huge snakes eating skeletons, birds of prey eating human hearts, and both canine and feline looking animals that appear to be marching.

In front of the main pyramid is an enormous central plaza that has many columns that were supports for a ceiling or roof, over 3,200 feet of benches for people to sit on, and it can hold 100,000 people. The benches have warriors carved on them, and it is believed that the ceremonies that were held here were often military-themed.

Today the energy at Tula is very calm, serene, and refreshing but there is an underlying tone of purposeful power, strategy, and preparedness, which is connected to the people who previously lived at Tula. This energy can be especially helpful if you're in the process of planning a big event or if you're conducting business where you need to have all of your I's dotted and T's crossed. It can propel you to success, especially in business, when dealing with your competition. This energy also has a calming effect if you're feeling stressed over completing tasks on time, or making sure everything is done for your event. It can help you find balance in the chaos of activity to ensure that everything goes according to plan.

35. VOLCAN MASAYA—NICARAGUA

Categories: Mythological Sites, Oracle Sites, Volcanoes/Volcano Cones

Volcan Masaya is located in the Department of Masaya in the municipality of Nindirí in the Masaya Volcano National Park in the Pacific region of Nicaragua. Volcan Masaya is an active caldera volcano, with a lava lake that is viewable intermittently, usually at times when the volcano is more prone to eruption. In the Chorotega language Masaya means fire. It is the most active volcano in Nicaragua and has a fluid basaltic lava flow. It is a basaltic caldera with steep sides about 985 feet tall and it is part of the Pleistocene Las Sierras pyroclastic shield volcano.

In the early 1500s, Spanish conquistadors discovered Volcan Masaya. At that time, the volcano had an easily seen and very active lava lake. The Spanish conquistadors, who called the volcano the Mouth of Hell, decided that it would be a good idea to take the molten gold from the volcano and Brother Blas del Castillo went down into the crater to retrieve it. Close to the same time Friar Francisco Bobadilla built a cross on the rim of the volcano in order to exorcise the devil from hell. Back then the lava lake was in the old Masaya crater, which is known as the Nindiri crater today. The lava lake has moved several times due to changes of the earth, which causes the lava to have to redirect itself to find another outlet for release.

The legend of the Witch of Chalchihuehue is associated with Volcan Masaya. According to the legend the chiefs of the tribes in the area would go to the crater of the volcano where a deity, which they called a witch, would emerge from the fire and give them predictions about upcoming events, similar to how an oracle would predict the future. In this case, the witch would tell when to expect earthquakes, eruptions of the volcano, droughts, and other types of natural phenomenon. In order to appease the witch, the native tribes would have elaborate ceremonies where they would sacrifice young children and teenagers by throwing them into the volcano. The Spanish conquistadors believed the witch was a devil. They described her as an old woman with breasts that hung to her navel, long fangs for teeth, and eyes that burned. Because of the Spanish conquistadors' disbelief, during her last appearance the witch told the chiefs of the tribes that they would never see her again during the predictions because they had not expelled the invaders from the territory. Today she is known as the goddess of water and rain, the Chalchihuehue, in Nahuatl mythology.[44]

As you might expect, the energy at Volcan Masaya is hot, volatile, and unpredictable. Have you ever had someone say to you that you need to light a fire under your butt? The energy at Volcan Masaya can do just that. If you're having issues getting started doing anything that you want or need to do, connecting to the energy of Volcan Masaya will give you the fire, passion, and motivation that you need to start, maintain, and be successful at whatever it is you choose to do.

44. Nicaragua Turismo e Inversión, "Masaya Volcano, Between Truths and Legends," February 28, 2017, http://nicaraguaturismoeinversion.com/masaya-volcano-truths-legends-2/.

Chapter 9
SOUTH AMERICA AND
THE CARIBBEAN

Imagine the wind in your hair, the sun on your face, and the ocean waters lapping across your toes. This is how the energy in the Caribbean and South American locations can give you a feeling of oneness with the universe, a calm inner perspective and a sense of relaxation. The wondrous locations from Boka Pistol in Curaçao, where the ocean energy rockets through the openings in the rocks to explode into the air, to Easter Island in Chile where the moai stand sentinel around the edge of the island, will open your eyes to energy connections you may not have thought about before now.

There are places of mystery, including Bimini in the Bahamas, where the edge of the Bermuda Triangle touches the area, with all of its paranormal and unexplained phenomenon occurrences and where some believe the city of Atlantis exists underneath the waves. Ecuador is home to the Galápagos Islands, where you can see the giant tortoises that can live to be 150 years old. Bragging rights to the largest pitch lake in the world go to Southwest Trinidad where La Brea Pitch Lake is located, and in Chile they have the Lake District, which has twelve large lakes with many smaller lakes and six volcanoes. The Nazca Lines in Peru are enormous pictures made in the earth by ancient man or, as some believe, possibly by aliens. Wherever you go in South America and the Caribbean, there are many opportunities to experience the powerful and transformative energy of earth's frequency.

Map key

1. Auyán Tepuí (Devil's Mountain) & Angel Falls—Venezuela
2. Ayo Rock Formations—Ayo, Aruba
3. Basílica Santuário Senhor do Bonfim —Brazil
4. Bimini—Bahamas
5. Boka Pistol—Curaçao
6. Ciudad Perdida (Lost City)— Columbia
7. Cochasqui—Ecuador
8. Colca Canyon—Peru
9. Cueva de las Manos—Argentina
10. Easter Island—Chile
11. Fernando de Noronha—Brazil
12. Fumaça Waterfalls—Brazil
13. Galápagos Islands—Ecuador
14. Iguazú Falls—Brazil/Argentina
15. Ingapirca—Ecuador
16. Isla de la Plata—Ecuador
17. La Brea Pitch Lake—Southwest Trinidad
18. Lake District—Chile
19. Lake Guatavita—Colombia
20. Machu Picchu—Peru
21. Manú National Park—Peru
22. Marajó Island—Brazil
23. Mount Roraima—Guyana
24. Ñacunday Falls (Salto Ñacunday) —Paraguay
25. Perito Moreno and Glaciers National Park—Argentina
26. Pintados Geoglyphs & the Giant of Atacama—Chile
27. Sacred Valley of the Inca—Peru
28. Salt Cathedral—Colombia
29. San Augustín—Colombia
30. São Thomé das Letras—Near Minas, Brazil
31. Saunders Island/Falkland Islands— Falkland Islands
32. Sete Cidades Rock Formations — Piauí, Brazil
33. Sun and Moon Islands in Lake Titicaca—Peru/Bolivia
34. The Nazca (Nasca) Lines—Peru
35. Tiwanaku—Bolivia
36. Valle del Encanto—Chile

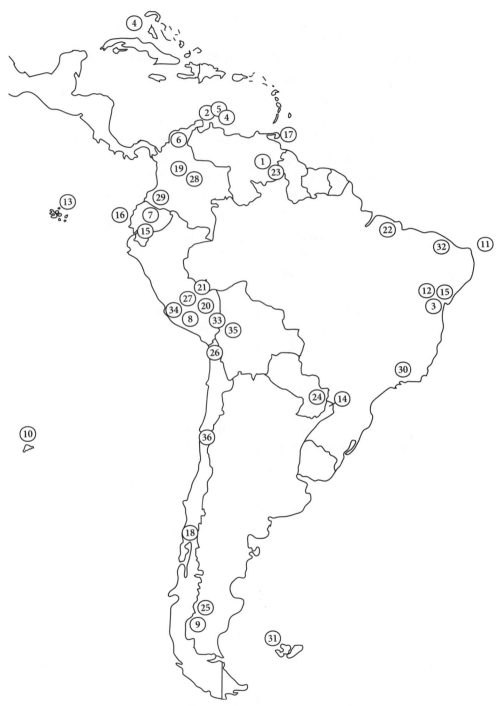

Map of South America and the Caribbean

1. AUYÁN TEPUÍ (DEVIL'S MOUNTAIN) & ANGEL FALLS–VENEZUELA

Categories: Bodies of Water/Waterfalls/Springs, Mountains/Mounds/ Cliff Locations, UFO/Extraterrestrial/Paranormal Sites

Auyán Tepuí is a table top mountain, called a tepui, which means the top is flat instead of being pointed, and is also referred to as a mesa, located in the Canaima National Park in Bolivar State. The Indigenous Pemon people called Auyán Tepuí "Devil Mountain" because they believed it to be evil. Along the top of the Auyán Tepuí flows a tributary of the Carrao River, part of Venezula's Orinoco River system. When the water flows over the side of Auyán Tepuí, it creates Angel Falls, which is the tallest waterfall on land. If you look at an aerial view of Auyán Tepuí, you will notice that it's heart-shaped. It also has a steep incline of 2,840 feet across the flat summit. On the north side is Devil's Canyon and to the east the summit is mostly rock but to the west there's some forestation. Auyán Tepuí is known as the House of the Gods to the Pemon people who live in the area.

From the ground, looking up at Auyán Tepuí and Angel Falls, it is a spectacular view. While there are over one hundred other tepuís in the Guiana Highlands, Angel Falls sets the Auyán Tepuí apart from the rest, even though the others may also have smaller waterfalls. A large portion of this mountain is still unexplored because the area is a dense rain forest. It is particularly interesting that the vegetation growing on the top of the tepuís in this area are all different and contain uniquely varied ecosystems specific to each tepuís summit, due to millions of years of isolation. The summits are often difficult to reach because they have very high cliffs that separate the flat tabletop summits from the jungle below.

The Angel Falls website credits the discovery of this spectacular waterfall to pilot Jimmy Angel who found it while flying over it in 1923.[45] The waterfall was named for him. From the top of the waterfall to the bottom is 3,212 feet, which makes it the highest waterfall in the world. It also has the longest uninterrupted drop, which is 2,647.64 feet.

According to local legend, in the Aonda canyon near Auyán Tepuí, there is the Canaima, a horrible spirit that represents death and chases people until it eventually finds and kills them. Paranormal activity is often experienced in this location.

---

45. AngelFalls.Info, "Angel Falls," http://www.angelfalls.info/Discovery.html

In order to get to Angel Falls, you have to journey through the jungle, which many people refer to as traveling through the lost world. The energy at Auyán Tepuí and Angel Falls is ancient. There is a combination of power yet submission, of darkness and light, and of stability and growth. There is a distinctive uniqueness to the energy that flows up, over, around, and down these mountains that have existed for millions of years. Connecting to the energy here allows you to express your own uniqueness, to find the power inside yourself that connects to your soul essence so you can bring forth your own ancientness of being.

2. AYO ROCK FORMATIONS—AYO, ARUBA

Categories: Islands/Reefs, Megalithic Sites, Petroglyph/Rock Art Sites, Power Places

Located off of the coast of Venezuela, the island of Aruba is part of the Lesser Antilles Islands, specifically the Leeward Antilles, in the southern Caribbean Sea. On clear days, you can actually see Venezuela from the island and vice versa.

On the east side of the island near Ayo village, are the Ayo Rock Formations and to the southwest of Hooiberg are the Casibari Rock Formations. These are extremely large monolithic boulders that the Caquetio Indians of the Arawak carved petroglyphs on thousands of years ago during the Pre-Ceramic period between 2500 BC and 1000 AD. The Caquetio considered both places to be sacred sites and it is believed they would climb to the top of these monolithic structures in order to listen for incoming storms or hurricanes. They were primarily hunters, fishermen, and gatherers. Because they lived on an island, they depended on the sea for food to survive. Their tools were made from stones and shells and they also made pottery. During the Ceramic Period, the people created five separate villages on the island where they grew yucca and corn.

These monoliths seem out of place on an island with sandy white beaches in the middle of the Caribbean. The boulders are very close together in unique designs. Some are shaped like dragons and others like birds. Some are as high as some of the modern buildings in the area. Scientists believe that these rock formations are the result of volcanic activity because there is a dormant volcano in the middle of the island. It is called the Hooiberg and is only 541 feet tall but in comparison to the flatness of the rest of the island it will grab your attention right away.[46]

---

46. ArubaBlog.net, "The Hooiberg, Aruba's Volcano," 2011, http://www.arubablog.net/the-hooiberg/.

There are differences in these two locations of rock formations. Ayo is less crowded than Casibari, which is a popular tourist attraction. At Casibari they have carved steps into the rocks, so the climb up to the top to get amazing views of the island is much easier. While you can still climb to the top of the monoliths at Ayo, there are no steps to help you get to the top so the climb is more difficult. At Ayo there are tunnels that meander through the boulders and some of the passageways are quite narrow. Both sites have a network of paved pathways around and throughout the stones. If you decide to visit either site, it is recommended to go early in the morning instead of the heat of the day. Avoid the area at night due to the animal life you could encounter. These sites are highly recommended by hikers and those who enjoy seeing the unusual.

The energy at the Ayo and Casibari rock formations is soothing, meditative, and relaxing. It is a warm, high frequency vibration that not only moves around you but also feels as if it moves through you. It is uplifting and can help you see that which has been hidden or that you have been denying. The energy here is clarifying, it can open your eyes so you see things as they are and not as you want them to be.

3. BASÍLICA SANTUÁRIO SENHOR DO BONFIM—BRAZIL
Categories: Marian Apparition/Miracles Sites, Pilgrimage Sites
The Basílica Santuário Senhor do Bonfim, is located in Salvador, in the province of Bahia of Brazil. It was originally built in 1669 and devoted to Jesus Christ, the Lord of Bonfim. It is the most famous Catholic Church in Bahia, is known as a shrine with the ability to cure people from ailments, and grants the fulfillment of wishes through the intervention of saints, which is physically represented by ribbons. Many people pilgrimage to the church from far and wide and leave these ribbons as symbols of their faith.

Fitas, which are also called Bonfim Ribbons or Measure of Bonfim (because they were forty-seven centimeters long, the length of the right arm of the statue of the Lord of Bonfim on the high altar in the church), is a tradition that started in 1809. These ribbons were originally made of silk but are now made of cotton and have *Lembrançe do Senhor do Bonfim da Bahia* written on them, which means "In remembrance of the savior of Bahia." They are said to have miraculous powers and will protect you from evil, heal you, and grant your wishes. Originally the ribbons were worn around the neck and people would attach medallions or other holy items to them, sometimes even little pictures or wax figures of the body part they wanted healed or that had been healed by the saints.

Today they're often tied to the church gates with three knots or worn as bracelets that wrap around the left wrist and are tied with three knots by one of your friends. Traditionally they're given as a gift and the person giving them ties them on your wrist; you can't do it yourself or your wishes will not come true. As each knot is tied you make a wish. You're not supposed to cut the ribbon off, but it is to wear away naturally. By the time it falls off of your arm, all your wishes are supposed to have come true. The color of the ribbon you choose is also important. For instance, white represents wisdom and inner peace while red represents passion and strength. The ribbons are available in a wide variety of colors to suit every need.

There is another tradition associated with the church called the Festa do Bonfim, which is when Bahia women wear a traditional white costume and, after mass at the Church of Conceição da Praia they walk to the Bonfim church where they wash the steps of the church and the square in front of it while singing, chanting, and dancing. The festivities last ten days and ends with mass in the Bonfim church. This tradition is Catholic and also has influences from the African religions in Bahia included.

The energy at Basílica Santuário Senhor do Bonfim is uplifting, spiritual, healing, and transformational. It can heal what ails you in mind, body, and spirit. The faith of the people who visit this church and their deeply positive beliefs that anything is possible has left an undeniable mark on the energy in this area. This energy can deepen your own beliefs in spirituality, universal consciousness, and your connection to the Divine. Whatever your truth, whatever your belief system, the energy of this place can strengthen you and transform negativity into positivity.

4. BIMINI–BAHAMAS

Categories: Islands/Reefs, Power Places, UFO/ Extraterrestrial/Paranormal Sites, Vortexes

Bimini is located in the Bahamas, which are approximately fifty miles off of the east coast of Florida, United States. Bimini is believed to be part of Plato's legendary lost city of Atlantis. Because of this, many people go to Bimini and participate in transformational and spiritual retreats.

There are two primary reasons that visitors go to the Bahamas, outside of taking a vacation of course, and they are because the Stones of Atlantis were found off the coast of North Bimini, and because the Bahamas make up one point of the Bermuda triangle. With so much mystery and intrigue surrounding these Bahamian Islands, there's no wonder that people feel drawn to investigate the energy here on their own.

The Stones of Atlantis, also known as Bimini Road, are enormous flat stones up to thirteen feet across and a half of a mile long placed in straight lines. Some were cut with right angles in them. Some think the road may lead to the Lost City of Atlantis. While skeptics dismiss the idea as nonsense, many people believe it is entirely a possibility. There have been a lot of civilizations discovered by archaeologists under layers and layers of ash due to volcanic eruptions, or that have been found deep in the jungles overgrown with vegetation. It is quite possible there are ruins of an ancient civilization, such as Atlantis, that are completely underwater, and Bimini Road might just lead to the lost city. Some people spend their lives researching the area around Bimini looking for clues to Atlantis by diving in the waters of the island. Geologists, archaeologists, and others in the scientific community have tried for years to determine if the stones that make up the Bimini Road are indeed proof of an ancient civilization buried deep beneath the Caribbean Sea or if it is just a natural phenomenon that occurred due to changes in the earth's surface. It hasn't been determined one way or the other and Atlantis is still a mystery waiting to be solved.

Connecting to part of the Bermuda Triangle is another reason people are drawn to the Bahamas. There have been hundreds of mysterious disappearances of aircraft or the malfunction of the instruments on planes, shipwrecks, and many other unexplained phenomenon such as pilots saying they felt like they flew through a black hole. Researchers and the public have come up with a number of reasons for these happenings; some are scientific and others are paranormal. Some blame the phenomenon on vortexes, UFO's, a space-time continuum, Atlantis, an electronic fog, earth's magnetism, or methane gas. Like Atlantis, the mystery of the Bermuda Triangle is still unsolved.

If you'd like to take a trip to Bimini in the Bahamas, you can participate in many of the spiritual, transformational, and healing retreats that tap in to the energy of the island. You can even swim with wild dolphins.

The energy in Bimini moves in a swirling and side-to-side motion. It is transformational, healing, and can be rejuvenating for mind, body, and spirit. Imagine swimming in the clear waters in a meditative frame of mind while aligning with your life purpose. The energy here can lift you up, bring enlightenment and clarity of vision, and when it comes to your own spirituality, it can show you the truth within yourself. The mystery of the Bahamas gives enlightenment so you understand the mystery that is you.

5. BOKA PISTOL—CURAÇAO

Categories: Caves, Geysers/Blowholes, Islands/Reefs

The Boka Pistol is located in the Shete Boka National Park at the Boka Tabla Cave in Curaçao, which is a Caribbean island owned by the Dutch and part of the Lesser Antilles islands north of the Venezuelan coastline.

Boka Pistol is where the sea is pushed through a narrow inlet and then shoots backward with enough force to cause the water to shoot straight up into the air like a blow hole. While Boka Pistol isn't officially named a blow hole, the effect of the water's movement is very similar. There is a cave under the Boka Tabla that you can walk into but use caution because it's very slippery inside the cave. Also pay particular attention to the tide at the time you plan to visit. If you go into the cave during high tide, you're going to get soaked, which could be fun. The cave is called the "sounds of nature" by the locals because you can watch and listen to the surf.

The Island of Curaçao is also known for its unique European architecture that was built on the Caribbean Island. The Dutch settled it in 1634 and they created the town of Willemstad around the harbor. This historic area is a world heritage site due to the unique Dutch buildings within four districts that distinctly show the historic development of the area over the centuries. The island is also known for its hundreds of species of Cactus and the Divi Divi Tree, a unique tree that grows upright and then horizontally, which makes it look like it is bowing to someone. This happens because of the trade winds that blow across the island from east to west so the branches are usually pointed to the west. If not for the trade winds, this tree could grow to be thirty feet tall. The island is home to many species of birds, reptiles, small mammals, and the white-tailed deer. It is thought that the Arawak tribe brought the deer with them when they originally settled the island.

The energy of Boka Pistol is joyous, lighthearted, and moves in swift, splashy movements similar to the way the water is propelled through the pistol. Being a part of nature and experiencing the power of the ocean as the water blows up into the air can help you connect to the core part of yourself. The wind is fierce and exhilarating, it whips around you with great strength, moving your hair and clothes in a rush of energy, which can, oddly enough, make you feel settled and calm inside. It can also make you feel as if you can conquer anything that life throws your way. It can lift you up, embrace you with its power, and fill you with the determination and excitement to do whatever it is you want to do in life. Embrace the powerful energy at Boka Pistol as you move along your path.

6. CIUDAD PERDIDA (LOST CITY)–COLUMBIA

**Categories: Ceremonial Sites, Mountains/Mounds/
Cliff Locations, Ruins/Archeological Sites**

Ciudad Perdida is located in Santa Marta, Magdalena, Columbia, in a very remote part of the northern part of the Sierra Nevada de Santa Marta Mountains. Known as The Lost City it is only accessible if you hike nearly twenty-seven and a half miles through the Colombian jungle to its location.

Archaeologists believe the beginnings of the city were 650 years prior to the Incan city of Machu Picchu in 800 AD by the Tayrona people. At that time, it was known as the city of Teyuna. Archaeologists believe that the ruins there today were built between the eleventh and fourteenth centuries. It is thought to be the largest pre-Columbian city of the area. Between four thousand to ten thousand people lived in the city. It is on a high ridge overlooking the Buritaca River Valley and was believed to be a commercial trading center due to its proximity to the river.

When the Spanish conquistadors invaded the area, the city was abandoned. It is believed that diseases introduced by the invaders eliminated the remaining people of the civilization. Over the years the jungle grew over the structures hiding the city from view. In 1972 grave robbers found steps on a steep ridge. They cut through the jungle foliage until they discovered the main part of the city, which by then were only plat-forms. Being grave robbers they dug up the graves and found golden idols and other artifacts that were buried with the people. There was a lot of fighting among those try-ing to rob the graves and it took three years before the government stepped in to main-tain order after some tourists and their guide were kidnapped on the way to Ciudad

Perdida.[47] There is still a large military presence for visitors who want to trek through the jungle to see the ruins because it still is not a particularly safe region.

The city consists of 1263 stone steps that begin at the river and go up to the main part of the city which contained over 169 terraces thought to be the foundations of houses, and open plazas, which are thought to have been used for ceremonial use, especially the ones at the center of the site. The city also had many stone pathways on the mountain, a water drainage system, and bridges. At the site there is a stone called la Piedra del Sapo which is representative of the animal gods worshipped by the Tayrona tribe. The chief's thinking chair, called la Silla del Mamo is also at the site.

At this time only 10 percent of the city has been excavated and the remainder is not expected to be excavated at any time in the near future because the indigenous people of the area do not want it to be disturbed.

The energy at Ciudad Perdida is quiet and peaceful which is a stark contrast to the safety issues surrounding the area. The energy here flows unobstructed across the mountains and through the valley. It moves at a slow, steady pace as if time has no meaning. Feeling the energy at the ancient ruins is like taking a deep breath, allowing the peacefulness of the energy to move through you, while it settles deep within your soul. The energy here can attune you to higher levels of enlightenment and bring you face to face with your spiritual self.

7. COCHASQUI—ECUADOR

Categories: Astronomical Observatories, Ceremonial Sites, Power Places, Pyramids

The Cochasqui pyramids are located in the Pichincha Province, in the Pedro Moncayo district, in the northern province of Ecuador in the Parque Arqueologico Cochasqui. The site has fifteen pyramids and twenty-one funerary mounds that were built between 500 and 1500 AD and covers approximately two hundred acres. Its location allowed the residents to monitor the activity of volcanoes in the area. The pre-Inca Quitu-Cara people lived at the site.

Today the pyramids and funeral mounds are covered up with dirt and grass. When archaeologists first began excavating the site they uncovered one side of the pyramid

47. Hudson, Shaney, "Trekking to Columbia's Lost City," August 1, 2012, http://www.bbc.com/travel/story/20120720-trekking-to-colombias-lost-city

that has stairs leading to the top where a solar and lunar calendar made of stones sits. The pyramids were constructed out of volcanic material called cangahua, which they made into blocks. Because the site is so close to the equator, archaeologists believe that the stones would fall apart if exposed to the elements so they stopped any further excavations of the site. They were also able to determine that most of the pyramids are connected by ramps.

There is a small archaeological museum on the site, which contains artifacts found during the excavations. It has pottery from other cultures, which may have been brought to the site to trade for other goods. The museum also contains the skeleton of a woman in the fetal position and surrounded by items that were buried with her. Other skeletal remains were found on the site but have been moved to other museums. There is an open air museum that shows ethnographic research about the site including details about how the people of the time lived. There's a botanical garden and a section where they keep llamas.

There are several theories on the uses of this particular site. Some believe that it might have been used as a ceremonial center. It is also thought that the structures here created an astronomical observatory, which was used by the Quitu-Cara people to watch the skies. Another theory is that it was simply a graveyard or a military training compound because over five hundred skulls have been found here.

The energy at Cochasqui flows upwards in surging pulses. As you look across Cochasqui you may think you're just looking at a hilly field without realizing that there is a city underneath the dirt and grass. Connecting to the energy here means seeing beneath the surface, to look within, and seeing that there are things going on behind the scenes that you are unaware of. This energy can bring clarity of mind, show you what is hidden, and make you firm in your resolve. It is meditative, which can help gain further enlightenment regarding your life path. This energy can help you get into deeper meditative states while energizing you to see clearly with your third eye into the Divine.

8. COLCA CANYON–PERU

Categories: Canyons/Gorges, Volcanoes/Volcano Cones

Colca Canyon is located in the Arequipa region of southern Peru in the Andean Mountains, also known as the Andes. It is the third most visited site in Peru and is the deepest canyon in the world at 10,725 feet. This is two times the depth of the Grand Canyon in the United States. The deepest part of the canyon is at an extinct volcano called Nevado Ampato, whose elevation is 20,630 feet.

One of the most fascinating attractions of the Colca Canyon is the Condor (Vultur Gryphys). This large, majestic bird is a scavenger that can find food from thousands of feet in the air due to a keen sense of smell and exemplary vision. It is considered a threatened species because there are ten thousand or less still in existence. This condor is the world's largest flying bird and also the world's longest living bird with a lifespan of over seventy years. The Condor is easily identifiable in the wild because it has a white ring of feathers around its neck, white feathers that stick out at the end of its wings, and the feathers along its wings closest to its body are white. When it is flying, the contrast of the white wings and its black body make it look like the letter T. The Condor was considered a sacred bird to the original inhabitants, Colca Canyon and is still considered sacred today.

Around the canyon you will find platforms that have been in existence since pre-Incan times Today's farmers tend the land using the same methods as their Incan ancestors did to grow food. The Colca Valley is home to the Cabana and Collagua cultures and was originally settled during Spanish colonial times between 1532 and 1572 AD.

There are many activities you can take part in at Colca Canyon. From bird watching to hiking or rafting down the Colca River, visiting La Calera Thermal Waters, or you can go zip lining. There are also some archaeological sites within the canyon to visit. Getting a guide is recommended in order to experience all Colca Canyon has to offer.

The energy in Colca Canyon is tranquil, relaxing, and peaceful. If you're looking for energy to slow you down and to relieve the buildup of stress that you may be feeling, then this is the energy to connect to. It feels light and airy, and can lift you up if you're feeling sad, and can make you see the positives more than the negatives in life. If you're involved in a situation where you're unsure of which direction to take, the energy here can help you take a step back, and slow down so you gain clarity of thought prior to moving forward. It can help make decision-making easier, relieve the clatter going on in your mind so that it's easier to relax, and rejuvenate you with its transformative abilities.

9. CUEVA DE LAS MANOS—ARGENTINA

Categories: Caves, Mountains/Mounds/
Cliff Locations, Petroglyph/Rock Art Sites

Cueva de las Manos is located in the Alto Rio Pinturas Area in the rural Patagonia Region in the northwest section of the Santa Cruz Province in Argentina approximately one hundred miles south of Perito Moreno. It is also located within the Francisco P. Moreno National Park in the Valley of the Pinturas River. It includes the cave with the ancient rock paintings, the cliffs surrounding the cave and the eaves in the area. The English translation of Cueva de las Manos is the cave of the hands.

The site was discovered in 1941 by a monk, was explored again in 1949, but it wasn't studied in earnest by archaeologists until the late 1960s. The site is comprised of a series of rock shelters on the outside of the cave, which is covered with hand stencils and other handprints. Archaeologists found pipes made of bone that people used to spray the paint through to create the stencil effect. By carbon dating the pipes they were able to ascertain that the hand stenciling and handprints were created between 7300 BC and 700 AD. The prehistoric site was used by Stone Age hunter-gatherers and is considered one of the most important prehistoric sites for pictographs and rock art created during that timeframe. The handprints were stenciled using hematite or red ocher to obtain the red pigment and charcoal or manganese to obtain the black pigment. One theory regarding the stenciling of the hands is that it was part of an initiation ceremony. The size of the hand prints are approximately the size of a 13-year-old boy's hand so it may have been a coming-of-age initiation ceremony.

There are paintings on the cave's walls that depict hunting scenes featuring humans and animals. There are also geometric patterns, red dots, images of the sun, and zigzagged shapes. Some of the scenes show the animals being driven into a ravine or brought down by a weapon with long cords and weights on it that was tangled up around the animal's legs.

The energy at Cueva de las Manos feels cool and smooth, is in forward motion, and means you're moving into new stages of development and accepting responsibility for yourself. It is like a strong pulse that captures your attention and motivates you. It feels like the positivity of growth and change as it lifts you into new realms of understanding. Whether it's a quest for new knowledge or to understand more of your own personal spiritual nature, the energy can broaden your scope of vision allowing you to see the past, as well as the present, in a more well-defined way. Think of the energy here like a candle that illuminates the darkness and lights your way, enabling you to find out more about yourself on all levels. The energy at Cueva de las Manos vibrates at a high frequency and is one of happiness, lightness of being, and joy.

10. EASTER ISLAND—CHILE

Categories: Astronomical Observatories, Ceremonial Sites, Islands/Reefs, Megalithic Sites, Power Places, Power Stones, UFO/Extraterrestrial/Paranormal Sites

Easter Island is located in the South Pacific between Chile and Tahiti and is owned by Chile. The island is approximately 2,300 miles from the West Coast of Chile and 2,500 miles from the East Coast of Tahiti and is approximately sixty-four square miles in size. The island was formed by volcanic eruptions and there are still volcanic cones at various points of the island today. The tallest is 11,674 feet above sea level. The island also has over seventy places where eruptions occurred prior to colonization. There hasn't been any volcanic activity on the island during the past 1,300 years.

The island was settled by the Rapa Nui people between 300 and 400 AD when King Hoto Matua landed on a white sandy beach called Anakena. No one knows why these Polynesian people left their home and headed out to sea but they did. At that time the island had a tremendous amount of plant life. The beach was important to the people, which is evident by the large number of moai erected in the area. At the height of the Rapa Nui civilization it is believed that between seven thousand and nine thousand people lived on Easter Island during the tenth to sixteenth century.

The Rapa Nui kept records of their language on what are called Rongo-Rongo tablets. Only a few of these tablets remain because, after the Peruvian slave traders captured most of the island's people, missionaries came to save the rest and ultimately destroyed almost all of the natives artifacts and wooden sculptures including the tablets.

Easter Island is famous for the giant stone figures called moai. They are about thirteen feet tall, weigh approximately thirteen tons each, and sit on ceremonial platforms. Scientists, researchers, and archaeologists have yet to determine why the people created so many of these statues and placed them around the island's coast. Easter Island has always been shrouded in mystery because of these enormous figures that look out to sea. While there have been a lot of different theories on how these massive structures were moved, the most well-known theory is that they walked to their final resting place.[48] This could have been accomplished by groups of people moving the moai using trees and ropes which would make it appear to someone watching from far away that the stone was indeed walking forward. Others believe space aliens helped move the giant moai across the island using some kind of advanced technology. Another theory regarding the creation and use of the moai is that they were sacred objects, which held the sacred spiritual essence called mana. It is also theorized that an astronomical observatory once stood on the island.

The energy at Easter Island is very spiritual, soulful, and ancient. It flows upwards from the center of the island and flows back down to cover the island all around it and into the ocean. The energy feels ever watchful, protective, and resolute. It is the type of energy that can help you be firm in your intention, and protective of your plan to progress toward your goals. This energy does not hold you back but instead grabs you by the hand and drags you along the path you have chosen and then pushes you to your final goal.

11. FERNANDO DE NORONHA—BRAZIL

Categories: Islands/Reefs, Volcanoes/Volcano Cones

Fernando de Noronha is part of the Mid-Atlantic Ridge in the South Atlantic Ocean, 220 miles from the coast of South America and three degrees south of the equator. It is the primary island in a twenty-one island archipelago that consists of islands, islets, and large rocks. The entire archipelago is also called Fernando de Noronha. It was originally named Ilha da Quaresma, which means Lent Island and there is some controversy around who actually discovered the island first. These archipelagos are actually the summits of a volcanic mountain range that exists underneath the water with the bottoms of the mountains being four thousand feet deep. It is believed that the islands formed between two and twelve million years ago.

Over the centuries, Fernando de Noronha was occupied by the English, French, and Spanish-Portuguese and was even used as a penal colony during World War II. They clear-cut the island of trees so the prisoner's couldn't make boats and escape. Today there are a lot of shrubs and some trees, but the island no longer has the type of

---

48. Thurtle, Estelle, August 19, 2014, "10 Fascinating Theories Surrounding Easter Island," http://listverse.com/2014/08/19/10-fascinating-theories-surrounding-easter-island/.

forestation that it had before being made into a prison. Instead, people brought other plants to the island. Today there are a plethora of fruit and nut trees including guava, banana, cashew, papaya, almond, mango, and coconut. You can also find Royal Poinciana, eucalyptus plants, and palm trees.

In 1988 about 70 percent of the island was named as a national maritime park in order to preserve the island, the sea around it, and the marine life, such as dolphins, lobsters, turtles, coral, sponges, and hundreds of species of fish. This is a wonderful place to go snorkeling and diving. Surfers enjoy large seven- to sixteen-foot waves that roll into the beaches of Cacimba do Padre, Biboca, Bode, Boldró, Cachorro, Conceicao, and Meio. Sometimes these beaches can get very crowded so plan your time accordingly.

If you are a birdwatcher, there are large populations of birds who live on the island year-round and other birds who stop there during migration. Because of this, the area is a Global Center of Bird Endemism.

Currently about 2,100 people live on Fernando de Noronha. They also limit the amount of tourists to about 270 per day (which is the number of the seats available on the plane that flies to the island) due to the delicate nature of the ecosystem for both plant and animal life, even though tourism is the way that most people survive on the island.

There are some unique features to the island in addition to the amazing beaches. For example, at Baia dos Porcos beach there are two large rock islands called the two brothers, which sit side-by-side. There is also a huge monolith named Morro do Pico, which is the cone of an extinct volcano and the tallest point of Fernando de Noronha Island at 1,060 feet.

The energy at Fernando de Noronha is calm, peaceful, and meditative as a connection to the natural world. It can guide you to understanding more about your own spiritual nature and help you focus on your life so you can clearly see the path before you. The energy here is spiritual and part of the universal sense of oneness we feel with the planet. If you're working on developing your intuition, clearing your chakras, or getting back to your true spiritual essence, the energy here can help make the journey smoother and brings faster results.

12. FUMAÇA WATERFALLS—BRAZIL

**Categories: Bodies of Water/Waterfalls/Springs,
Mountains/Mounds/Cliff Locations**

The Fumaça Waterfall, also known as the Cachoeira da Fumaça, is located close to the small village of Fumaça (the village is named after the waterfall) in the Chapada Diamantina National Park in the mountain region in the state of Bahia, Brazil. The Fumaça Waterfall is one of the primary attractions in these mountains because it is one of the tallest waterfalls in the country at 1,115.50 feet.

The Chapada Diamantina mountain range consists of mountains, escarpments, valleys, canyons, plateaus, and very tall cliffs. The mountains were formed millions of years ago out of agglomerate and cuarcite rock that has an orange color. In addition to the waterfall, you'll also find monoliths, rivers, other waterfalls, and many systems of caves that were formed by the rivers. The highest point of the mountain range is a little over 6,500 feet above sea level. Almost all of the mountains in the range are flat on top. There is an abundance of vegetation and wildlife in the area. It is also home to anteaters and jaguars. The area gets its name from the diamonds that were mined extensively in the 1900s. Chapada Diamantina is known for having the best hiking in Brazil, with lots of natural pools where you can swim and caves you can explore.

To reach the Fumaça Waterfall requires several hours of travel by car depending upon your starting point. Once you reach the path to the waterfall, you'll have to walk about a mile to reach it. Timing your visit in accordance with the weather is important. If it hasn't rained, the waterfall dries up so you'll only see the face of the cliff that it flows over. If it has been raining a lot, then you'll need to make sure you're wearing good boots because the path to the waterfall will be very wet and muddy. If the sun is out, you'll need to wear a big hat and wear sunscreen because there isn't much shade on this particular path. If you want to go to the summit of Fumaça Waterfall it is suggested that you only go with a guide or tour group because it is very dangerous and you could fall, especially when the surrounding rocks are wet.

Have you ever seen a waterfall that goes up instead of down? Fumaça Waterfall is unique because at times the wind blows the water sideways or up into the sky. The water from this waterfall never hits the ground because it turns into a mist before it can reach the earth below and is often blown away by the wind.

The energy here is ancient, stable, and emits a quiet yet potent vibration. Walking through the forest and viewing the waterfall fills you with a serene, powerful peacefulness. You can feel its vibrancy in the world around you, and as you allow your energy to become one with the forest and the waterfall its effervescence moves through you at a soul level. The energy here feels comforting, as if you're where you should be and that all is right in your world.

13. GALÁPAGOS ISLANDS—ECUADOR

Categories: Islands/Reefs, Volcanoes/Volcano Cones

The Galápagos Islands are an archipelago in the Pacific Ocean that are 620 miles from the coast of Ecuador. The group includes nineteen islands and numerous islets. The Galápagos Islands and the sea surrounding them are both protected World Heritage sites. They are believed to be 3.2 to 4.2 million years old and the submerged part beneath the surface could be fifteen million years old.

Approximately five to ten million years ago the summits of underwater volcanoes appeared above water where the Pacific, Nazca, and Cocos tectonic plates joined and formed the Galápagos. Some of these volcanoes are still active today and occasionally erupt. At that time, the summits were barren rock. The plant and animal life that currently thrive on the island were believed to have arrived there in a number of different ways. Some of the sea animals like sea lions and sea turtles just swam there, birds flew there, and reptiles such as lizards and iguanas, along with rats, probably floated there on tuffs of vegetation. The seeds of plants could have been attached to the animals that arrived there and, in the case of birds, have also been in their guts and excreted there or they could have floated to the island by sea. The majority of the seeds for the plants on the island are salt tolerant. Other plants, for instance the many dandelions that are on the island, could have arrived by floating along on a breeze until landing on the island.

The Galápagos Islands and surrounding sea are home to over four hundred species of fish, eight hundred different types of mollusks, and the only iguana or lizard in the world that can swim and eats seaweed, called the marine iguana. But the islands are most famous for three other species of animals. The first are the giant tortoises, which can live to be 150 years old and can weigh nearly six hundred pounds. The second are the boobies. There is the blue-footed booby, who indeed has blue feet. There are also red-footed boobies and Nazca boobies on the islands as well. The third are the penguins. The

Galápagos Islands are the only place you can see penguins in their natural habitat in the northern hemisphere. Because the animals aren't afraid of humans, there are rules in place for visitors to the islands that protect the animals.

The landscape of the Galápagos Islands is always changing Archeologists have determined that the older islands in the archipelago are beginning to sink back into the ocean. While the older islands sink, the younger ones are being lifted higher out of the ocean.

The energy of the Galápagos Islands is slow moving, mindful, and strong. If you live and work in a hectic environment, as many of us do, visiting the Galápagos Islands is like going from the fierceness of a hurricane into the quiet eye of the storm. This refreshing energy can bring balance back to your life by helping to rejuvenate your mind, body, and spirit. It is a high frequency vibration that can help you slow down and become more aware and attuned to the world around you, your spiritual essence, and enables you to experience the transformation that mindfulness can make in your life.

14. IGUAZÚ FALLS—BRAZIL/ARGENTINA
Categories: Bodies of Water/Waterfalls/Springs, Power Places, Rainforests

Iguazú Falls, also known as Iguassu Falls and Iguaçu Falls, which mean "big water," is located in Misiones Province in Argentina and the State of Paraná in Brazil in Iguazú National Park, which is largely a rainforest. According to Patagonia-Argentina.com it was discovered in 1541 by the Spanish conquistador, Álvar Núñez Cabeza de Vaca.

There is a legend associated with Iguazú Falls. It is said that a huge, ferocious snake lived in the river and the people named it Boi. Each year to appease the snake and keep it happy, the indigenous people would sacrifice a woman to the snake. But one year a brave man from the tribe saved the woman and escaped with her down the river. With tremendous anger, Boi rose up from the river and bent its body, which split the river and separated the man and woman, creating the Iguazú Falls.[49]

Named as one of the new Seven Wonders of the World, Iguazú Falls is breathtaking to behold. It is nearly two miles across and is formed in a half-moon shape. It separates the Iguazú River into an upper and lower section. There are 275 individual waterfalls that make up Iguazú Falls. The largest and main waterfall is called Devil's Throat, which has a drop of 262 feet and the widest water curtain, and includes fourteen individual waterfalls.

---

49. Wander Argentina, "Iguazú Falls: The Fury of Nature," https://wander-argentina.com/iguazu-falls-the-fury-of-nature/

The number of total drop points changes based on the season as does the volume of water tumbling down the waterfalls. You may see fewer waterfalls during the dryer season than you would in the rainy season. During the rainy season there can be as much as 459,090 cubic feet of water flowing over the falls every second. On a typical day, it averages 52,972 cubic feet of water per second. Iguazú Falls is three times as wide and twice as tall as Niagara Falls.

What makes Iguazú Falls so impressive, breathtaking, and awe-inspiring is its half-moon shape and the fact that you see so many individual waterfalls within one enormous waterfall. They are at varying levels; some are wide and robust while others are thin and look more delicate.

You can easily access Iguazú Falls from both the Brazilian and Argentinean sides. From the Brazilian side you can see panoramic views of all of Iguazú Falls. Seeing it in this way gives you a deeper appreciation of the magnificence of this power place. On the Argentinean side, you can walk along boardwalks and get up close to the falls. If you choose the boardwalks, know in advance that you will get wet. You can also go out on a speedboat, which will take you right underneath the waterfalls where you will get completely drenched.

Seeing Iguazú Falls can cause you to feel a lot of strong emotions even if you're just looking at a video. The energy here is radiant and glorious and is a divine connection to the universal consciousness that we each carry within us. Listening to the thundering sound of the falls and feeling the mist of the water against your skin is a transformational experience. One that fills you with hope, inspires you, and makes you feel as if nothing is impossible.

15. INGAPIRCA—ECUADOR

Categories: Astronomical Observatories, Monasteries/Temples, Mountains/ Mounds/Cliff Locations, Relic Sites, Ruins/Archeological Sites

The Ingapirca Archeological Site is located in the Andes Mountains of the southern region of Ecuador in the Cañar province. Ingapirca is the largest known Inca ruins site in Ecuador. It overlooks the surrounding valley and was settled by the Hatun Cañari tribe prior to the arrival of the Incas. They constructed the Temple of the Moon, whose ruins are also at the site. The Hutan Cañari fought against the Inca invasion and weren't conquered by them until late in the fifteenth century. After winning the battle with the

Hatun Cañari, the Inca built Ingapirca together with them as a show of respect. The Temple of the Sun was built to complement the Temple of the Moon. The other buildings at the Ingapirca Archeological Site were built around the same time.

There is a general consensus among archaeologists and historians that the site was built by order of the Inca Huayna Cápac. It is believed that the site was used for military meetings but it was also used for ceremonies to worship the Sun god called Inti, and was also known as Apu-punchau. The Incas believed that the Sun god was one of their ancestors and they often represented him during their ceremonies by having a man wear a mask that had pieces of gold shaped in a zigzag pattern coming away from the center to represent flames or rays of light. Sometimes there were even small faces made into the gold at the end of the sunburst. Other masks were shaped like a disk with carvings representing flames and light going to the edge of the disk. The Incas believed Inti to be very generous but if he was angered, he showed it through a solar eclipse. When this happened the people felt they had to give sacrifices in order to win back his favor. It is believed that the sacrifices were women because female skeletons have been found at the site.

The Ingapirca Archaeological Site is comprised of roads, storage chambers, observatories, and the Temple of the Sun, which is also called El Castillo, "the castle." The Temple of the Sun is the central building in the complex and is the only remaining sun temple of the Inca Empire. It was built with very thick walls that were carved so precisely that mortar wasn't needed, and because of its strategic location high above the valley it is thought to have also had a military purpose. Near the Temple of the Sun is a V-shaped rock that is believed to have been used for both human and animal sacrifice and beside that is a large stone that is thought to be a calendar. There is a museum on site with artifacts and relics including sculptures, tools, and a skeleton, among other things.

The energy at Ingapirca vibrates at a high spiritual frequency and is peacefulness in the face of opposition, working together even if you have opposite views, and working together as one for the best interest of all. The energy here can help you get along better with others, enables you to look at different peoples point of view, and allows you the inner strength to move past negative feelings you may harbor against others in order to seek a positive resolution for all involved. This is an uplifting energy that can inspire and motivate you to become more involved in your community.

16. ISLA DE LA PLATA—ECUADOR

Categories: Islands/Reefs, Mythological Sites

Isla de la Plata is an uninhabited island located off of the coast of Ecuador northwest of Puerto Lopez, a small town in the Manabi Province on the north coast, and is in the Machalilla National Park. To reach Isla de la Plata it is an hour and a half boat ride from Puerto Lopez.

The island is known by a couple of different names with the most recent being the poor man's Galápagos. It is also known as Silver Island because it is believed that Sir Francis Drake buried treasure there, although treasure has never been found, and many people believe this to be a myth. It's also called Silver Island because of the vast abundance of birds who cover the island in white poop.

The reason that the island is called the poor man's Galápagos is because many of the animal species found in the Galápagos Islands also live on Isla de la Plata. For example, there are blue-footed boobies (which are in abundance here), pelicans, frigatebirds, and petrels. Dolphin are abundant in the ocean surrounding the island and quite often you will also see groups of up to ten humpback whales swimming around.

Snorkeling around the island reveals a plethora of fish in every color imaginable. The coral around the island is no longer colorful but the bright colors of the fish make up for it. Often sea turtles can be seen while you're snorkeling or you might even encounter a giant manta ray.

The island is relatively small, there is no shade, and the terrain is rough so you have to come prepared. It's important to take sunscreen, raingear, and wear good shoes for hiking the trails. In order to visit the island you will have to take a tour with a guide due to the hour and half boat ride to get there. If you enjoy scuba diving, there are also diving tours that go to the waters around the island. On the guided tour, your guide will escort you along trails on the island, some of which are sometimes closed in order to protect the animals or the area. After the tour most of the tour companies offer lunch and then you go snorkeling before returning to Puerto Lopez. Sometimes the trip to and from the island is just as exciting as visiting the island itself because you may see orcas, humpback whales, and dolphins along the way.

The energy at Isla de la Plata is invigorating and yet at the same time is calm and peaceful. Being able to interact so closely with the birds on the island, who walk right beside you, can also be a moment when you can use animal frequency to connect to the energy of the blue-footed booby who is often particularly interested in people. The energy here is ancient, deep, and moves at a slow pace. Its frequency beats steadily, which enables you to become more grounded and secure within yourself.

17. LA BREA PITCH LAKE—SOUTHWEST TRINIDAD

Category: Pitch Lakes

Located off of Southern Main Road in Brighton, La Brea Pitch Lake is a natural lake of asphalt, the largest in the world. It is one of only three asphalt lakes in existence. La Brea Pitch Lake was discovered by Sir Walter Raleigh in 1595. He used asphalt from the lake to repair his ship. It is located on 109 acres, is 250 feet deep in the center, and is believed to contain approximately 100 million tons of naturally formed asphalt. It is about 1,200 yards from the sea below a hill that is 140 feet high. Artifacts have been found in the pitch lake including Amerindian pottery, a mastodon tooth, and the remains of prehistoric animals including a giant sloth.

The lake is believed to have been formed when the Caribbean continental plate collided with another of earth's tectonic plates, which created fault lines and fissures. Oil rose to the surface, filling a volcanic crater. When the mixture made contact with the air, the oil's lighter elements evaporated leaving behind a heavy crude oil, clay, and water, which created the heavy asphalt. The asphalt still moves very slowly, replenishing itself and moving its contents from bottom to top and back again. You can even see the flow lines on the top of the lake. From time to time this movement causes things that are beneath the surface of the lake to emerge and then disappear again; for example, in 1928 a prehistoric tree thought to be four thousand years old appeared and a piece of it was taken before it disappeared back into the asphalt depths.

The lake has so much asphalt that it is able to supply it to markets all around the world. The asphalt from La Brea Pitch Lake has been used to pave places like the LaGuardia Airport in New York, the road in front of Buckingham palace in England, and the Lincoln Tunnel which runs from New York to New Jersey, in addition to numerous other roads and airport runways internationally. It is also used as an ingredient in other products such as underbody coating for vehicles, seam sealants, and anticorrosive black paint just to name a few.

La Brea Pitch Lake has sections of semi-hardened asphalt, channels, and mineral pools. People can walk on the semi-hard surfaces, which occasionally bubble up as gasses are forced through the asphalt, and some people will even swim in the pooled water because it is believed that the high levels of sulfur and minerals can heal joint pain, skin problems, and other types of aches and pains.

The energy at La Brea Pitch Lake is, like the asphalt itself, slow moving and flows in an up and down motion. It is thick, smooth, and grounding—a connection to the inner workings of both the planet and, on a spiritual level, the inner essence within you. As you grow spiritually, you are continually moving, taking what feels right to you at the moment that enables your spiritual growth, and making it your own. Some spiritual concepts that aren't right for you at this moment in time will come back around some day, just as the asphalt lake constantly moves its contents, and when they do, they may make perfect sense to you at that time. The energy here is one of growth and renewal, of being flexible but firm in order to create wonders that you may have once thought were only attainable in your dreams.

18. LAKE DISTRICT–CHILE

Categories: Bodies of Water/Waterfalls/Springs, Healing Springs, Mountains/ Mounds/Cliff Locations, Regions, Volcanoes/Volcano Cones,

The Lake District is located in the southern part of Chile in the Andean foothills. The term Chilean Lake District is often used by travel companies to describe the region and all of the different lakes in this area. Geologists and scientists prefer the term Zona Sur, which means "southern zone," and is one of five named natural regions in continental Chile. Its borders are the Bío-Bío River to the north, the Indian mountains to the east, the Pacific Ocean to the west, and the Chacao Channel to the south. It is approximately six hundred miles long. The entrance to the lakes is at the city of Puerto Varas, which is known for its view of the two snowcapped volcanoes, named Osorno and Calbuco, surrounded by an ancient forest and flanked by lakes. It is considered one of the most beautiful areas in all of Chile.

In the Lake District, the Andes Mountains are very close to sea level. There are hundreds of rivers in the mountains that flow to this area of Chile. Many of the rivers form deep lakes, some of which are in the mountains, while other rivers flow directly into the Pacific Ocean. The southern zone of Chile is often referred to as the rainiest place in the world and has a diverse geography throughout the zone. The area has twelve primary lakes and many smaller lakes, waterfalls, dense forest, and a total of six volcanoes in the region. Many people say that the setting here, and the views of the scenery, is similar to Switzerland. Because of the large amount of water in the area there is also an abundance of fog, which makes the Lake District look intriguing, mysterious, and otherworldly.

The Lake District is well known for adventure sports and has many national parks, forest reserves, protected parklands, and even small areas of protected coastal rain forest where you can participate in a variety of outdoor activities. If you are an adventure sports enthusiast visiting the Lake District you can climb a volcano, go hiking, mountain biking, or horseback riding. If you visit during the winter months you can even ski down the slopes of the volcanoes. If you enjoy water sports there are plenty of opportunities to go rafting or kayaking. Due to the amount of lakes in the area, fishing is a popular sport and many people enjoy fly-fishing for the variety of trout and salmon species that are available in the lakes. If you spend a day out hiking or participating in any type of rigorous activity, you might also enjoy relaxing and soaking in some of the hot springs in the area afterwards.

The energy in the Lake District is peaceful, quiet, and meditative yet there is an undertone of high-frequency movement that propels you to take action. Walking through the forests or along the side of a volcano will enable you to explore the meditative part of this energy, however the high-frequency undertones will also affect you in a way that makes you not only contemplate the things you want to achieve but enables you to put a plan of action together while you're thinking about them. The energy here is all about taking action and putting things in motion that will have a positive outcome for what it is that you desire.

19. LAKE GUATAVITA—COLOMBIA
Categories: Bodies of Water/Waterfalls/Springs, Ceremonial Sites

Lake Guatavita is located in the widest section of the Colombian Andes known as the Cordillera Oriental, in the Cundinamarca Department, Almeidas Province, in the municipality of Sesquilé in Columbia. Because of its perfectly round shape the lake was once thought to be the result of a meteorite impact or that it was a volcanic crater that filled with water.

The area surrounding the shores of the lake was inhabited by the Muisca people, a tribe indigenous to the Andes, who named the lake. It was a sacred lake to them and they worshiped the goddess of the water there. They often conducted rituals and ceremonies that involved the lake. One of those ceremonies led to the legend of El Dorado. During the ceremony to appoint a new ruler, known as a zipa, of the southern part of the area, they would cover the new ruler in a dusting of gold powder. He would then get on a ceremonial raft, which was full of precious artifacts, jewelry, and other items, and go out to the middle of the lake where he would dive into the water, effectively washing off the gold. He would then climb back onto the raft and throw all of the items that he carried out there with him into the water. Worshipers who remained along the shores would also throw jewelry, trinkets, and other offerings that were special to them into the lake. Spanish conquistadors saw this ritual and they called the zipa, El Dorado. The legend of the city of gold was born.

Because of the legend, during the 1500s there were two attempts made to drain the lake but both times the lake levels only went down by small amounts. A few artifacts were found but they weren't of great value. Then in the 1800s it was believed that the lake held over $300 million of gold so it was drained through a tunnel to a depth of about four feet of mud. Very few artifacts were found. Finally, in 1965 the government protected the lake and made it illegal to try to salvage anything from the lake or to drain it again.

About thirty minutes from the sacred lake is the town of Guatavita. The original town was completely flooded when they built a reservoir in order to generate power and increase the water supplies to surrounding areas. The town was rebuilt in the 1960s as a replica of the colonial Spanish town. Today it is a popular attraction. The town has a bullfighting ring, the Main Street, the town church, a museum, there are a few restaurants, handicraft stores, and you can even go boating or skiing on the reservoir or visit Lake Guatavita, for which it was named. To get to the lake you have to climb 150 steps and it's about a half hour hike after you arrive there by car.

The energy at Lake Guatavita is clear, light, and healing. The silence of the area can help you to quiet your mind and feel the lightness of being within yourself. This is a healing energy that can help you look within and transform whatever's holding you back in life, be it negativity caused by fear or the way you look at life in general. The energy here brings clarity of purpose and helps you see where you should go on your spiritual path so you can become all you're supposed to be during this lifetime.

20. MACHU PICCHU—PERU

**Categories: Ceremonial Sites, Earth Chakras (Sacral), Monasteries/
Temples, Mountains/Mounds/Cliff Locations, Pilgrimage Sites,
Power Places, Ruins/Archeological Sites, Vortexes**

Machu Picchu, also known as the Lost City and one of the Seven Wonders of the World, is located in the Cusco department of Peru in the Urubamba province and in the Machu Picchu Archaeological Park. It is on the eastern slopes of the Cordillera de Vilcabamba mountain range in the Peruvian Andes. The Urubamba River, which was considered sacred to the Inca, encircles Machu Picchu. When viewed from above you can see that Machu Picchu sits on a high ridge of the mountain almost at the summit. The people who lived there were obviously not afraid of heights.

The city has over 600 terraces, thousands of steps, 170 buildings, 16 fountains, several temples, a water drainage system, and a water supply system nearly a mile long. The stones used to build the city were taken from the rocks on the mountains. The stone fitting was so precise that you can't even slide a pin or anything else between them today and they were built without iron tools or wheels. They didn't use mortar but instead used river rocks to carve the larger stones so they fit perfectly together. The terrace system was used to grow crops and kept the city from sliding down the mountainside, due to the large amount of rainfall in the area. The terraces were seven feet tall and ten feet wide and built with a drainage system within them that used larger rocks at the bottom then smaller rocks, a gravel layer came next, then a layer of sand and finally a layer of topsoil.

When Machu Picchu was discovered, there were many different theories as to what it was and the purpose it served. Some believed that it was a hub for trade similar to many other ancient cities, others believed it served as a prison, there is also the thought (based on the amount of terraces) that it was a place where new crops were tested. Some thought it was a retreat for women or a nunnery due to the amount of female skeletons found at the site. Some believed it to be a spiritual site that was a place of pilgrimage or that it honored the rising and setting of the sun, which aligned with nearby mountains that had religious importance to the Incas, especially during solstices and equinoxes. The current and most popular belief model of archaeologists today is that it was a Royal retreat for the fifteenth century Inca Emperor Pachacuti, where he would go to entertain guests with his royal court, to relax, and maybe go hunting. Some archaeologists believe that all of these different theories could have happened during the history of Machu Picchu.[50]

The energy surrounding Machu Picchu is considered a vortex that resonates with all the chakras within the human body. The frequency of the energy is so high, there is a divine connection and the energy is considered transformational. Because of the high amplification of the energy at this vortex if you are an intuitive, particularly an empath, you may want to shield yourself spiritually by building protective walls around you as you venture into the site and then gradually allow those walls to come down as you adjust to the change in frequency. You're also at a high elevation which can affect you physically. The energy here is so amplified because there is a lot of quartz in the area, which aids in healing, clarity, harmony, cleansing, and balance. After visiting Machu Picchu, or connecting with the energy there, do not be surprised if you experience transformations in everything you're doing including an increase in your understanding of metaphysical topics, a higher level of accuracy in your intuition, and an enhanced ability to simply to know things while experiencing enlightenment.

21. MANÚ NATIONAL PARK—PERU
Categories: Mountains/Mounds/Cliff Locations, Rainforests, Regions

Manú National Park is located in Madre de Dios, Peru. This is a very isolated area that contains one of the most bio-diverse ecosystems in Peru, South America, and quite possibly the world, including the Amazon Rainforest, Andean forest and grasslands, low land rainforests, Yunga forests, and mountain cloud forests. It is a national park, one of the largest in South America, which is home to over 1,025 different species of birds, more than anywhere else in the world. This is because there's a wide range of elevations throughout the park that are suitable for the many different species.

In fact, jaguars, giant otters, and more than 200 species of other mammals make Manú National Park their home. There are also 77 different species of amphibians, 68 species of reptiles, and so far 1,300 species of butterflies have been recorded. It is believed that there are hundreds of thousands of other arthropods such as insects, spiders, or crustaceans that live in the park and haven't been recorded yet. When it comes

---

50. Than, Ker, "What Was Machu Picchu For? Top Five Theories Explained," July 22, 2011, https://news.nationalgeographic.com/news/2011/07/110721-machu-picchu-100th-anniversary-archaeology-science/.

to plant life, there are more than 5,000 different species. An interesting fact about Manú National Park is that scientists seem to be continually discovering new species of animal and plant life in the park.

Manú National Park is also home to approximately 1,000 of the indigenous people called the Matsigenka. They live in the forest, farm crops, and hunt for their food. While the rules of the park allow the Matsigenka to do these things for their own use, the people are not allowed to hunt with guns or to sell anything from the park without the park's permission. Many of these people still gather plants for medicine, grow yucca and other crops, and hunt with bows and arrows.

While the actual national park does not allow visitors, there are some areas that are called the reserve zone at the edge of the park where you are allowed to go. There are several lakes that you can visit, you can go rafting along the rivers or take tours where you can visit and spend the night in the cloud forest in the high jungle or stay in lodges in the low jungle. The energy in this national park is one of unity. There is no separation between mind, body, and spirit but it is all a collective universal consciousness of the Divine. The people who live in the park respect all of life in every form and understand the ebb and flow of positive and negative energy within all that is. Connecting to this energy will enable you to experience spiritual growth at all levels, it will allow you to see what you fear and release that fear.

22. MARAJÓ ISLAND—BRAZIL

Categories: Burial Sites, Islands/Reefs

Marajó Island is located in the Amazon River Delta in the estuary where the Amazon flows into the Atlantic Ocean. It is an island produced by sediments from the Amazon River, which passes north of the island. Other channels send water into the Pará River on the south side of the island, effectively separating it from the mainland. This type of island is called a fluvial island, also known as a river island, and Marajó Island is the largest one in the world at 15,483 square miles. Approximately 250,000 people live on the island. The main town is Soure where there are no traffic lights on the roads. There are few vehicles in the town and most people use bicycles or walk.

There are two sections to the island. To the west there are swamp forests and to the east are grassy savannas. There are numerous tidal rivers that flow into the island, which can cause flooding, especially during the rainy season where some areas are flooded for six to eight months out of the year. For thousands of years, the people of the area have burned the savannas in order to flush out the wildlife, especially turtles, for food. Today farmers let water buffalo and cattle roam over the area, which destroys growing plant life. Some areas of the island have been logged until some species of trees became extinct on the island, then the loggers move on to another species of tree.

There are approximately one hundred pre-Columbian archaeological mounds on Marajó Island that have been dated to 400 to 1500 AD.[51] These mounds were believed to be funerary mounds and contained artifacts such as pottery objects. Scientists and archeologists excavated the mounds in the savannas, which were between thirty-two and thirty-nine feet high, some so extensively that they were completely destroyed. It was determined that the mounds used as houses were found around mounds used as burial sites. Archeologists also decided that the same civilization of people lived all across the island but there were variations found in the pottery styles from groups in different locations and the pottery styles changed over time.

The energy at Marajó Island vibrates at a slow rate. It is in an unhurried forward motion; constantly moving and changing but taking its time to do it. This energy is helpful when you need to slow down, to cast off that which no longer serves your best interest, and to take time for yourself. If you feel yourself getting bogged down in mire, or stuck in a rut, the energy here can flood you with positivity, like the island when it floods with rain or tidal water, so that you become unstuck and can move more freely. Once you are lifted from the mire by the flow of energy you can pick up your pace until you are standing on clear solid ground again.

23. MOUNT RORAIMA—GUYANA
Categories: Mountains/Mounds/Cliff Locations, Mythological Sites

Mount Roraima, is a flat-topped mountain, also called a tepuy or mesa, in the Pakaraima Mountains in the Guiana Shield, which is a Precambrian geological formation that is 1.7 billion years old and part of the South American northern coast. Mount Roraima is also in the Canaima National Park. Mount Roraima marks the borders of Brazil, Guyana, and Venezuela (where two thirds of the mountain is located) at a point in the

---

51. Rossetti, Dilce de Fátima, Góes, Ana Maria, and Mann de Toledo, Peter, "Archaeological Mounds in Marajó Island in Northern Brazil," 2009, Wiley Periodicales, Inc., http://www.dsr.inpe.br/Marajó/ Archaeological.pdf.

center of the mesa's summit. Of the three countries, it is the highest mountain in Guyana but not in Brazil or Venezuela.

This mesa is surrounded with myth and legend, especially among the Pemón indigenous people who live in the area. According to their legends, Mount Roraima was once a huge tree that held all of the fruits and tuberous vegetables in the world but one of their ancestors cut the tree down causing a terrible flood. It is often referred to as the Lost World because Sir Arthur Conan Doyle depicted ascending Mount Roraima in his 1912 novel *The Lost World*, which described dinosaurs and other extinct animals living on the isolated summit of the mesa.

The summit of Mount Roraima is 9,094 feet in elevation and is nine miles long with its highest point being in the Venezuelan section at Maverick Rock, which has an elevation of 9,219 feet. It can only be accessed from Venezuela where there is a naturally formed ramp that goes to the top. The rest of the mountain has vertical cliffs all around the sides that are 1,312 feet high. The summit is home to many plants that can only be found on the mesa because it's so isolated. One of the plants, Drosera Roraimae, is carnivorous. The terrain of the summit is very rough and can be dangerous because it has many gorges. There are also pools of water and in some areas gardens of wildflowers. Because of the elevation, if you were standing on top you'd see clouds below you and it rains on the summit daily. The rainwater produces gorgeous waterfalls, some of the tallest in the area, and many occur randomly depending on the amount of rainfall. Waterfalls that are there today may be gone tomorrow and a new one can show up in a different place. The rainwater feeds many rivers and streams including the Amazon River.

If you decide to visit Mount Roraima, it is best to hire a guide to take you on a tour. The path getting to the summit has lots of markers so you can find your way, but that's not why you need the guide. Once you reach the summit there is constant cloud cover, which can make it difficult to find your way. Guides know the area well so you will not get lost or suddenly find yourself at the edge.

The energy at Mount Roraima is cool, crisp, and mysterious. It feels like you stepped into a different dimension and as if eyes are watching you as you make your way tentatively around the area. It feels all-knowing, expectant, and is infused with ancient power. This energy feels charged and deep, as if you're just waiting for some epiphany. Harnessing the powerful energy of Mount Roraima can help you find peace within yourself, enhances your intuitive abilities, and enables you to let go of drama in your life and embrace a satisfied calmness of simply knowing.

24. ÑACUNDAY FALLS (SALTO ÑACUNDAY)–PARAGUAY
Category: Bodies of Water/Waterfalls/Springs

Located in Alto Paraná, Ñacunday District on the Ñacunday River is the Niagara of Paraguay, Ñacunday Falls, which is inside Ñacunday National Park. Ñacunday Falls is almost two miles from the juncture of the Ñacunday and Paraná rivers. The water at Ñacunday Falls forms a single curtain that cascades over a balsalt step. It has a drop of approximately 115 feet and is 361 feet wide. Paraguay is a landlocked country bordered by Bolivia, Brazil, and Argentina in the central part of South America. The country itself has a very diverse ecosystem that ranges from wilderness, wetlands, forests, and has plenty of rivers and waterfalls.

The Ñacunday National Park encompasses an area that is twenty square miles. Within the park, there is a wide variety of all kinds of wildlife including birds, reptiles, rodents, mammals, and insects. Ñacunday Falls is the biggest attraction in the park. You'll know you're getting close to the waterfall because you can hear it from a third of a mile away.

Ñacunday Falls is a great place to watch the river otters who live around the falls. The banks of the river are steep at the waterfall and there are many species of orchids and epiphytes growing in the area. This is due to the high humidity and mist created by the waterfall. If you're feeling adventurous you can walk behind the falling water to an island that was created when fallen trees went over and behind the waterfall. If you visit this island, you can see the waterfall from the inside. You can also walk from one side of the river to the other by taking the route behind the waterfall.[52] At different points around the waterfall, you can always see a rainbow on sunny days.

During the rainy season, the falls will often be muddied and brown. The volume of water flowing over the falls increases dramatically. During the dry season (which just means there is less rain than during the rainy season because it's still rainy) the water going over the falls is clear and the volume is lower.

---

52. Morales, Octavio, "Las Maravillas de los Saltos," 2014, http://promosaltos.blogspot.com/p/saltos-del-tembey.html.

The energy at Ñacunday Falls is adventurous and fun. Imagine yourself walking through the forest while hearing the roar of the waterfalls ahead of you. Feel the anticipation, the expectation, and the joy coursing through you as you wait to appreciate the unknown. Upon viewing the beauty of the falls you feel overcome with a sense of excited happiness. You trek down to the river and slip behind the curtain of water into the cool shade of a hidden island-like setting. Connecting with the energy of Ñacunday Falls can add excitement and happiness to your life. If you've been feeling bored or as if life is dull then the energy here can liven you up and heighten your awareness which allows you to better appreciate everything in your life.

25. PERITO MORENO AND GLACIERS NATIONAL PARK–ARGENTINA

Categories: Bodies of Water/Waterfalls/Springs, Glaciers

In the Austral Andes in Argentina, on the border of Chile and within the southwest part of the Santa Cruz Province, you'll find the Los Glaciares National Park, which is so named because there are over three hundred glaciers in the park, forty-eight of which are in the Patagonian Ice Field. It is the largest national park in Argentina and a federally protected area. Typically, glaciers start around 8,200 feet in elevation, but the glaciers here begin at a height of 4,900 feet.

The ice caps in the Patagonian Andes are what feed the glaciers, which cover more than half of the park, and the South Patagonian Ice Field feeds most of the glaciers. This ice field is a relic of the Quaternary Period, which is well known as the great Ice Age. Due to the high elevations and all of the glaciers, the area here is difficult to access.

One of the most well-known glaciers at Los Glaciares National Park is Perito Moreno, which is often called the most beautiful glacier in the world. It is located in the southern part of the park and is across from the Magellan Peninsula. This glacier is constantly moving forward which causes large chunks of ice to break off and fall into the lake water in front of it. It is nearly two hundred feet tall at the water's edge. Perito Moreno is nineteen miles long and encompasses ninety-seven square miles. While it is one of the forty-eight glaciers in the Patagonian Ice Field it is also an extension of the Andean Ice, which is shared with Chile.

One unique feature of the Perito Moreno glacier is called rapture. This is when the glacier moves over the southern tip of Lake Argentina and acts like a dam blocking the outflow of water, separating the lake into two sections. Lake Argentino can rise nearly one hundred feet above its normal level. The pressure eventually causes the glacier to crumble down into the lake, which is rapture. This occurs every 4 to 5 years and thousands of people visit to see it happen.

There are two large lakes located within Glaciers National Park. These are Lake Argentino and Lake Viedma. Both of these lakes drain into the Atlantic Ocean. Lake Argentino is enormous at 20 miles wide, has a maximum depth of 1,600 feet, and takes up 546 square miles. Lake Viedma is 50 miles long, 9.3 miles wide, and takes up 420 square miles. Ice from the glaciers break off into these lakes creating lots of icebergs.

If you decide you would like to visit Los Glaciares National Park you can go hiking on Perito Moreno. Currently there are two different types of hiking tours available. The first time you go out on the ice for about an hour, for the second you go out for five.

The energy at Perito Moreno and Los Glaciares National Park, is a slow vibration, yet it is crisp and clear. It feels as if you took a deep breath of clean, cold, winter air. The energy here is fresh as the old transitions to the new. Just as the glacier breaks apart into the waters of the lake to begin a new path, you too can break away from old patterns that have been holding you back to embark on a new journey that can lead you to new discoveries.

26. PINTADOS GEOGLYPHS & THE GIANT OF ATACAMA−CHILE

Categories: Gigantic Landscape Carvings, Pilgrimage Sites, UFO/Extraterrestrial/Paranormal Sites

Located in the Atacama Desert at Cerro Unitas, in the Region de Tarapaca of Chile, are the Pintados Geoglyphs including the Atacama Giant. The Atacama Desert is west of the Andes Mountains and goes across parts of Argentina, Bolivia, Peru, and Chile. This desert is very harsh and dry. The terrain is stony and is made up of felsic lava, sand, salt lakes, and is pretty much a barren environment. It is believed that the Inca or the Tiwanaku, who lived in this region thousands of years ago, created the images.

Over five thousand Pintados geoglyphs are in the Atacama Desert and they represent a wide range of images. Some are geometric, others anthropomorphic (have human characteristics), and others are zoomorphic (have animal characteristics). Archaeologists believe that the geoglyphs were made between 600 and 1500 AD. However, due to the problematic nature of dating geoglyphs, these figures could be much older than originally thought or they may be younger. These desert geoglyphs were made in one of three ways. In the additive technique, the people would have found stones and other material to create a raised image or an outline of an image. In the extractive technique, they would dig out the topsoil to expose the lighter soil underneath, leaving an image in the dirt. The dirt they dug out may have been piled up around the edges to also help create an outline of the image. They also used both techniques at the same time within one image, which is called the mixed technique. For example, they may have dug out the main part of the image, then stacked rocks inside of it to create another image, and then stacked rocks around the edge to create an outline of the larger image.

The Atacama Giant was constructed on the side of a hill called Cerro Unitas. It is an anthropomorphic geoglyph, with a square head that has four lines protruding from the top and from each side. It also has a rectangular body, skinny legs, and arms that are bent in the shape of the letter V. The eyes and mouth are square and there are lines protruding from the hips and knees. It also has lines for feet, which may represent boots. It also looks like it has a small animal with a curved tail beside it and a circular image above it. It is the largest known geoglyph ever found in the world to date. There are many theories regarding the Atacama Giant. Some believe it is an astronomical moon calendar, others believe it is a deity the people worshiped and possibly even a pilgrimage site. Some believe it is a site for extraterrestrial visitation, or is related to an ancient language or a map for travelers. We may never know for sure.

The energy surrounding the Pintados geoglyphs and the Giant of Atacama is smooth, dry, and moves at a high vibration. You feel the energy shimmering from the ground into the air like a lot of thin zigzagging bolts of golden red light. This energy is good for getting your creativity flowing, to help you make something from nothing, which will stand the test of time. This could apply to a business or any other situation where you create something that you will eventually be known for. Connecting to the energy of this place will energize, uplift, and inspire you.

27. SACRED VALLEY OF THE INCA–PERU

Categories: Burial Sites, Fertility Sites, Regions, Ruins/Archeological Sites

The Río Urubamba Valley is known as the Sacred Valley, in the foothills of the Andes Mountains about 9.3 miles from the town of Cuzco and is accessible by driving along a narrow road filled with very sharp turns.

People have lived in the Sacred Valley since the earliest time of the Incan settlement. During that era, the valley was a buffer between the city of Cusco and the Antis tribe who would occasionally try to raid the city. The land was fertile and they could grow crops that wouldn't grow higher in the mountains, but that could be transported to cities at higher elevations.

Today there are colonial type towns and isolated villages where weaving is done. There are street markets as well as tours offered to the three main Incan archaeological sites of Ollantaytambo, Pisac, and Chinchero. The Sacred Valley is still a fertile area that supplies Cusco with fruit, vegetables, corn, and other produce.

Ollantaytambo is in the northern section of the Sacred Valley and was an administrative city for the Inca civilization, as well as the route to the Incan inhabited eastern part of the Amazon Incan Empire known as Antisuyo. It was the last stronghold during the Spanish invasion and today you can visit the fortress at Temple Hill. This fortress is made up of many enormous terraces that were used to grow crops. It was also the site of a famous battle where the Incas flooded the valley and forced the Spanish to retreat but they returned and defeated the Incas later. From here, you can also visit the Inca Trail or catch a train to Aguas Calientes. There is an incomplete Temple of the Sun here that had sundials and other features that enabled the Incans to use it as a calendar.[53]

There are also ruins at Picas of the citadel that controlled the route to Paucartambo. The stonework here is astounding and is cut from solid blocks of rock. There is a water duct system, a Sun Temple, and ancient burial sites.

Chinchero is a small Andean Indian village with views that overlook the Sacred Valley. According to legend, Chinchero is the birthplace of the rainbow. The people who live here today still use the agricultural terraces that were built by the Incans and they built a church on the foundation of an Incan temple. The energy of the Sacred Valley and surrounding areas is one of simplicity, fertility, abundance, and calmness.

---

53. The Only Peru Guide, "Ollantaytambo Ruins," https://www.theonlyperuguide.com/peru-guide/the-sacred-valley/highlights/ollantaytambo-ruins/.

It flows around the valley at a high frequency vibration but in slow movement (so it's moving slow but vibrating fast). The energy is helpful to you when you need to slow down and enjoy the fruit of your labors, to simplify your life and to let go of stress so you feel calm and content. There is abundance all around you if you'll only settle into this energy and reach out for it.

28. SALT CATHEDRAL—COLOMBIA

Category: Caves

Located in Zipaquira in the Cundinamarca Department, thirty miles from Bogotá, Columbia, the Salt Cathedral is built inside a rock salt mine so you have to walk to a depth of 590 feet underground in a halite mountain in order to see it. Halite Mountains were often underwater at some point in history in order for the rock salt to form. Approximately three thousand people visit the Salt Cathedral every Sunday.

The Muiscas, a Pre-Columbian people, were mining salt from this mountain since the fifth century BC. Salt was an important trade product for them. Sometime in the centuries since then, the miners carved a small church and altars in the mine where they would pray each day for their own safety while mining the salt.

The church was expanded between 1950 and 1954. In 1990 it was closed down due to structural problems which would put the people visiting in danger. So they built the Salt Cathedral that is there today between 1991 and 1995. This new cathedral is two hundred feet deeper than the older one, which is directly above it.

As you enter the Salt Cathedral, there are metal arches that support the tunnel through the mountain of salt. The mining tunnels are illuminated with neon lights until you get to the main cathedral. As you walk inside you'll discover fourteen small chapels called the Stations of the Cross which represents the birth, life, and death of Jesus Christ and his journey to the cross. All of these chapels are connected by tunnels.[54] It is a Roman Catholic Church but there isn't a bishop so it's not officially a cathedral according to the religion's standards and they do not perform weddings or baptisms there. They do offer the sacraments of the Eucharist and confession.

In the main part of the cathedral, the ceiling is dome shaped with an enormous cross that is fifty-two and a half feet high and nearly thirty-three feet wide as the cen-

---

54. Miguel in Bogotá, "Salt Cathedral in Zipaquira," April 25, 2017, https://www.youtube.com/watch?v=XOlocOeXVTY.

tral focus. There are lights illuminating the cross that change colors. In other parts of the cathedral there is a strobe light effect when the colored lighting changes. There is also a last supper table in the main cathedral that is made out of thirty-six tons of salt. Throughout the cathedral, you'll see many sculptures depicting angels and other religious scenes that are carved out of salt or are a combination of marble and salt. Some pews and altars are made out of salt and others are made out of wood. As you exit the cathedral there are also a lot of shops where you can buy souvenirs.

The energy at Salt Cathedral is inspiring, spiritual, and creative. It moves at a medium speed, and vibrates at a high frequency. It is uplifting and humbling. Connecting with the energy here can help you become more in tune with your own spiritual nature, including your core spiritual essence and higher self. It can help you grow on your path, spark your creativity, and lead you in a positive direction that is filled with hope for the future.

29. SAN AUGUSTÍN–COLOMBIA

Categories: Burial Sites, Ceremonial Sites, Megalithic Sites, Pilgrimage Sites, Power Places

San Augustín is located in the Huila Department of Columbia near the town of San Augustín in the San Augustín Archaeological Park. It is also in the Colombian Massif of the Colombian southwestern Andes. It is believed to be the world's largest necropolis and contains more megalithic sculptures and monuments than any other archaeological site in South America. San Augustín Archaeological Park covers an area of 250 square miles and contains one third of the areas known statues and half of the known burial mounds in the Alto Magdelena region, which has a total of six hundred statues and forty burial mounds.

It is believed that societies developed in the area around 3,300 BC. Between the years 1 and 900 AD the indigenous people created amazing stone carvings, the majority of which are in San Augustín but many are also in the surrounding area. The details in these carvings show the high level of craftsmanship and creativity of these ancient people. Archaeologists believe that the site was abandoned around 1350 AD. Then in the eighteenth and nineteenth centuries, it was rediscovered and grave robbers disturbed many of the monuments.

The site is thought to have been a place of pilgrimage and of worship and was considered a sacred land. Artificial platforms, drainage ditches, and funerary monuments can be found all over the area. Some of the funerary monuments are over thirteen feet tall and are carved out of volcanic rock that weighs several tons. Due to their placement, archaeologists determined that they were used to protect the burial sites and funeral rooms. However, no one really knows their true purpose. There is very little folklore or legend surrounding this area or the people who lived here. Some believe that these carved figures were also spiritually charged with specific purposes (like you would clear or charge the energy within a crystal or stone today) or that they acted like batteries providing energy to the area.

When I looked at the statues, one thing really jumped out at me—each face feels like it draws you to it and each mouth has a set of upper and lower teeth that are long and pointed. This made me wonder if the people actually had big sharp overgrown teeth like that back then or if they filed their teeth in some way. You can feel the energy of the statues just by looking at their pictures. Some look angry with their fists clenched and their eyebrows pulled together while others look like children with a goofy smile on their face while they're holding a doll. Another looks like an old man who is sitting down resting his weary bones. To me, it almost seems as if these statues represent an actual person who lived during this time.

There is a range of energy at San Augustín and overall it is powerful and positive. The energy surrounding some of the statues feels very upbeat and positive, some feel lonely and sad, while others feel fierce, like a warrior about to go off to battle. Still others touch a happy place within your soul or make you smile. Looking at the carvings at the site can enhance your own energy in a number of ways. It can help with your creativity, you can heighten your intuition, and it makes you think of the people of the past and how they lived. This can be applied to how you live and changes that you can make in order to have a simple, productive, and happy, joyous life.

30. SÃO THOMÉ DAS LETRAS—NEAR MINAS, BRAZIL

**Categories: Caves, Power Places, UFO/Extraterrestrial/
Paranormal Sites, Vortexes**

São Thomé das Letras is a municipality located in the state of Minas Gerais in the southeast region of Brazil. The town is known as a mystical location due to the energy here. It attracts both the scientific and new age communities.

The São Thomé das Letras has quite a few legends surrounding it. One says there was a mystic named Chico Taquara who could control the animals and one day he mysteriously vanished inside of a cave. The other legend references a slave who ran away from a plantation owned by the Baron of Alfenas. The slave found a letter written in calligraphy beside a statue of Saint Thomas. He gave the letter to the Baron and he was so amazed by it that he freed the slave and built a church at the site where the statue and letter were found. Others say the word letras in the town's name refers to strange inscriptions found inside local caves. It is said that Carimbado Cave leads to a hidden civilization of people who live underground and that it shares a source of energy with Peru's Machu Picchu. There are also many stories of UFO sightings in São Thomé das Letras and people climb a hill that is close to Casa da Pirâmide just to look for strange objects in the sky.

Another fact that draws people to this location is that São Thomé das Letras is built on a mineral deposit of quartzite. This metamorphic rock is made when quartz sandstone is exposed to high temperatures and pressure within the earth. Quartzite stones amplify the energy of an area just as quartz does. It also shares the same characteristic of being easily programmable with the intentions and for the purposes that you need. It is often white, although it can have other colors depending upon the amount of other mineral deposits within it. Quartzite has a high vibration and can be used to raise your own frequency or during chakra work. It's known for helping you learn to understand your emotions and aids in helping you understand your life lessons. With a whole town being built on a quartzite deposit, and used in the construction of the streets, homes and other buildings, the energy here is very intense, strong, and vibrant. One of the buildings here is a house made entirely of quartzite called the Pyramid House. They mine the stone today so you'll see machines and signs associated with the mining industry in the area.

The energy at São Thomé das Letras is at a very high vibration due to the amplification of the natural energy by the quartzite. It is light, bright, and moves in a spiraling motion around the town. It feels like a vortex energy that is pulled from deep within the earth and then spirals outward. Connecting to this energy can help you with obtaining any type of spiritual or metaphysical knowledge and helping you to put that knowledge into practical use. It will help you grow on your spiritual path, find balance within yourself, and enable you to experience spiritual and intuitive events that you may have been unknowingly blocking.

31. SAUNDERS ISLAND/FALKLAND ISLANDS– FALKLAND ISLANDS

Category: Islands/Reefs

Located off of the southern tip of Argentina in the South Atlantic Ocean on parts of the Patagonian Shelf, which is part of the South American continental shelf, are the Falkland Islands, which are also known as the Malvinas. The primary islands are East Falkland and West Falkland but there are an additional 776 islands that make up the entirety of the Falkland Islands. Saunders Island, also known as Isla Trinidad, is the fourth largest of the Falkland Islands and is located northwest of West Falkland.

Saunders Island has been farmed since 1948 and it was purchased in 1987 by the Pole-Evans family, who currently operate a sheep farm on the island with over six thousand sheep. It is open to the public from September 15 to April 30, which is when the area is abundant with wildlife, for which the island is well known, and includes many species of penguins including king penguins, macaroni penguins, gentoo penguins, and southern rockhopper penguins. You can also view sea lions, elephant seals, ruddy-headed geese, black-browed albatross, Falkland steamer ducks, white-brindled finches, hawks, eagles, kites, falcons, herons, egrets, cormorants, boobies, and vultures, just to name a few. There are more than 225 species of birds that call the Falkland Islands home, thus making it a birdwatcher's paradise. Whales and dolphins come into the bay to feed, and you can observe them from Saunders Island. If you enjoy hiking, there are plenty of opportunities to walk around and explore the island and its wild inhabitants.

The location of the Falkland Islands is so remote that you will not find any big name chain stores or restaurants on the islands. Instead, you'll find privately run eateries and shops on East and West Falkland which adds to the unique feeling of being at home and one with the natural energy of the place. On Saunders Island, there is a settlement shop where you can buy food if you're spending the night on the island. There are four locations where you can book overnight stays. The most popular locations are at the neck and rookery because you can see so much wildlife right outside your door and you can really relate to the unique frequency of the land, sea, and animals. There is also a refurbished bunkhouse near the original British settlement or you could also choose to stay at the Stonehouse located inside the settlement. It is one of the oldest houses on the island. Day trips to the neck and rookery are offered if you stay at the settlement accommodations.

Experiencing the energy of Saunders Island can help you feel settled within yourself, it can help you find peace when it feels like your world is crumbling around you. It is a calm closeness with the land, feeling the power of the island emerging from the sea, and feeling the power of the sea itself as you look out across its never-ending movement that flows around the island and around you. It embraces you at a soul level and fills you with the universal power that is part of the whole, of all that is. It invigorates the spiritual essence within you to empower you to come back to yourself and be all that you were and more.

32. SETE CIDADES ROCK FORMATIONS—PIAUÍ, BRAZIL
Categories: Caves, Healing Springs, Mythological Sites, Rock Formations

In the northeast part of Brazil is the state of Piauí, which is known for its national parks, is the *Parque Nacional de Sete Cidades*, which translates to "National Park of Seven Cities."

The Sete Cidades rock formations are located within the national park. The stone formations are natural and are approximately 190 million years old. The locations of the rocks are grouped together into what looks like small cities, thus the reason that it is said they are the only stones remaining of the mythical Seven Lost Cities and the reason for the name of the park. There are also approximately 1,500 man-made paintings that were created on some of the rock formations between three thousand and five thousand years ago. Many of the formations also look like they are covered in black scales, which is a unique feature of these stones.

The formations are in an abundance of different and unique shapes. Let's take a look at some of the shapes you'll see in each of these cities. In the first city you'll find petrified prehistoric trees and the Pool of Miracles. This is a continually flowing spring that has water even when other springs in the area run dry. Here you will find formations that look like a snake, an open-mouthed frog, a sewing machine and one that is described as the town square.

In the second city you'll discover the library which looks like stacked books, the Arc de Triomphe which resembles the Paris monument of the same name, an amphitheater, soldier, giant's foot, stone phallus and the mount of olives. The highest point in the park is located in this city.

In the third city are the devil man, a seahorse, a map of Brazil with the states included, three wise men, the stone kiss, the finger of God, and the Rock of Our Lady. The largest cave in the park is located in this city and is called the Cave of the Stranger. One of the formations looks like the head of the Emperor Dom Pedro I.

In the fourth city are an eagle head, two lizards, two brothers, and a lion laying down. In Archete there are prehistoric paintings and in the Grotto of Catirina is where the healer of the Seven Lost Cities, Jose Catirina, lived. A formation of Brazil also exists but this one only has the state of Ceara instead of all of the states.

The fifth city contains prehistoric paintings on the Stone of Inscriptions. At Furna do Índio are more paintings which show hunting rituals of the ancient people who lived in the area. Other formations include a king wearing a crown and robe, a camel, and the House of the Guard.

The sixth city has three primary formations, which include the dog, the elephant and Turtle Rock, which resembles a turtle's shell. The seventh city is known for the Shaman's cave, which has a lot of different inscriptions within it and a formation that looks like a Chinese dragon above it. This city is also an ecological reserve that can only be visited with prior permission in order to preserve the natural plant and animal life that live there as well as the ancient paintings and inscriptions.

If you plan to visit all of the cities, it will take you all day with lots of hiking. It's recommended to hire a guide to make sure you see all of the stone formations and the spectacular waterfalls.

The energy throughout the cities at Sete Cidades feels deep, ancient, and mysterious. The energy feels very pure and radiant. At some points it is light and airy and at other places it feels heavy. Both types of energy draws you into a meditative state where you may find yourself thinking deeply about your own spirituality, life purpose, and individual path. It is easy to connect to your core spiritual essence in this quiet tropical climate, as you listen to the songs of the birds, the whisper of the wind, and view the spectacular rock formations all around you.

33. SUN AND MOON ISLANDS IN LAKE TITICACA–PERU/BOLIVIA

Categories: Bodies of Water/Waterfalls/Springs, Earth Chakras (Sacral), Healing Springs, Islands/Reefs, Monasteries/Temples, Power Places

The largest freshwater lake in South America lies at 12,500 feet above sea level, on the plateau of Collao between Peru and Boliva, and is named Lake Titicaca. Of all of the lakes in the world, Lake Titicaca is one of the deepest and largest and is at the highest elevation. The color of the lake is a deep blue year round. The mountains Ancohuma and Illampu soar high above the lake, are often covered by mist, and were where the weather gods and nature spirits lived. Archeologists recently found a temple submerged in Lake Titicaca that is believed to be between 1,000 and 1,500 years old.

Prior to the arrival of the Incan civilization, the area was inhabited by the Tiahuanaco between 100-700 AD. The Incans believed that the great condors protected the mountains, and the spirits who lived there, and were messengers of the gods who could communicate through shamans. Archeologists have found evidence that ancient people climbed as high as 18,000 feet up these mountains to ask the gods and spirits for rain to sustain them and their crops.

For the Inca civilization, Lake Titicaca was thought to be the center of the universe and was where the sun, moon, and stars originated. It was also believed the human race began from the waters of Lake Titicaca and their spirit would return to the lake when they died. The whole area of the lake and the islands within it was a very sacred site for the Incans.

Two of Lake Titicaca's forty-one islands held more sacred prominence than the others. The Island of the Moon was believed to be the home of the Incan goddess Mama Quila, who was the wife and sister of Inti, the sun god. She was the goddess of marriage and a protector of women. She also ruled over the menstrual cycle and the Inca calendar. It was said that Mama Quila was extremely beautiful and cried silver tears. To honor her, the Incans selected women to live on the Island of the Moon called Virgins of the Sun, who lived a meager existence, conducted ceremonies to worship the sun, and were priestesses to Mama Quila. The Inca believed that a lunar eclipse was the result of Mama Quila being attacked by an animal.

The Island of the Sun is on the Bolivia side of the lake and is the largest of all the islands. It was believed to be the home of the Incan sun god Inti. The Incans built a large labyrinth made of stone (called Chinkana) outside of the town of Challapampa, which is on the north side of the island. On the path between the two you will find a sacred rock that the Incans carved to make it look like a puma, and two large footprints, which the Incans thought were made when the sun stepped on the earth to give birth to Manco Capac and Mama Ocllo, who were the son and daughter of Inti. They were born to earth to help the human race by teaching them to live by rules, to worship the sun god, to plant and harvest, and to build homes. On the opposite side of the island is the town of Yumani, where the Incans built 206 steps that lead to a sacred fountain, often called the fountain of youth, under which are three natural springs. There are also stone towers on this island that are believed to be where they buried people.

The energy of Lake Titicaca and the Sun and Moon Islands is tranquil, serene, and yet invigorating at a spiritual level. Walking among the labyrinth or resting at the sacred puma rock allows you to feel a deeper connection to your own core essence and you can feel a divine arc between your spirituality and the natural world. The energy here can calm, balance, and ground you. Sitting at a higher elevation and staring out across the lake brings a sense of inner peace that can help you connect to your life's purpose. It is a sacred experience that helps you remember your spiritual self, that you are part of the universal whole, and allows you to feel at one with all of existence.

34. THE NAZCA (NASCA) LINES—PERU

Categories: Fertility Sites, Gigantic Landscape Carvings, UFO/Extraterrestrial/Paranormal Sites

Located in the southern portion of the Libertadores, Wari Region of Peru, in the Pampa Coloroda coastal plain and the river basin of the Rio Grande de Nasca approximately 249 miles from Lima, are an amazing number of giant geoglyphs known as the Nazca Lines. Some of these lines are several miles long and the collection of geoglyphs in this area are unrivaled due to their sheer size and number.

According to the UNESCO, these lines and geoglyphs were created between the eighth century BC and the eighth century AD by pre-Hispanic cultures that lived in the area. Archeologists also believe the Nazca people who lived in the area between 1 and 700 AD created the majority of the lines. The lines were made by removing the top layers of earth until the lighter colored bedrock underneath was revealed. In the two-thousand-plus years since the creation of the first lines, they have turned to a rusty color, but if you were to removed the top layer again, you'd find the lighter colored bedrock underneath.

The best way to view the geoglyphs is from an airplane. When viewed from above, the lines reveal huge images of animals, people, plants, and geometric shapes. Some of the creations include a monkey, hummingbird, condor, astronaut, dog, spider, whale, trapezium, flamingo, parrot, lizard, and labyrinth to name a few. Due to the desert conditions and low rainfall rates, which limit erosion, the lines have stayed virtually the same as when they were originally created.

The Nazca lines have often been shrouded in mystery; many UFO theorists believe that the images were made as a way to communicate with alien beings from other planets. These theorists think that some of the lines are landing zones for alien aircraft. It is also believed that they may have been created as paths to water in ancient times, or as paths to gathering places so the people could perform ceremonies to appeal to the fertility gods or to the gods of rain to ensure population growth and the ability to feed the people.

The energy at the Nazca lines feels open and freeing. There is a sense of ancient, otherworldly, and mystical sensations in the area. Walking along the lines, with the sun warming your skin, you will feel a deeper connection not only to the earth and sun but to universal consciousness as well. It's as if you're just a small dot in the bigger picture that you're examining from the ground, even if you can only see a small portion of that picture, but yet you still feel part of all of it. From the air, you feel wonder and awe, a deep respect for those who took the time to create these images and appreciation that they have lasted for you to see. Feeling the energy of the Nazca lines will help you feel more settled, yet they also expand your intuitive ability to rise above situations you're in so that you can see the bigger picture.

35. TIWANAKU—BOLIVIA

**Categories: Ceremonial Sites, Megalithic Sites, Monasteries/
Temples, Mountains/Mounds/Cliff Locations, Power Places,
Ruins/Archeological Sites, Vortexes**

High in the Andes Mountains about thirteen miles from the southeastern point of Lake Titicaca in the Ingavi Province, La Paz Department of Bolivia, is the town of Tiwanaku.

Between 500 and 900 AD, the Tiwanaku, a pre-Hispanic culture, created their capital near the sacred Lake Titicaca. The capital was named Tiwanaku for their culture and because it was their center for spiritual ceremonies and for politics.

Today, a modern city stands where the ancient adobe city was once located. The ceremonial center and monumental stone buildings survived and are now protected as part of an archeological site. Andean scholars consider Tiwanaku one of the most influential cities for culture, religion, and trade prior to the arrival of the Incas. These buildings show the development of the Tiwanaku culture at various times. Based on the location and the surrounding land, it is believed by archeologists that agriculture was an important part of the daily life of the inhabitants.

The public can visit several protected areas of the ancient city. Some of these areas open to visitors are the Akapana, which is a cross-shaped pyramid type structure that has a sunken court in the middle. Archeologists have determined that this structure is entirely manmade from blocks of earth that were excavated from a moat that encircles the site. The Akapana East is on the eastern side of the city and was the boundary between the ceremonial center and the homes where the people lived. It was made of both yellow and red clay for decorative purposes. The Pumapunku is a terraced mound of earth on which megalithic blocks were placed to create a platform. At this structure, you'll also find courtyards, some with walls around them and others without walls. The most significant part of the Pumapunku is the stone terrace, which was created with stone blocks, including the largest stone block onsite. This terrace is called the Plataforma Lítica.

Gateways, open doorway structures, are found in several locations on the site with the most impressive being at the Kalasasaya Pyramid. This structure has a long courtyard above stone steps and the Ponce Monolith, a stone carving of a person, from certain viewpoints, appears to fill the open area of the gateway even though it is set back from the structure. It is customary and a sign of respect to the spiritual energy of the place to ask permission to enter before crossing the gateways.

The Subterranean Temple has rock walls with 175 protruding faces created from rock. Each face is different and unique from the others and are believed to represent the many different races of people who gathered at this location during ancient times. Some archeologists believe that this structure may be seventeen thousand years old.

The energy of the area is one of warmth created from the red adobe of which the structures are made. The frequency is of a high vibration and feels very spiritual, as if it has a direct connection to universal energy. When visiting Tiwanaku you may feel as if you've entered a vortex and can feel the spiraling energy move both around and within you. The energy feels radiant and you may even feel a little light headed as you interact with the energy. Due to the water channels beneath the area, the energy is amplified, which makes it easier to experience.

36. VALLE DEL ENCANTO—CHILE

Categories: Canyons/Gorges, Ceremonial Sites, Petroglyph/Rock Art Sites, Regions,

The Valle del Encanto (Enchanted Valley) National Monument is located between three and eleven miles west of the city of Ovalle, Chile, in South America. This valley is in a tributary canyon of the Río Limarí River, which has been dry for many years with the exception of a small section along an eastern slope that has never dried up completely, even during times of drought. Archeologists discovered the valley in 1946 but it was well known to the local people long before its scientific discovery. The area was occupied by the Molle people between 500 and 700 AD and it was known to hunter gatherer people for almost four thousand years prior to the arrival of the Molle.

The valley is filled with rocks and there are thirty that contain pre-Colombian petroglyphs, many of people wearing ceremonial masks, as well as pictographs of people. The petroglyphs are carved into the stone and the pictographs are pictures that were painted onto the stone. The pictographs are easier to view later in the afternoon due to the way the sun hits the rocks at that time of day. The quality of some of the pictographs are poor due to their age, making them harder to see. Another unique feature of the Valle del Encanto are the piedras tacitas, which are flat rocks along the riverbed that have round indentations in them. There are hundreds of these unique rocks, one of which has forty-two of these cuplike holes in it.

As with any enchanting place, there is a local legend about the valley. In the eastern part of the valley, there is a rock known as the Rock of the Charm and the legend is known as the Charm Valley Maiden. It is said that a blonde witch used to practice magic there due to the rock's powerful energy and she could make glowing orange orbs of light move between her hands. When someone intruded upon her doing her magic at the rock, she and her orbs of light disappeared into thin air. Another version of the story is that a man came upon the maiden doing her magical ritual and fell in love with her. He waited for her to return and after several days she did. He threw himself at her and tried to possess her but a bright flash of orange and gold light blinded him. That night his vision returned to normal but he was so upset that she had rejected him that he jumped off a rock and killed himself.

The site at Valle del Encanto is believed to have been a place where the ancient local people went to conduct both spiritual and magical religious ceremonies. The large amount of ceremonial headdresses carved into or painted on the stones, shows these people practicing their beliefs. The energy in this valley is one of serene reverence and respect. You feel the magical quality of the stones, the high vibration of the earth and the air, and an appreciation for the energy of the water that used to flow over these rocks, and for those who created these lasting representations of their life. The Valle del Encanto holds powerful energy of positivity and a connection to higher consciousness. Take a moment to reflect, meditate, or simply connect to your soul song.

CONCLUSION

I hope you have enjoyed traveling around the world with me and visiting sacred sites, power places, and energy vortexes. There are so many unique and interesting locations that are overflowing with the positivity of the earth's energy. I hope the exercises proved helpful to you and that they were a catalyst to your own intuition and ability to connect to the frequency of the places we visited.

Energy is and always will be the source of our spiritual power, just as it is the source of the earth's power. Making a conscious choice to connect your frequency with earth's frequency will empower you along your spiritual path and aid in your spiritual growth. Sometimes you'll click right away with a place's power and other times it takes a longer session to really feel it deep inside. Give yourself time, be patient, and enjoy the wonderful effects that earth's frequency can bring into your life. Let earth's frequency become one with your inner essence. It can be life-changing.

BIBLIOGRAPHY

Barlow, Bernyce. *Sacred Sites of the West*. St. Paul, MN: Llewellyn Publications, 1996.

Bellows, Keith. *100 Places That Can Change Your Child's Life: From Your Backyard to the Ends of the Earth*. Washington, DC: National Geographic, 2013.

Boardman, John. *The Oxford History Of Classical Art*. New York: Oxford University Press Inc., 1993.

Brockman, Norbert C. *Encyclopedia of Sacred Places*. Oxford, UK: Oxford University Press, 1998.

Cali, Joseph and John Dougill. *Shinto Shrines: A Guide to the Sacred Sites of Japan's Ancient Religion*. Honolulu, HI: University of Hawai'i Press, 2013.

Carr-Gomm, Phillip. *Sacred Places: Sites of Spiritual Pilgrimage from Stonehenge to Santiago de Compostela*. London, UK: Quercus, 2009.

Dale, Cyndi. *Llewellyn's Complete Book of Chakras: Your Definitive Source of Energy Center Knowledge for Health, Happiness, and Spiritual Evolution*. Woodbury, MN: Llewellyn Publications, 2016.

Darvill, T. *The Concise Oxford Dictionary of Archaeology*. New York, NY: Oxford University Press, 2002.

Davey, Steve. *Unforgettable Places to See Before You Die*. Woodlands, London: BBC Worldwide, A Firefly Book, 2004.

DeSanctis, Marcia. *100 Places in France Every Woman Should Go*. Palo Alto, CA: Solas House, 2014.

———. *100 Places in Greece Every Woman Should Go*. Palo Alto, CA: Solas House, 2016.

Devereux, Paul. *The Sacred Place: The Ancient Origin of Holy and Mystical Sites.* London, England: Cassell & Co., 2000.

———. *Secrets of Ancient and Sacred Places: The World's Mysterious Heritage.* London, England: Blandford, 2000.

Douglas, David. *The Atlas of Sacred and Spiritual Sites: Discover places of mystical power from around the world.* London, UK: Octopus Publishing Group Limited, 2007.

Evans, Susan Toby, David L. Webster (Editors). *Archaeology of Ancient Mexico and Central America: An Encyclopedia.* New York, NY: Garland Publishing, Inc. 2001. Accessed online at: https://books.google.com/books?id=vZ3DAAAAQBAJ&pg=PA95&lpg=PA95&dq=Capacha+%E2%80%93+Colima,+Mexico+Ancient+Shaft+Tombs&source=bl&ots=AdFjKxyoB2&sig=rhA0lMhdrQQFUov2wY65Cl8rw1A&hl=en&sa=X&ved=0ahUKEwit3P6d67rVAhUU5mMKHac7B6EQ6AEITTAJ#v=onepage&q=Capacha%20%E2%80%93%20Colima%2C%20Mexico%20Ancient%20Shaft%20Tombs&f=false

Flood, Josephine. *Archaeology of the Dreamtime: The Story of Prehistoric Australia and its People.* New Haven, CT: Yale University Press, 1990.

Frutos, Robert. *Hawai'i: Sacred Sites of the Big Island Places of Presence, Healing, and Wisdom.* Self-published at CreateSpace Independent Publishing Platform, 2014

Genzmer, Herbert. *100 Sacred Places: A Discovery of the World's Most Revered Holy Sites.* Parragon Books, 2011.

Global Volcanism Program, 2016. *Report on Masaya (Nicaragua).* In: Venzke, E (ed.), Bulletin of the Global Volcanism Network, 41:8. Smithsonian Institution.

Grant, Rachel A. *Changes in Animal Activity Prior to a Major (M=7) Earthquake in the Peruvian Andes.* 2015 Elsevier Ltd. (accessed 10-31-2016 online at http://www.sciencedirect.com/science/article/pii/S1474706515000236).

Gray, Martin. *Sacred Earth: Places of Peace and Power.* New York, NY: Sterling Publishing Co., Inc., 2007.

Greenberg, Peter. *The Best Places for Everything: The Ultimate Insider's Guide to the Greatest Experiences Around the World.* New York, NY: Rodale, 2012.

Guilliford, Andrew. *Sacred Objects and Sacred Places: Preserving Tribal Traditions.* Boulder, CO: University of Colorado Press, 2000.

Hall, Judy. *Crystals and Sacred Sites: Use Crystals to Access the Power of Sacred Landscapes for Personal and Planetary Transformation.* Beverly, MA: Fair Winds Press, 2012.

Harrison, P. *The Lords of Tikal: Rulers of an Ancient Maya City.* London, UK: Thames & Hudson Ltd., 1999.

Hitching, Francis. *Earth Magic: The astounding mystery of the greatest of all lost civilizations.* New York, NY: William Morrow and Company, Inc., 1977.

Hughes, Holly and Julie Duchaine. *500 Places to See Before They Disappear.* Hoboken, NJ: John Wiley & Sons, Inc., 2012.

Houston, Jeffrey. *Ancient Egypt Secrets Explained!: The Influences Behind Egyptian History, Mythology & The Impact On World Civilization.* FFD Publishing, 2016.

Janusek, John Wayne. *Ancient Tiwanaku.* New York, NY: Cambridge University Press, 2008.

Kennedy, Frances H. *American Indian Places: A Historical Guidebook.* New York, NY: Houghton Mifflin Books, 2008.

Kramer, Samuel Noah. *The Sumerians: Their History, Culture, and Character.* Chicago, IL: University of Chicago Press, 1971.

Lake, Col. Carrol A. *Coral Castle Book.* The Historical Museum of Southern Florida, Miami, FL, 1950.

Lambert, Peter, and Andrew Nickson. *The Paraguay Reader: History, Culture, Politics (The Latin America readers).* Durham, NC: Duke University Press, 2013.

Lee, Ilchi. *The Call of Sedona: Journey of the Heart.* New York, NY: Scribner, 2011.

Lujan, Nathan K. and Jonathan W. Arbruster. "13: The Guiana Shield (PDF)." In James S. Albert and Roberto E. Reis, *Historical Biogeography of Neotropical Freshwater Fishes.* The Regents of the University of California, 2011.

Mann, A. T. *Sacred Landscapes: The Threshold Between Worlds.* New York, NY: Sterling Publishing Co., Inc., 2010.

Martin, Thomas R. *Ancient Greece: From Prehistoric to Hellenistic Times.* New Haven, CT: Yale University Press, 2013.

Meaden, Terence. *The Secrets of the Avebury Stones: Britain's Greatest Megalithic Temple*. Berkeley, CA: Frog Books, Ltd. 2000.

Meddens, Frank, Colin McEwan, Katie Willis, and Nicholas Branch. *Inca Sacred Space: Landscape, Site and Symbol in the Andes*. New York, NY: ACC Publishing Group, 2014.

National Geographic. *100 Countries 5000 Ideas*. Washington, DC: National Geographic Society, 2011.

————. *Complete National Parks of the United States, 2nd Edition: 400+ Parks, Monuments, Battlefields, Historic Sites, Scenic Trails, Recreation Areas, and Seashores*. Washington, DC: National Geographic Society, 2017.

————. *National Geographic Concise History of World Religions: An Illustrated Time Line*. Washington, DC: National Geographic Society, 2011.

————. *Destinations of a Lifetime: 225 of the World's Most Amazing Places*. Washington, DC: National Geographic Society, 2015.

————. *Drives of a Lifetime: 500 of the World's Best Most Spectacular Trips*. Washington, DC: National Geographic Society, 2010.

————. *Journeys of a Lifetime: 500 of the World's Greatest Trips*. Washington, DC: National Geographic Society, 2007.

————. *Sacred Places of a Lifetime: 500 of the World's Most Peaceful and Powerful Destinations*. Washington, DC: National Geographic Society, 2008.

————. *Secret Journeys of a Lifetime: 500 of the World's Best Hidden Travel Gems*. Washington, DC: National Geographic Society, 2011.

————. *The World's Most Romantic Destinations: 50 Dreamy Getaways, Private Retreats, and Enchanting Places to Celebrate Love*. Washington, DC: National Geographic Society, 2017.

————. *Timeless Journeys: Travels to the World's Legendary Places*. Washington, DC: National Geographic Society, 2017.

————. *Visual History of the World*. Washington, DC: National Geographic Society, 2005.

National Geographic. *Wild, Beautiful Places: Picture-Perfect Journeys Around the Globe.* Washington, DC: National Geographic Society, 2016.

―――. *World's Best Travel Experiences: 400 Extraordinary Places.* Washington, DC: National Geographic Society, 2012.

Naquin, Susan and Chün-Fang Yü. *Pilgrims and Sacred Sites in China (Studies on China).* Los Angeles, CA: University of California Press, 1992.

O'Brien, Henry. *The Round Towers of Ireland : or, The History of the Tuath-De-Danaans.* London, England: W. Thacker & Co. 1898

Olsen, Brad. *Sacred Places North America: 108 Destinations.* San Francisco, CA: Consortium of Collective Consciousness, 2008.

―――. *Sacred Places: 101 Spiritual Sites Around the World.* San Francisco, CA: Consortium of Collective Consciousness, 2000.

Ondaatje, Michael, Joseph Marshall III, Paul Theroux, Andrew Motion, Jan Morris, Mark Tully, and Alexander McCall Smith. *100 Journeys For The Spirit.* New York, NY: Stirling Publishing Co., Inc., 2010.

Palmer, Martin and Nigel Palmer. *The Spiritual Traveler: England, Scotland, Wales: The Guide to Sacred Sites and Pilgrim Routes in Britain.* Mahwah, NJ: Hidden Sprint, 2000.

Parker, Philip. *World History: From the Ancient World to the Information Age.* London, UK: DK Penguin Random House, 2017.

Parragon Books. *Mysteries in History: A Journey Through the Great Unanswered Questions of our Time.* New York, NY: Parragon Books Ltd., 2015.

Pinch, Geraldine. *Egyptian Mythology: A Guide to the Gods, Goddesses, and Traditions of Ancient Egypt.* New York, NY: Oxford University Press, 2004.

Potter, Merle C., Ph.D. *Thermodynamics Demystified.* New York, NY: The McGraw-Hill Companies, 2009.

Pryor, Damien. *The Lalibela Handbook (Great Sacred Sites).* New York, NY: Threshold Publishing, 2014.

Roaf, Michael. *The Cultural Atlas of Mesopotamia and the Ancient Near East.* Oxford, UK: Facts On File, Inc., 1990.

Roberts, David. *In Search of the Old Ones: Exploring the Anasazi World of the Southwest.* New York, NY: Simon & Schuster, 1997.

Rodgers, Nigel and Dr. Hazel Dodge. *Ancient Rome: A Complete History of the Rise and Fall of the Roman Empire, Chronicling the Story of the Most Important and Influential Civilization the World Has Ever Known.* London, UK: Southwater Publishing, 2013.

Schultz, Patricia. *1000 Places to See in the United States and Canada Before You Die.* New York, NY: Workman Publishing, 2007.

———. *1000 Places to See Before You Die: A Traveler's Life List.* New York, NY: Workman Publishing, 2003.

Scott, Michael. *Ancient Worlds: A Global History of Antiquity.* New York, NY: Basic Books/Hachette Book Group, 2016.

Shunxun, Nan (Professor) and Beverly Foit-Albert. *China's Sacred Sites.* Honesdale, PA: Himalayan Institute Press, 2007.

Silva, Freddy. *Legacy of the Gods: The Origin of Sacred Sites and the Rebirth of Ancient Wisdom.* Charlottesville, VA: Hampton Roads Publishing Company, Inc., 2011.

Silverman, Helaine and William Isbell. *Handbook of South American Archaeology.* New York, NY. Springer Science + Media LLC. 2008.

Singh, Upinder. *A History of Ancient and Early Medieval India: From the Stone Age to the 12th Century.* London, UK: Pearson Publishing, 2009.

Smithsonian. *Timelines of History.* London, UK: DK Penguin Random House, 2015.

Stokstad, Marilyn. *Art: A Brief History.* Pompton Plains, NJ: Pearson Education, 2016.

Thorley, Anthony and Celia M. Gunn. *Sacred Sites: an Overview.* The Gaia Foundation, 2007. Accessed online on 11-05-2016 at http://www.sacredland.org/media/Sacred-Sites-an-Overview.pdf

Taylor, Anthony. *The Sacred Sites Bible: The Definitive Guide to Spiritual Places.* Cardiff, UK: Sterling Publishing, 2010.

Travel & Leisure Editors. *100 Greatest Trips: From the Editors of The World's Leading Travel Magazine.* New York, NY: American Express Publishing Corporation, 2007.

Van De Mieroop, Marc. *A History of the Ancient Near East, ca. 3000-323 BC (Blackwell History of the Ancient World)*. West Sussex, UK: Wiley-Blackwell, 2015.

Verschuuren, Bas; Jeffrey McNeely, Gonzalo Oviedo, and Robert Wild (editors). *Sacred Natural Sites: Conserving Nature and Culture*. New York, NY: Routledge, 2012.

Verschuuren, Bas and Naoya Furuta. *Asian Sacred Natural Sites: Philosophy and practice in protected areas and conservation*. New York, NY: Routledge. 2016.

Wagers, Robert and Judy Wagers. *Mysteries of the Marfa Lights Revealed: Guide to the History, Mystery, Science, and Viewing of the Marfa Lights*. Richardson, TX: R & J Books Unique, 2012.

Westwood, Jennifer (editor). *The Atlas of Mysterious Places: The World's Unexplained Sacred Sites, Symbolic Landscapes, Ancient Cities and Lost Lands*. New York, NY: Weidenfeld & Nicolson, 1987.

Westwood, Jennifer. *On Pilgrimage: Sacred Journeys Around the World*. Mahwah, NJ: Hidden Spring / Paulist Press, 2003.

Wheeler, Tony and Maureen Wheeler. *The World: A Traveller's Guide to the Planet*. London, UK: Lonely Planet Publications Pty Ltd., 2014.

Willis, Jim. *Ancient Gods: Lost Histories, Hidden Truths, and the Conspiracy of Silence*. Detroit, MI: Visible Ink Press, 2017.

Wilson, Colin. *The Atlas of Holy Places & Sacred Sites: An Illustrated Guide to the Location, History and Significance of the World's Most Revered Holy Sites*. New York, NY: DK Publishing, 1996.

WEBSITE RESOURCES

"AG Africa Geographic," Africa Geographic, https://africageographic.com

"Ancient Egypt Online," Dirk Laukens, http:// ancient-egypt-online.com

"Ancient History Encyclopedia," Ancient History Encyclopedia Limited,
     https://ancient.eu

"Ancient Origins," Stella Novus, http:// ancient-origins.net

"Ancient UFO," Ancient UFO, http://ancientufo.org

"Archaeological Survey of India," Government of India, http://asi.nic.in

"Art Encyclopedia," Encyclopedia of Art Education, http://visual-arts-cork.com

"Atlas Obscura," Atlas Obscura, http:// atlasobscura.com

"Australia: The Land Where Time Began," M.H. Monroe, http://austhrutime.com

"Australia," Tourism Australia, https://australia.com

"BBC News," BBC, http://news.bbc.co.uk

"Beautiful World," Beautiful World, https://beautifulworld.com

"BuddhaNet," Buddha Dharma Education Association Inc., https://buddhanet.net

"Canada's Historic Places," Canadian Register of Historic Places, http://historicplaces.ca

"Coral Castle Museum," Coral Castle, http://coralcastle.com

"Discover More with Science Direct," ScienceDirect, https://sciencedirect.com

"Discovering Ancient Egypt," Discovering Egypt, https://discoveringegypt.com

"Earth Chakras," Robert Coon, http://earthchakras.org/Locations.php

"Ecuador," Ecuador Channel, http:// ecuador.com

"Encyclopedia Britannica," Encyclopedia Britannica, Inc., https://britannica.com

"Encyclopedia of Myths," Advameg, Inc., http://mythencyclopedia.com

"Encyclopedia.com," Birdie Media, http://encyclopedia.com

"English Heritage," English Heritage, http://english-heritage.org.uk

"Explore Japan," Japan-Guide.com, https://japan-guide.com

"Exploring South America," ExploringSouthAmerica.com, http://exploringsouthamerica.com

"Fraser Coast Queensland: Where Nature Comes Alive," Fraser Coast Tourism & Events, https://visitfrasercoast.com

"Geology Page," Geology Page, http://geologypage.com

"Great Barrier Reef," Welcome to the Great Barrier Reef, http://greatbarrierreef.org

"Greek Gods & Goddesses," Greek Gods & Goddesses, https://greekgodsandgoddesses.net

"History," A & E Networks, http:// history.com

"India," India WebPortal Private Limited, http://india.com

"Just Another Day In Western Australia," Tourism Western Australia, https://www.westernaustralia.com/us/Pages/Welcome_to_Western_Australia.aspx#/

"Kia Ora Welcome to New Zealand," New Zealand Government, https://newzealand.com

"Lilianfels Blue Mountains Resort & Spa," Escarpment Group, https://lilianfels.com.au

"Live Science," Purch, http://livescience.com

"Lonely Planet," Lonely Planet, http://lonelyplanet.com

"Losglaciares.com," Prodig Multimedia Consulting, http://losglaciares.com

"Mayan Ruins," Welcome to Mayan-Ruins.org, http://mayan-ruins.org

"Megalithia," Richard M., http://megalithia.com/index.html

"Mommy Mystic," Lisa Erickson, https://mommymystic.wordpress.com

"Mungo National Park," Office of Environment and Heritage, http://visitmungo.com.au

"Mysterious Places," MysteriousPlaces.com, http://mysteriousplaces.com

"Mythical Ireland," Mythical Ireland & Anthony Murphy, http://mythicalireland.com

"National Geographic," National Geographic Partners, LLC, http://nationalgeographic.com

"National Park Service," U.S. Department of the Interior, https://nps.gov

"National Trust," National Trust, https://nationaltrust.org.uk

"Norway Powered by Nature," Innovation Norway, https://visitnorway.com

"NSW National Parks and Wildlife Service," NSW Government, https://nationalparks.nsw.gov.au

"Paranormal-Encyclopedia.com," Paranormal-Encyclopedia.com, http://paranormal-encyclopedia.com

"Queensland," Tourism and Events: Queensland, https://queensland.com

"Reference Information You Can Trust," Encyclopedia.com, https://encyclopedia.com

"Renown Travel," Renown Travel, https://renown-travel.com

"Sacred Land Film Project," Sacred Land Film Project, http://sacredland.org

"Scientific American," Scientific American, A Division of Springer Nature America, Inc. https://scientificamerican.com

"Smithsonian.com," Smithsonian Institution, https://smithsonianmag.com

"Smithsonian Institution National Museum of Natural History Global Volcanism Program," Smithsonian Institution, https://volcano.si.edu

"SouthAfrica.com," South Africa Channel, http://southafrica.com

"Taktsang (Tiger's Nest) Monastery," Little Bhutan, https://tigersnestbhutan.com

"The Ancient Wisdom Foundation," Ancient-Wisdom, http:// ancient-wisdom.com

"The History Hub Historical Facts," Part of Buzz!Fy Media, https://thehistoryhub.com

"The Islands of the Bahamas," The Islands of the Bahamas, https://bahamas.com

"The Mayan Ruins," MayanRuins.info, http://mayanruins.info

"The Megalithic Portal," Andy Burnham, http://megalithic.co.uk

"The World's 1000 Wonders," TheWorldWonders.com, http://theworldwonders.com

"Tour Egypt," Tour Egypt, http://touregypt.net

"Travel Channel," The Travel Channel, L.L.C., http://travelchannel.com

"Traveller," Fairfax Media, http://traveller.com.au

"Uluru Australia's Iconic Red Center," Uluru Australia, http://uluru-australia.com

"UNESCO," UNESCO World Heritage Centre, http://whc.unesco.org

"Viking Denmark," EssentialContent.com, http://vikingdenmark.com

"Volcano Discovery," Dr. Tom Pfeiffer, https://volcanodiscovery.com

"Wairakei Terraces & Thermal Health Spa," Wairakei Terraces, http://wairakeiterraces.co.nz

"Welcome to Sacred Destinations," Sacred Destinations, http://sacred-destinations.com

"Welcome to the Vredefort Dome," Crusse Trade Enterprises c.c., http://vredefortdome.org

"Wondermondo Wonders of the World," Wondermondo, http://wondermondo.com

"World Atlas Explore the World," WorldAtlas.com, http://worldatlas.com

"World-Mysteries," World Mysteries, http://world-mysteries.com

INDEX

TO WRITE TO THE AUTHOR

If you wish to contact the author or would like more information about this book, please write to the author in care of Llewellyn Worldwide Ltd. and we will forward your request. Both the author and publisher appreciate hearing from you and learning of your enjoyment of this book and how it has helped you. Llewellyn Worldwide Ltd. cannot guarantee that every letter written to the author can be answered, but all will be forwarded. Please write to:

Melissa Alvarez
℅ Llewellyn Worldwide
2143 Wooddale Drive
Woodbury, MN 55125-2989

Please enclose a self-addressed stamped envelope for reply,
or $1.00 to cover costs. If outside the U.S.A., enclose
an international postal reply coupon.

Many of Llewellyn's authors have websites with additional information and resources. For more information, please visit our website at http://www.llewellyn.com

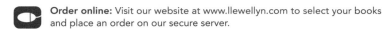

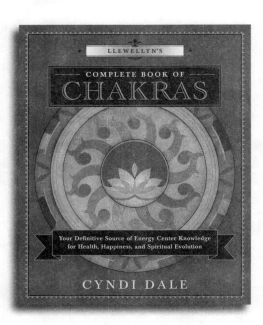

COMPLETE BOOK OF

CHAKRAS

Your Definitive Source of Energy Center Knowledge
for Health, Happiness, and Spiritual Evolution

CYNDI DALE

Llewellyn's Complete Book of Chakras
Your Definitive Source of Energy Center Knowledge
for Health, Happiness, and Spiritual Evolution
Cyndi Dale

As powerful centers of subtle energy, the chakras have fascinated humanity for thousands of years. *Llewellyn's Complete Book of Chakras* is a unique and empowering resource that provides comprehensive insights into these foundational sources of vitality and strength. Discover what chakras and chakra systems are, how to work with them for personal growth and healing, and the ways our understanding of chakras has transformed throughout time and across cultures.

Lively and accessible, this definitive reference explores the science, history, practices, and structures of our subtle energy. With an abundance of illustrations and a wealth of practical exercises, Cyndi Dale shows you how to use chakras for improving wellness, attracting what you need, obtaining guidance, and expanding your consciousness.

978-0-7387-3962-5, 1056 pp., 8 x 10 **$44.99**

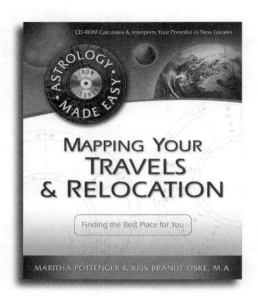

CD-ROM Calculates & Interprets Your Potential in New Locales

ASTROLOGY · MADE EASY

D-ROM SERIES

MAPPING YOUR TRAVELS & RELOCATION

Finding the Best Place for You

MARITHA POTTENGER & KRIS BRANDT RISKE, M.A.

Mapping Your Travels & Relocation
Finding the Best Place for You
Maritha Pottenger
Kris Brandt Riske MA
Cosmic Patterns

Changing your location changes your horoscope, whether through a change of residence or even a weeklong vacation. Knowing how a move will affect you can help you choose a location that will maximize the positive and minimize problem areas indicated in your birth chart. It's your opportunity to supercharge your entrepreneurial and vocational endeavors, love and romance opportunities, scholarly success, and more. The included Windows-based CD will calculate different charts and print out interpretative reports so you understand in advance the effects of a changed location on your life.

978-0-7387-0665-8, 240 pp., 7 ½ x 9 ⅛   **$19.95**

MELANIE BARNUM

PSYCHIC
VISION

DEVELOPING YOUR CLAIRVOYANT
AND REMOTE VIEWING SKILLS

Psychic Vision
Developing Your Clairvoyant and Remote Viewing Skills
Melanie Barnum

Imagine being able to see people, landmarks, or objects in a far away location without physically going there! Offering a unique combination of intuitive and analytical guidance, *Psychic Vision* includes everything you need to know about using clairvoyance and remote viewing to enhance your life. With chapter-by-chapter exercises created specifically to take you on a clairvoyant journey—as well as instructions for the exact protocols used by government intelligence agencies—*Psychic Vision* is an indispensible guide to developing your psychic sight. Sharing true stories of actual remote viewing events, this book provides practical applications for clairvoyance and introduces you to an extraordinary and inspiring spiritual awareness.

978-0-7387-4623-4, 216 pp., 6 x 9   **$16.99**

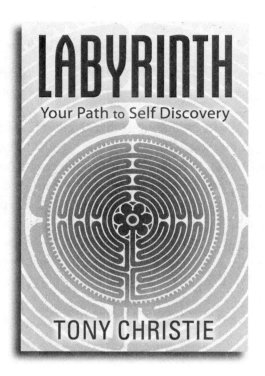

Labyrinth
Your Path to Self-Discovery
Tony Christie

The labyrinth is an enigma, a seemingly ordinary symbol that has the power to open the gateway to profound self-discovery. Within its coils and turns, secret wisdom is revealed that has the potential to help humanity on its journey toward spiritual advancement. In this book, spiritual teacher Tony Christie shares new information and powerful techniques for exploring the labyrinth as a source of wonder, wisdom, healing, and enlightenment.

Discover how to work with labyrinths to quiet your mind and gain insights and answers for the questions that matter most to you. Use the labyrinth as a safe container for letting go of your troubles and finding that peaceful place within yourself. Learn about the fascinating connections between the labyrinth and tarot, alchemy, crop circles, and the cosmos. With the right guidance and intention, every step you take in a labyrinth can bring you greater understanding of your life's purpose on your own sacred journey.

978-0-7387-5661-5, 312 pp., 6 x 9   **$21.99**

---

365 WAYS

to

RAISE YOUR

FREQUENCY

Simple Tools to Increase Your
Spiritual Energy for Balance,
Purpose, and Joy

MELISSA ALVAREZ

365 Ways to Raise Your Frequency
Simple Tools to Increase Your Spiritual Energy for Balance, Purpose, and Joy
MELISSA ALVAREZ

The soul's vibrational rate, our spiritual frequency, has a huge impact on our lives. As it increases, so does our capacity to calm the mind, connect with angels and spirit guides, find joy and enlightenment, and achieve what we want in life.

This simple and inspiring guide makes it easy to elevate your spiritual frequency every day. Choose from a variety of ordinary activities, such as singing and cooking. Practice visualization exercises and techniques for reducing negativity, manifesting abundance, tapping into Universal Energy, and connecting with your higher self. Discover how generous actions and a positive attitude can make a difference. You'll also find long-term projects and guidance for boosting your spiritual energy to new heights over a lifetime.

978-0-7387-2740-0, 432 pp., 5 x 7   **$17.99**
